Charles Adamson Salmond

For Days of Youth

A Bible Text and Talk for the Young for Every Day in the Year

Charles Adamson Salmond

For Days of Youth
A Bible Text and Talk for the Young for Every Day in the Year

ISBN/EAN: 9783337170240

Printed in Europe, USA, Canada, Australia, Japan

Cover: Foto ©Lupo / pixelio.de

More available books at **www.hansebooks.com**

> "I live for those who love me,
>   For those who know me true;
> For the heaven that smiles above me,
>   And waits my coming too;
> For the cause which needs assistance,
> For the wrong which needs resistance,
> For the future in the distance,
>   And the good which I can do."

For Days of Youth

A Bible Text and Talk for the Young

for

Every Day in the Year

BY THE

REV. CHARLES A. SALMOND, M.A.
EDINBURGH

"Give us day by day our daily bread"

EDINBURGH & LONDON
OLIPHANT ANDERSON & FERRIER
1896

All Rights Reserved

MORRISON AND GIBB, PRINTERS, EDINBURGH.

Author's Preface

THERE are many books of Daily Readings for older people, but few, if any, which are specially meant for the Young. It is therefore hoped that, in days when so many books are prepared for the latter, and enjoyed by them, there may be a place and a welcome for the present volume.

The subjects of the Readings are varied, and their length is moderate. It has been sought to brighten most of them by anecdotes and other illustrations; because teaching or counsel, even when founded on a text from the Best of Books, is little likely to be favourably received by young people if it is prosy and dull. A few of the 366 Talks have appeared in a more fugitive form already; but they will not be less liked on that account by any Young Reader who may happen to recognise one here and there.

Though the volume is designed for individual use,—morning or evening as may be found best,—it may have a use in the home circle as well.

The Author hopes that the Texts and Talks will sometimes be read aloud at family worship, as other books of Daily Readings often are. Perhaps it will be found that, while particularly adapted for those still in their teens, these brief Addresses are not altogether unwelcome, when printed as well as spoken, to some young people even whose teens have now to be spoken of as "fifty years since."

Contents

JANUARY

		PAGE
1.	The Days of thy Youth (Eccles. xii. 1)	1
2.	A Gift God Asks (Prov. xxiii. 26)	3
3.	The Advocate (1 John ii. 1)	4
4.	Knowing our Way (Job xxiii. 10)	5
5.	A Prayer and a Resolve (Ps. cxix. 117)	6
6.	A Strange Command (2 Pet. iii. 18)	7
7.	A Special Promise (Prov. viii. 17)	8
8.	The First Preacher (Heb. xi. 4)	9
9.	God Sees (Gen. xvi. 13)	10
10.	Not Living to Ourselves (Rom. xiv. 7)	11
11.	The Fowler's Snare (Ps. cxxiv. 7)	12
12.	A Little Minister (1 Sam. ii. 11)	13
13.	The Wishing Gate (Prov. viii. 11)	14
14.	Good Scholars (John viii. 31)	15
15.	Hid in the Heart (Ps. cxix. 11)	16
16.	Shine (Matt. v. 16)	17
17.	The Beloved (Eph. i. 6)	18
18.	My Jewels (Mal. iii. 17)	19
19.	Poor Balaam (Num. xxxi. 8)	20
20.	The Broken Heart (Ps. li. 17)	21
21.	The Whole Heart (Ps. cxix. 2)	22
22.	The Highest Rank and the Grandest Title (1 John iii. 1)	23
23.	Rich toward God (Luke xii. 21)	24
24.	Behold the Lamb (John i. 29)	25
25.	Whom do you Serve? (Matt. vi. 21)	26
26.	The Secret of Paul's Life (Gal. ii. 20)	27
27.	Joyful Progress (Prov. iv. 18)	28
28.	Look unto Me (Isa. xlv. 22)	29
29.	An Unsparing God (Rom. viii. 32)	30
30.	With Him—all Things (Rom. viii. 32)	31
31.	Marked in the Ear and in the Foot (John x. 27)	32

Contents.

FEBRUARY

		PAGE
1.	Giant Hermon (Luke ix. 28)	33
2.	The Trustee and the Treasure (2 Tim. i. 12)	34
3.	Good Running (1 Cor. ix. 24)	35
4.	Christ our Captain (Heb. ii. 10)	36
5.	Satisfied at Last (Ps. xvii. 15)	37
6.	The Name to be Remembered (Ps. xlv. 17)	38
7.	Kept from the Evil (John xvii. 15)	39
8.	Meeting Places for all (Prov. xxii. 2)	40
9.	On Earth, as in Heaven (Matt. vi. 10)	41
10.	Turn (Ezek. xxxiii. 11)	42
11.	The Best Boast (Ps. xxxiv. 2)	43
12.	Good Success (Josh. i. 8)	44
13.	Watch (Mark xiii. 37)	45
14.	Ready Reckoning (Rom. viii. 18)	46
15.	Vanishing Goodness (Hos. vi. 4)	47
16.	Christ the Door (John x. 9)	48
17.	Choice (Ps. cxix. 30)	49
18.	Jesus and the Children (Matt. xviii. 2)	50
19.	Persevere (Rom. ii. 7)	51
20.	A Soul in Prison (Ps. cxlii. 7)	52
21.	Cruel Cain (Jude 11)	53
22.	Dorcas (Acts ix. 36)	54
23.	Ready (Rom. i. 15)	55
24.	The Lord knowing them that are His (2 Tim. ii. 19)	56
25.	The Lord's showing that they are His (2 Tim. ii. 19)	57
26.	Greater than Solomon (Matt. xii. 42)	58
27.	The Hope, and the Reason for it (1 Pet. iii. 15)	59
28.	The Sin of Neglect (Heb. ii. 3)	60
29.	Be Diligent (Prov. x. 4)	61

MARCH

1.	Emmanuel (Matt. i. 23)	62
2.	A Puzzle for Many (Matt. xxvii. 22)	63
3.	A Dangerous Levity (Matt. xxii. 5)	64
4.	The Great Physician (Jer. xvii. 14)	65
5.	An Echo of Jesus (1 John iii. 11, etc.)	66
6.	Worthy Living, and Gainful Dying (Phil. i. 21)	67
7.	Remember the Sabbath (Ex. xx. 8)	68
8.	A Beautiful Biography (Gen. v. 24)	69
9.	Our Substitute (Rom. v. 6)	70
10.	It cometh from Above (Jas. i. 17)	71

Contents.

		PAGE
11.	A Good Keynote (1 John iv. 8, 16).	72
12.	Faithful though not Famous (Acts i. 26)	73
13.	A Cloud of Witnesses (Heb. xii. 1)	74
14.	Not Yours, but You (2 Cor. xii. 14)	75
15.	Myself and Thyself (Job xxxiv. 32)	76
16.	The Best of Friends (Matt. xi. 19)	77
17.	More Precious than Gold (Ps. cxix. 72)	78
18.	A Wonderful Key (1 John iv. 19)	79
19.	Complete Confidence in Jesus (Matt. xiv. 12 and Luke ix. 10)	80
20.	Seeking the Lost (Luke xix. 10)	81
21.	No more Sea (Rev. xxi. 1)	82
22.	The Brightness of the Firmament (Ps. viii. 3, 4)	83
23.	The Best Guide (Ps. xxiii. 2)	84
24.	In Christ, Early (Rom. xvi. 7)	85
25.	A Lesson from Carmel (1 Kings xviii. 21)	86
26.	The Wise (Prov. xi. 30)	87
27.	The Fool (Luke xii. 20)	88
28.	By and By (Acts xxiv. 25)	89
29.	Christ is Risen (Matt. xxviii. 6)	90
30.	The Best Gift (John iv. 10)	91
31.	The Tables Turned (Matt. xix. 30)	92

APRIL

1.	True Courage (2 Tim. iv. 17)	93
2.	In the Morning (Ps. cxliii. 8)	94
3.	The Nearness of Christ (Phil. iv. 5)	95
4.	God Hears (Mal. iii. 16)	96
5.	Taking the Census (Ps. lxxxvii. 6)	97
6.	A Capital Exercise (Acts xxiv. 16)	98
7.	The Fear that casts out Fear (Ps. lxxxv. 9)	99
8.	A Visitor at the Door (Rev. iii. 20)	100
9.	A Wise Prayer (Luke xvii. 5)	101
10.	A Covetous Man (2 Kings v. 20)	102
11.	Who has Won? (Phil. iii. 8)	103
12.	Growth and the Secret of it (Hos. xiv. 5, 6)	104
13.	Strange Perversity (John v. 40)	105
14.	Work Away (John ix. 4)	106
15.	Your Garden and Mine (Song of Sol. i. 6)	107
16.	The Head (Col. i. 18)	108
17.	A Rich Legacy (John xiv. 27)	109
18.	Broken Cisterns (Jer. ii. 13)	110
19.	A Lesson from Mount Rephidim (Ex. xvii. 15)	111
20.	Bringing us to God (1 John v. 12 and Eph. iii. 12)	112
21.	Beholding and Trying Men (Ps. xi. 4)	113

Contents.

		PAGE
22.	Sowing and Reaping (Gal. vi. 7)	114
23.	Christ's Brothers and Sisters (Matt. xii. 50)	115
24.	The Way of Life (Ps. xvi. 11)	116
25.	The Path of Death (Prov. xii. 26)	117
26.	Martyr Stephen (Acts xxii. 20)	118
27.	A Good Soldier (2 Tim. ii. 3)	119
28.	Good Company (Prov. xiii. 20)	120
29.	A Wise Servant (Matt. xxiv. 45)	121
30.	Trusting the Pilot (Isa. xii. 2)	122

MAY

1.	A Perfect Likeness (Col. i. 15)	123
2.	A Beautiful Vision (Isa. lx. 8)	124
3.	The Face of Christ (2 Cor. iv. 6)	125
4.	Caught in the Meshes (Mic. vii. 2)	126
5.	Christ's Property (Mark ix. 41)	127
6.	The Character of Isaac (Gen. xxi. 3)	128
7.	True Gratitude (Ps. cxvi. 12)	129
8.	A Lesson from Sinai (Ex. xx. 5)	130
9.	Grieving our Best Friend (Eph. iv. 30)	131
10.	For Christ's Sake (Eph. iv. 32 and 2 Cor. xii. 10)	132
11.	What she Could (Mark xiv. 8)	133
12.	The Father Himself (John xvi. 27)	134
13.	Looking up (John xvii. 1)	135
14.	A Free Salvation (Mark x. 17)	136
15.	How to be in a Majority (2 Chron. xxxii. 7, 8)	137
16.	Two Lovely Sisters (John xi. 1)	138
17.	The Proper Standard (Acts ix. 6)	139
18.	Pleasing God (Heb. xi. 6)	140
19.	The Name above every Name (Matt. i. 21)	141
20.	A Noble Aim in Life (Acts x. 38)	142
21.	Something to be Sure About (Num. xxxii. 23)	143
22.	A Free Pardon (Isa. lv. 7)	144
23.	John the Beloved (John xxi. 20)	145
24.	The New Heart (Ezek. xxxvi. 26)	146
25.	Honest Work (Ex. xxv. 11)	147
26.	Crossing the Jordan (Josh. iii. 4)	148
27.	Weighed in God's Balances (Dan. v. 27)	149
28.	Rebuked by an Ass (2 Pet. ii. 16)	150
29.	The Eleventh Commandment (John xiii. 34)	151
30.	Shadows (Song of Sol. ii. 17)	152
31.	After many Days (Eccles. xi. 1)	153

Contents.

JUNE

	PAGE
1. The Lessons of the Rainbow (Gen. ix. 14, 15)	154
2. God's Banished brought Back (2 Sam. xiv. 14)	155
3. The Exile Home (2 Cor. v. 8)	156
4. The Two Suns (Matt. v. 45 and Ps. lxxxiv. 11)	157
5. A Fearless Confidence (Ps. xxvii. 1)	158
6. Who is King? (Matt. ii. 1, 2)	159
7. A Living Way (Heb. x. 20)	160
8. A New Song (Ps. xl. 3)	161
9. The Lion, yet the Lamb (Rev. v. 5, 6)	162
10. Not Uncertain, though Unknown (1 John iii. 2)	163
11. Honour to and from God (1 Sam. ii. 30)	164
12. On Pisgah's Height (Deut. xxxiv. 1)	165
13. A Stern Opponent, yet a Real Friend (Ps. lxxxv. 10)	166
14. A Way of Escape (1 Cor. x. 13)	167
15. Our First Home (Gen. ii. 15)	168
16. Hiding from God (Gen. iii. 8)	169
17. Our Last Home (Rev. xxii. 14)	170
18. Lazarus of Bethany (John xi. 11)	171
19. Not (Ps. i. 1)	172
20. But (2 Kings v. 1. and 2 Tim. iv. 16, 17)	173
21. Laying Past (Luke xii. 21)	174
22. "Abba," Father (Rom. viii. 15)	175
23. Looking unto Jesus (Heb. xii. 2)	176
24. Nailed to the Doorpost (Ex. xxi. 5)	177
25. Weakness in Strength (Judg. xvi. 7)	178
26. Strength in Weakness (Judg. xvi. 28)	179
27. Christ's Feast and Banner (Song of Sol. ii. 1)	180
28. Everyone from his Place (Zeph. ii. 11)	181
29. Holy Anger (Gen. vi. 7)	182
30. Think of Others (Phil. ii. 4)	183

JULY

1. The God of Hope (Rom. xv. 13)	184
2. Work for Everybody (Acts ix. 6)	185
3. A Rich Inheritance (1 John v. 11)	186
4. The Master (John xi. 28)	187
5. A Walk on Olivet (Luke xix. 29)	188
6. The Secret of a Happy Home (Josh. xxiv. 15)	189
7. A Hard Life (Prov. xiii. 15)	190
8. Salvation by Grace (Eph. ii. 9)	191
9. Faithful in Little and in Much (Matt. xxiv. 45)	192

Contents.

		PAGE
10.	ACQUAINTANCE WITH GOD (Job xxii. 21)	193
11.	A LIE IN THE RIGHT HAND (Isa. xliv. 20)	194
12.	LOVING MUCH (Luke vii. 47)	195
13.	SAD IGNORANCE (Luke xix. 44)	196
14.	THE VOYAGE OF LIFE (1 Tim. i. 19)	197
15.	BECOMING STARS (Dan. xii. 3)	198
16.	A LESSON FROM MOUNT MORIAH (Heb. xi. 17)	199
17.	LIVING TO PURPOSE (Gal. vi. 9)	200
18.	THE NAZARENE (Matt. ii. 23)	201
19.	AS LIGHTS IN THE WORLD (Phil. ii. 15)	202
20.	A RANSOM FOR MANY (Job xxxiii. 24)	203
21.	OUR DUTY (Luke xvii. 10)	204
22.	GOD UNDERSTANDS YOU (Ps. cxxxix. 2)	205
23.	A MAN OF PROGRESS (John iii. 1)	206
24.	MOUNT ZION (Heb. xii. 22)	207
25.	PRISONERS OF HOPE (Zech. ix. 12)	208
26.	TRY IT FOR YOURSELF (Ps. xxvi. 1)	209
27.	THE GREAT LEVELLER (Isa. xiv. 11)	210
28.	FILIAL LOVE (Eph. vi. 2)	211
29.	NOT MUCH TIME (1 Cor. vii. 29)	212
30.	THE ONLY BEGOTTEN (John iii. 16)	213
31.	CONSTANT PROTECTION (Ps. cxxi. 5)	214

AUGUST

1.	A HAPPY HOLIDAY (Zech. viii. 5)	215
2.	LEAVING OUR MARK (1 Kings xi. 12 and 2 Kings xiii. 2)	216
3.	WHO WILL MISS YOU? (2 Chron. xxi. 20)	217
4.	A TRUE OBEDIENCE (Ex. xix. 5)	218
5.	IDOLS IN THE HEART (1 John v. 21)	219
6.	A LESSON FROM MOUNT HOR (Num. xx. 28)	220
7.	BIBLE ADDITION (Matt. vi. 33)	221
8.	A BOUNTIFUL HARVEST (Gal. vi. 9)	222
9.	GUIDED WITH GOD'S EYE (Ps. xxxii. 8)	223
10.	ONESIMUS OF COLOSSE (Philem. 10)	224
11.	WAS IT BY CHANCE? (Ruth ii. 3)	225
12.	THE BRAZEN SERPENT (Num. xxi. 8)	226
13.	THEREFORE (Ex. xxxi. 14)	227
14.	RETRIBUTION (Ps. ix. 16)	228
15.	BIBLE MULTIPLICATION (Prov. xi. 24)	229
16.	CHRIST THE PROPHET (Acts iii. 22)	230
17.	ONE OF GOD'S FORGET-ME-NOTS (Isa. xliii. 1, 2)	231
18.	LOVE IN ANGER (Ex. xxxii. 19)	232
19.	BIBLE SUBTRACTION (Luke viii. 18)	233
20.	NOAH'S SERMON (2 Pet. ii. 5)	234

Contents.

	PAGE
21. THE SECRET OF SAFETY (Ps. xvi. 1)	235
22. CHRIST THE PRIEST (Heb. iv. 14, 15)	236
23. SUBMIT (Jas. iv. 7)	237
24. VULGAR FRACTIONS (Matt. vi. 32)	238
25. CHRIST THE PRINCE (Acts iii. 15 and v. 31)	239
26. CHRIST OUR SURETY (Ps. cxix. 122)	240
27. PHŒBE (Rom. xvi. 1)	241
28. A WITNESS TO BE RELIED UPON (Rom. i. 9)	242
29. NO DIFFERENCE (Rom. iii. 23)	243
30. THE SPRINKLED BLOOD (Ex. xii. 13)	244
31. BALANCE (Mark viii. 36)	245

SEPTEMBER

	PAGE
1. SPIRITUAL PHOTOGRAPHY (2 Cor. iii. 18)	246
2. THE LIVING AND LIFE-GIVING ONE (1 Cor. xv. 45)	247
3. NOT ASHAMED TO PRAY (Dan. vi. 10)	248
4. GIVING UP FOR GOD (1 Kings xvii. 13)	249
5. THE ATONEMENT (Rom. v. 11)	250
6. THE VALLEY OF ACHOR (Hos. ii. 15)	251
7. THANKFULNESS (Col. iii. 15)	252
8. QUARTUS, A BROTHER (Rom. xvi. 23)	253
9. THE TEST OF FAITHFULNESS (Gen. iii. 3)	254
10. COME WITH US (Num. x. 29)	255
11. FIRE FROM HEAVEN (Gen. xix. 24)	256
12. AT ONCE (Mark i. 18)	257
13. COUNTING OUR STEPS (Job xxxi. 4)	258
14. THE LORD REIGNETH (Ps. xcvii. 1)	259
15. ROBBING GOD (Mal. iii. 8)	260
16. CHRIST THE ROCK (1 Cor. x. 4)	261
17. THE TESTIMONY OF THE DUST (Luke ix. 5)	262
18. DOUBLE-MINDEDNESS (Jas. i. 8 and Gen. xlix. 4)	263
19. CHRIST WITH US IN THE SHIP (Matt. viii. 26)	264
20. LOVING BACK AGAIN (1 John iv. 19)	265
21. YOUR NAME, SIR? (Gen. xxxii. 27)	266
22. SYMPATHY (Gal. vi. 2)	267
23. SELF-HELP (Gal. vi. 5)	268
24. SUPPORT (Ps. lv. 22)	269
25. SON, REMEMBER (Ps. lxxvii. 11)	270
26. WHAT LIKE IS THE FRUIT? (Matt. vii. 20)	271
27. LED TO DESTRUCTION (2 Tim. ii. 26)	272
28. THE FINDING OF MOSES (Ex. ii. 6)	273
29. A CHEERFUL GIVER (Matt. x. 8)	274
30. FITLY SPOKEN (Prov. xxv. 11)	275

Contents.

OCTOBER

	PAGE
1. A Welcome to the King (Ps. xxiv. 7)	276
2. Settling Accounts with God (Eccles. viii. 11)	277
3. Respect unto the Lowly (Ps. cxxxviii. 6)	278
4. On the Way to Greatness (Ps. cxix. 141)	279
5. The Christian's Heritage (1 Cor. iii. 21)	280
6. Christ the Sun (Mal. iv. 2)	281
7. The New Testament Passover (Ex. xii. 26)	282
8. None like God (Ex. xv. 11)	283
9. A Selfish Choice, and What Came of It (Gen. xiii. 11)	284
10. Join Hands (Ps. cxxii. 1)	285
11. What is your Price? (Zech. xi. 12)	286
12. Simon Peter (John i. 42)	287
13. Ready for Either (Rom. xiv. 8)	288
14. Reading (1 Tim. iv. 13)	289
15. How God Tempts (Gen. xxii. 1)	290
16. Beware of Wrong Beginnings (Mic. i. 13)	291
17. The Folly of Earthly Greed (1 Tim. vi. 7)	292
18. Christ the Truth (John iii. 2 and xiv. 6)	293
19. Lessons from Babel (Gen. xi. 9)	294
20. Staying the Flood (Isa. lix. 19)	295
21. Self-made Men (1 Pet. i. 14)	296
22. Confessing Christ (Matt. x. 32)	297
23. Be Pitiful (Eph. iv. 32 and 1 Pet. iii. 8)	298
24. Be Courteous (1 Pet. iii. 8, 9)	299
25. Son Timothy (1 Tim. i. 18)	300
26. Not Hidden, or Far Away (Deut. xxx. 11)	301
27. In the Wrong Slot (Isa. lv. 2)	302
28. Be Content (Heb. xiii. 5)	303
29. The Place of Safety (John x. 28, 29)	304
30. Which Twilight? (Rom. xiii. 12)	305
31. Bread from Heaven (Ex. xvi. 4)	306

NOVEMBER

1. The True Test—"Daily" (Ps. lxi. 8 and Luke ix. 23)	307
2. Shoes or Sermons (Rev. xx. 13)	308
3. The Raven and the Dove (Gen. viii. 7, 8)	309
4. Be Reverent (2 Sam. vi. 7)	310
5. The Unspeakable Gift (2 Cor. ix. 15)	311
6. Cursing the Deaf and Tripping the Blind (Lev. xix. 14)	312
7. An Upsetting Sin (Prov. xxiii. 31)	313

Contents.

	PAGE
8. Not Worth the Candle (Hag. i. 9)	314
9. The Mindfulness of God (Gen. xxi. 17)	315
10. God Lives (Ps. xviii. 46)	316
11. Heavenly Armour (Eph. vi. 13)	317
12. Giving to God (1 Chron. xxix. 14)	318
13. Our Marching Orders (Mark xvi. 15)	319
14. Bad Coins (Jer. vi. 30)	320
15. Swifter than the Telegraph (Neh. ii. 4)	321
16. The True Vine (John xv. 1)	322
17. Crossing the River (Isa. xliii. 2)	323
18. Sin's Bitter Fruit (Gen. iii. 24)	324
19. Keeping your Temper (Prov. xv. 1)	325
20. To what Purpose? (Jer. vi. 20 and Matt. xxvi. 8)	326
21. Water from the Rock (Ex. xvii. 6)	327
22. A Queen who Lost and Kept her Crown (Esth. i. 12)	328
23. Led at Christ's Chariot Wheel (2 Cor. ii. 14-16)	329
24. A Member of the Aristocracy (Jer. ix. 23, 24)	330
25. Stirring up the Nest (Deut. xxxii. 11, 12)	331
26. Selling the Birthright (Heb. xii. 16)	332
27. Touching the Sceptre (Esth. v. 2)	333
28. God Holding our Right Hand (Ps. lxxiii. 23)	334
29. The Slander Book (1 Pet. ii. 1)	335
30. The Wonderful Name (Isa. ix. 6)	336

DECEMBER

1. Surely and Quickly (Rev. xxii. 20)	337
2. A Dark Path to a Bright Career (Gen. l. 20)	338
3. Gathering to Christ (Gen. xlix. 10)	339
4. Seeking one another (Luke xix. 3, 5)	340
5. Epaphroditus (Phil. ii. 25)	341
6. Eyes to the Blind (Job xxix. 15)	342
7. Pilgrims to Canaan (Num. x. 29)	343
8. Hard to Blot out (Ps. li. 9)	344
9. The Three R's (Luke i. 1)	345
10. Closed Eyes opened (Ps. cxix. 18)	346
11. Partakers of Others' Sins (1 Tim. v. 22)	347
12. Be Honest (Ps. li. 6)	348
13. Using the Means (Acts xxvii. 31)	349
14. The Filling of the Cup (Luke xiii. 8)	350
15. In His Steps (1 Pet. ii. 21)	351
16. The Common Lot (Gen. v. 5, 8, 11)	352
17. Amid Changeful Weather (2 Tim. ii. 13)	353
18. A Helpful Master (Isa. xli. 10)	354
19. I must Work (John ix. 4)	355

Contents.

		PAGE
20. There also (John xii. 26)	. . . .	356
21. Shutting the Door (Gen. vii. 16 and Matt. xxv. 10)	. . .	357
22. Now (2 Cor. vi. 2)	. . . .	358
23. Heirs of God (Rom. viii. 17)	. . . .	359
24. The Safe Refuge (Ps. xlvi. 1)	. . . .	360
25. The Young Child (Matt. ii. 14)	. . . . . .	361
26. The Kindest Wish (3 John 2)	. . . .	362
27. A Pressing Invitation (Rev. xxii. 17)	. . . . .	363
28. Hitherto (1 Sam. vii. 12 and John xvi. 24)	. . . .	364
29. Henceforth (2 Cor. v. 15)	. . . .	365
30. The Sin of Ingratitude (Ps. ciii. 2)	. . . . .	366
31. The Story of Life (Ps. xc. 9)	. . . .	367

For Days of Youth

The Days of thy Youth.
January 1

"Remember now thy Creator in the days of thy youth" (Eccles. xii. 1).

THY youth! As the old preacher utters his counsel, he calls to mind his own youth with a sigh. It is for ever gone. Its days, and years too, are like a short-lived dream of the long ago. But *thy* youth is still thine, though its days are hurrying by. Remember God in them, he says. Let no day pass without thinking of Him, and of what you owe to Him. Hear His loving-kindness in the morning—in the morning of your life—in the free bright morning time, before the noisy voices of earth can claim and keep your ear and heart. And as you hear His loving-kindness every morning, let your life each day speak forth His praise!

"The days of thy youth"—how precious they are! They are happy days, influential days, fleeting days.

(1) *Happy days*—surely you feel them to be that! No doubt youth has its own troubles; its sorrows, losses, disappointments. It is not all brightness. But there is in it far more of the sunshine than of the shadow. Youth's tears are quickly dried; and there is soon again the clear shining after rain. One thing you may be very sure of—that, if you are spared to be old, you will look back upon the days of your youth as very gladsome days. "The days of our youth"—when we looked with new eyes upon a new world that met us with a smile—when the earth seemed so beautiful, and men so true, and women all so good—when we marched to the music of hope, with few burdens upon the back, and few cares upon the

The Days of thy Youth.

heart, to make the wealth of life our own—what wonder that we who are older look back upon them even now with a peculiar pleasure! They were for us what God and all the good desire that they should be for you—happy days.

(2) *Influential days*: yes, they are that too, even when you are least thinking of it. Youth is undoubtedly the seed-time for the harvest that is to follow. The babe has been called "a bundle of *possibilities*." In youth you have already begun to determine what you are *actually* to be. Your heart is now open to impressions which will leave their mark on all your future life. The choices you now make, the friendships you form, the patterns you accept, the habits you acquire—tell me these, and I may with much confidence predict what sort of man or woman you will be. Now is the time for high thoughts and noble purposes. Now is the time for seeking a lifelong friendship with Him who will enable you to realise them.

(3) *Fleeting days*—how swiftly fleeting! You are anxious to grow quickly older? That is a wish very sure to be fulfilled. The year just gone—how short it seems to look back upon! The years will ever seem to vanish more swiftly as they go. The days of youth will speedily pass into other days. But they need not be "evil days"; and will not be, if we have Him with us who has promised to be with His people "*all the days* even to the end." With a heart kept young by His presence even to old age, you will have the best of life—an immortal youth—before you still.

> "Then be thou zealous in thy youth;
> Fill every day with noble toils;
> Fight for the victories of Truth,
> And deck thee with her deathless spoils."

A Gift God asks.   January 2

"My son, give me thine heart" (Prov. xxiii. 26).

This, dear young people, is a season for giving as well as receiving gifts. You have got some, I doubt not; and you may have given some. I wonder if you have yet acted on the invitation of this text? If you have not, do it now! Then there will be joy among the angels of heaven, and yours will be indeed a Happy New Year.

We find here (1) *God asking something*. Is not this unusual—God, who is always giving, and to whom the earth belongs and the fulness thereof, asking something? But the wonder grows when we see (2) *from whom He asks it*. If you were told of some person that he had a gift to bestow that the Queen was very anxious to possess, you would at once say that surely he must be very rich or great. But if you wish to know the person from whom the King of kings asks this that He so much desires, you have not far to go; for it is from *you*. And now notice very specially (3) *what He asks*. It is something that He values more than all the money in all the banks in all the world. It is not things you have, your possessions, that He seeks. These are His already. They have been only lent to you. What He longs for is—yourself.

We are told of the great teacher Socrates, that, at the beginning of the session, all the scholars brought to him their gifts. But there was one who hung back when the others advanced with their presents to their loved master. It was seen that tears were coursing down his cheeks, when suddenly he sprang forward, and, flinging himself at the feet of Socrates, exclaimed—"Master, I have nought to offer thee. But I give thee myself!" This was the most valued of all the gifts. And Socrates answered, "I will give thee back thyself, better than when I received thee!"

To satisfy His own love, to secure your safety and happiness, God is saying to you, in view of the future year and the future life, "My son, my daughter, give me thine heart!" You will not be in any sense the worse, but in every sense the better, for giving obedience now to this gracious call.

The Advocate.

"We have an Advocate with the Father" (1 John ii. 1).

THE word "Advocate" here means *one called to help* another. It is now chiefly used of one who pleads a cause. And in this sense, as well as in the wider one, Jesus is our Advocate.

Have you ever been in a law court, I wonder? There you will see the judge upon the bench, looking very solemn but very calm: at the side, the culprit at the bar, looking very anxious and perhaps downcast; and, in front of the bench, the advocate, busy with his papers, and very eager to make the most of his case.

Now, our text speaks of a case being tried. Who is the Judge? God, the Judge of all the earth, seated on His eternal throne. And who is the culprit? You, or I, who have broken God's holy law. And who is the Advocate? Ah, who? Not ourselves—not any other man: else there can be but one sentence—*Death!* But here there is One we can trust, Jesus—whom multitudes have trusted, and not in vain.

Men esteem an advocate who is *able, earnest, fair, successful*; and "Jesus Christ the righteous" is all this.

1. He is infinitely *wise*. When any case is committed to Him, He can take in all its bearings at a glance, and knows exactly how to represent it.

2. He is entirely *earnest*, and pleads as though He were pleading for His own very life.

3. He is absolutely *fair*, and does not attempt to hide the very worst that can be truly said against those He argues for.

4. And He is always *successful*. Millions have looked to Him for aid, and He never once has lost a case He undertook. For He has an argument that cannot fail, and that is—Himself, as the sacrifice for sin.

Will you not commit yourself to Him, saying—"Lord Jesus, be my Advocate?" Not only will this give you boldness in the day of judgment—it will give you present peace.

Knowing our Way.

January 4

"But He knoweth the way that I take" (Job xxiii. 10).

THESE are the words of Job, when he was in great perplexity and distress. He was troubled, because he could not find God, to speak with Him, and get his difficulties cleared away. Whether he went backward or forward, he could not perceive Him: whether he looked to the left hand or to the right hand, he could not see Him. But he falls back at last on this comforting thought—Whether I see Him or not, He sees me! "He knoweth the way that I take."

When you are sailing towards the Kyles of Bute, it seems at one point as though your farther progress were completely barred. Your vessel appears to be bearing down upon a small land-locked bay; and, standing upon the deck, you cannot see how it is possible for you to get along much farther. But on the ship glides, under the skilful direction of the pilot; and just when you reach the point at which your way seemed "hedged up so that you could not pass," you perceive a narrow opening to the left, along which the vessel is smoothly guided into the larger room beyond.

Even so may it be with you sometimes in your future life. There may seem to be so many difficulties ahead of you, as completely to hem you in. But if you have Christ with you in the ship, not only will He know the way you take, but He will guide you in the right way. With Him as your Pilot, you will find that your difficulties marvellously disappear, and that, just where you expected your progress to be stopped, He gives your course a new direction, that will bring you through scenes of beauty and of peace to the larger liberty beyond. When you come to the most difficult part of your passage, and are called to launch out into the great unknown sea, you will be comforted to see your Pilot face to face, and to know that He, not you, will still be at the helm.

You remember the beautiful hymn of Tennyson which closes with the words—

> "For though from out our bourne of Time and Place
> The flood may bear me far,
> I hope to see my Pilot face to face
> When I have crossed the bar."

January 5 — **A Prayer and a Resolve.**

" Hold Thou me up . . . and I will have respect unto Thy statutes continually "
(Ps. cxix. 117).

In the heart of every prayer, there ought to be a resolve. And the Psalmist here utters both. He gives us—

(1) A good *New Year's prayer*: "Hold Thou me up, and I shall be safe." This expresses our dependence upon God. When you were learning to walk, you were glad of even a finger to support you. When some of you boys were being taught to swim, you were thankful for the float, or for the belt and cord with which your teacher held you up. Now you are called to go in the path of duty, and you may have to climb amid difficulties and dangers. You are to set forth on the ocean of life, and you may have often to swim in weariness against the tide. Commit yourself to Christ. If he holds you up, you will be safe, and your progress will be sure.

But remember the *and* with which duty is linked to privilege, as the Psalmist gives us—

(2) A good *New Year's resolve*: "And I will have respect unto Thy statutes continually." By God's *statutes* are meant His fixed rules, those laws of His which He will not and cannot relax in order to please us. If we break these, we dishonour Him, and at the same time injure ourselves. Our true safety and well-being cannot be secured except by *having respect* to God's statutes. What is meant by this? It means that we shall not only learn them, but that we shall constantly remember and act upon them.

That word "continually" is an important word. A traveller is climbing a difficult mountain, along with an experienced Alpine guide. He is careful for the most part; but at one point he fails to have respect to his guide's instructions, and sinks into a deep crevasse. The momentary carelessness has cost him his life. You have the Best of all Guides, All-Wise and Almighty. But the heights of holiness are hard to climb. The hill of perfection is higher than Mont Blanc. Follow the Lord fully. Cleave to Him closely. Have respect to His statutes continually.

A Strange Command.

"Grow in grace, and in the knowledge of our Lord and Saviour Jesus Christ"
(2 Pet. iii. 18).

ONE of the most interesting things about you young people is, that you are growing; and growing up, not down. Your parents like to see that. You yourselves like to know it. Very probably there is a door or a post somewhere, on which there are marks which tell you how much you have grown in height from time to time.

Now it is pleasant to see you boys growing—big, and strong, and manly. May you at the same time grow brave, and pure, and wise. Above all, seek that you may grow in the grace and in the knowledge of our Lord and Saviour Jesus Christ.

We read of one little boy, that "he grew, and the Lord was with him." That was Samuel: and when his mother brought him a new and larger tunic year by year, she found that he had grown in more ways than one, and was better fitted to be a good and valiant servant of Jehovah. Of another boy we are told, that he increased not only in stature, but "in wisdom, and in favour with God and man." That was Jesus Himself, the boy of Nazareth.

Make it your ambition to be like them. What a grand thing it will be, if you are found growing more Christlike, the older you grow. This is really what is meant by growing in "grace." For grace means *beauty*—and the highest of all beauty, girls, is the grace, the loveliness of Christ. This is the sort of beauty you are to covet and to seek.

It may seem a strange command this—"grow." You cannot by taking thought, by wishing it, add a single inch to your height. And yet you can help on your growth. You can avoid what will hinder it. And by taking good food, breathing pure air, and having plenty of exercise, you may promote it. So, too, with your spiritual growth. If you feed on God's Word, breathe the air of God's fellowship, and enjoy the exercise of doing good, then you will grow in heavenly stature. But remember, that in order to growth there must first be life: and it is only from Christ that either life or growth can come.

January 7

A Special Promise.

"Those that seek Me early shall find Me" (Prov. viii. 17).

These are the words of Wisdom, whom we learn to know better in the New Testament as the Lord Jesus Christ. Some put "earnestly" instead of "early" in the text; but we shall keep it as it is, and take the words as a loving promise to the young from the kind Saviour, who long afterwards said, "Suffer the little children to come unto Me." He is the same yesterday, to-day, and for ever; and He is saying to you, "Those that seek Me early shall find Me."

If we seek, it means either that we have lost something that we need, or that we are without something that we wish. Now it is the case that we have lost God through sin, and are in a very real sense ourselves lost. Well for us all to feel our loss, and to seek after Jesus as One we dearly wish to call our own! For if with all our hearts we truly seek Him, we shall surely find Him. And there is this special encouragement for *you*, "Those that seek Me early shall find Me."

Jesus is seeking *you*: and there are special reasons why you should seek Him "early." (1) It will be *safer for you*. You know not when you may be called away from earth. There are little graves as well as big ones in the cemetery; and the reaper Death gathers the "flowerets" as well as the bearded grain. But, with Christ as your Saviour, you will be ready, and you need not fear.

(2) It will be *happier for you*. Your whole life on earth will be the brighter if you give yourself to Jesus now, instead of waiting till old age—even if you were sure that you would be spared so long, or sure that you would find Him then. And besides this,

(3) It will be *happier for Christ*. You will rejoice His heart by coming early to Him: and surely you would like to make Jesus glad? The Good Shepherd yearns over His lost lambs. The loving Saviour will be at least as glad as you can be if you seek and find Him *now*. How joyful for you both, if you are able to say—

> "I've found a Friend; Oh such a Friend!
> He loved me ere I knew Him;
> He drew me with the cords of love,
> And thus He bound me to Him."

The First Preacher.

"He, being dead, yet speaketh" (Heb. xi. 4).

This is said of Abel. He had his place far up the stream of time: so that much can be said of him that can be said of nobody else.

He was *the first brother*: the first to whom anyone on earth could turn and say, "my brother." No doubt, for a time at least, Cain was glad to have one to speak to and play with, whom he could call by that sweet name. He was *the first shepherd*, too. The names of other Bible shepherds will occur to you—Jacob, Moses, David, and Jesus, "that great Shepherd of the sheep." It was from his flock that Abel brought the offering whose acceptance by God cost him life, but gained him life eternal. For He was *the first to die*. In Abel it was that Adam and Eve first had their hearts pierced at the sight of death. The first to die was not an old person, but a youth slain by an envious brother's hand. But, then, he was *the first to enter heaven*. When he went there, he was for a time the only human inhabitant of the heavenly palace. How the angels must have looked at him! How the Son of God must have rejoiced to hear his solitary note of praise, knowing that, by and by, there would be attuned to it the songs of "an exceeding great multitude whom no man can number!"

And, lastly, Abel is *the first preacher*. "By it"—that is, by his faith—"he, being dead, yet speaketh." He speaks still to us, of One who is a Brother, "bone of our bone, and flesh of our flesh"; of One who is a Shepherd, "the Good Shepherd," who gave His life for the sheep, but took it again, that He might lead them to green pastures and bring them to living fountains of waters; of One who is a Priest and also a Lamb, to whom the offering of Abel pointed forward, and through whose Sacrifice it was that Abel got to Heaven, and all poor sinners that have ever been admitted there. Abel did not know that he was preaching by his faith, or that his sermon would be listened to so long. What kind of lesson does *your* life speak?

God sees!

"Thou, God, seest me" (Gen. xvi. 13).

WHERE is God? *In heaven*, one answers. *Everywhere*, says another. *Here*, replies a third. And all are right. But the last answer is, in some respects, the best.

A sceptic—a proud careless man who said, not only in his heart, but with his tongue, that there is "no God"—had printed over his study mantelpiece the words: "God is no-where." His little daughter was one day playing in the room, when her eye caught the words hung upon the wall. She began to spell them out. "G-O-D, God; I-S, is; N-O-W, now; H-E-R-E, here—God is now here." She spelled them differently from her father, but more correctly than he! And her simple, artless words, spoken half unconsciously aloud, sunk deep into his heart.

Now, when Hagar gave this name to God—"Thou, God, seest me," she felt and was thankful that God was near. These words, as used at first, do not come as a warning, but as an encouragement.

They do give a note of warning. They remind us that God sees us everywhere and at all times, that He looks us through and through. Man looks upon the outward appearance, but God looks into the heart. As with certain beehives made of glass, in which all the operations within are disclosed to view, so is it with our hearts. Everything within is naked and open to the eyes of Him with whom we have to do. "Live guiltless: God is looking," was the motto of Linnæus, and is a suitable motto for others beside.

But "Thou, God, seest me" should bring us not warning only, but comfort. He looks upon us, not with the cold eye of a detective, but with the eye of a Friend and Father, who is deeply interested in our good. He whose eye followed poor fleeing Hagar, the slave, and whose voice spoke a word of comfort to her in her distress, is looking down upon you in love. If you are relying upon Him as your Father in Heaven, it will be with a thrill of thankfulness, and not with a shudder of guilty fear, that you turn to Him and say—"Thou, God, seest me!"

"*None of us liveth to himself*" (Rom. xiv. 7).

THIS is true in a sense of everybody. None of us could live only to himself, even if he tried. We are all influencing one another. The lives of different people are so interlaced with one another, that one cannot be good without benefiting others, or bad without hurting somebody else.

But it is specially true of Christians, so far as they are worthy of the name, that "none of *us* liveth to himself." Certainly Christ did not. He came not to be ministered unto, but to minister, and to give His life a ransom for many. He both lived and died for others. And if we are to be worthy followers of His, we, too, shall be found living, not for self, but for others.

The selfish life is a miserable, unhappy, and, in the end, unsuccessful life. You may remember the story of Ralph the Rover, who, to serve his own ends, cut away the bell that used to warn mariners away from the fatal Inchcape Rock. He hoped to secure plunder from the wrecks. But one night, in a dreadful storm, his own ship struck upon the self-same rock, from which the bell might otherwise have warned him; and, as he and his crew sank beneath the waves, they were taught in a terrible way what a wretched doom awaits the selfish life.

The truly Christian life, on the other hand, takes as its motto—"As we have opportunity, let us do good unto all men." It finds, it contrives to make, such opportunities. And in helping others, the follower of Christ is helped himself. For Christian service is twice blessed. Any deed of love you render will not only benefit him you seek to aid, but it will prove a blessing to yourself. You will not be thinking of recompense, but Jesus will see to it that, if you give even a cup of cold water in His name to a thirsty soul, it shall not be left without reward. One of your hymns appropriately prays—

"God make my life a little song
That comforteth the sad,
That helpeth others to be strong,
And makes the singer glad."

The Fowler's Snare.

"Escaped as a bird out of the snare of the fowlers" (Ps. cxxiv. 7).

Do you know what a fowler is? He is one who catches fowls, *i.e.*, what we now call birds or "fowls of the air." This he does in a variety of ways. Sometimes he spreads a net with very fine meshes over some tempting grain; or he sets gins or traps for his feathery victims; or he spreads quicklime on spots where they are likely to settle, such as the tops of poles or tree branches, which holds them fast. And then, he has often what are called "decoy birds," —that is, birds which he has already caught, and tamed, and trained to sing, so that they may tempt other birds into captivity.

Now there is one great fowler, against whom you must be upon your guard. His name is Satan, the enemy of our souls. A clever fowler is he. He spreads his grain. He sets his snares. He has his decoy birds, too, in readiness. Alas for you, if he gets you fairly entangled in the meshes of evil habit, or fettered in the quicklime of despair! Yet even then there is hope for you in Christ, who has come to destroy the works of the devil, and who delights to set the captive free.

The saddest captivity is that which has so broken the spirit of the prisoner that he no longer has the heart to care for freedom. A man who had been himself a captive in a foreign land once saw an eagle, chained by the foot within a large iron-barred cage. He resolved to buy for the noble bird his freedom. So, having paid the price, he had a door of the cage flung open, and the fetter removed. But, to his disappointment and the surprise of the onlookers, the eagle never stirred. It had been so long in slavery that it knew not what freedom meant. But in a moment or two, a wing was stretched out, then the other, and the king of birds looked up to the sky. The love of liberty was waking in his breast. A minute more, and the disused pinions began to flap; and soon he was mounting upward to the azure blue.

May the Lord deliver you from every snare and evil work, and give you to know the freedom wherewith He makes His people free, —to rise higher and higher in the enjoyment of a heaven-bought liberty.

A Little Minister.

January 12

"*The child did minister unto the Lord*" (1 Sam. ii. 11).

This is said of little Samuel, when he was living at Shiloh with old Eli. It was not much that he could do, at that time, in the way of service. He was not very strong, and he had not much experience. But he had the desire within him to be useful, and he was able every day to gratify that desire. He could open the door of the tabernacle; he could trim the sacred lamps; he could in many ways be a help and a comfort to God's High Priest. And in all this, he was "ministering to the Lord." He was a little minister, or servant, of Jehovah.

Now there is great room still in God's world for "ministering children." There are words of love that none can speak so well as they. There are deeds of kindness that can best be wrought by little hands. There are messages of mercy on which little feet, better than any other, may speed.

The great poet Wordsworth once wrote in a child's album these words, which you should learn by heart—

> "Small service is true service while it lasts:
> Of friends, however humble, scorn not one.
> The daisy, by the shadow that it casts,
> Protects the lingering dewdrop from the sun."

Certain it is, that Jesus does not despise any of His friends, however humble. The smallest servant, and the littlest service, is noted and valued by Him.

If, however, you are to serve Christ, you must give yourself to Him. "Whose I am" should come first, and *then* "whom I serve," in the motto of your life. But if this be so, you will not only be found *doing* helpful things, but *being* a real help wherever you go. "This is the little boy that helps the minister," said the pastor one day, laying his hand on Johnny's head. The mother looked surprised, but he continued—"Yes: for I see his eager attentive face looking up at me week by week; and he helps me to preach the better for it." So Johnny ministered to the minister, you see, and through him to the Lord.

The Wishing Gate.

"Wisdom is better than rubies" (Prov. viii. 11).

THERE is a gate in the Lakes District in England called the Wishing Gate. To it the young country people are said to resort, in the belief that whatever wish they express while standing by it is very likely to be granted.

If you could be brought to such a wishing gate, where what you most desired was sure to be given, I wonder what your greatest wish would be? To live long, to have plenty to eat and nothing to do? Surely not. To be a grand lady, with rich dresses, a fine carriage, a beautiful house, and plenty of servants? Something better, surely, than this. To be a mighty hero, famed for conquest, and held in honour by a grateful and admiring nation? Something better yet than this.

Young Solomon made a wise choice, when he was brought to the wishing gate. God said to him in a dream (1 Kings iii. 5)—"Ask, what I shall give thee." And Solomon asked *wisdom*. God approved his choice, and told him that, along with wisdom he would get riches, and honour, and other things, which he had not asked. And Solomon saw no reason afterwards to regret the choice. He says, in the light of experience, concerning wisdom, that it is "better than rubies." And so it is. Riches in the pocket, or a jewelled diadem upon the head, is not to be compared in value to the riches of the heart. What we have is of little account compared to what we are.

Therefore, choose Wisdom. I write it here with a capital letter; because, while wisdom has been called "the choice of the best ends and of the best means of attaining them," Wisdom is also a Person. Again and again in the Book of Proverbs you find Wisdom so represented; and in this eighth chapter there are things said of Wisdom that are true only of God's own Son. Choose *Him*. Take Christ to your heart. If His Spirit dwell within you, yours will be a happy life, a peaceful death, a glorious eternity. If you choose Him, everything really desirable which you have not asked will be also given to you by God.

Good Scholars.   January 14

"If ye continue in My word, then are ye My disciples indeed"
(John viii. 31).

To whom was this spoken? Was it to the Twelve? No: it was to "the Jews who believed on Him." So that, you see, those who believe in Jesus are disciples: and all of them should seek to be disciples indeed. Some are old disciples, like Mnason (with whom Paul lodged, Acts xxi. 16). Others are young disciples, like Timothy. Some have been long in Christ's school; others only a short time. But all, old and young, have much to learn yet from such a Master, and ought to be eager to make the most of their opportunities.

The word "disciples" means *learners*, or *students*, if you like. Now we know that there are students *and* students at college; just as there are scholars *and* scholars in every school. Some are content to have merely the name; others do some work now and again, by fits and starts. The true students, or scholars, are those who love truth, and are patient in the pursuit of it.

Jesus wishes you to be good scholars in His school. If you have believed in Him, you have obtained an entrance to His school, as a beginner, in the lowest form. And perhaps you have risen somewhat already. Go on learning, He says; keep at it. Continue in My word. Learn more and more, and live by what you learn. If you are a humble, persevering learner and doer of My will, then you will be a scholar worthy of the name, "a disciple indeed."

It is one of the great secrets of getting on in any art, to put in practice what you have already learned. An old proverb says, "Practice makes perfect." Well, religion is both a science and an art. It invites you both to know and to do. You must therefore seek to know more and more of the will of Jesus, and at the same time to do it more perfectly; and, as He Himself tells you, the more diligently you do it, the better you will understand His teaching. What a wonderful privilege for you, to be an everyday scholar in such a Master's school!

January 15 — Hid in the Heart.

"Thy word have I hid in mine heart, that I might not sin against Thee"
(Ps. cxix. 11).

WHY do you hide a thing? Either because you value it very much, *or* because you are ashamed of it. The mother of Moses hid her babe, because "he was a goodly child," and very dear. Moses, long after, hid the Egyptian in the sand, because he was afraid to have his deed of blood made known.

A boy or a girl has done something wrong. *Shame* says, "Hide it." A boy or a girl owns something precious, that is in danger of being taken away. *Love* says, "Hide it." May you have little to hide this year in the first sense, else you are sure to be unhappy. See that you hide God's Word in the second sense, as a precious treasure in the heart, and all your days will be joyous in the sunshine of His love.

"In the heart." Why *in the heart*?

(1) Because the heart is the inmost, *safest place*. A little girl in a popish country was presented with a Bible. She learned through it to know and love the Saviour. The promises of Scripture were her comfort, and the pattern life of Jesus her constant study. But people in that country were forbidden to read God's Word. What did the little girl do to keep her Bible safe? She *buried it in the garden*: and she used to go as often as she could to dig up her treasure, that she might enjoy the reading of it. Now, *you* have not to hide God's Word in the garden. But you should hide it deep and safe within the heart. An Irish boy whose Bible was burned by his priest was able to tell him—"But you can't burn these chapters that I have learnt by heart!" And you are to hide God's Word there—

(2) Because the heart is the place of *greatest influence*. There is no part of the body so all-important as the heart. If it be sound, a person as a rule is strong. If it be wrong, nearly everything goes wrong. For the heart has to "circulate," or send round, the blood to every member of the body. Now, just so is it with the spiritual life. The state of "the heart" affects everything. From it goes forth an influence which is felt on all that a person is and does. See that you have God's Word then hidden there! And remember that "the Word" means sometimes not the Book, but the Son of God (John i. 1). To have Him hid in the heart will be the secret of a happy year and a happy life.

"*Let your light so shine before men*" (Matt. v. 16).

SHINING is here brought before us as a duty. This verse tells us—

(1) *Who* is expected to shine? You! Of course you must be lit first, before you can shine. But if you are Christ's, you will be found shining to some extent in His light. He says of Himself, "I am the light of the world." But he also says to His people, "Ye are the light of the world." And their business is, like the reflector on the lighthouse tower, to send Christ's light out upon a dark world.

(2) *Where?* In "the world"; and that just means, your own little world, wherever it may be. If the right spirit is in you, if love shines out from you, it will reach somebody for good. A believer once said despondingly—"I have no more influence than a farthing rushlight." The answer was—"Well, a farthing rushlight can do a great deal. It could set a haystack on fire, or burn down a house; and it can do more and better than that—it can help some poor creature to read God's word, and to learn the way to heaven."

(3) *How?* Through "good works." There must be not only kind wishes in the heart, but kind deeds in the life; for it is these only that can be seen. Light itself is invisible. But we perceive its presence in the objects it reveals. Now a very simple action, done from a loving heart, may shed a deal of light on some darkened life. A poor sufferer said—"That pretty posy in the cracked tumbler by my bedside was brought to-day by a little girl, who said it was all she had to bring. But it is worth a great deal to know I am remembered. And that flower has made me think all day of the green fields and posies I used to know when I was young; and it has reminded me of what a wonderful God we have. If this flower was not beneath His making and care, He will not forget or overlook the humblest of His children."

(4) *Why?* You are to shine, not that you may be admired, or your goodness talked about, but that God may be glorified. An architect once built a great pier, and put the king's name upon it with words of honour. But after some years passed, the waves washed off the concrete from the surface. And there, graven into the stone, was the architect's own name in large letters seen! Let not yours be a mock humility like this. Be sure *so* to shine that your Father, not you, may be glorified.

The Beloved.

"Accepted in the Beloved" (Eph. i. 6).

THIS beautiful name makes us think of two things about Christ.

First, it makes us think of *the love of His Father for Him.* God is love; and He loves all the creatures He has made. But there is One Being He loves above all else—the Son who dwelt in His bosom from all eternity. Others are beloved; but this is *the Beloved.* "My Beloved Son, in whom I am ever well pleased." Can you wonder at it? Oh how God rejoiced to have such a Son!

Second, this name makes us think of *the love of Christ's people for Him.* There are many whom they love on earth, and some have gone to heaven. But He is to them "the chief among ten thousand, the altogether lovely." He has the supreme place in their hearts. And do you know the secret of it? He has been more to them, and done more for them, than any other could. He has been their Saviour. He has opened the gate of heaven for them. They are "*accepted* in the Beloved."

There is often a great love for Jesus in a little child's heart—a love greater than for the nearest earthly friend. It is told of a great philosopher, whose child lay dying, that, taking her hand, he said in tears, "Do you love me, darling?" "Yes," was the answer, "but *I love Jesus more.*" And that sorrowing father could not, in that moment, be jealous of that love.

A little boy of five was reading to his mother one day, about the Son of Man, who had not where to lay His head. He stopped for a little, and said, with much emotion—"Oh, mother, if I had been there, I would have given Him my pillow!" Is Jesus your Beloved? And are you His? Are you doing anything to show how much you love Him? Remember that He says—"If ye love Me, keep My commandments." May it be yours to say to Him in all sincerity—

> "My joy is in Thy beauty
> Of holiness divine;
> My comfort in the duty
> That binds my life in Thine.
> Oh for a heart to love Thee
> More truly as I ought,
> And nothing place above Thee
> In deed, or word, or thought."

My Jewels.   January 18

"In that day when I make up My jewels" (Mal. iii. 17).

The word "jewel" is derived, through the Italian *gioella*, from the word joy (*gioja*). It thus means, something that we rejoice in. It commonly stands for precious stones or trinkets, used as ornaments for the person, which many people are very fond of, and set a great value upon.

Now, the jewels of God are not precious stones or ornaments of gold, but the souls of His beloved people. In the great day, when much that is worthless shall be destroyed by fire, He will see to it that *they* are kept safe. Not one of His people shall be amissing in the day when He makes up His jewels.

A very little consideration will show you how unspeakably precious the souls of His people are to Jesus.

Think of *the price He paid* to redeem them. It was not corruptible things like silver and gold that He gave, but His own precious blood.

Think of the *search He made* to recover them. He came all the way from Heaven—He who humbleth Himself to behold the things which are upon the earth—that He might search for His jewels in the mud and grime of this sinful world until he found them.

Think of the *care He takes* of them. How He guards them, as with His very life! He is resolved that, whatever happens, they shall be safe. And He says: "None shall be able to pluck them out of My hand . . . and out of My Father's hand." Both His hand and His Father's hand are about them: so precious are His jewels.

Think of *the preparation He bestows* on them. Never did a jeweller bestow such pains on getting a precious stone ready for its place, as Jesus, by His Spirit, bestows on the souls He has redeemed.

And think of *the setting He has in store* for them—a place in His own glorious crown. They are His joy and "crown of rejoicing." Oh, what an honour to have a place in the everlasting diadem of Christ!

January 19. Poor Balaam.

"Balaam also, the son of Beor, they slew with the sword" (Num. xxxi. 8).

Such was the end of this remarkable but unenviable man. Looking at Balaam, we feel inclined at first to admire him; but we soon see reason not, after all, to envy him.

He was (1) *a very majestic, but a very hollow man.* You may have seen a tree, tall and stately, with spreading branches and beautiful green leaves, and you said—"A noble tree!" But by and by the woodman comes, and taps it with his axe. There is decay within. There is a canker at its heart. It is, with all its fine appearance, a rotten shell. Such was Balaam.

Then he was (2) *a very clever, but a very foolish man.* He knew a great deal more than other people. He was looked up to as a sage. He could work wonders, and was counted a great magician. He "could look after number one," and was very shrewd. He was eloquent, and could even prophesy. But, after all, he was not wise; for to be wise and to be clever are two different things. With all his knowledge, he did not know himself; and he did not truly know God. With all his shrewdness, he did not lay out his life well. He lived for a wrong end, and he used wrong means. Therefore he was not wise.

He was, moreover, (3) *a great gainer, but a greater loser.* No doubt he was a successful man in a way, but not in God's way. He was like a child giving up a valuable jewel for some toys. When the toys were broken, or you had grown tired of them, you might cry out for your jewel again in vain. So was it with poor Balaam. He gained large influence—great fame—much gold—kingly company and favour. But he lost God's favour. He lost his own soul. So, what profit had he?

The saddest thing about Balaam is, that (4) *he was very near the kingdom of God, and yet outside.* He came into close contact with God's people, and, in spite of himself, admired them. He blessed instead of cursing them. He had much religious knowledge, and could utter a pious wish about his death. But he fell fighting against the cause and people of God, after tempting Israel to gross sin. How sad—to be so near and yet outside! How sad—when a great vessel goes down just outside the harbour!

The Broken Heart.

"A broken and a contrite heart" (Ps. li. 17).

IT is not the case with many things that they are more valuable after being broken. But of some things this is true.

It was true of *the alabaster box of precious ointment*, which the woman brake (Mark xiv. 3). Had she kept it whole, it might have been worth three hundred pence, as Judas said ; but when she broke it, its fragrance filled the world, and its value could not be set down in pence, or in pounds either.

It is also true of *the body of Christ*, that precious temple in which the Holy Ghost dwelt, and which He had specially prepared for the pure soul of Jesus to inhabit. Precious in itself, it became infinitely more precious for us sinners, and therefore for Christ Himself, when He could speak of it as " My body broken for you." For, through the breaking of His body,—that is, His death upon the tree,—He purchased our salvation.

And it is also true of *the sinner's heart*. The Bible says that, while unbroken, the heart of the wicked is " little worth " (Prov. x. 20). But, when broken, it is something which God will not despise. On the contrary, He greatly values it. Much can be made of it *then* which could not have been made of it before. And much *is* made of it. For God makes it His *dwelling place*. He says : " I will take up my abode in that broken heart. With that man will I dwell, who is of a humble and contrite heart." God also makes of it His *garden*. It was too hard and stony before, to admit of beautiful flowers growing in it. But when it is broken, the soil becomes soft and open ; and the fair graces of the Spirit thrive within it.

When the great preacher Whitefield was at Exeter, a man in the audience had his pocket full of stones, which he intended to throw at the preacher. He waited through the prayer ; and, as the text was about to be announced, he pulled out a stone. But God sent the sword of the Spirit into his breast ; and the stone was never thrown. He went up to Whitefield after the service, saying—" Sir, I came here intending to give you a broken head ; but God has given me a *broken heart*." The man proved himself afterwards a good and useful Christian.

It is a good prayer for each of us—" May I indeed have, O Lord, the broken and contrite heart ! "

January 21 — The Whole Heart.

"Blessed are they that seek Him with the whole heart" (Ps. cxix. 2).

THE broken heart, as we saw yesterday, is of much value in the sight of God. But there is a sense in which God values the whole heart too. He likes the sinner to have a broken heart. But when that is accomplished, He likes him as a believer to have a whole heart. To this end God sends His Spirit, that He may renew the heart of the penitent, and make it whole again,—though not in the old hard sense,—that it may be wholly given to God.

If you ask what the whole heart *is*, and *does*, I will tell you.

It is a *soft* heart still: not cold, and selfish, and hard, but tender toward God and man. It is a *sound* heart. Its beat is healthful. Not weak and irregular, but strong, and steady, and true. It is a *single* heart. Not divided in its loyalty, as with those of whom it is said, "Their heart is divided, they are found faulty"; but single in its attachment to Christ. And it is a *satisfied* heart. Not fluttering about, vainly seeking rest and finding none; not longing, as a great man did, who had tasted all that worldly success and praise could give him, for a short return to the earlier days of youth and love which could never be recalled; but a heart satisfied in Christ, to whom a great sinner in the early days, who afterwards became a great saint (Augustine), addressed these true and memorable words—"Thou hast made us for Thyself; and our hearts are restless, until they find rest in Thee."

As to what the whole heart *does*, I will mention only three things. It *seeks God fully*, and in doing so is blessed (Ps. cxix. 2) It *praises God constantly* (Ps. ix. 1, cxi. 1, cxxxviii. 1), and in doing so is made glad. And it *obeys God cheerfully* (Ps. cxix. 69), and, keeping thus the precepts of God, it glorifies Him and does good to others.

If you have received the broken heart, then ask that you may also have the whole heart, which God delights to see in His own people. Make up your mind that, whatever others may be, you are not to be a "half-hearted" Christian. Be out and out for Christ!

The highest Rank and the grandest Title. January 22

"That we should be called the sons of God" (1 John iii. 1).

You young folks know what is meant by calling people names. Those whom you love you call by good names. Those whom you dislike or are angry with, you sometimes, I am afraid, call by bad names. But *our* calling people names does not make them to be what we call them. Though we give them a good name, that does not always imply that they are really good. And your calling a companion by a "nickname" does not necessarily mean that he deserves it. It may tell more about you, and the state of your heart, than about him.

But when God calls anybody by a certain name, it always means a great deal. You may be sure that it is a name that applies to the person to whom He gives it.

Now God here calls those whom He loves by a good name. Their name is "Sons of God." No wonder the Apostle John holds up his hands in amazed thankfulness; for those who get this name from God Himself have the highest rank and wear the grandest title. "Behold, what manner of love the Father"—that is, Christ's Father, and the Father of those who have Him as their Saviour and Elder Brother—"hath bestowed on us, that we should be called the sons of God!"

When our Sovereign wishes to show her regard for one of her subjects, she sometimes gives him a new name, or what is called "a handle to his name." She summons him into her presence; he goes down upon his knee before her; she touches or gently strikes his shoulder with a sword, saying, "Arise, Sir John"; and although when he knelt he may have been plain John Smith, he rises to his feet a Knight. The Queen has called him so to good purpose. In naming him a knight, she has made him one.

Even so, if God calls you something, you are sure to be it, if you are not so already. Have you any reason to think that you are among the "us" of whom the verse speaks?

January 23   **Rich toward God.**

"*And is not rich toward God*" (Luke xii. 21).

THIS *not* applies to the man of whom these verses speak. He was very rich in this world's reckoning. He had lands. He had barns. He had grand crops. He had plenty of money. He had so much of this world's good, that he was actually put about by it. He needed to pull down his barns and build greater; and the time for real enjoyment seemed to him to be still in the future—after he had actually managed this, and so had secured a time of happiness. But he was, after all, a very poor rich man. For he had no higher thought than for the things of earth. All his plans were bounded in by time. And with all his shrewdness, there was one thing he forgot to take into account : and that was, what God might have to say to his arrangements. This was a terrible mistake, as he very soon and sadly found. *And he said:* " I will do this and that, and then I shall be quite happy, and I will say to my soul, Take thine ease, eat, drink, and be merry." *But God said:* " Thou fool, this night shall thy soul be required of thee." And so God came that night, and called his soul away. " He died rich," said the world. " He died poor," said God.

I have known, dear young people, one who was rich in a very different sense from this. His wealth lay, not in the beauty of his Scottish estate on the banks of the Tummel, where at an early age we buried him, but in the wealth of a nature which God, who made him, had wonderfully endowed, and God, who redeemed him, had unspeakably enriched. He was rich in a faith which, in early days, had held out the hand to receive God's greatest Gift, and which nerved him for duty and supported him in trial in after days. He was rich in a love to the Saviour and to all, a love which flowed forth wherever human sympathy might find its opportunity. He was rich in good works : so that, though his ministry was short, he lived much if not long, and left many behind him to bless his name.

> "We live in deeds, not years; in thoughts, not breaths;
> In feelings, not in figures on a dial;
> We should count life by heart throbs. He lives most,
> Who thinks most, feels the noblest, acts the best."

Let it be your aim and mine, so to live as to be rich toward God !

Behold the Lamb!

"The next day John seeth Jesus, and saith, Behold the Lamb of God"
(John i. 29).

Do you know what John's finger was pointing at when he spoke these words? Was it a flock of sheep? No. It was some men passing; and it was one of them whom he singled out, saying, "Look, that is the Lamb of God!" What could he mean?

You know what a lamb is: one of the most innocent, meek, modest, pure beings you can see. Now Jesus was all this. But John means more than this when he points to Him and calls Him the Lamb of God.

Also you know that a "lamb" is a term of endearment. Your mother sometimes calls you "my lamb," because she is so fond of you. And God loves Jesus dearly—far more than ever mother loved her child; but that is not why He is called God's Lamb.

To understand it, you must read the Old Testament. There you often find lambs mentioned in connection with sacrifice. If you had been a Jewish child, instead of a British one, you would have been taken, not to church, but to the tabernacle or the temple; and instead of hearing a sermon, you would have seen one.

Standing among the worshippers, you would have seen the minister, or priest, offering up a lamb upon the altar, in room of the sinful people. Could that save them? No; but it pointed them to One who could. It spoke to them of God's Lamb, whom, in the fulness of the time, God was to deliver up to the death for us. It told them of Jesus, who was to bear upon the cross of Calvary the punishment due for our sins.

Long, long before, Abraham had said to his son Isaac, while they were climbing Mount Moriah together—"My son, God will provide Himself a Lamb for a burnt-offering." And now, John, many generations after, is perceiving the deepest meaning of Abraham's words. "This," he says, pointing to Jesus, "is the Lamb of God, which bears, and bears away, the sin of the world."

Behold Him, young reader. Trust Him. Love Him. Follow after Him. For, if you follow the Lamb whithersoever He goeth, He will lead you at length into the throng who surround "the midst of the throne" (Rev. v. 6).

January 25 — Whom do you serve?

"No man can serve two masters" (Matt. vi. 24).

THERE are several things we ought to bear in mind with regard to service.

(1) *We are all serving some master.* People sometimes do not acknowledge this. They boast of their freedom. So was it with the Pharisees in the days of Jesus upon earth. They proudly declared —"We are Abraham's seed: *we* never were in bondage to any man." But what does Jesus say? "Whosoever committeth sin is the servant of sin." They thought themselves free; but they were all the time slaves of the worst of masters. The question is—Who is our master? We are certainly serving someone.

(2) *Some are trying to serve two masters, but cannot.* The two are, Sin and God. But to serve both with the heart is impossible. Each demands all our time and gifts. And their errands are in such different directions that we cannot be giving obedience to both. Nay, so opposed are the two, that, if the one have our heart, the other may be, to a large extent, shut out of our thoughts. "If any man love the world, the love of the Father is not in him." Robert Hall wrote the word G-O-D on a slip of paper, and then put a sovereign over it, to illustrate how completely the world may, to an earthly mind, shut God out from view. Even a farthing, if brought close to the eye, will hide entirely the glorious sun.

(3) *There is only One Master whom we ought to own and obey.* He is not a tyrant, but our Father. He does not give wages, as Sin does, whose wages is death. But, being our Father, He gives us food, and home, and comfort, and everything. He says to us, as His children in Christ, "Son, all that I have is thine." And what He expects from us is—the free, and joyous, and interested service of a son in the Father's house.

Whom, then, do you serve? Is Sin to have your heart, whose service is the worst of slavery? Or is God to have it, whose service is perfect freedom?

"*I live by the faith of the Son of God, who loved me, and gave Himself for me*" (Gal. ii. 20).

PAUL here lets us into the secret of his life. When the physicians were probing in the breast of one of Napoleon's veterans for the bullet which was lodged there, he said, with a faint smile, "A little deeper, and you will find the emperor." And so, when you probe to the heart of the Apostle Paul, you find—King Jesus. The uppermost thought with him ever is—" He loved me, and gave Himself for me. And now He is my life."

It is told of a Roman servant, that, knowing that the enemy were searching for his master to put him to death, he dressed himself in his master's clothes, and, being mistaken for him, was captured and put to death in his room. This was wonderful devotion; and it is no wonder that the master should have erected a monument of brass in remembrance of such a servant. But here is something more wonderful far—the Prince of Heaven taking upon Him the form of a servant, that He might suffer in the sinner's stead. "He loved me, and died for me."

Whenever Paul's love is in danger of growing cold, he has just to remind himself of this—"*He* loved *me*." Whenever his faith is getting weak, he falls back on this for his strengthening—"He gave Himself for me." When his hope is threatening to grow dim, this revives it—"He loved me, and gave Himself for me." If He did this for me, He did it for a great end, which is sure to be attained. Having conquered death, He ever lives to be my Helper. Why should I fear? Oh, it is a blessed thing to have such a Saviour to trust in, and such a faith to live by. It is not the strength of your faith, remember, that saves you, but the strength of Him on whom it rests. It was said to a good Christian woman once—"And are you the woman with the great faith?" She answered—"No; but I am the woman with a little faith in the great Saviour." How strong is the life that is lived by the faith of the Son of God! How happy is the death which is died in the faith of Him who loved us, and gave Himself for us!

Joyful Progress.

" As the shining light, that shineth more and more unto the perfect day "
(Prov. iv. 18).

This is the kind of life I would wish for you; this is the sort of path which I hope yours is to be—"the path of the just," or righteous. By these are meant those who are accepted for Jesus' sake, and in whose heart have been implanted the beginnings of holiness. They are trusting Jesus, and becoming more like Jesus day by day.

The life of such, we are here reminded, is (1) A *bright* life. It is set in opposition to the way of the wicked, which is as darkness. The two are as unlike as day and night are. Once the Christian, too, was in darkness. But now he is light in the Lord; and his is a bright, joyous, gladsome life. But, further, it is (2) a *helpful* life. The sun does not shine up in the sky for himself. He shows forth the glory of God, and he does, at the same time, good to men. So, if your path is to be "as the light of dawn," you will not be shining only for yourself, but for others. God will be glorified in you, and others blessed. Your cheerful radiance will shine out upon a world of sin. Yours will be a gladdening, light-giving life. You will be among the joy-bringers. And, then, we are here taught that the Christian life is (3) a *growing* life. Just as the light of dawn shines more and more unto the perfect day, so your life should grow in beauty and in splendour with the years. It should be like the path of the sun as he mounts upward to the meridian of his strength.

But at this point the figure fails. For the sun, as we know, begins to decline again, when the zenith has been reached. But whatever may be said of his outward bodily life, the inner life of the Christian—the life of his soul—should never know decline. "I will constantly go on," should be his motto. "From glory to glory," should be his path of happy progress. His is a life that leads to the perfection of beauty—where God shines. There is no night there, and no possibility of even the most short-lived eclipse. May the good Spirit lead you on to that land of uprightness!

Look unto Me! January 28

"Look unto Me, and be ye saved, all the ends of the earth" (Isa. xlv. 22).

ONE wintry day, 15th December 1850, a boy of sixteen who had intended to go to a church farther away, but was prevented by the snow, went into a little Methodist Chapel in the town of Colchester, in England. He was the son of pious parents, and was longing after the truth; but latterly he had been in great darkness and distress of mind. A thin, pale man entered the pulpit: and, after giving out the text (as above), he turned to where the youth was sitting and said—"Young man, you are in trouble. You will never get out of it until you look to Christ. Look! Look! Look!" The youth afterwards tells: "I had been waiting to do fifty things; but when I heard this word 'Look,' what a charming word it seemed to me. Oh, I looked until I could almost have looked my eyes away; and in heaven I will look on still, with joy unutterable."

Do you know who that boy was? His name was Charles Haddon Spurgeon, the greatest English preacher, in some respects, of this or perhaps any century. The thin, pale Methodist preacher did a good day's work, by the blessing of God, when he pointed him, and multitudes through him, to the Saviour, that snowy Sabbath morning in Colchester.

And now, he being dead yet speaketh. The message of his ministry, so greatly blessed of God, and the message from his grave at Upper Norwood to every boy and girl who reads this, is—"Look! Look to Christ! There is life for a look at the Crucified One."

This is a call to be addressed to "all the ends of the earth," because this is something which people everywhere need, and need more than anything else—to be "saved." And, dear young reader, is it not a wonderful and a blessed thing that this great need can be so very simply met? It has cost God a great deal to provide salvation: His own Son had to die in the room of sinners in order to secure it. But all that is asked of you, in order that you may have it, is a look—a simple look of trust to Jesus as your Redeemer. He has been lifted up that He might draw not only men and women, but boys and girls to Himself

January 29. An unsparing God.

"He spared not His own Son" (Rom. viii. 32).

GOD is the great sparer. He is sparing of His children (Mal. iii. 17). When He calls them to serve, He does not lay upon them an unaided and overwhelming task. And when He calls them to suffer, He does not permit them to be tried above that which, by His help, they are able to bear. He "tempers the wind to the shorn lamb."

But God is also the great giver; and, for what He deemed a worthy end,—the salvation of poor lost souls,—He was found ready to give the very best He had to give, with unsparing hand.

This is the great wonder of the Bible. It is the wonder of Heaven. It will be the wonder of eternity:—"God spared not His own Son."

We cannot understand it. Your father and mother might be able to tell a little of what it means, if you were to propose to go to the heart of Africa where fever rages, or to some island where poor lepers dwell, in order that you might do good among your fellow-creatures. Would it not cost them a sore pang to part with you, even for so good an end? I know a mother who gave a bright young son to the mission-field in Africa. He laboured on for the good of the poor black people there for a number of years, often in complete solitude, sometimes in privation and in weakness. Then the time for furlough came, and he had actually entered the steamer to start down the lake toward home. But the people, fearing Arab attacks, implored him to remain, and he had his luggage taken ashore again. Then, after a time, fever laid hold of him, and, at the age of thirty-one, he died in the midst of those he longed to save, giving his last thoughts to the work for which he had given his life. Can you wonder that a mother, while thankful to have such a son, and thankful that he had given himself so nobly to the service of Christ, should have a sore, sore heart in being called to part with him?

But even a case like this falls far short of what our text relates. No son was ever to an earthly parent what God's *own* Son was to Him; and never was there love such as the Father had for Him. Yet, marvel of marvels, "for us" God spared not His own Son!

"*How shall He not with Him also freely give us all things?*" (Rom. viii. 32).

This is what the apostle argues from the fact that was under our consideration yesterday, that "God spared not His own Son." Is He likely, then, asks Paul, to grudge us anything else that will be for our proper good? If He has given this great and unspeakable proof of His love for sinners, is He likely to withhold smaller tokens of it?

A friend pays your debt of £1000, let us say, to get you out of prison. Is he likely to grudge you enough to keep you in life till you are able to find work again? Or someone gives you a rich jewel, worth more money than you could easily count. Is he likely to grudge the casket which is needed to protect it?

If the Queen conferred on a poor subject a rich estate, would the royal treasury be taxed severely in order to pay his railway fare to the place? If your father plans by night and works by day in the sweat of his brow to provide you with food, clothing, and education for your future calling, would it not be surprising—nay, quite incredible—if he were to grudge you a drink of water? And if God spared not His own Son, the giving of whom cost Him more than tongue can tell, will He refuse to you, who, in accepting Christ, have become one of His children, that which costs Him next to nothing? Surely not.

"How shall He not *with Him*?" Ah, this is the important word for us all—*with Him*! With Him, or without Him—which are you to-day? Is *He* yours, or is He not?

Without Him—that means a haphazard, risky life. No matter what else you may have, you cannot be really satisfied; and you have no security for even the lesser good you enjoy. With Him—you have fulness of provision, and complete security of good. You can never exhaust the love that has bestowed upon you Christ. And nothing can ever separate you from that love. People speak about "insuring their lives." With Him, your life is well insured; and your endless happiness too.

January 31   **Marked in the Ear and in the Foot.**

"My sheep hear My voice, and I know them, and they follow Me"
(John x. 27).

WHEN Christ speaks, some do not listen; others do. When He calls, some do not follow; others do. As an old writer, Jay of Bath, quaintly says, "The sheep of Christ are marked in the ear and in the foot." You know to whom sheep on a hillside belong by the mark or brand upon them; and this is how Christ's sheep are known to be His—"They hear His voice, and they follow Him."

Are you able to recognise Christ's voice? Have you ever heard it? Is there anything in its tones that appeals to something in your breast?

Many years ago, a farmer in the backwoods of America was out working in the fields with his sons. His wife was away to the village; and at home there was a young child, with her older sister Regina left in charge. The latter was sitting down to teach the child a little hymn which she had often heard her mother sing, when, suddenly, the barn is seen ablaze! The Indians are upon them. The father and brothers lie bleeding. And Regina and her little sister are carried off to the Indian settlement. Ten years pass. By that time Regina's mother is old and careworn; and she herself is a tall Indian girl, though she still remembers some of the texts and hymns she learned in earlier days. A successful war has been waged against the Indians, and they have agreed to restore all white captives by a certain day, at a certain fort. There are two hundred of these; and friends, including Regina's mother, are there to claim their own. But the poor old woman does not see Regina, and Regina does not know her; and the disappointed mother is in tears. "Is there nothing she will remember you by?" the captain asks. The mother thinks. "Possibly the hymn I used to sing to her at her cradle." And immediately her voice quavers forth—

> "Alone, yet not alone, am I,
> I find my Saviour ever nigh;
> Though in this solitude so drear,
> He comes the weary hours to cheer.
> I am with Him, and He with me;
> Even here, alone I cannot be."

The old familiar verse, sung out, though more feebly, by the old familiar voice, did its appointed work. It struck a chord of memory in a young breast; it made a bright pair of young eyes to glisten; and soon a handsome young woman had stepped from the group of rescued captives and flung herself upon her mother's neck. Regina required no pressing to follow her mother home. She heard her voice, and followed her. So may it be with you and Christ!

He took Peter and John and James, and went up into a mountain to pray" (Luke ix. 28).

So Luke introduces to us the scene of Christ's Transfiguration. Both Matthew and Mark speak of it as "an *high* mountain *apart*," and we gather from the former that it was in the north, in the region of Cæsarea Philippi. Hence it is now generally believed to have been Hermon rather than Tabor, which was a good deal farther south, and the summit of which was not a place of solitude in our Lord's time, but the site of a considerable fortress and town.

He went up "to pray." For the Son of God was a man of prayer, and many a mountain-top in Palestine is hallowed ground, because there He poured out His soul in communion with His Father. Often Jesus had not where to lay His head; but He always found a place for prayer, and ofttimes, we are told, He spent "all night in prayer"—not for Himself alone, but for those whom God had given Him in the world, that they might be kept from the evil in it.

"And as He prayed, the fashion of His countenance was altered, and His raiment was white and glistering." What a sight awaited the astonished eyes of the three sleeping disciples when they were awakened from their slumber! For they saw their Master then as they had never seen Him before. They were eye-witnesses of His majesty. They had a glimpse of the Prince of Heaven, with His earthly guise for a brief season thrown aside. They saw the Man of Sorrows clad in His native livery of heaven, and with a joyous kingliness upon His face that spoke of His coming victory through death.

"And behold there talked with Him two men, which were Moses and Elias." With what rapt interest would the three privileged disciples listen to the converse which passed between their Master and these two glorified saints, as they spake together of the decease which He should accomplish at Jerusalem! Moses and Elias! It would be a deeply moving sight to see these noble servants of the olden time, with Jesus in the midst; and we cannot wonder that Peter would fain have continued on the mount.

But, suddenly, when they looked round, the glorious scene had vanished! "They saw Jesus only with themselves," and the mountain slope was bare and ordinary as before. "Jesus only"! But was not He enough? "Hear ye *Him*," the Father's voice from heaven had said to them and us. The Transfiguration scene has served its purpose for Jesus and for them; so let it pass. And as the Saviour steps from the mount of glory into the vale of tears below, let them not imagine that His true glory is in anywise left behind. It consists, not in radiant apparel, but in the divine nature, so full of sympathy and power, which shines through His every look and act, and which forthwith finds an object for itself in the distressed lunatic boy just at the foot of the Transfiguration Mount.

February 2   **The Trustee and the Treasure.**

"*I know whom I have believed*" (2 Tim. i. 12).

THIS is very often misquoted—"I know *in* whom I have believed." But an old saint, who was at the same time a scholar, was right when he said—"No; leave out the *in*. I cannot allow even a preposition to come in between me and my Saviour. I know *whom* I have trusted." It was Professor (or "Rabbi") Duncan who said that.

Paul here speaks of Christ as the Trustee to whom he had committed something that he was sure would be quite safe in His keeping. It was something so very precious that he could not dare to keep it himself, and there was no one else but One only to whom he could entrust it. But in the keeping of that One, he knew, no evil could befall it. For that One he knew well, and knew how worthy He was of the fullest confidence.

You may have heard of the Kohinoor Diamond, which was in the possession of Dhuleep Singh. The name means the Mountain of Light, and the precious stone was valued at £120,000. It now belongs to the British Crown. Well now, suppose you had that wonderful diamond put into your hand, and were strictly charged to keep it safe for a month or a year—how would you feel? Rather uncomfortable, I should say. To have charge of it even for a day would be torture. You would be afraid to carry it about with you, and afraid to leave it anywhere, in case it should be stolen. But if you handed it over to your father, and he put it into his "safe," which fire could not enter, and thief could not break into, your mind would be at ease; for you know your father, whom you trust, and you have confidence that he is able to keep things of the greatest value safe.

But now there is something far more precious than the Kohinoor; and that is your immortal soul. You dare not try to keep it yourself. Even your father or your mother cannot undertake to keep it for you. But Christ can. And if you go to Him, and say from the heart, "Lord Jesus, I commit my precious soul to Thee," He answers, "Be not afraid. None shall be able to pluck you out of My hand."

Good Running.

"So run, that ye may obtain" (1 Cor. ix. 21).

If you are to run to any good purpose in a race, there is one thing you must *be very clear about* to begin with, and that is, *the goal you wish to reach.* The apostle lays stress upon that in this chapter; and he is able to say of himself, that he does not run "as uncertainly." He is quite decided as to the point he is aiming at, and the prize he hopes to win. He does not go zigzag on the course, or pursue his way with halting and uncertain step, but he presses straight toward the mark.

Another thing, as he tells us elsewhere (Heb. xii. 1), which we must be careful about, is—to " lay aside every weight." Earnest runners in a race *strip off all unnecessary burdens*; and the man that carries a needless load upon his back is too much handicapped to hope for much success. A long, trailing robe would be specially hindersome, and would certainly be flung aside by one who meant business in his running. Even so with the Christian race. We must not allow ourselves to be encumbered, either by the cares or by the pleasures of the world; and we must put from us the entangling robe of unbelief, which so easily besets us, to trip us up at every step.

And, again, having the right goal in view, and having stripped off what would hinder, you must *run with patience* (Heb. xii. 1) the race that is set before us. The word means what you boys would call "staying-power." In order to attain it, you sometimes go into "training" for your competitions, and exercise a good deal of self-denial, so as to strengthen your powers of endurance when the testing-time arrives. Some, as you know, in an ordinary race, go bravely from the starting-place; and it seems at first as if they were to carry all before them. There is a grand spurt. But then, alas! all is over with them. They get "puffed out," they lose heart, and are soon outstripped by those whom they headed at the start. Let it be different with you. See that you run with "staying-power"; for, if this is needed anywhere, it is certainly needed in the Christian race. That you may have it, keep "looking unto Jesus," who is able by His Spirit to give you courage and strength, day by day, and moment by moment, as you need it.

February 4   ## Christ our Captain.

"The Captain of salvation" (Heb. ii. 10).

WE hear a good deal in these days of the "Salvation Army"; and perhaps you may have seen some of its curious "regiments" passing along the streets. Whatever may be said of these people and their strange ways, they have got hold of a right idea. The followers of Jesus are an army—striving to subdue the whole world to Him.

Much might be said of this army. Let me just ask you to remember what their banner is—Love; their music—Hope; their weapon—Truth; their enemy—Sin; their field of battle—Everywhere; their Captain—Christ.

How it encourages the Church to know that their great Leader is with them. When Wellington's men were wavering one day in battle, he himself rode forward into their midst. One of the men, seeing him, cried—"There's the Duke! God bless him! I had rather see his face than a whole brigade." Then followed a tremendous cheer; and at once the tide of battle was turned. So is it with the Captain of Salvation. When we have such a Leader, victory is sure. He Himself has borne the brunt of battle. On Him, made perfect through suffering, the enemy tried his worst in vain. He died to conquer, and rose again to reign. He can never know defeat.

Will you not join this army of Christ, battling against sin and wrong, and trying to bring in righteousness and peace in all the earth? Perhaps you say—"I can't do much as a soldier." But there is one fortress you ought to ask strength from Him to take and keep. It is mentioned in Proverbs xvi. 32; and to take and keep it may be harder than to take a city. But Jesus can enable you to overcome, and to drive out the pride, selfishness, hatred, envy, and other enemies that are lurking there. And if you desire to promote His kingdom among others, He will help you by His Spirit to do that too.

Satisfied at Last.   February 5

"I shall be satisfied, when I awake, with Thy likeness" (Ps. xvii. 15).

THERE is a sense in which it is true that we ought to live in contentment—to be "content with such things as we have." I hope you will never be found among the grumblers, who are never thankful, but always complaining, and who, miserable themselves, do their best to make everybody around them unhappy too.

But there is, also, a sense in which the Christian even cannot be fully satisfied, so long as he is here. He is discontented : not with his surroundings, however, so much as with himself. His heart is craving after something, which he never perfectly attains on earth ; and that thing is the thing which he most of all longs for.

We are all wishing something more than we yet have. And what we are wishing most, reveals what sort of persons we are. Here is a boy whose one desire is to grow up rich and famous. That tells me what sort of boy he is, and what kind of man he is likely to be. Or here is a girl, whose crowning anxiety is to grow up tall and beautiful, so as to be envied and admired. That tells me what sort of girl she is, and what kind of woman she is likely to become. But even if such things as these could be attained by you, at their best, would they really satisfy your heart ? No ; for over every fountain of mere earthly satisfaction the words are written—"He that drinketh of this fountain shall thirst again."

But now, there is in the true Christian's heart a desire which tells us what sort of person he now is, and is not only likely but sure to become. It is a desire which, when fulfilled, will bring him full satisfaction—the desire to be made like to Christ. The words of Augustine are worth repeating here—" Thou, O Lord, hast made us for Thyself ; and our hearts are restless till they find rest in Thee." And though the soul that trusts in Christ does have some taste, even on earth, of the sweetness of rest in Him, the believer is never completely satisfied here below. *With Christ, and like Christ*, is to him the guiding star of hope. "I shall be satisfied, when I awake, with Thy likeness."

February 6   **The Name to be Remembered.**

"I will make Thy name to be remembered in all generations" (Ps. xlv. 17).

WHATEVER other name may be in view in this psalm, it refers especially to the name of Christ. A greater than Solomon is here. The King of whom this ancient song speaks is fairer than the sons of men. His bloodless victories are still going on. His army is always receiving fresh recruits, and never wants for officers from age to age. Instead of the fathers He takes the children, to make them princes in all the earth. And, though unseen, He continues to live in the hearts of multitudes. The promise is fulfilled—"I will make Thy name to be remembered *in all generations.*"

When Jesus was on earth, if anybody had said that His name would be thus enshrined in the memories and hearts of men in all succeeding ages, he would have been laughed to scorn by the great ones of the time. Many learned men lived then who thought themselves far more worthy of being remembered; but their names are quite forgotten. And so with many powerful men, who figured largely in the public eye in their day, but have now sunk into complete oblivion. Yet the name of Jesus has not lost any of its lustre. It rather grows in glory and in preciousness with the years. Napoleon was right when he contrasted the fame and influence of Jesus with his own, and with that of Alexander and other mighty men before him. "We founded our empires upon force; but on what was the empire of Jesus founded? Upon love; and I tell you that, to this day, millions would die for Him!"

In what way does God cause the name of Christ to be always remembered? He does it in His Word. It lives for ever; and the name of Christ lives with it. In its every part, indeed, the Bible is meant to point and to lead up to Jesus. But He especially makes Him to be remembered in the living souls which hail Him as Saviour and as King. He shall have a seed to serve Him in all generations. Are you to be among those who, by what you are and say and do, make the name of Christ to be remembered, and thought upon, and loved in your own day and generation upon earth?

Kept from the Evil.

"I pray not that Thou shouldest take them out of the world, but that Thou shouldest keep them from the evil" (John xvii. 15).

SOME years ago, away in the desert of Judea, I visited a strange, solitary place, inhabited by a number of strange, solitary-looking people. It was a monastery called Marsaba; and those who lived in it were what are called monks—persons who live apart from their fellow-men, and think in that way to become holier and better. They were curious-looking mortals, in their long and not over-clean robes. Most of them were already old; and it could be seen upon the faces of many of them that, in earlier days, they had known a good deal of the world and of sin. Yet there they were, trying in in their own way to be good.

Theirs was not, however, Christ's way. He desires His people to be good, not by going out of the world, but while remaining in it. You will not shut out the bad heart by shutting yourself up in a monastery. But if you have God's Spirit dwelling within you, and keeping you from the evil, then you may be in the world and yet not of it. Like the diver when he goes down into the depths of the ocean, and yet by his tube apparatus is kept in communication with the upper air, so you, by prayer, may even in the world breathe the atmosphere of heaven. For His people's own sake, and for the world's sake—for their education, and for its good—Jesus desires, not that His people should be taken out of the world, but that they should be kept in it from the evil.

This is the very prayer your mother offers for you. Slipping up to your room, after you are asleep perhaps, she tells Jesus of her anxieties about you. "Mary—Johnnie—not out of the world, Lord, for how sorely I would miss them; but oh, keep them from the evil!" It was your father's prayer for you, perhaps, when you were sent first to school; or when, later on, you had to set forth into the greater school of the world.

Make it your own prayer. "Lord, help me to live in the world so as to please Thee. I am surrounded by sin, and there is sin in my heart. But do Thou save me and keep me; and so I shall be truly safe and happy, now and for ever."

February 8 — Meeting Places for All.

" The rich and poor meet together: the Lord is the maker of them all"
(Prov. xxii. 2).

THIS verse reminds us that, though people are divided into rich and poor, and though class is separated from class in some respects in human society, there are certain ties which bind all men together, and certain places in which the rich and the poor do meet.

The first of these which I would mention is—(1) *The Cradle.* To be born into this cold and sorrowful world, is much the same experience for the rich man's as for the poor man's child. There may be a little softer down on the cradle of the one, and more ornamentation round the cradle-head. But, to make up for this, the poor child has often more of the mother's bosom and loving care. And the earliest lessons of life are much the same to both. The mysteries of the alphabet and of the multiplication table are no easier to the peer's son than to the peasant's. They are equally dependent, in the matters of food, sleep, opening intelligence; and they both need the same schooling in obedience, to fit them for their future place in life. There is no royal road to learning.

(2) The *Cross* is another place where rich and poor meet together. Their paths may lead them apart, after early youth is past; but in the heart of them they are not so very far away from one another. In one thing, at anyrate, they are alike: they have both met temptation, and fallen before it. They have both sinned, and are sinners in the sight of God. And if they have been brought to realise this, there is one, and only one way of salvation for them. "God be merciful to me, a sinner," is as suitable a cry for a young princess as for a poor outcast of the city slums. Both need the cleansing blood. There is a meeting place at the Cross.

(3) The *Church* is another place where rich and poor gather together. Jesus welcomed to Him the rich nobleman and the beggar at the gate, the woman who was a sinner and the ruler of the Jews; and those who believed in Him were prized by Him, for something else than their worldly rank. So should it be in His Church. Though differences of wealth and worldly position remain, and must remain, they must not be allowed to estrange hearts from one another, through either the rich man's or the poor man's pride. Those who sit at the one Communion Table should be brethren in Christ.

(4) The *Cemetery,* too, is a place where all must meet. One may be buried in an oaken coffin, and another in a pauper's shell. But death is no respecter of persons, and "dust to dust" applies to all. And looming out beyond the cemetery is the Judgment Seat, where "small and great" must stand, before the great white Throne.

On Earth, as in Heaven.

"Thy will be done in earth, as it is in heaven" (Matt. vi. 10).

THERE are two places mentioned here, which are very different from each other. The difference is not so much that the one is a place of brightness and joy, and the other a place of toil and trouble. It consists, first and chiefly, in this—that in the one God's will is done, and in the other it is not. This is where the great difference lies between heaven and earth.

You know what a "will" is. In one sense it is a document left behind a person who is dead, to let others know what he wishes, or wills, should be done with his possessions. But, in its first and proper sense, it is a power within us, by which we choose and determine that certain things shall, if we have our way, be done. Our will directs our limbs; a general's will directs his army; God's will directs the universe.

Now it is certain that on earth a great many things do obey the will of God. He makes the winds His messengers, and flames of fire His ministers or servants. All nature around us is obedient to God's voice; and when we look up to the sky, we see the orbs of light, harmoniously though silently singing their Creator's praise. But there is one thing, alas! which we find set in opposition to the will of God. And that is, the will of man—by which I mean the will of boys and girls, as well as of grown-up men and women. This is a sad and dreadful state of matters; more sad and hurtful than if your limbs some day refused to obey *your* will, or the soldiers of an army to obey their wise and brave commander.

Now, if you sincerely pray, "Thy will be done in earth, as it is in heaven," you must begin with yourself, and try daily and constantly to observe God's will.

Why should you obey God? Not merely because He is an Almighty Governor, who can compel obedience, and who will punish you if you trample on His authority. Not merely, that is, because you fear Him. But because He is "Our Father in Heaven," whom you love; who loves you, and cherishes you; who is so good that He never will ask you to do anything wrong; who is so wise that He never will tell you to do anything not fitted to promote your highest interests.

And *how* should you obey God? Like the angels; or, as a little boy once answered, "Without asking any questions"—promptly and fully. Like Jesus, rather let me say. You cannot go up to heaven, to see how the angels obey; but God's Son has come down to earth, and shown us in Himself the beauty of the heavenly life. In doing, or in suffering, seek to obey *as Jesus did*.

February 10 — Turn!

"Turn ye, turn ye . . . for why will ye die?" (Ezek. xxxiii. 11).

A YOUNG soldier, who had led a careless life, but had become afterwards a Christian, described very well the change that had been wrought in him when he said—" Jesus Christ said to me, *Right about face!* And I heard and obeyed Him, in my heart." That is exactly what we call "conversion." It is a turning-about of the face—from the world to God. But with the face, it is a turning also of the heart. "Ye turned to God from idols," says Paul to the Thessalonians (1 Thess. i. 9). The idols that they formerly loved and trusted in were as nothing to them now, in comparison with God. The current of their affections was not diverted away from Him now by other objects; but it set toward Him. They had been converted—turned round. Face and heart had both been turned to God.

So is it with every Christian; and everybody ought to be a Christian. It is especially sad when it is true of boys and girls brought up in a Christian country, and in a Christian Church, and perhaps in a Christian family, that they are not so.

You will observe that God's call to "turn" implies that our faces are in the wrong direction to begin with. This we know, too well, to be true. The most innocent-looking child, when it grows a little older, is found seeking after what is evil—with its face turned away from God, and toward the world and sin. If you have a wooden boat with some lead in one side of it, when you place it in the water, it will heel over to the side where the lead inclines it. So, in our nature, the heavy, evil thing called sin draws our life over to its own side; and this wrong tendency is in us all.

But God wants us to be turned in the right direction. He has no pleasure in wickedness, and no pleasure in the death of the wicked. It grieves Him to see our faces and our hearts averted from Him; and it is not only displeasing to Him, but deeply dangerous for ourselves. Therefore He cries, with all the earnestness with which you might cry to a blind or a senseless man making straight for a precipice, "Turn ye, turn ye: for why will ye die?"

"My soul shall make her boast in the Lord" (Ps. xxxiv. 2).

Boys and girls are sometimes given to boasting. They boast about themselves, perhaps, or about their possessions, or their friends. They even have boasting matches occasionally. I remember one little boy boasting to me, when we were children, that he had more mice at home than we had; and I had to acknowledge on that score defeat! The habit of boasting is a foolish one, especially if it be about what *we* have and we can do. Those who have most, and can do best, are usually those who say least about it.

But to boast in the Psalmist's sense is not a wrong thing. If your heart is very full of anything, or anybody, you cannot help speaking of them; and it is a very pardonable thing, when a boy or a girl, full of love and admiration for father and mother, for example, is fond of speaking to a companion in their praise. Now, the heart of the Psalmist is here bursting with gratitude; and out of the abundance of the heart his mouth speaketh. He is so full of what the Lord is and has done for him, that he cannot help speaking of Him. So he says—"My soul shall make her boast in the Lord."

This is the safe and proper boast. Is it yours? Have you found such a friend in the Lord that you feel inclined to bless Him at all times, and rejoice when you can get somebody else to magnify Him along with you? Do you feel that He has done so great a thing for you, and wrought such a deliverance for you, that you cannot be silent about it?

In the great American War, a touching incident happened. The father of a large family was called out to join the troops. But a friend of his, who was unmarried, came forward and said—"I wish to go instead of you: let me be your substitute"! The wish was granted, and this noble friend fell in battle. Can you wonder that he in whose stead he fought and fell, was very grateful? He often used to tell, what he also had printed upon his tombstone—"He died for me!"

I do not wish you to speak about Christ what you don't feel; but I hope you do rejoice in Him as your Substitute. If so, your soul may well "make her boast in the Lord," saying—He died for me!

February 12. Good Success.

"Then thou shalt have good success" (Josh. i. 8).

You would like, I am sure, to succeed in life. This is a natural and proper wish, and, to fulfil it, will require both prayer and pains. Success is seldom or never given to the idler. "It is lesson after lesson with the scholar, blow after blow with the labourer, crop after crop with the farmer, picture after picture with the painter, step after step and mile after mile with the traveller, that will secure what all desire—success."

But you are especially to be mindful that there are two kinds of success. There is a *bad* success, which some men are winning or have won: bad in its means, and bad in its result. Satan himself tasted it in Eden, when he succeeded in tempting Eve. Judas Iscariot tasted it, when he succeeded in betraying Christ. The man tastes it who becomes rich through fraud, and the boy or girl who gets to the top of the class through cheating a neighbour. Whoever gains one or other of the world's prizes at the cost of principle, tastes it, only to find that what he sought so eagerly as luscious fruit, is like the apples of Sodom—ashes between his teeth. In such success may you never share!

Good success is what you are to covet: a success whose object is good, a success which is attained by worthy means, a success which will bear the light of eternity. And if you seek it, as Joshua did, then you will attain it, whatever may be the world's opinion of you, or its verdict upon your life.

What, then, is the secret of such success, as told to Joshua? It is found, first, in *courageous and constant observance of the will of God* —"That thou mayest observe to do according to all that is written in this book of the law." And, second, in *having the presence of God with us in all our life*—"As I was with Moses, I will be with thee. I will not fail thee, nor forsake thee. The Lord thy God is with thee, whithersoever thou goest."

Consult God's will then, day by day. Seek the blessedness of those who not only know, but do what He commands. And plead for His constant presence with you. Then, whether your life-work is to be a long or a short one, *you* will have "good success."

Watch! February 13

"I say unto all, Watch" (Mark xiii. 37).

The duty of watchfulness is often urged in the Bible. There is something you are to watch over, something you are to watch against, and something you are to watch for.

1. You are to watch *over* yourself. Our hearts are so wayward, and so deceitful, that we need to maintain a constant watch over them, else they will be sure to lead us wrong. Bad words and wrong deeds take their rise from bad thoughts and evil feelings in the heart. Some are fond of watching over other people's character and conduct, not their own. "I must have closer attention," said the teacher, "and wish none of you to look off your books. The first that sees another do so will please let me know." Harry said to himself, that he would watch Joe, whom he did not like; and in a little while he was heard crying to the teacher—"I saw Joe Simmonds, sir, looking off his book!" But Harry himself was caught. He had been more careful to watch over others than himself.

2. You are to watch *against* temptation. Beware of the beginnings of evil. Be on your guard against the approaches of sin. The Christian has been compared to a sentinel upon the walls, not only because he is expected to be alert and constantly on the outlook against the enemy's approach, but because it is his wisdom not to attempt to ward off the foe in his own strength, but to tell his commanding officer. When temptation comes, when sin approaches, at once tell Jesus, the Captain of Salvation. In His strength you will overcome.

3. You are to watch *for* opportunity. That is, you are to be on the outlook for the chance of doing good. If you wish and seek for this, you are sure to find it. Somewhere, there is somebody whom you can benefit and cheer. Be like John Newton, who said—"I perceive that there is a heap of happiness in the world, and a great heap of misery; and my aim in life is, to take some few grains at least from the latter, and to add some grains to the former heap." By watching for opportunities this devoted man was enabled, in a wonderful way, to fulfil the purpose of his heart.

February 14 — **Ready Reckoning.**

"I reckon that the sufferings are not worthy to be compared with the glory"
(Rom. viii. 18).

Paul was a good arithmetician. He could deal correctly and effectively with very large sums. And he knew well what he was here speaking about. He knew well both what is meant by "suffering," and by "glory."

There are few men who have known what suffering means better than Paul did. You boys like tales of adventure. Where will you find a true story that is more thrilling than the short account Paul is able to give, in the 11th chapter of 2nd Corinthians, of his life's experience since he became a Christian? "In labours more abundant, in stripes above measure, in prisons more frequent, in deaths oft. Of the Jews five times received I forty stripes save one. Thrice was I beaten with rods, once was I stoned, thrice I suffered shipwreck, a night and a day I have been in the deep; in journeyings often, in perils of waters, in perils of robbers, in perils by mine own countrymen, in perils by the heathen, in perils in the city, in perils in the wilderness, in perils in the sea, in perils among false brethren; in weariness and painfulness, in watchings often, in hunger and thirst, in fastings often, in cold and nakedness." This is a long list of adventures. But it is not a case of "an old salt, drawing the long bow," about his hairbreadth escapes. It is all literally true. Paul had endured all this, in addition to his daily anxieties about the interests of all the different Churches he had been the means of planting here and there. He knew suffering well.

But he also knew the meaning of "glory," as few men on earth have known it. He was himself caught up to the third heaven, into Paradise (2 Cor. xii. 3-4), and he there saw sights and heard unspeakable words, which he could not relate to any other. What he does feel at liberty to tell is, that what the prophet said of old is quite true—"Eye hath not seen, nor ear heard, neither have entered into the heart of man, the things which God hath prepared for them that love Him."

And what he tells you, if you are one of those who love God, is that, as the result of his comparing and computing, he reckons the sufferings of the present, no matter how great and varied they may be, as not worthy to be compared with the glory which shall be revealed in us. They are out of all proportion to one another. There is no comparison really between them.

Vanishing Goodness.

"Your goodness is as a morning cloud, and as the early dew" (Hos. vi. 4).

IN hot eastern countries, especially at some seasons of the year, the appearance of a cloud is very welcome, as the promise of a refreshing shower. And the dew which falls upon the tender herb is counted of the greatest value. But very often, as the sun rises in the sky, the morning cloud, from which the eager farmer hoped for the reviving rain, passes away; and, to his regret, he sees the morning dew quickly dried up under the scorching rays of the sun. It is to this that God likens the goodness of Ephraim. It had been full of promise, but it had quickly vanished. It had melted like the morning cloud, and been dried up like the early dew.

Is it not sometimes so with you? You begin the day well, with good desires and holy resolutions. But, before long, the world's influence is upon you. Hot temptation scatters the good thoughts and feelings; the glowing pleasures of earth absorb and dry up the dewy freshness that was upon your spirit in the morning. By night your heart is hard and dry again. And what you find to be true of a single day is too often true of a whole life. It began full of promise. There seemed to be a great deal that was good about it. The character appeared to be fresh, and innocent, and fair. But by and by the early promise disappeared. The field which had glistened with pearly dewdrops lay hard, and sodden, and barren afterwards.

You may have heard the story of young Giuseppe, a beautiful boy who lived near Naples. An artist saw him one day, and was so much attracted by him that he painted his portrait, and, hanging it upon his wall, called it Innocence. He wished to get a companion picture, to set in contrast with it, under the name of Guilt; but, for long years, he searched without seeing a face bad and repulsive enough to suit his purpose. At length he saw a scowling criminal, lying in a Roman jail awaiting execution; and he said—"That is the face I have been searching for: that will do for Guilt, to set alongside of my picture Innocence!" What was the artist's surprise to find, on inquiry, that the wretched felon awaiting his death was none other than the once fair, young Giuseppe!

The Lord direct *your* heart into the love of God, and keep you in it! Then your goodness will *not* be as the morning cloud and early dew, which quickly pass away.

February 16   **Christ the Door.**

"*I am the Door*" (John x. 9).

Is not this a strange name which Jesus gives to Himself here—the Door? What does He mean by it?

He is speaking of the sheepfold—the place of peace and plenty for His people—in which they are "safe" and "find pasture." And He says, "You can get in there only by me: I am the Door."

Suppose that, wandering one day in the grounds of a palace which you were anxious to reach, you were lost. If one met you in the guise of a shepherd-guide, and, in answer to your bewildered look and question, said, "I am the *way*," you would know what he meant. You would know that he intended to assure you that *he* was the one to bring you to the palace. And if, on reaching it, as you sighed and said, "Oh, what a lovely palace! Would that I could get in!" he were to show you on his hand a princely signet-ring, and say, "I am the Door," you would know that what he meant was, "It is I who have the right, the power, to let you in."

Now, what is called the sheepfold here is elsewhere represented as a palace. In both cases, what it means is, Christ's true Church. To His people on earth, that is very much what the fold is to the sheep; but, in heaven, it will have not only the peace and safety of a fold, but the splendour of a palace, and all God's people will live there as children of the King. And Jesus, who now meets you as the Shepherd-Guide, and says, "Come with Me: I am the Way"—if you believe in Him and follow Him, will, as you near heaven's entrance, reveal Himself to you as the Prince, and, saying to you, "I am the Door," He will let you in.

If Christ is the Door, what is the key? I will tell you. It is Faith, so that the entrance is sometimes called the "Door of Faith." See if you can find a verse where it is told as a wonderful thing, that God has opened that Door to the like of you and me.

"I have chosen" (Ps. cxix. 30).

The power to choose is one that you young people have, and like very much to exercise. It is a great gift; but it is one not to be lightly used, because we shall have to answer to God for the use we make of it.

All through life we are called upon to choose, but it is especially in early days that important choices have to be made. You will soon be at the parting of the roads, if you have not reached it already, where you will have to make up your mind which way you are to go. And everything depends, under God, on whether you choose the way of life or the way of death. There is a famous picture by Sir Noel Paton, called The Choice, in which a youth, clad in armour, is being called upon to choose which path he is to follow. A handsome but gay and luscious-looking female figure, with a foaming goblet in her hand, is trying to tempt him along an easy, flowery path—which, however, as we see, leads down to a dark abyss. A fair angel form, on the other hand, is beckoning him to enter upon a steep and narrow path, which, climbing upward in the rocky defile, leads to a far-off realm of light and peace. And we see from the expression on the young warrior's face, that his resolve is taken. He will not listen to the temptress, but, shaking himself from her grasp, he is minded to follow the angel upward, in face of whatever difficulty, to the region of purity and light.

There meets you, dear young reader, not an angel merely, but God's own Son; and He says to you, at the parting of the ways, "Come with me." The world, in its most alluring strains, and exposing to view its most tempting attractions, says, "Nay; come with me!" Which are you to follow? Which do you choose? Choose Christ! For though the path in which He leads may seem rough and steep, it is a path which leads to glory; while the way of sin, however broad and easy, is a way that leads down to death.

February 18   **Jesus and the Children.**

"And Jesus called a little child unto Him" (Matt. xviii. 2).

Jesus and the children — how close the ties between them were when He was here on earth! And we know that He is "the same yesterday, to-day, and for ever."

1. He was Himself a young child; and He grew up like other children. He learned His lessons, enjoyed His games, climbed the hills with His companions, just like the rest. Only in one thing He was different: "He knew no sin, neither was guile found in His mouth." No bad deeds marred His life, no false words escaped His lips, no impure thoughts lurked within His heart.

2. The children were the first to suffer for His sake. Soon after His birth, you remember, the cruel decree of Herod went forth, that all the little boys in and around Bethlehem, of two years old and under, should be put to death. Jesus escaped, for He was by that time safe in Egypt. But a cry of anguish rose upon the air, which shortly before had echoed with the angels' song. Many mothers were weeping for their little ones, and would not be comforted.

3. The children had much that was attractive in the eyes of Jesus afterwards. He called a little child to Him one day, and made him the text of a beautiful sermon, which we have, in outline, in the beginning of the eighteenth chapter of Matthew. He told the disciples that, in order to enter the kingdom of heaven, they must needs be as humble and trustful as that little child, and that the lowliest in heart were they who should really have the highest place within His Kingdom.

4. The children were not only interesting to Jesus, however, but they were very dear to Him. He was much displeased when the disciples sought to keep them at a distance, fearing that they would be an annoyance to the Master. He took the little ones in His arms, and blessed them, and drew them close to His heart. He said, "Whoso shall receive one such little child in My name, receiveth Me."

5. The children, too, on their part, were interested in Jesus, and felt that there was something in Him which drew them to Him. Their young hearts were filled with His praise; and there was no praise He valued more than theirs. When they shouted their Hosannas, the chief priests and scribes might be "sore displeased" (Matt. xxi. 15); but Jesus loved to hear them. It seemed to Him the most perfect praise He had heard on earth: not so much an echo of the older people's welcome, as an echo of the angels' song.

Persevere!

"*Patient continuance in well-doing*" (Rom. ii. 7).

WELL-WISHING is good; but well-doing is far better; and patient continuance in well-doing is better still. This last is what the follower of Christ must try to maintain. He must seek to be like Him who had to "endure the contradiction of sinners against Himself," but who, in spite of opposition and discouragement, went about continually doing good. The patience of Christ is one of the most needful, but one of the most difficult lessons for the Christian.

Over the doorway of one of the oldest houses in the High Street of Edinburgh—that old historic street, where the noble families of Scotland used to dwell—this legend is engraven, "He that tholes overcomes." "Thole" is an old Anglo-Saxon word, meaning "to bear"; and the motto is intended to teach, that patience is the road to victory. Perhaps you have found this already to be true among your companions. A bad-tempered comrade has taken "an ill-will" against you, and has set himself, in every way possible, to annoy and vex you. But if you have been enabled to "thole" it all in a spirit of meekness, he has at last become ashamed of himself; and the victory is yours.

The precise lesson of our text, however, is, not merely that we are to bear trouble patiently, but that we are to persevere in actively doing good in face of every discouragement.

When Abraham Lincoln was asked if he expected to end the great American War while he was in office as President, he said "he didn't know." When further asked what he meant to do, he answered, "To keep pegging away, sir—pegging away." And we know what came of it. You remember the story, too, of Robert the Bruce, when, sorely disheartened, he had to take refuge in a barn. Lying on his back, he noticed a spider endeavouring to attach its web to the top of a beam. Twelve times it tried and failed; but, at the thirteenth time, it succeeded. "I will follow its example,' he said. "Twelve times I have been beaten, the thirteenth I may succeed." So he arose, and did likewise.

Even so, many a spiritual victory is awaiting the young Christian worker and warrior who, in the strength of God, is determined to persevere.

February 20   A Soul in Prison.

" Bring my soul out of prison " (Ps. cxlii. 7).

IT is a sad enough experience for the body to be in prison. But it is far worse to have an imprisoned soul. What is a prison? It is a place devoid of *comfort*. It is the very opposite of a home. The prison fare is poor. The prison bed is hard. Little sunshine visits the inhabitants. The whole life within is, and is intended to be, comfortless and dreary.

It is a place devoid of *company*. Or, if company there is, it is of the worst and most undesirable sort. You have heard stories of the Bastile in Paris, where for long years prisoners were kept entirely apart, and were thankful for a few pins to amuse themselves with, to keep them from going mad. And you have also read of the Prisoner of Chillon.

It is a place, especially, that is devoid of *liberty*. The inmates cannot do anything that is not allowed by the jailer. Their life is most monotonous and joyless. It is like tramping always upon a treadmill, with no variety in it, and little that is good coming out of it.

If you were put into a prison, how would you feel? You would be very apt to feel degraded, disgraced, miserable. And yet the body may be imprisoned while the soul remains free. Paul and Silas knew true liberty at Philippi, when their feet were fast in the stocks, in the inner prison. Their souls rose to fellowship with God, and the other prisoners at midnight heard a sound strange to their ears in such a place—the song of heartfelt praise. Bunyan, too, was free in spirit, when, in Bedford jail, he wrote the wonderful story of the Pilgrim's Progress from the City of Destruction to the Celestial City; and, with the spiritual companionship he enjoyed, he could not be comfortless or solitary.

The worst imprisonment is that of a soul which feels itself shut out from God and shut in with sin. No wonder that, when the horror of this experience is felt, the cry goes forth, "Take my soul out of prison!" Some may have to pray this prayer for the first time; for they have never escaped from bondage at all. Others may have to pray it over again; because they have fallen, and been ensnared by evil habit, and feel themselves hemmed in on every side.

The key of escape from the prison is prayer. He who Himself cried, "My God, my God!" can give the opening of the prison door. May we know the freedom wherewith Christ maketh His people free!

Cruel Cain.   February 21

" They have gone in the way of Cain" (Jude 11).

Two lives, like two rivers, may rise within a few feet of each other—from the same home, perhaps, or from beside the same watchful mother's knee. But they take different directions from the first. The one turns toward God, the other to worldliness and sin. It may be a very small watershed that separates them, to begin with; but, while the one flows on its smiling course till it is merged in the summer ocean of endless felicity, the other flows sullenly on its troubled bed, then rushes heedlessly forward, till it is engulfed in the region of never-ending storm.

As for Cain, his mother expected great things of him. He was the first little boy the world ever saw. Eve was naturally very fond of him. She called him "possession," or "darling"; and gave as her reason, that she had gotten "the man" from the Lord, who, she hoped, would be the promised Deliverer. But alas! she was to be sadly disappointed. Soon she saw that sin was in his heart; and she was grieved to find that this child of her bosom was on the devil's side.

This did not appear all at once. At first, it showed itself in little acts of self-will and disobedience. Then perhaps, after Abel was born, in envy and selfishness when the two little boys were at play: "that's mine"—"you shan't have that"—"I'll strike you!" And then the day came which was clearly to reveal the characters of the two—when they were grown lads, with the duties of men, and were called to sacrifice to God. It showed Cain in the worst possible light.

While Abel came, feeling and telling God that he was a sinner, and implored forgiveness, Cain would only come, confessing that he depended on God for his daily food. If he had plenty of that, he did not care about sin, and salvation. His heart was hard, and his will stubborn and unsubdued. And when he saw that God was well pleased with Abel, but not with him, Cain's brow darkened. He was angry with God, and wild with envy toward Abel. And, since he could not strike God, he watched his opportunity, one day in the field, and slew his brother.

Thus, from being the first little boy, Cain became the first *murderer* the world has seen. And "the way of Cain" became a way of weary wandering from God—the life of a "vagabond," with a brand upon his brow, and a bad, accusing conscience in his breast. Oh, what a terrible thing sin is. Beware of the beginnings of evil. Beware of the first steps in "the way of Cain"!

February 22.   Dorcas.

" A certain disciple named Tabitha . . . by interpretation Dorcas" (Acts ix. 36).

THE life of Dorcas was a humble, but a very beautiful one. Her story in the Bible is quite short. Yet there are several things about her to be remembered.

1. Her *name*. She was called Dorcas, or "the gazelle"; and she was well named. The gazelle is wonderfully clear-sighted, and so was she—quick to perceive, not the faults of others, but their wants. The gazelle is noted for its nimbleness; and so was she—always ready to run with light foot on God's errands of mercy. The gazelle is distinguished for its grace; and so was she—for she shone in the beauty of holiness and loving-kindness, whether or not she had a handsome face. Unlike some other people, in the Bible and out of it, she was worthy of her name.

2. Her *school*. We are told that she was a *disciple*. This means, that she was a learner. But in what school? In a school which has an unseen Teacher—whom, having not seen, the scholars love; no fees—the only thing you have to pay being "attention!"; exercises for the heart, rather than merely for the head; and scholars of all ages under training, from the youngest to the very oldest. It is called the School of Christ. We are not told of what age Dorcas was; but I am sure she was in an advanced standard in the school. Have *you* entered it yet? Have you heard the Master say, "Learn of Me? Have you gone to Him with the prayer, "Teach me, O Lord"?

3. Her *hobby*. It is said that everybody is better to have some hobby or other. That is true, if only it be as good a hobby as Dorcas had. "She was full of good works, and alms deeds which she did." She was always trying to do good to somebody. That was her hobby. She was full of it; her heart was in it. She bestowed thought, and care, and labour for the poor; and if she could not *give* much, she could ply her needle for them, and take pains to find out those deserving of relief.

4. Her *history*. That is soon summed up. Dorcas, though in a quiet sphere, lived a life of remarkable usefulness; and when she died she was greatly missed. Probably nobody would have been more surprised than herself, to have witnessed the scene of genuine sorrow which followed on her death. But her history did not end there. God raised up her life—so valuable was it in His sight, and so much worth restoring. "And many believed on the Lord." Nor has the history of Dorcas ended yet. Such a life never dies. She lives still on earth in the "Dorcas Societies" which bear her name; and she lives on high, serving in His presence the Lord she loved and served below.

"*I am ready*" (Rom. i. 15).

It is a good motto on one of the beautiful stained-glass windows of Glasgow Cathedral, the legend of an ancient Scottish family—"Ready, aye Ready!" That is a very suitable watchword for a Christian. It is a motto to which Paul's life at least was true. He could say, as few Christians can, "I am ready."

He was ready for *service* (Rom. i. 15). Wherever there was an opening for the gospel, Paul was eager to enter in and possess the land for Christ. He did not grudge any amount of time, and trouble, and fatigue in the service of his master. He would undertake any length of a journey—to Rome, or to Spain, or anywhere—for the sake of the gospel cause. He did not merely stand by and direct others; but, in his eagerness, he put to his own hand, and worked, seeking, as he had opportunity, to do good unto all men.

So should it be with us. No true Christian will count good hard work for Christ, or the good of others, beneath him. It is told that Washington was one day going round the encampment, when he came upon a small group of soldiers, trying, with a cord and pulley, to raise a great beam to a certain place. Strain themselves as they might, they could not get it quite up to the desired level. Their petty officer, a pompous little corporal, was standing by, crying—"Heigh-ho, there she goes!" but never putting out so much as a finger to help them. Washington quietly stepped forward, and, laying hold of the rope, gave the men such a lift with their work that the beam was at once raised and adjusted to its place. The corporal, rubbing his hands, asked the stranger in civilian clothes, "to whom they might be indebted for this polite assistance"? With a strange look on his face, and a tone in his voice that brought confusion to the little man, Washington answered, as he turned away—"Whenever help is needed again, send for me to the quarters of the Commander-in-Chief. I shall be ready!" So we should be "ready to every good work" (Tit. iii. 1).

Paul was ready, too, for *suffering or even for death*, for Jesus' sake. When others besought him to keep out of danger, he told them it would "break his heart" not to witness for the Master wherever duty called. "I am ready not to be bound only, but also to die for the name of the Lord Jesus" (Acts xxi. 13). It seemed strange, no doubt, to many; but he actually took pleasure in reproaches, persecutions, distresses for Christ's sake. And when the time for dying came, he was "ready to be offered." It was with him as with John Knox, who, when they said to him, as he entered the dark valley, "Hast thou hope?" pointed upward, and so died.

February 24 The Lord knowing them that are His.

"The Lord knoweth them that are His" (2 Tim. ii. 19).

DOES the shepherd know his sheep? Does the miser know his gold? Does the mother know the children of her love? Much more does the Lord know them that are His. He knows that they are His; and He knows everything about them. Nobody can set such a value on anything as Christ puts upon His ransomed ones. He has done so much to make them His: every one of them has cost Him so very much, that it is no wonder that He knows and values each, and never lets any of them out of sight or out of hand. He gave Himself for them. He bought them with His blood. And He tells us how much He loves them. We have no measure for such a love; but what He says is—"As the Father hath loved Me, so have I loved you" (John xv. 9). The love of Jesus for His people, that is to say, is like the love of God the Father for His only-begotten and well-beloved Son!

Yes; other people may make mistakes about who belong to Christ and who do not. But the Lord Himself never does. It was John Wesley, I think, who said—"When I get to heaven, I shall be greatly surprised at two things—at the presence of some whom I did not expect to see there, and at the absence of some whom I had confidently expected to meet in the fellowship above; and the greatest marvel of all will be, that such a sinner as I should ever have been admitted there." No doubt there will be such surprises to the servants at the last. But there will be no surprises of the kind for Christ. "He knoweth them that are His."

There is a mark on each of them which tells to His eye that they are His property. It is the brand or "seal" of the Holy Spirit. Down at the wharf you may see a great deal of property, lying huddled together and commingled in apparent confusion; yet in a little while it is cleared away and sent to its proper owners, because on the different bales of goods the stamp was found which told to whom it belonged. So, in this world, society is so mixed up that to our eyes it is not always easy to say who are Christ's and who are not. But He knows, and He has His eye all the time on every soul that is sealed with His Spirit. All such will be gathered safely home. There will be none of the Lord's precious property amissing in the great Day.

The Lord's showing that they are His. February 25

"And, let everyone that nameth the name of Christ depart from iniquity"
(2 Tim. ii. 19).

It is a solemn, and may be a comforting thought, that the Lord "knows them that are His." We may know it too, and should not be content without knowing it about ourselves. Have I accepted Jesus as mine? Have I given myself to Him? These are questions which, in our own hearts, we ought surely to be able to answer; and to which we should be satisfied to give, in humble sincerity, only one answer.

But if we do belong to Christ, we should not be content with merely knowing it ourselves. We should live so as to show it also to others.

Now, it is not merely by speaking that you will be able to do this. There may be occasions when you will be called upon to let it be known on whose side you are, by so many words; and I hope you will have courage and modesty to do this aright at such times, "in meekness and fear." But words alone will not count for much. As an old Scotchwoman used to say, "the wind of your mouth costs you little." Your character and your conduct, as well as your lips, must speak. You are to be yourself "a living epistle," as Paul puts it. You are to *be* a person on whom, as a living letter, the writing of Christ—that is, the influence of the Holy Spirit—shall be so plainly seen as to be known and read of all men. You are to be dissatisfied with yourself unless the marks of the Lord Jesus are so plainly discerned upon you that even your enemies will have to say—"That is one of the company of Christ. He has been with Him: he *is* with Him. That is a Christian, and no mistake!"

One thing which the world will rightly look for in you will be, to see you turning your back upon sin. If you fall before temptation, you will be heartily sorry for it; and you will really wish and strive to be done with everything mean, and impure, and unworthy. The remembrance that you are Christ's, and that He is looking on, will help you in this. When tempted to sin, by evil companions or by your own evil heart, you will say, like young Joseph, "'How can I?' If I were my own, I might. But I am not my own: I am Christ's. And it pleases me most to do always those things that please Him!"

The hidden seal of the Spirit—that is the heavenward side, seen by God. And this is the earthward side, seen by the world—"Let everyone that nameth the name of Christ depart from iniquity."

February 26   ## Greater than Solomon.

"Behold, a greater than Solomon is here" (Matt. xii. 42).

THERE is a contrast drawn here between the great Solomon, the magnificent monarch, and—Jesus, the carpenter of Nazareth. And the contrast is all in favour of the humble Nazarene.

Solomon was great in his *dominion*. Under him, the prosperity of Israel reached its greatest height ; and, following upon the conquests of his warlike father David, Solomon ruled a kingdom that extended far beyond the borders of Palestine. Many foreign tribes owned his sceptre. He ruled from sea to sea, and from the river to the ends of the earth. But Jesus is greater still in His dominion. For the earth is the Lord's, and the fulness thereof. And the hosts of heaven own His sway. He is King of kings and Lord of lords, doing His will among the armies of heaven and among the inhabitants of earth.

Solomon was great in his *wisdom*. He was a man of wide knowledge, of deep penetration, of wonderful practical sagacity. He showed this early in his reign, and by and by his wisdom grew so famous that people travelled long distances to hear him. The Queen of Sheba went all the way from Arabia for this purpose ; and she was so greatly impressed, that she counted the very servants happy who stood continually before King Solomon and heard his wisdom. But Jesus is wiser far. He knows all the secrets of earth and heaven. He is "the Wisdom." That is one of His names. His judgments are unsearchable. The depth of the riches both of His knowledge and of His wisdom cannot be fathomed. And He can do what Solomon never could : He is able to make others wise unto salvation.

Solomon was great in his *glory*. The splendours of his Court, the grandeur of the house that he had built, the number and the apparel of his retainers were such that the Queen of the East, rich as she herself was, felt herself completely overwhelmed by the sight. "There was no more spirit in her." But all this was not worthy of being named with the glory of King Jesus. To Him, in His heavenly palace, myriads of angels and ransomed saints give their united homage. "*Thou* art the King of Glory, O Christ."

Solomon, alas ! was *not* great after all in *character*. The story of his later life was one of miserable selfishness, and backsliding, and disappointment. But Jesus was spotless in character, perfect in purity, as rich in sympathy and self-giving love as He was great in wisdom and in power. Truly a greater than Solomon is *here* ! Shall we not seek Him ?

"A reason of the hope that is in you" (1 Pet. iii. 15).

WHAT is *the* hope that is in you? You have many hopes, far and near, small and great. Some of you are looking forward with expectation to the Easter holidays. Some of you, taking a wider sweep, are thinking and planning about what you are to be and to do, when you are a man or a woman. But *the* hope that is in you, your brightest and best hope, goes beyond all that, I trust: it is the hope that you will get to heaven.

A youth was speaking with a Christian friend once about his prospects. His friend asked him what he was to be. "A student," he said. "What then?" "A lawyer." "What then?" "I shall make speeches, and win fees, and with them a great name." "What then?" "I hope to become a judge, and sit upon the Bench." "What then?" "In old age I shall retire, in honour, for the enjoyment of a well-earned repose." "What then?" "Why, then I suppose I shall die, like other people; and I hope there will be many to show respect at my funeral." "And what then?" Ah, here the young man paused. He had not thought of what was coming after death; and he had made no provision for it. If *you* cherish a hope beyond the grave, you have, in that respect, a truer view of life than that young man had; for this life, at the longest, is very short, and is only a preparation for a longer.

But, let me ask, what is the *reason* of the hope that is in you? This is a very important matter. If there is one man more to be pitied than he who is in despair, and has no hope at all, it is the man who is cherishing a false hope—a hope that is not resting upon a sound and solid foundation. Your hope of reaching heaven is of this sort, if it is resting on anything in yourself: on your good character, and your determination to work your way thither. There is only one good foundation for such a glorious hope.

A poor dying Bengalee was able to point to the right reason for it. A missionary found him lying by the wayside, and at first thought him to be a devotee upon pilgrimage, worn out with his march. But, seeing him to be really dying, he bent over him with the words—"Brother, what is your hope for eternity?" With a look of delighted surprise he answered faintly, as he pointed to a leaf of the Bengalee Testament by his side—"The blood of Jesus Christ, His Son, cleanseth us from all sin!" And, in a little moment, the soul of that unknown believer had passed within the heavenly gates.

February 28 **The Sin of Neglect.**

"How shall we escape, if we neglect so great salvation?" (Heb. ii. 3).

If you were on a sinking ship, and a lifeboat were brought alongside, what would be needed in order to your being drowned? Would it be necessary for you flatly to refuse to step into the boat, or to laugh and mock at those who brought it near to you, for their pains? No. The only thing necessary to secure your destruction would be, to "neglect" the opportunity of safety—to pay no attention to those who invited you to secure it.

Or, if you had a garden with some flowers in it, and also some strong bad weeds, what would be necessary in order to have your garden completely spoiled? Would it be needful for you to care for and water the weeds, and to sow more weeds, along with them, in different parts of the garden? Not at all. By simply "neglecting," paying no attention to the presence and the growth of the weeds already there, you would secure the ruin of your garden. It would in course of time, perhaps speedily, be completely overrun; and the flowers would hardly have a chance to grow in the dirty soil.

Now, this sin of neglect—just failing to "pay attention"—is a very common fault among you young people. It is a frequently heard excuse—"Oh, I didn't mean to"; or, "I just forgot"; or, "I wasn't thinking"; or, "I was thinking about something else." The habit of thoughtlessness may, however, lead to very serious consequences; and this is specially true in matters of the soul.

There is one thing above all others that you cannot afford to be careless about; and that is, "the great salvation." It is a great thing, wrought out by a great Captain (verse 10), who suffered much to secure it. And it is great, whether you consider the depth of misery from which it rescues the sinner, or the height of glory to which it brings him. Now, in order that your soul may be lost, you have not to scoff at Christ, and to make a mock at the salvation He brings. You have simply to neglect Him, and it. That is all.

Go, rather, to Him and say—"I deserve punishment; I thank Thee for bearing it. I have done what is bad, and I am bad; help me to become better. I want to step into the lifeboat : I want to have my heart cleared of weeds, and made a garden of the Lord. I want to escape the doom of the wicked. I will *not* neglect so great salvation."

Be Diligent!

"The hand of the diligent maketh rich" (Prov. x. 4).

THE word "diligent" is derived from a Latin verb meaning "to select," and then "to love." Thus it describes a person who has made up his mind about the object he wishes to attain, and who pursues that object with eager devotion. Now, the words of our proverb are true of different kinds of riches. Wealth of the pocket, wealth of the intellect, wealth of the heart—if any or all of these be desired, they must be sought with diligence; and diligence in seeking any of them is sure in the longrun to have some measure of success.

The fruits of diligence are often such as to be quite surprising to idle people. An amusing story is told by the Roman historian Pliny, of a man named Cressin, whose ground yielded such an abundant crop, while the lands around were poor and barren, that his neighbours not only envied him, but accused him of using magic arts for his own enrichment and their disadvantage. Cressin, in pleading his case before the judges, pointed to his comely daughter as his fellow-labourer, and said—"Come, see our implements of husbandry; and go with us to the fields, and behold how they have been fenced in, tilled, manured, weeded, watered. In these things, you will behold all the magic arts and charms which Cressin has used." Not only was he acquitted by the judges, but his lazy and silly accusers were put to shame.

It will not be the cleverest of you boys and girls who will necessarily do best in your future life, but the most diligent. Those who begin with fewest advantages sometimes score best in the end. A queer, awkward-looking boy, with a squint eye and a hissing, indistinct manner of speech, was brought into a school one day. His clothes were poor, and he had considerably outgrown them. The other boys at once made him a laughing-stock. But this did not last for long. He turned out a capital scholar, and mockery soon made way for envy. By and by, he became a professor, as the reward of his diligence, while those who idly laughed were never heard of.

Be sure to make a good choice of the kind of riches you are to seek. Covet earnestly the best gifts. Be diligent to attain them; and ask God to bless and crown your efforts with success.

Emmanuel.

"They shall call His name Emmanuel" (Matt. i. 23).

"EL" means God. It is part of a great many Bible names, some of which, such as Elijah, it begins, and others of which, such as Samuel, it ends. "Emmanu-el" means, "With us, God." The name is found, not only in Matthew's Gospel, but in the ninth chapter of Isaiah. Some people think that it was the name given by the prophet to one of his own sons. Names in those days meant something; and it is quite possible that Isaiah may have called his little boy *Emmanuel*, to show his trust in Jehovah, and to keep him in mind, in days of trouble, of *God with us*. But there was not only present comfort but future hope in this word, for Isaiah and the faithful in Israel. It pointed them forward; and it had its true fulfilment long centuries after in Bethlehem, when the Holy Child was born, who was at the same time—think of it!—the Eternal Son of God.

And is it not a comfort for Christ's people to know that this is a name which is truly His in every age? "Lo, *I am with you alway, even to the end of the world.*" When they are tossed on the dangerous tempest still, He is with them in the boat. When they are in sorrow, He is with them to comfort them. When they have to go through the dark valley of death, even then they need not fear, when they can say, "*For Thou art with me.*"

Is Jesus *your* Emmanuel? Do you ask Him to be with you every day, and all the day? A godly man was seen starting from his home one morning—then returning to his room—then setting out again; and being asked the reason, he replied, "After I got out, I found Jesus was not with me. I could not go on without Jesus; so I went back to my closet to seek Him. Now He is with me, and I can go." Can you not understand something of what that man felt? It is the presence of Jesus that makes the day bright, and the spirit strong.

A Puzzle for Many.

March 2

" What shall I do then with Jesus?" (Matt. xxvii. 22).

THE speaker is Pilate, the rough Roman governor. The person spoken about is "Jesus" (Saviour), who is called "Christ" (or Messiah, the Anointed). The question is—What is Pilate to do with Jesus? His judgment says one thing, and his personal inclination, to some extent, supports his judgment. But selfish interest appears to say another thing. And so Pilate, though he evidently knows what he ought to do, does the very opposite. To please the Jews, he scourges Jesus, and gives Him up to be crucified. And then he washes his hands—as though that would make them clean!

A great many people are like Pilate—perplexed about what they are to do with Jesus. Some even who would like to forget Him cannot get rid of Him. His name is always turning up. They are constantly meeting Him, and being forced to meet this question—"What *shall* I do then with Jesus?"

If this is a question that you have not properly solved yet, I should like to help you to the right answer. There are four things that you young people ought to do with Jesus, and which it should be not less, but in some respects more, easy for you than for older people to do.

You should *trust* Him. He is well worthy of your entire confidence. You have not learned to distrust others so much yet as you may by and by be constrained to do. But here, at anyrate, is One who never disappoints. He is strong, and He is faithful. In His arms you will be safe.

You should *love* Him. Your young hearts are full of love. The cold world has not chilled them with its coldness yet. You love those who love you. And here is One who yearns over you with pure affection. "He is kind above all others: Oh how He loves." Will you not love Him in return?

You should *follow* Him. You are fond of imitating others. It is sometimes amusing, and sometimes sad, to see how apt young people are to imitate those whom, rightly or wrongly, they admire. Here is One whom you may safely imitate in *everything*. He has left us an example, that we should follow in His steps.

You should *serve* Him. How happy you are, to be able to do a service to your mother or your teacher! If you would have a truly blessed and worthy life, take the Prince of Wales's motto, and use it in a Christian sense—*Ich dien,* "*I serve*—I serve Jesus, who is called Christ."

A Dangerous Levity.

" But they made light of it " (Matt. xxii. 5).

THOSE of whom this is said put far too much weight on some things, and far too little weight on others. They were so much taken up with ordinary daily concerns, that they despised the invitation to the marriage of the King's Son. And so some of them "went their ways, one to his farm, and another to his merchandise," while the rest, annoyed at the repeated and urgent invitations of the King's servants, actually turned upon them, and put them to death. So little did they make of human life, so light did they make of sin! But when the King in wrath sent forth his armies and destroyed them and their city, they had reason to view things differently.

These are the two things which people often, most foolishly, make light of still, to their own undoing.

They make light of *the King's invitation*. God has, at great cost, prepared the gospel feast. He has sent forth His servants to announce that all things are ready, and to give a free and hearty invitation to sinners everywhere, to come and share the blessings offered to them in Christ. But multitudes turn a deaf ear to the gospel message. They consider the most ordinary affairs of life a far more practical concern; and if they do not turn upon God's messengers, and entreat them spitefully, they at anyrate "go their ways," and spurn the invitation which would have brought them truest happiness.

They make light also of *sin*. Apparently they forget what a hateful thing it is in God's sight; and what a heavy thing, too, it must be, if it needed God's own Son to come that He might, even at the cost of life, bear it, and bear it away in His own body on the tree. And so they trifle with it, not remembering what a dark blot it is upon their life, and what a terrible and growing power it is within their hearts.

A gentleman in India had a cub tiger as his pet. It was always with him, and was treated by him as a plaything. One day, as he was lolling in his room, his frolicsome companion came and licked his hand, which was hanging over the side of the arm-chair. It licked and licked, till he felt a stinging sensation; and, glancing down, he discovered to his horror that the skin was broken and the blood had come! The flashing eyes of the tiger told him that the brute nature in it had been thoroughly aroused. There was nothing for it but to lay hold of his revolver with his other hand, and shoot his dangerous playmate through the heart. Do not make light of sin!

"*Heal me, O Lord, and I shall be healed*" (Jer. xvii. 14).

This is a prayer from a sinner to God, who is the sinner's only help. There are different ways of addressing Him, and different sides on which to lay hold of His help. Here He is approached as the Great Physician, who can bring healing to the soul. I wonder if you have ever felt your need to make this prayer your own.

We have here suggested, first, *a disease* which is incurable by man. That word "incurable" is a terrible word; and to be put into the hospital for "incurables" is a very sad experience. There was one disease in Bible times that was especially feared and loathed, because of the desperate hold it took of the sufferers from it, and because the skill of man could do so little for its relief. This was leprosy. The poor leper was "a walking sepulchre." He has also been called "a walking parable"; because, as he lived apart, with his head uncovered and his garments rent, and as he cried when any would have approached him, "Unclean, unclean," he reminded people of a yet worse and more incurable disease than leprosy—the terrible disease of *sin*.

Dear young people, this is a disease we all suffer from; for we have all been born with it. I would not be long with any of you without discovering "symptoms," plague spots, telling of the evil within. That boy's bad temper, that girl's foolishness or selfishness, these bad thoughts which come into the mind, these evil desires you give way to, these impure or angry words you speak—what of these? They tell others, and may warn yourself, of the terrible disease that is in your heart.

But we are reminded, further, of *a Physician* who can cure what to all others is incurable. This is Jesus, who saves His people from their sins.

In a doctor, what would you like to have? One ready to run at your call; one skilful to discover your trouble, and to apply the remedy; one kind and sympathetic with you, in your suffering; and yet, one strict in his treatment, to subdue and get rid of the disease. Now, Jesus is all this. He is waiting to hear the sufferer's call; He knows what is in man, and the very cure man needs; He is full of compassion; yet rigorous in dealing with this terrible evil of sin (Matt. v. 29, 30).

What you, the patient, have to do is—to call in the Doctor; to trust Him, and have full confidence in His skill; to take kindly to Him, and not hinder His operations by alarm; and to obey Him, putting yourself entirely in His hands, and acting up to His instructions. If in this spirit you cry to Jesus, "Heal me," then you shall be healed; and "He will be your praise."

An Echo of Jesus.

"Love one another" (1 John iii. 11, iii. 23, iv. 7, 11).

It is told of the Apostle John, who had been the youngest of the disciples, and long outlived the rest of the Twelve, that when he was an old man, and unable any longer to address the company of Christian believers at Ephesus, he used to be carried into the midst of the assembly of worshippers on the Lord's Day; and the only words the venerable saint uttered, with outstretched hands, were these—"Little children, love one another."

You cannot but be struck with the frequency with which these words occur in this letter of him who is called the Apostle of Love. And what is the reason? It is just this, that there were certain words of Jesus, spoken long before, which had sunk deep into the memory and heart of John, and which find their echo here—"Love one another."

In some of the mountain passes of Switzerland you come to a point where your guide calls a halt; and one of the natives, putting a horn or a bugle to his lips, sounds forth a few clear, melodious notes. You listen; and you hear the same notes echoed and re-echoed with wonderful distinctness among the successive peaks and valleys.

Or, to turn from nature to art, you have before you a phonograph. A distinguished man, living hundreds of miles away, or perhaps dead years ago, has spoken into the instrument. And, as you listen, the words are permitted to escape again. They come forth exactly as he spoke them. If you knew his voice in life, you can have no difficulty in recognising it here. The words he uttered are reproduced, and in the very tone he used. You could almost fancy you were listening to himself.

Even so it is here. Aged John is going back in thought to the Upper Room at Jerusalem. "Love one another, as He gave us commandment" (John xiii. 34), he says. And, as he repeats these words, so distinctly engraven upon his memory and heart, we at once recognise "the eleventh commandment," and seem to hear the very cadence of the Master's voice.

Worthy Living, and Gainful Dying. March 6

"To me to live is Christ, and to die is gain" (Phil. l. 21).

LOOKING at you young people, two questions rise to the mind. First, What is life to be to you? You have *life* before you: of what sort is it to be? And second, there rises, unbidden, the other question, What is *death* to be to you? You have eternity before you: on what sort of eternity is death to usher you?

If you would live a worthy life,—then, as with the apostle, to you to live should be *Christ*. What Paul meant by this was, not only that in Christ he had the source of his true life, depending upon Him, as the branch depends upon the vine, for life and nourishment, but that the love of Christ was his ruling motive, and the glory of Christ his great end.

Pierce your way into the Christian's heart, the heart of one like Paul, and you will find enthroned a better than any earthly king; love to whom is a purer impulse, and has been a more powerful and blessed influence than love to any other—the love of Christ.

And with Paul, whether he was preaching in the synagogues, discussing in the streets, or making his tents at Corinth—this was his crowning aim, to subserve the glory of Christ. If a man is very much bent on anything, we say it is "his very life." Of one, we say that business is his very life; of another, society, or pleasure; of another, politics; of another, religion. What is *your* life to be? If it is to be worthy of you, it will be—*Christ*.

Then for you, as for the apostle, this word "to die" need have no terrors, but may rather have attractions. For it will mean, more of Christ. It will be, to depart and to be with Him; and if life is good, why, death is better. "To-day shalt thou be *with Me* in Paradise." Will not that be gain? What an exchange! Death for life; darkness for light; sickness for health; poverty for wealth; night for day; solitude for company; chains for liberty; toil for rest; hunger for satisfaction; perpetual trouble for endless peace.

Who would not be like the apostle? But, remember, if Christ be not your life, then death will be, for you, not gain, but awful loss.

Remember the Sabbath.

"Remember the Sabbath day, to keep it holy" (Ex. xx. 8).

You know what is meant by the Sabbath day. It means the day of *rest*. No work, no worry is expected on that day; but quiet, and calm, and peace. But I wonder if you know what is meant by keeping the Sabbath "holy"? It means keeping it *for God*. This is the day which He intends you to set apart specially for Him, for His worship and service. In its sacred hours you should think much of God and heaven, and sing songs of praise to Jesus.

The other days are given us to work in. In them we go to school or business, and do our best to get on in the world. But we need also to think of the world to come: of heaven, and how we are to get there. And every time the Sabbath comes round, it says—"Stop and think! Stop and think!"

What a blessing the Sabbath is to us, even in our bodies and in our minds! It comes in like the winding up of a clock, and sends many weary workers forward on their way with new vigour and hope. And what a blessing it is especially to our souls, if it brings us near to God, and leads us to taste true rest in Him! Yet many people go on with their worry and bustle, planning for gain and plunging into worldly pleasure on the Lord's Day, without ever knowing what a Sabbath really is. They are very foolish for their own sakes, and they are at the same time dishonouring God. They have only a Sunday at the most; and the Sabbath does not bring them true peace or real rest, because they disobey the command of God, and refuse to keep it holy.

"*Remember* the Sabbath day, to keep it holy." How short our memories often are, where religious things are concerned! A gentleman on his way to church was asked by a passer-by if he had seen three men, as he came along, making for the country. "Yes," he replied; "and one of them has a blue coat, and they all have short memories." "How do you know that?" said the other, smiling. "Because," said the gentleman gravely, "God has said 'Remember the Sabbath day, to keep it holy,' and they have quite forgotten it." It is a sin to have a short memory here, when God has specially reminded us.

"Keep the Sabbath *holy*." That does not mean—Keep it unhappy, with your face long, and the blinds down, and the house dark. Rather—Keep it bright and cheerful and joyous: as the glad day when the Saviour, who rose a conqueror on the first day of the week, is ready to meet with you. "We will rejoice and be glad in it!"

A Beautiful Biography.

"And Enoch walked with God; and he was not, for God took him" (Gen v. 24).

THERE have been very many biographies written since Enoch's time. But there has never been a more striking and beautiful one than his, though it is so very brief. In reading over the long list of names here, about which so little that is good or noteworthy has to be told, it comes over the heart like a breath of Paradise again, to read—"And Enoch walked with God; and he was not, for God took him."

It was a long walk this of Enoch's—lasting some 365 years. But it was not a tiresome one. For it was in the very best of company, and on terms of real friendship. It is not said of Enoch merely that he walked "before God," as beneath His eye; or "after God," as seeking to follow in His steps; but "with God," as you might walk with your father, holding by his hand and looking up into his face, telling him all that is in your heart, and hearing him speak to you again.

"Can two walk together except they be agreed?" No; they may drag on together, but not walk together in this sense. We gather certainly from what is told of Enoch here, that there was peace between him and God; and not only peace, but sympathy, and frank, loving intercourse. Is this true of you? Has the enmity been slain in your heart toward God and that which is good? Have you truly learned that God was in Christ, reconciling the world unto Himself? Are you among the reconciled ones, who know the joy of friendship and communion with our Heavenly Father day by day? Then the rest of Enoch's biography will also be true of you. God will one day take you to be with Himself for ever, in the Father's house of many mansions.

"He was not, for God took him." One day Enoch was missed. What had become of him? Death was not so familiar then as it is now. Jared, the father of Enoch, lived 962 years; and Methuselah, his son, 969 years; so that, at 365, Enoch was still comparatively young. And when he disappeared, people would not so readily as we, think of death as the explanation. No; and Enoch had not died. God would somehow let it be known that he had taken him to heaven by a brighter portal. And not only the men of Enoch's time, but many since his day, have had their thoughts and desires lifted upward by what is told of this friend of God, whom He loved so much, and of whom it was true, that, when he "was not" to the eyes of men, he had gone to be with God.

Our Substitute.

"Christ died for the ungodly" (Rom. v. 6).

You boys know what it is "to provide a substitute," or, another who shall, on a certain occasion, fill your place and do your part. You are expected to play in a football match; the captain of the team is counting upon you. If, through cold or other illness, you cannot be present on the appointed day, you undertake to provide a substitute.

Now, in Christ Jesus we have the sinner's Substitute. As a poor believing negro once expressed it, "He die : me no die." God's own Son, though He knew no sin, consented to take the place of the vilest sinners, and to be "made sin"—that is, to be regarded and treated as if He were utterly sinful, as sin itself—for them. He died in room of the ungodly. Our sin could not go unpunished; but He has borne sin's worst punishment, and has opened the gate of Heaven to all believers.

The captain of a vessel running to the Cape of Good Hope was suddenly taken ill, and laid upon the bed of death. When the mate entered his cabin for orders, he said to him—"I am dying; you must command the ship; I shall never go on deck again. But oh! can you—can you help me to appear before God?" The mate could give him no comfort about such a matter. The second mate was equally helpless, when called; and so with others of the officers and crew. At last the cabin-boy was summoned. His name was William Smith; and he was on his first voyage. It was with fear and trembling he came into the captain's presence; but, to his surprise, it was not to get rebuke, but to give help he had been called. "I've got a Bible which my mother gave me; shall I fetch it?" "Yes, boy." "Where shall I read, captain?" "Where you used to read to your mother!" "Shall I read as she taught me?" "By all means."

The boy proceeded—"But He was wounded for William's Smith's transgressions; He was bruised for William Smith's iniquities; the chastisement of William Smith's peace was laid upon Him; and with His stripes William Smith is healed." "Stop," said the captain; "put my name in, and read slowly." The boy did as he was told, and soon John Davis, the dying captain, was rejoicing by faith in Christ, his Substitute. Young reader, *put your own name in!*

"Every good gift, and every perfect gift, is from above" (Jas. i. 17).

WHEN John Wesley was preaching at Doncaster, he told of a poor Romanist woman, who, having broken her crucifix, went to her priest in great distress, crying—"I have broken my crucifix! I have broken my crucifix! I have now nothing to trust in but the great God!" Wesley added, "What a mercy she had a great God to trust in!" And these simple words were so blessed to a Romanist hearer in the audience, that he was led to put an undivided trust in the Lord Jesus.

Our text reminds us, and the context suggests, that everything good comes to us from God, and that nothing but what is good comes to us from His gracious and bountiful hand. If we are His children, then, even what is for the present unwelcome has love in it, when He sends it. We often change, but He does not. He is not like one of the heavenly bodies, such as the moon, liable to eclipse, or to cast a shadow through turning. But He is the Father of lights, ever full and serene in His shining. Clouds may come between Him and us; but they proceed, not from heaven, but from earth. For our own sakes He may have to vary His treatment of us, in order to our higher good. But "though His dispensations vary, His disposition toward His children does not change." Even when your Father metes out chastisement to you, He loves you still; and His heart is never tenderer toward you than just at such a moment.

A little French boy, called Peter, was enabled to keep hold of this truth, which his dying parent had taught him as they parted. And whatever was sent to him, he was in the habit of saying, "It cometh from above."

So long as it was a case of receiving a sou or a franc or some other gift, it sounded all right; but sometimes his refrain had a remarkable, though to others an unexpected, application. One windy day, little Peter was knocked down by a plank in the street. "It cometh from above," he said; and the passers-by smiled. But not far ahead, as he passed on, three men were killed by the fall of a roof, at a spot which Peter had been prevented reaching just by the tumble which had delayed him. He had many such experiences through life, which led him to stick to his chosen motto, to abide in his trust toward God in all circumstances, and to see his Heavenly Father's hand in everything. He became a rich merchant; and, when prosperity flowed in, he still humbly said, "It cometh from above."

March 11   A Good Keynote.

"God is Love" (1 John iv. 8, 16).

IT is very important that the song of your life should be set to a good keynote. And the Apostle John supplies you with that. His keynote is—Love.

This is the keynote to which his own *character* and life were set. He was "the beloved disciple," and the most intensely loving of the disciples. You must not think of him as a soft, weak man, but as a strong man, of a soaring, powerful nature, like the eagle. And whether his fervour showed itself in the proposal to bring down fire on the heads of those who slighted his Master, or in the eager desire for close, warm communion with Him on whose breast he leaned at Supper, the supreme governing note to which his heart kept true was the same—love to Christ!

Love is the keynote of John's *teaching* too. He became "the Apostle of Love." His Gospel is the one which shows us most of the heart of Christ. And if faith is Paul's distinctive keynote; hope, Peter's; obedience, James's—love is the keynote, and the constant refrain, of these letters by John. "God is Love." "Love is of God." "He that dwelleth in love dwelleth in God; and God in Him." "He that loveth not, knoweth not God; for God is Love."

It has been said of love, that in it you have the blending of all the perfections of the divine nature; and that, as the diamond is white because you have all the colours harmoniously united in it, so, if you wish one expression for the nature of God, and wish to say in a word what God is, it is here you must find it—God is *Love*.

Thus, if you would be like God, you are not to be so anxious to be clever or to be powerful, as to be loving. It is here that true kinship with Him comes out; and "of all earthly music, that which reaches farthest into heaven is the beating of a loving heart." This is true, just because such music is not earthly music after all. It is of heaven; and its echoes reach back to heaven again. Boys and girls are often far more taken up about who is to be counted the cleverest, than about who is the most loving among them; and men and women are apt to be the same. But "in the next world God will put the tape, not about men's heads, but about their hearts."

Faithful though not Famous

"And the lot fell upon Matthias" (Acts i. 26).

Of this Matthias, who, after the miserable death of Judas Iscariot, "was numbered with the eleven apostles," we know comparatively little. We do know that he was a steadfast follower of Jesus: he was one of those whom Peter described as "men who have companied with us *all the time* that the Lord Jesus went in and out among us." We also know that he was a man much esteemed among his brethren; he was one of two who stood so high in their regard that they had no doubt about one or other of them being the best man to fill the place left vacant by the Apostle Judas. And Matthias was, accordingly, set apart by lot to the high office of the apostleship; for it was upon him, and not upon Justus, that the lot fell.

This is really all we know about the life of Matthias. Not a syllable of his history afterwards is recorded; there is no record on earth of his good deeds, or of his subsequent service to the Christian cause. Yet we have learned enough of him to be sure that he was a good man and a true, and that, somewhere and in some way, he would do all he could while he lived to promote the glory of Christ and the good of men.

From the brief appearance of Matthias on the canvas of early Church history, and his absolute disappearance again from view, we may learn this lesson—that our great concern should be, to do our part well in our place, wherever it may be, without caring whether we and our work are much or at all heard of among men. It is often the best sign of a man and of his work that they are little spoken about. If there is good in either, the day of eternity will fully declare it, and bring it to its proper issue.

It was a becoming spirit which Sir Henry Lawrence, one of the great men of India, revealed in the choice of his epitaph, as he lay a-dying. "I wish this," he said, "to be on my tombstone, 'Here lies Henry Lawrence—who tried to do his duty.'" By "duty" we mean what is due, to God and man. Seek ever to do yours, content, if God sees it best, to be among "the unnamed forces of the universe." No honest service, though it may seem unnoted, is either lost or forgotten.

"Honour and shame from no condition rise,
Act well your part: there all the honour lies."

A Cloud of Witnesses.

"*We are compassed about with so great a cloud of witnesses*" (Heb. xii. 1).

THE picture suggested here is of the runners in a racecourse, with a definite goal to be reached, and a crowd of interested spectators looking on. The path of life, the way of God's commandments, is the course. Heaven, not death, is the goal. For see! beyond the dark porchway—within—the victors are being crowned. And the picture is given that we may be induced to join in the race, if we have not done so yet, and may be encouraged to hold on in it, if we have already begun.

The chapter before this, the 11th of Hebrews, gives a glorious muster-roll of saints and heroes of the olden time who have run the race before us, and run it well. It is one of the most beautiful chapters in the Bible; and you ought to learn it off by heart.

Far up in the earliest reaches of time, you see Abel bending heavenward—whither the murderous hand of Cain only hastened him the sooner. Then Enoch, who in his common daily life walked with God, till one day he was missed by his fellow-men, because God had taken him to be with Himself for ever. Then Noah, whose path led him through the deep. Then Abraham, whose road led him to and beyond a far unknown country of promise, which became to his seed for a possession. Then the rest of the patriarchs; and Moses, whose course brought him through a desert land—with many a doubting and weary wandering, ere, from the top of Pisgah, he was ushered upon the true home of his desire. Then the whole army of prophets and martyrs, of whom the world, which scorned and persecuted them, was not worthy.

All these, and many besides,—a glorious company of veterans, including some whom we ourselves have known,—are witnesses to us that God is faithful who hath promised, and that, when the heat and dust and weariness of the race are over, He will be the rewarder of all them that diligently seek Him. And we may even think of them, for our encouragement, as looking down upon us, in loving interest, as the former pupils of your school do sometimes at your contests, in the anxious hope that we shall run well.

Not yours, but you.   March 14

" I seek not yours, but you " (2 Cor. xii. 14).

How true this was of Paul! Some of the Corinthians seem to have been foolish enough to think that he was anxious to make a gain of them. But this was far from being the case. With gifts like his, and openings such as had been available for him, if gain had been his object, he might have attained it in a much easier way than by becoming a poor missionary of the Cross. Rather than be burdensome to these Corinthians, Paul had worked as a tentmaker at Corinth. He could look them, and all to whom he preached the gospel anywhere, honestly in the face, saying—"I seek not yours, but you."

And how true this is of Paul's Master! Jesus came, not to be ministered unto, but to minister, and to give His life a ransom for many." Though He was the Prince of Heaven, and had a right to the very best that earth could furnish to Him, He often had not where to lay His head. The foxes and the birds of the air were richer in that respect than the homeless Wanderer. Yet there was never a murmur on His lips. He went about, not continually complaining, but continually doing good; for what He was in quest of was something else than bodily comfort for Himself. Even if all the wealth of the world had been poured by men at His feet, that would not have satisfied the heart of Christ, which was hungering for their salvation. His answer still would have been—"I seek not yours, but you."

I have read of an Indian chief, who, under deep conviction of sin, came to a missionary and offered him his much-valued belt, that he might please God. The missionary shook his head; and the Indian went anxiously away. Soon he returned, and laid at the missionary's feet his gun, and the booty he had taken in the field. But still the answer was—" This is not the offering Christ will have from you." Ere long he came back; and this time he said, "I give wigwam, wife, child,—everything I have,—to please God." But again the missionary made reply—" With these the Lord Jesus will not be satisfied." And thereupon the chief, bursting into tears, raised his eyes heavenward, crying with deep emotion—" Then, Lord, take poor Indian too!" And he went joyfully back to his home, an accepted man.

Myself and Thyself.

"That which I see not, teach Thou me" (Job xxxiv. 32).

It was a good prayer, uttered by a servant of God, "Lord, shew me myself, and shew me Thyself." It was a prayer every boy and girl might very well take and use. And these were the two things that Job most needed to have shown clearly to him, when he said to God, "That which I see not, teach Thou me."

1. *Myself.* Show me this more fully, Lord! Job was a good man, but not so good as he thought he was. There was far more evil in his heart than he knew about. When God afflicted him, he thought he did not deserve at all to be chastised; and so, pride and rebellion rose within. But when God sent His light in, the evil was revealed.

A room sometimes seems wonderfully clean. But, let a bright sunbeam stream in through the side of the blind, and motes of dust are seen floating everywhere. Water may sometimes look wonderfully pure. But if it is submitted to the microscope, it may be full of loathsome insects. So when God's light shines in, and the microscope of God's law is applied, there may be much that is evil discovered in what seemed a comparatively pure heart and life. When we are inclined to think too well of ourselves, God sometimes has to bring us to see this.

2. *Thyself.* Lord, show me more of Thee! This is a prayer we need constantly to use. For there is more, and ever more, in God for us to know and to adore. His wisdom is unsearchable, and so are the riches of His love. You can never exhaust this subject. It will be always full of freshness, and interest, and comfort for you. So Job found. Though he was sinful, far more so than he had thought, God did not cast him off or refuse to speak with him, but revealed to him His marvellous goodness. He showed Job that even in trying him He had been showing His interest in him and love for him. He had been seeking all the time to free him more perfectly from sin, and to prepare him more fully for Himself. May God so deal with us! The sight of ourselves only might sink us into despair. But the sight of Him, too, will bring us hope and joy.

The Best of Friends. March 16

"A friend of publicans and sinners" (Matt. xi. 19).

THIS was what we would call "a nickname" for Jesus at first. But, like some other nicknames, it was more full of honour than of shame; and there was no name which Jesus Himself delighted more in than this—the Sinner's Friend. He was both a Friend *to* sinners and a Friend *of* sinners. He sought them; and they drew near and clung to Him.

You know already what a "friend" is, boys and girls, and you know what you like to have in a friend. Here is the kind of Friend Jesus was:—

1. A *loving* Friend. He was full of tenderness to the most despised of outcasts. His heart yearned over them in love, and their sorrows made Him weep.

2. A *true* Friend. He was their Friend behind their backs as well as to their faces. We often find Him standing up for them, against those who treated them with unkindness and disdain.

3. A *fast* Friend. He was not ready to take offence, but long-suffering and good; and, though there was much in sinners to offend Him, He was slow to turn His back upon them.

4. A *candid* Friend. He told sinners their faults openly, but in a kindly, not a sneering way. It was to better, not to embitter them, He spoke; and they could not but feel that kind and faithful were the wounds of such a Friend.

5. A *helpful* Friend. He was always ready to put forth His hand to lift a burden off; and He even died to free poor sinners from their load of guilt.

Are you a sinner? Then this is the Friend for you. Take everything to Him; for He loves you, and is waiting to hear whatever you have to tell him. A child was overheard asking another who had lost her mother—"What do you do without a mother to tell all your troubles to?" "Mother told me, before she died, to whom to go," was the answer. "I go to the Lord Jesus. He was my mother's Friend, and He is mine." Was it not well that the little orphan could say this? She had a Friend that sticketh closer than the nearest and dearest of earth—a Friend that death could never take away from her.

March 17   **More Precious than Gold.**

" The law of Thy mouth is better unto me than thousands of gold and silver"
(Ps. cxix. 72).

You have no doubt heard of Jenny Lind, the Swedish nightingale, as she was called. There have been many great singers in the nineteenth century, but probably she excelled all others. When she came over to London, in 1846, she captivated everybody, from the Queen downwards, who were privileged to hear her. For three years she continued to draw immense audiences, and her popularity, if possible, only increased; when, somewhat suddenly, in May 1849, it was announced that she had appeared upon the stage for the last time.

"Folly!" said the British public, "to retire, when she had the ball of fortune so completely at her foot! What madness to throw away such a chance of making thousands of gold and silver, to say nothing of adding constantly to her personal fame!" But what was her own explanation of it? You shall hear. A friend found her one evening, soon after her retirement, sitting by the seaside with a Bible in her lap, gazing wistfully across the sea at the glories of the setting sun. In the course of conversation, the friend ventured to ask her, what had led her to do what had taken all England by surprise—to withdraw from public life at the very moment when her popularity was at its height? The quiet but decided answer came—"When every day the theatre made me think less of *this* (laying her hand upon the open Bible), and nothing at all of *that* (pointing to the going down of the sun), what else could I do but give it up?"

Here was a woman to whom God's word was "more to be desired than gold, yea than much fine gold." The law of God's lips was "better to her than thousands of gold and silver." What was the applause of the multitude to her, in comparison with His approval, and the joy of cultivating His acquaintanceship? Was she not right, to count all things else but loss for the excellency of the knowledge of Christ Jesus her Lord?

Money can do a great deal; but there are some things it cannot do. It cannot satisfy the heart. It cannot bring true peace to the life. It cannot prepare the soul for a blissful eternity.

A starving Arab, fainting upon the desert, saw, as he was just sinking upon the sand, a wallet near by. He clutched eagerly at it, thinking it was full of bread. But it was only a bag of gold.

A Wonderful Key.

"*We love Him, because He first loved us*" (1 John iv. 19).

You know what a key is. It is an instrument to fit into a lock, in order to get into a place to which, without it, you would have no access. There is a cupboard, or a secret drawer, which you wish to open. How are you to get in? You must find the key. If you do, the rest is easy.

Now, our verse tells us of a key that God Himself has used to good purpose, and which His people too are invited to use. It is the Key of Love. Our hearts were shut and locked against God. But He has opened them, and has obtained an entrance for Himself through His divine irresistible love. He might have crushed and shattered us by His power; but how many a heart, like Lydia's, has been opened by the love of God in Christ—and laid for ever open afterwards to the sweet restoring influences of His grace! But for this, we would never have loved Him. We do love Him now, because He first loved us, and made us feel His love.

"Why is it, Mary," asked one of a little girl, "that you are always so happy?" "I suppose," was the innocent reply, "I suppose it is because I love everybody." There was a great deal of truth and wisdom in that answer. Love to God and to everybody is the key to true happiness. But our main point just now is, that it is the key to real, Christ-like influence.

There was a lady with three cherished children of her own, who once, in the kindness of her heart, took a poor little orphan girl into her home to stay with them. The young stranger at first was very shy, and could not be induced to come out of the corner of the room, to play with the other children. Their mother, however, said that she knew the secret of bringing her out. It was a word of four letters, and she asked them to guess what it was. The first said D-o-l-l, and brought her *doll* to the little orphan, but without effect; the second tried offering her her *muff*, with a like result. But the third went forward with a kind smile, and put her arms round the orphan's neck and kissed her; and, where everything else had failed, *love* conquered. Try that key, young people, oftener than you are wont to do!

March 19 **Complete Confidence in Jesus.**

"They went and told Jesus" (Matt. xiv. 12). *" When they returned, they told Him all that they had done "* (Luke ix. 10).

WHEN the disciples had any special trouble weighing upon their hearts, they went and told Jesus. Or when they had anything noteworthy to relate, either about the difficulty or about the success of their work, they went and told Jesus. They knew that in Him they had a Friend of such perfect sympathy that they could come to Him at any time and with everything. Whatever was of concern to them was of moment to Him. He would not turn a deaf ear to them, or bid them go away and not trouble Him. They were sure of comfort, guidance, help from Jesus, as they needed it.

We, too, are invited to turn to the same Friend, with everything and for everything. He will never be found so occupied with other people as to have no time to listen to what we have to tell Him. He will never be found so taken up with weightier concerns as to have no thoughts to bestow on what is of concern to the very smallest and humblest of His disciples. Nothing pleases Jesus more than to know that His is such a place in your heart that He is the One to whom you naturally turn, as the Friend in whom, above all others, you can confide.

James Gilmour of Mongolia, the intrepid missionary, who went alone into the heart of Asia, carrying the gospel to the wandering half-savage tribes there, had himself a great, living trust in Jesus. He wrote to his two boys in England—" Cheer up, my dear sonnies, we shall see each other some day yet! Tell all your troubles to Jesus, and let Him be your Friend. Sometimes, when I am writing a letter to you, and come to the foot of a page, I don't take blotting-paper and blot it, but kneel down and pray while it is drying." How well it was for these boys to be directed and commended to a Friend who, even after father and mother had forsaken them in death, would abide as their ever-present Help!

Jesus invites your full confidence; and He offers you His full sympathy. Tell Him not only of your troubles, but of your joys. Tell Him not only of your wishes, but of your resolves. Tell Him not only of your successes, but of your failures; aye, and of your sins. His is an ear into which you may breathe what you could tell in no other ear but His. Go day by day to Jesus, and tell Him *everything.*

Seeking the Lost.   March 20

" The Son of Man is come, to seek and to save that which was lost "
(Luke xix. 10).

You must have sometimes seen a poor, lost child upon the street. It is crying bitterly. A crowd begins to gather round, and kind people ask it, " What is the matter ? " And they try to comfort it. But all in vain ! The tears still flow, and the wail of distress refuses to be hushed. For the little one is lost, and feels that it is lost ; and the shop windows and the other sights that were such an attraction a short while ago, as it wandered unthinkingly onward, have altogether ceased to charm. It will not be comforted.

But suddenly the little face brightens ; the eyes glisten with delight through their tears ; the yammering of sorrow is broken by a short, eager cry of joy. What means this ? The child's restless eye has found what its heart has been longing for; and in a moment, radiant with delight, it is clasped in its mother's arms.

How sad to see upon the street a helpless little one, in distress because it knows that it is lost ! But to me it is almost more pitiful to see one lost without knowing or heeding it—going gaily onward for a while, but sure to waken at last to the discovery that it has lost its mother and its home. And are not some boys and girls just like this with God. Ah, yes ! They are wandering from Him who loves them with more than a mother's love ; and they do not know their loss. But the time will come when they will miss Him. Then they will seek Him, if haply they may find Him. And shall they find Him ? Christ's answer for you to this question is— " They that seek Me early shall find Me." And the Bible warning is—" Seek ye the Lord while He may be found ; call ye upon Him while He is near."

Our seeking, even after we had discovered that we were lost, would be of little avail if that were all. But Jesus too, for whom the heart of the lost but awakened sinner craves, is seeking, that He may save just such as you are. The Good Shepherd, who laid down His life for the sheep, but took it again, is not, you may be sure, careless about the lambs. Oh what delight it would give Him to bear you upon His shoulder rejoicing ! And the joy in His heart, and in yours, would find an echo among the angels in heaven.

No more Sea.

"And there was no more sea" (Rev. xxi. 1).

THIS is part of St. John's inspired description of heaven. If you ask "What is heaven?" the Bible answers shortly—"Where Jesus is." That is heaven. But it is also, Where certain other things are not. And among these, this is one, "No more sea."

Now, I do not know if you would be quite disposed to include this in your idea of heaven. You love the sea, with its rippling waters and its pleasant breezes. You delight to go to the seaside in the summer time, to sport upon the sands; and you afterwards carry a bright picture of it in your heart.

This prophecy certainly shows that the "new earth" must be very different from this one; for more than half the surface of this old earth of ours is covered by the sea. And so important are the uses of the sea, that, as things exist, we could not do without it. It is the great *purifier*. Without the sea, into whose briny depths so much of the world's filth is received in order to be cleansed, the earth would be scourged with pestilence. It is also the great *rain-giver*. It is from the sea that most of the moisture is drawn upwards by the sun, to descend again in refreshing showers to water the earth. And another of the many good uses of the sea is, that it *tempers* the climate in different quarters of the globe, where without it the land would be either baked with heat or frozen up with perpetual cold.

But, in the new earth, such uses will be no longer needed. There will be no impurity and no sickness there. The inhabitant shall not say, "I am sick": he will be in the enjoyment of perfect health. There will be no drought; for "the river of the water of life" will irrigate the whole of that fair land. There will be the warmth of comfort, but no scorching heat; and "neither cauld nor care, in the Land o' the Leal."

And then, three things, which, as you get older, you may learn to think of when the sea is mentioned, will not be found in heaven. Here a mother's heart is often yearning after her boy in a far-off land; but a great stretch of waters rolls between. Yonder the members of God's family will be divided by no sea of *separation*. Here we sadly read of the dangers of the deep—its shoals and reefs and storms. Yonder, there will be no sea of *peril*. Here the moaning, troubled sea, like a restless conscience, never is at peace. But yonder there will be no sea of *unrest*. There will be perfect union, safety, peace—in the world with "no more sea."

"*When I consider Thy heavens . . . What is man?*" (Ps. viii. 3, 4).

You know what the "firmament" is, you young people. It is the blue vault of heaven above us, mentioned, you remember, in the first chapter of the Bible, where we are told of its being stretched by God's own hand.

And you know what the stars are. A little girl once described their *appearance* very prettily when she said, "They are gimlet holes in the floor of heaven, to let some of the light shine through." But I do not need to tell you that they are among the things which "are not what they seem." They are not gimlet holes, but great worlds, as you well know; some of them vastly bigger than the world we live in, though their distance from us makes them seem so very small.

You might profitably read all the verses you can find in the Bible about the stars. What God says to Abraham, for example, about them; what David, the shepherd-king, who so often saw the stars above his head at Bethlehem, says in the 8th Psalm that they made him think about and wonder at, as he looked up at them at night; and what we are told in the Gospel about the wonderful star which guided the wise men to the humble manger where the Creator of all worlds lay as a little Babe. Then some of you may be able to tell where it is that Jesus—"the Dayspring from on high," as he is called in Luke—is foretold by a strange prophet in the Old Testament, as "a star" that would one day "rise out of Jacob."

There are many things that a look up at the starry sky on a quiet night will suggest to the thoughtful heart. It will make you admire the greatness of Him "who created these things, and calleth them all by names." It will excite your wonder at the condescension of the great God, in stooping to visit man, even fallen and sinful man, and in caring day by day for you. And it may also suggest to you the glory that awaits those who are wise unto salvation; for they, as the Bible tells us (Dan. xii. 3), "shall shine as the brightness of the firmament." When you look up next at the starry canopy of heaven, let it remind you of the vault of God's great spiritual temple, His purified and glorified Church; and covet for yourself a place in that bright sphere, which will be far more gloriously beautiful than the resplendent dome of the sky.

The Best Guide.

"He leadeth me" (Ps. xxiii. 2).

WHO is "He"? It is the Good Shepherd, Jesus, who guides and guards His sheep, and gives them all they need, not for safety only, but for satisfying.

Who is the "me"? It is David; but also every believer—every true follower of Jesus, every sheep and every lamb in the Good Shepherd's flock.

I hope the *me* here means *you*. Apart from the Saviour's leading, you will wander far astray upon the barren moors, weary of heart often, with none to restore your soul; and without Him to bring you thither, you can never possibly reach the one safe fold at last.

Can you say from the heart, "*He* leadeth *me*"? Not merely, "He leads His flock"; or, "He is willing to lead me"; but, "He leads me"; "I am under His leading"? If you can, you are under the best of all guides; and all the comfort which this wonderful 23rd Psalm is fitted to give is meant for you, just as much as for him who was inspired to write it at the first. A wonderful psalm indeed—generally the first that children learn beside the mother's knee, and very often the last that the dying believer quotes, as he enters the dark valley and gets beyond the hearing and help of all other friends but One!

"*He* leadeth me." This means, that there is a very *close personal tie* between you and Jesus. He is not only the Shepherd of Israel, but you can say of Him, "The Lord is *my* Shepherd."

"He leadeth *me*." This means that *you* are an object of *particular interest* to Him. He has a great flock; but He has as much loving care over you as if He had no other to lead and to provide for.

"He *leadeth* me." This means that your life is continual *progress toward the goal of blessedness*; and it implies, that where He leads you are ready to follow. How often you have used these words in repeating this old psalm! I hope they do mean, every time you use them, that you are one of those who listen to Christ's voice, love His word, walk in His footsteps; who desire to be near Him, to be like Him, and at length with Him for ever.

"Andronicus and Junia, who also were in Christ before me" (Rom. xvi. 7).

PAUL was not an envious man, at least after he became a Christian. But there were some whom, even then, he felt disposed to envy. Andronicus and Junia, mentioned here, were among them. They were those who were "in Christ" before him.

"In Christ" meant for Paul, safety, joy, life; "out of Christ," danger, misery, death. To be "a man in Christ," or a real Christian, meant to him the true and proper manhood. His great joy was, to be in Christ. His chief regret as a Christian was, that he came so late to be in Christ. The life he spent before that, he felt to have been a comparatively wasted life.

And Paul's advice to you young people is—Come to Jesus *early!* Do not delay; but come at once. If you put off, perhaps you may never come at all. If you do come later, it will be a lifelong regret that you did not come before.

Now, what is meant by being "in Christ"? There are two ways in which we may look at this, as suggested by the Bible. The believer is in Christ as Noah was in the Ark; he is also in Christ as the branch is in the Vine. How well it is for any of us to be in Christ in both of these respects!

You need to be *in Christ as the Ark of safety.* You are guilty before God. You have sinned; and you have a sinful heart. And God has revealed His wrath from heaven against all unrighteousness of men. Therefore, out of Christ you are exposed to the tempest of divine indignation, which, like a flood, will sweep the impenitent transgressors to destruction. But in Christ there is safety for you. Believe in Him; commit yourself to Him. Step into the Ark; and God will shut you in, beyond the reach of the flood that is to destroy the ungodly.

You need to abide *in Christ as the True Vine.* The life of your soul comes from Him, and He must sustain it. Just as the branch apart from the vine would be a poor withered worthless thing, so would your soul speedily languish, and wither, and die, but for Christ's life being imparted constantly to you. Without Him you can do nothing. But "in Christ" you will be a living, fruit-bearing branch. The fair blossoms and precious fruits of a real Christianity will be seen in you; and Christ's Father, and yours, will be glorified.

March 25 A Lesson from Carmel.

"How long halt ye between two opinions ?" (1 Kings xviii. 21).

SUCH was the question addressed by Elijah to the waverers, in the course of the great conflict between himself and the prophets of Baal upon Mount Carmel.

It appears at first sight a strangely unequal contest. On the one hand you see a great company, representing the Court religion, and resting under the smile of the king, and of the fawning courtiers who surround him. On the other hand you see a solitary man, simple and uncouth in his attire, with no favour from outward patron resting on him, but with the strength of faith in his heart, and its resolution in his face, and with the favour of Jehovah resting upon him. Unequally matched they are, in verity; but not in the sense in which they seem to be. Power in this conflict lies not in numbers or in outward might, but in the force of truth and the exercise of faith. It is the kind of contest to be decided, not by the clash of arms, or the collision of serried hosts, but by an appeal to an Unseen Power, real though invisible, who will make Himself felt at the proper moment, and unmistakably. And it is a case in which the one is right against the many; the solitary combatant, the victor.

"How long halt ye between two opinions?" cried Elijah to the swaying multitude, who were neither loyal to Jehovah nor much in in love with Baal. Be one thing or another, he says: make up your minds as to whom you ought to serve, and serve Him with all your hearts.

The same question and appeal come to us to-day. Are you still, young reader, halting between two opinions—like a bird "hopping from branch to branch," as the word means—with your heart not at rest yet in its allegiance, and the energies of your life not directed deliberately and consistently to a worthy end? This is surely most unsatisfactory. It means weakness; and "to be weak is miserable." Ay, and it is sinful. For your mind ought to be made up. You have been gifted with the power of choice. "God or the world, Jehovah or Baal—whom shall I follow, whom shall I serve"? There is only one right choice possible. For your own sake as well as God's, make it heartily and at once. To refuse to choose, remember, is to make the wrong choice. Not to be for God is to be against Him.

"*He that winneth souls is wise*" (Prov. xi. 30).

WHAT is meant by *wisdom*? It is different from *knowledge*. Many a man knows a great deal who is far from being a wise man. Here is the best general definition I have seen of wisdom — "Wisdom consists in the choice of the best ends, and of the best means of attaining them." A person who has a bad end in view, no matter how clever he may be in reaching it, is not wise; nor can he be called wise who, having set before him a good object, attempts to attain it by stupid or unworthy means. The end must be good, *and* the means appropriate.

Now, our text points us to one kind of person whom it pronounces without hesitation *wise*. Who is it? The person who has set before him as his great end the winning of a great fortune, or of a great name for himself? No. Many of those who are doing that are anything but wise, even though they may be very cleverly succeeding in their work. But "he that winneth souls" is wise, for he has set his heart upon an object that is well worthy of the best and most constant endeavours of a consecrated life. And, thank God, there are many who are wise in this sense to-day. You will find them not only in our pulpits, but in the destitute slums of our great cities, and in the far-off fields of heathendom. They are men and women to whom God has revealed something of the meaning of that terrible word *lost*—a *lost* soul; and who, having been made wise unto salvation themselves, are bending all their energies to the great end of winning souls, for the crown and kingdom of the Lord Jesus.

It *needs* a wise man to win souls. This is another way of looking at the text. We may read it, not only as a *declaration* that he is wise who gives his life to the securing of so enduring and immortal a treasure, but as an *admonition*, that he who would be successful in such work must needs be wise, with a wisdom higher than that of earth. Christ makes His disciples fishers of men; He sets them to the work, too, of shepherding souls. But what gracious tact the fisher needs! What patient skill, the shepherd! This wisdom cometh from above; and it is to be had for the asking. If your own soul, once lost, has been won, may you not do something, by kind word and Christlike deed, to win others to the Saviour. If any feel his lack of wisdom, let him ask of God. Has not your Heavenly Father promised to give the Holy Spirit to them that ask Him?

March 27   The Fool.

"*But God said unto him, Thou fool!*" (Luke xii. 20).

THIS is not a name to be bandied about lightly from one to another, as boys and girls sometimes do. But it is a name which God very solemnly applies to certain people. You have them mentioned in the beginning of the 14th Psalm; and you have, in this parable in the 12th chapter of Luke, a full-length portrait of a fool, drawn by the divine hand of Christ Himself. From it we learn that the fool is—

1. *One who ignores God.* He lives upon God's bounty day by day. He spends the time God has given him, he uses the faculties with which God has endowed him, for purposes of his own. Yet all the while he lives and plans and resolves and executes, without so much as once consulting God. He lives as though there were no divine Being to whom he is accountable. God is not in all his thoughts; or, if the thought of Him does steal in, he tries to smother it, saying in his heart, "There is no God," and plunging all the more eagerly into the absorbing pursuits of earth. Self is the only God he will recognise. "And *he* said, This will *I* do: *I* will pull down *my* barns, and build greater; and there will *I* bestow all *my* fruits and *my* goods. And *I* will say to *my* soul"—and so on. It is all "I"—"I"—"I." But *God* said—"Fool!"

2. *One who excludes eternity.* The fool may be far-sighted enough so far as this world is concerned. He may be counted very shrewd among his neighbours. His schemes for increasing his wealth and power, and securing a continuance of his worldly pleasures, may be very well laid and eminently successful. But he is very short-sighted after all. For his horizon is bounded in by time. He deliberately excludes eternity from view. He forecasts for himself many years of earth, and lays up in his extended barns large provision for long-continued ease and merriment. But eternity is upon him before he is aware. He has grievously miscalculated. He has been occupied only about the preface, and a poor preface he has made of it. He has forgotten all about the volume that is to follow.

3. *One who despises the true riches.* The fool may have plenty of riches of a kind. But they are of the sort that can be gathered into barns, and to which a match may be put for their destruction. They cannot endure the fervent heat of the day of the Lord. The fool has none of the enduring riches, the riches of the heart. He has no treasure in heaven, which moth and rust and thief cannot touch. He is like Bunyan's man with the muck-rake; and, however many of the sticks and straws of earthly fortune he may scrabble together, he writes himself down a fool, for he is oblivious of the celestial crown.

" When I have a convenient season, I will call for thee " (Acts xxiv. 25).

THE man who uttered these words to the Apostle Paul was called Felix, "the Happy." But he was sadly misnamed. He and true happiness were utter strangers. He had, indeed, been successful in a sense. Beginning life as a slave, he had gained his freedom, and won position, wealth, and Court favour. But he had continued to be a slave in heart,—mean, self-seeking, cruel, lustful,—hated by others, even when they flattered him, and inwardly despised by himself.

He was, in short, a really bad man; and no bad man is ever truly happy. He might try to drown his senses in debauchery, and smother his conscience in worldly mirth. But secretly he was ill at ease. And we see him here, while the prisoner at his bar is reasoning of righteousness, temperance, and judgment to come, cowering and trembling in his presence, and anxious to get Paul taken out of sight and hearing of him. If I were to ask you which of the two was really Felix, "the Happy," you would not have difficulty in answering the question. Not the exalted Roman judge upon the bench, with outward fortune smiling on him, but with hell within his heart; but the poor Hebrew prisoner at the bar, whom he was to leave for years longer in his bonds, but who had Jesus for his Friend!

Yet Felix, too, might have shared the peace and heavenly joy that Paul knew, had he only received the message the apostle brought him "concerning the faith in Christ." He was unwilling, however, to give up sin just yet. By and by he might yield his heart to God; but let him enjoy the pleasures of sin still for a season. And so, he put off the proper settlement of his soul's affairs to a more convenient time, which never came.

The lesson from Felix for you is—Now is the accepted time! Beware of delay. There is no season *so* convenient as *just now*!

A minister dreamed one day that he was listening to the lost spirits in hell, devising how they might best ruin the souls of men. One rose and said, "I will go and tell men that the Bible is all a fable." Another said, "I will tell them that there is no God, no heaven, no hell"—at which words a fiendish smile lit up their faces. But it was agreed that men could not generally be got to believe them. At last one rose and suggested, serpent-like—"No; I will journey to the world of men, and tell them that there *is* a God, that there *is* a Saviour, that there *is* a heaven—yes, and a hell too; but that *there is no hurry*, and to-morrow will do." And they sent him. What multitudes have believed that messenger, to their own undoing!

March 29   **Christ is Risen.**

"He is not here: for He is risen, as He said" (Matt. xxviii. 6).

THERE is a church in Jerusalem, at this day, called the Church of the Holy Sepulchre. It is a building into which a great many marvels have been crowded, for the benefit of the sightseer, by the sects that have possession of it. But there is one object in particular, to look upon which multitudes of pilgrims travel from long distances every year, namely, the little chapel in the centre of the big church, which is supposed to mark the spot "where the Lord lay." It is more than doubtful whether it is the real site of Joseph's emptied tomb; but it is touching to see the crowds of devotees flocking to see it, and kissing the marble slab, as some of them do, which rests upon a place to them so sacred. And certainly it is a great and blessed truth, that somewhere in that neighbourhood, at anyrate, the Son of God, who had died for our sins, rose again. Whether we visit Jerusalem or not to see the place, and whether we observe the date or not in an Easter celebration, we may well rejoice in the rising again of the Lord Jesus Christ.

The Resurrection of Jesus is one of the best-attested facts, and, taken in connection with His death, it is the most important fact in history. If the Syrian stars still looked down upon a lonely grave, from which He had never risen, our Christian hope would indeed be vain. But Christ is risen. And the resurrection on the third day meant—(1) That Jesus *had triumphed over all His foes.* It seemed as if He had been beaten. The hopes of His disciples appeared to have been buried with Him in the tomb. But He rose a Conqueror, and wrested from the last enemy what had only seemed his victory.

(2) That Jesus *had secured salvation for His people.* He had died to purchase it; and His resurrection meant, that God had accepted the payment as a payment in full. He was now justified in appearing before God as the sinner's Surety. He was raised again for our justification; and because He lives, we who believe in Him shall live also.

(3) That Jesus *had opened a pathway for us to heaven through the grave.* It is a dark portal, but it leads to a bright place. In His rising He became "the first-fruits of them that slept." He is the Forerunner of His people; and them also who sleep in Jesus shall God bring with Him. He has changed for believers what would otherwise be only the graveyard, the place of death, into "the cemetery"—the sleeping-place, from which there will be for them, too, a bright resurrection morn.

The Best Gift.   March 30

"*The gift of God*" (John iv. 10).

GOD is the great Giver; and all the gifts He sends us are good and perfect in their kind, however we may spoil them in their use. But there is one Gift which far transcends them all. For it is *the gift of God*, the gift of His Son, and of salvation in Him.

1. It is a *gift*—because freely given, as every real gift must be. There was nothing compelling God to give us Jesus Christ; and nothing but His own wonderful love impelling Him to bring salvation to us. We had not deserved the boon; we could not work for it; we could not purchase it. God gives, He does not sell, His blessings. He is too rich and great for that.

"Would that I had some of these luscious grapes," thought a poor woman, "for my dear sick one at home!" She gave a modest knock at the hothouse door. "May I buy some of those grapes," she said, "for my poor fevered boy?" "We don't sell grapes here; and so begone," said the gardener, as he shut the door. The woman turned sadly away; but the door was quietly opened again, and a girl kindly asked her what she wanted. "I wished to buy some grapes, miss, for my dying child; but the man says they are not to be sold." "No, you cannot buy them, my poor woman. My father is too rich to sell his grapes; but he is kind, and if I ask him he may give you some." The young lady vanished, and in a few minutes reappeared, with joy upon her face, and a mellow cluster in her hand, which the mother, who could not purchase it, received with tears of thankfulness as a free *gift*!

2. It is *the* gift—because it is the greatest we could possibly receive. It is the most precious in itself; and if we get it and treasure it in our hearts, it will bring all other good things with it, and make them ours for ever. No other gift in our possession is worth half so much. It is of infinitely more value than all the rest.

3. It is *the* gift *of God*—because only He could give it, and it is the very greatest gift that even He could give. It is as though a king, not content with giving you—a beggar—food and raiment and every kind of comfort, took the richest jewel from his crown, or the signet from his finger, and gave it to you, as what he prized most, and what would do you most good, in making sure to you all other gifts. Nay, it is far more than that. There was no jewel in the universe to compare with God's Son. To part with Him was to give up His very best possession. Yet He so loved us that "He gave His only-begotten Son." Oh what love! Oh what a Gift!

The Tables Turned.

"But many that are first shall be last; and the last first" (Matt. xix. 30).

Just as in a race it is not always those who get the best start who come in first at the goal, so is it often in life. It is not always those who have most advantages that succeed best; or those of most promise who in the end of the day turn out the best. And what is true of time is no doubt true in eternity. You remember Wesley's saying, that in heaven he would have three things, he believed, to wonder at. The greatest marvel would be, that he himself, so great a sinner, had been admitted there; but he would also be surprised that some whom he confidently expected to be there were absent, and that some were there whom he never had expected to see in heaven. There will be a great "turning of the tables" in the next world. Many who were first shall be last; and the last first.

But, even on this earth how often we see this saying of the Lord's fulfilled. We who are older, when we go back in memory to our schooldays, can recall many illustrations of its truth. Some whose start was vigorous and bright have fallen sadly behind in the race, if they have not altogether dropped from sight. They are struggling hopelessly behind others now whom once they counted unpromising and dull. And these—though in temper and circumstances and prospects undoubtedly inferior then—are now far ahead. Every township, every circle of friends, every class, almost every family, illustrates the same thing; and no doubt it will be as true by and by of you and your mates as it has been of those who have gone before you, that "many that are first shall be last; and the last first."

Some lives are like a day whose dawn is fair and bright—not a cloud to dim the horizon, or a breath to tell of coming storm. But too soon the fogs begin to gather, and ere long fair heaven is shut from view, and the dingy earth is shrouded in its clammy covering. Other lives have a less promising dawn. There are threatening clouds floating here and there, and an unpleasant drizzle which seems to say the storm is at hand. But the sun's genial rays break through; and lo! Nature seems to revel in the near companionship of earth and sky.

May your path be that of the shining light! Cast in your lot heartily with Christ. Allied in love, duty, destiny with Him, you will begin, continue, and finish well.

True Courage.

"The Lord stood with me" (2 Tim. iv. 17).

THERE have been many brave Christians. Luther, for instance, was a brave man. On his way into Worms he said to his anxious friends, who were fearing for his safety—"I shall go; though there were as many devils as there are tiles upon the roof-tops, it would not keep me back." And having declared his beliefs in presence of his most powerful enemies, he said, "Here I take my stand; I cannot otherwise; so help me, God!" Knox, too, was a brave man; so brave that it was truly spoken over his grave, "Here lies the man that never feared the face of man." And there have been other Christians ready to face anything for the sake of their Redeemer. But there has never been a braver Christian than the Apostle Paul. One is almost inclined to think, that if *he* had been among "the Twelve," he would not have forsaken Christ and fled.

What was the secret of Paul's courage? It did not lie in himself. No doubt he was, by nature, a man of firm mould. But that is not the explanation of his marvellous fortitude. Here it is— "The Lord stood with me, and strengthened me." It was this that made him calm, where others would have trembled. There was One standing by him, whom others could not see, but who was far more real to him than the great Emperor Nero was—"the Lord"— the King of kings—the Lord Jesus Christ. He endures, as seeing Him who is invisible. Looking to the past, he can say with thankfulness, "I was delivered out of the mouth of the lion." Looking to the future, he can add with confidence, "The Lord *shall* deliver me."

How inspiring has been this example of Paul the aged,—a prisoner at Rome, forsaken by his friends, lied against by his enemies, about to confront a second time the most cruel of despots; yet full of thankfulness and invincible resolve! Another early Christian, Chrysostom, the "golden-mouthed," had caught a like spirit when he said to them that threatened him—"Banish me? The earth is my Father's house. You cannot banish me. Slay me? Nay; my life is 'hid with Christ in God,' where you cannot touch it. Take my treasures? I have none that you know of, or can take; my treasure is in heaven. Drive me from men, where I shall have no friend left? Nay, for I have a Friend from whom nought can sever me!" Thus does the courage which is added to faith overcome the world.

In the Morning

"Cause me to hear Thy loving-kindness in the morning" (Ps. cxliii. 8).

This is part of a beautiful prayer uttered by the Psalmist, which he sums up, at the 11th verse, in one word—"*Quicken* me, O Lord, for Thy name's sake." Make me "quick"—alive—to hear, to see, to do the right.

It is a prayer which he offers in the morning; and it is a prayer suitable for you to offer in the morning too. You may offer it this morning, and the day will be the better for it; for if you come to God in the freshness of the dawn, you will have your recompense in the hours that follow. You may well offer it in the morning of your life, and all the life will be the better for it. When, amid the heavy responsibilities that may await you in maturer years, you are bearing the burden and the heat of the sun, there still will linger on your spirit some of the dewy freshness of the early consecrated life, made "quick" by God's own Spirit to hear and see and do.

"Cause me to hear Thy loving-kindness in the morning." How deaf men often are to the voice of God, just because it is a still small voice, in comparison with the noisy voices of earth that claim our ear. In the morning of the day and of the life you have a favourable opportunity of listening to it, before the world's din has confused and deafened you. It is too good a chance, young friend, to throw away. The voice of God is a voice of loving-kindness, the music of which, if you catch it early, will be ever welcome afterward to your well-accustomed ear, and will bring strengthening and consolation, in many a weary hour, perchance, on the bustling thoroughfares of after-life.

"Cause me to know the way wherein I should walk" will have its answer too. Under the clear morning sky, as you lift your soul to God, He will give you light, and set your footsteps in a way of peace, from which, even when the smoky mists of earth have descended, He will not suffer you to wander. His Spirit, who is good, will lead you upwards to "the land of plainness"—the high, level pasture-land for flocks to lie down in. And at evening time it will still be light.

"Teach me to do Thy will." Made quick to hear, and alert to know, you will be also made expert to do God's will. "Learn young, learn fair." Practical obedience to the loved One who is unseen, if you learn it in the morning, will be the habit and the delight of a devoted life on earth, and the preparation for an eternity of blissful service before the Throne.

"*The Lord is at hand*" (Phil. iv 5).

Though Jesus is not now on earth in His bodily presence, He is not far away from His people, but very near. He is true to His own word of promise—"Lo, I am with you alway, even to the end of the world."

He is within *seeing* distance of us. He knows our downsitting and our uprising, and is acquainted with all our ways. He sees us well enough to count our steps (Job xxxi. 4). He notes the changing expression on our faces; and, more than this, He looks into the heart, and can read off all the thoughts and desires that may be hidden there. What a comfort for Christ's people it is that, when they are in perplexity or danger, they are still under His eye.

He is within *speaking* distance. He can make His voice heard by us; and He does it, not in the loud accents of Sinai, which struck terror to the heart, but in the still small voice of His Spirit, which, "soft as the breath of even," speaks within the breast. It is well for us ever to remember, that He is near enough to speak to us. And it would be well if our desire and request were oftener that of little Samuel—"Speak, Lord : Thy servant heareth."

He is within *hearing* distance. Not only can He make His voice reach us, but He is so near that even our feeble voice can reach Him. You have not to move from the spot where you are sitting or standing now, in order to get near enough for Christ to hear you. Speak to Him where you are, and He will listen, and take in well your meaning. Even a poor dying child of His, too weak to speak to anyone else, can gain His ear. For He even heareth the *desire* of the humble (Ps. x. 17).

And He is within *helping* distance. A friend may be standing on the shore, within seeing, speaking, hearing distance of a loved one struggling in the water, and yet not be within helping distance; and he might have the pain of seeing that loved one, though so near, go down to death. But it is not so with the Lord in whom we trust. He is at hand; and when we are ready to sink, and the cry goes forth, "Lord, save me," He stretches out to us, as He did to Simon Peter on the stormy waters, His strong right hand of help. He says, "Fear not : I will uphold thee with the right hand of My righteousness." And, grasping that strong but tender hand, we are comforted.

April 4   God Hears!

"And the Lord hearkened and heard" (Mal. iii. 16).

SOME time ago I was in a curious place—the great underground quarry or cavern at Syracuse, called "the ear of Dionysius." It was here that the tyrant used to keep his captives confined. The peculiarity of the cavern is the echo, which makes the slightest whisper below distinctly audible, it is said, away up in a chamber near the roof. The crafty king used to sit concealed, we are told, in the dark recesses of this chamber, that he might hear what the prisoners below were whispering to each other about himself. And then he would drag them forth to punishment.

It is well for us to bear in mind that there is another—a King unseen—listening to all we say, and taking note, not only of what we do, but even of our secret thoughts. He is not, however, a cold and crafty and cruel King like Dionysius, but a King of infinite love and grace as well as knowledge. Those who wilfully despise Him will find how terrible a thing His vengeance is. None will be able to stand before it. He will strike through kings in the day of His wrath. But He knoweth the way of the righteous. The Lord is mindful of His own. And if you are among those who fear Him, and think upon His name, you are among those He loves and cherishes, as jewels which to Him are beyond all price.

If you love Christ, who first loved you, and are showing day by day that you truly desire to please Him, then you may be sure that the Father Himself loves you. And you are to think of God as One who is watching you continually, not with the malice of a tyrant, but with the interest and affection of a Heavenly Father. His heart is toward you for good—His ear is quick to catch every word of truth and kindness that you speak—His eye is keen to discover in your breast right feelings toward Himself. How it should encourage us in what is good, and keep us back from what is evil, to know that God is near us, within hearing distance in whatever company we may be! Has He got nothing to write yet in His book of remembrance about any of us, that we shall be glad to hear read off in the day when the secrets of all hearts shall be revealed?

Taking the Census.

" The Lord shall count, when He writeth up the people, This was born there "
(Ps. lxxxvii. 6).

Once every ten years in our country the Census is taken. A great staff of clerks is employed in every town and district, to call at every house, and take down the name, and age, and birthplace of every man, and woman, and child who has slept overnight in each dwelling. This is done, that the Sovereign and Parliament may know how many in the Three Kingdoms are the subjects of the Crown.

Now, in the text, Jehovah, the King of Israel, is by a bold image represented as taking the Census of His true people. He does not require a great army of special secretaries and accountants to help Him. But He Himself knows, and notes exactly, who those are that belong to the spiritual Zion, and are citizens of the Heavenly Jerusalem. Some of them are to be found in most unlikely places. In Rahab—that is, in Egypt—in Babylon, in Ethiopia—among the descendants even of cursed Ham—God has a seed to serve Him, who shall be counted to the Lord for a generation. So says this old psalm. And, as we know from the New Testament, there were saints of Christ even in Cæsar's household (Phil. iv. 22), where the atmosphere was most hostile to Christian piety. But wherever they may be, whether recognised by men or not, God sees and values them all. His most distant and most hidden ones are written in His book, as surely and as gladly as those born in the confines of Palestine.

By God's taking note of your name, is meant His taking full account of your spiritual history. "This is a true child of Zion : he was born into My kingdom *there*!" Can that be said of you? Have you Zion's King enthroned in your young heart? He is a crucified King; and the crown upon His head, when He was here on earth, was a crown of thorns. But He is now a glorified King; and the crown He wears on high is a diadem, in which the jewels are the souls of His redeemed. Is your soul to be among them? Can the Lord, looking abroad upon the world, say of you—"That is one of Mine?" Or must He pass you over, saying—"That one is of the heathen still!" Where were you born? Have you one birthplace, or two? "Once born, twice die; twice born, once die." How much depends upon being born into the spiritual Zion!

A Capital Exercise.

"Herein do I exercise myself, to have a conscience void of offence" (Acts xxiv.16).

You are all fond of exercise, you young people. The spring-time is now here, and you are finding an outlet for your youthful energies in different sorts of outdoor games. Even when the weather is bad you show, as the old folks sometimes know to their cost, that indoors, if not outside, such an outlet *must* be found. Healthy life and healthful activity always go together.

Now, the text speaks of a kind of exercise which everybody whose soul is healthy engages in, and which everyone who would like his soul to become more healthful still will not omit. It is, moreover, a sort of exercise with which the change of seasons does not interfere. You may and ought to have it in winter as well as in summer—in the house as well as in the playground—in the school, in the church, in the street, and wherever you may be. Like Paul, you ought to *exercise* yourself to have a conscience void of offence.

What *is* "conscience"? Every smallest child knows something of what it is, though the oldest of us would take a long time to *explain* what it is. It is the strange, mysterious "something," which says within the breast "right!" or "wrong!" to the different thoughts we think, words we speak, and acts we do. It is the voice of God within the heart. The word "con-science" means "knowledge with" another—namely, with God, who knows us through and through.

What is an "offended conscience"? It is a conscience offended or "hurt" because we have not taken its counsel, but have stifled its voice, and have been content, in wounding it, to displease and grieve God, for whom it speaks. Oh, seek to have your conscience "void of offence," both in what you do and what you are, toward God and toward man.

Pray and strive that your conscience may be kept tender and pure. And if at any time it should be wounded and defiled, be thankful *not* to feel happy till you have gone down upon your knees and obtained forgiveness of God for Jesus' sake, who can alone "give the guilty conscience peace, and wash away the stain." A hurt conscience is bad. But there is a worse thing than that—a conscience first neglected, then stifled, then seared and dead. A conscience that cannot be offended any more! It is a terrible possession. God save us from it!

The Fear that casts out Fear. April 7

'Surely His salvation is nigh them that fear Him" (Ps. lxxxv. 9).

THE wise man has said that "the fear of man bringeth a snare, but whoso putteth his trust in the Lord shall be safe." How often has this truth been illustrated upon both its sides! The Israelites, when near to Canaan, on hearing the report of the spies about the giants, feared them so much that they were ensnared into forty years of wandering in the wilderness; and, with the exception of Caleb and Joshua, the whole of the faithless generation lost the Promised Land. The Hebrew youths in Babylon, on the other hand, feared God so much, with the fear both of reverence and of trust, that they could brave the worst threats of Nebuchadnezzar; and in the fiery furnace they were safe,—for One "like the Son of God" was with them, and brought them out unto great honour. Simon Peter illustrated in himself the fear which bringeth a snare, when he followed Christ afar off, and ended by denying his Lord, in weakness and shame. He afterwards illustrated in himself the boldness of a well-grounded confidence in Christ, when, along with John, he defied the Sanhedrim to browbeat him into silence about his Lord: "and they took knowledge of them, that they had been with Jesus."

Look, too, at the Apostle Paul. However strange it may seem, it was fear that was the secret of his consistent courage. His fear of God cast out all other fear. The one thing he was afraid of was —that he should even seem to doubt or deny Christ. He would dare anything to be delivered from that evil. Can you understand something of his feelings? You should be far more afraid, boys and girls, of doing what is wrong, than of suffering what is wrong. If others call you names at school, or overreach you, or tell lies about you, just bear in mind what a good man said—"I expect to suffer a thousand ills, but none so great as to do unjustly."

A boy was playing with two others in a woodshed, now a good many years ago, when suddenly, checking his merriment, he said, "Oh, I forgot something this morning." They saw him retire, heedless whether they laughed or no, to a corner of the shed, where he knelt down, and reverently repeated his morning prayer. Then he came back with a bright face, and joined his comrades at their play again. Years passed. That brave boy became a gallant captain, and fought and fell for his country in the storming of Sebastopol. Best of all, he was a good soldier of Jesus Christ—never ashamed to own his Lord, and true to His colours to the last. Fearing God, he knew no other fear; and even in death he was "preserved unto the heavenly Kingdom."

April 8

A Visitor at the Door.

"*Behold, I stand at the door, and knock*" (Rev. iii. 20).

HERE we have a shut door, and somebody knocking at it. It is a door that has been long shut, as you can see from the weeds, and the moss, and the ivy that have clustered all about it. I wonder if He that is knocking at it will manage to get in?

The door, dear young friend, is the door of your heart. *The door*—the front door. There is a back door, and there are side doors, which are open enough, and through which strange visitors sometimes get, that do your heart no good. But this is the front door, which, with some of you, has never been opened yet at all; and, remember, He who is knocking *won't go in at any but the front door*.

Let us ask, concerning this Visitor — (1) *Who* knocks? and (2) *Why* does He knock?

(1) He who knocks is a Pilgrim, in a long robe of purity, woven throughout, without a seam, or flaw, or stain. If you look at His sandalled feet, you will see nail-prints on them, as if they had been scarred and bleeding. And see, what is that upon His head? It is a crown—but a crown of thorns; for He is a King. A King—and He won't go in at any but the front door. Who, then, is He? He is the Son of God, who became also the Son of Man. He is the King of Grace; He is the King of Glory. *This* being He who knocks—will you not fling wide the door?

(2) Why does He knock? That is the second question; and it is an important one. When anyone taps, you first naturally ask, "Who's there?" and then you next inquire, "*What are you wanting?*" Perhaps sometimes, if your mother is out, you are not very sure about opening the door; and you try to peep through the key-hole first, or out at one of the windows, to see who the visitor is, and guess what his errand may be.

A Protestant minister, some time ago, in the south of Ireland, heard a knocking at his door, late one Sabbath night. The district was "disturbed"; so he cautiously asked first, before he drew the bolt, who knocked, and why? "We are friends; and we knock to get in." He was suspicious, and refused. A bullet then whistled in past his ear; and, with a curse, his strange moonlight "friends" went upon their way. But *you* need not have any fear this time. This is not One to do you harm. He comes to be your real Friend. This is what He asks. "If any will open, I will sup with him, and he with Me." The King begs for admittance, because He wishes "to be friends" with you. What an honour! What a joy! He will share whatever you may have to give to Him; and He has much to give to you. Won't you let Him in?

A Wise Prayer.

"*Increase our faith*" (Luke xvii. 5).

IF we have learned to trust God at all, this is a wise and should be a natural prayer. Now—

(1) *Why* should we seek to have our faith increased? In the first place, because want of faith dishonours God. Think how your father would be grieved, if he saw you did not trust him. And do not dishonour and grieve your Heavenly Father, who is so worthy to be trusted, by giving *Him* no more than a half-hearted confidence. In the second place, seek more faith, because little faith means little strength, little comfort, little success in the Christian life. Here, as always, the honour of God and our own good are bound up close together, and cannot be disjoined.

(2) *How* are we to seek faith's increase? We are to do it by doing what the disciples did, by praying for it. By this I do not, of course, mean that you are merely to use these words,—"Increase my faith,"—but that you are *to pray* them, really and with all the heart. If you do this, day by day, there are *two* things you will be in earnest about daily—to know God better, and to practise faith more. For thus it is that faith will find increase.

"*Acquaint thyself with God*," the Bible says. It is because you do not know, or because you forget who and what God is, that you lack confidence in Him. A lady was once taught this truth in a very simple but striking way by her husband. They were on board a vessel in mid-ocean, when so terrible a storm arose that anxiety showed itself even on the sailors' faces. The lady was frantic with alarm. Her husband, who was a soldier, suddenly drew his sword, and pointed it at her heart. She looked up inquiringly, but showed no fear of the glittering blade. "You do not shrink before my sword?" "Nay, why should I? Is it not in the hands of one who loves me?" "You trust *me*, beloved," he answered; "and will you not trust *Him*, who holds the sea in the hollow of His hand, and without whose knowledge not a hair of your head can perish!" Christ invites our full confidence: "It is I; be not afraid." Seek to know God better, that you may trust Him more.

And remember *to exercise the faith you have*—to put it in practice day by day. Confidence grows with use. I remember being taught, when a boy, to swim. At first it needed some courage to go down into the water at the master's bidding; but he had tied about my waist a life-preserver, and was ready, besides, to come at any moment to my rescue. One trial brought some confidence, and each successful trial made me less and less afraid to sink. Put faith in practice; and, with exercise, both strength and courage along with it will grow. Praying thus, you shall have an answer to the prayer—"Lord, increase my faith."

April 10 ## A Covetous Man.

"As the Lord liveth, I will run after him, and take somewhat of him"
(2 Kings v. 20).

THESE are the words of Gehazi, the servant of the prophet Elisha. He is sorry that his master has not used his opportunity better, in the way of securing a reward at the hands of Naaman, who, in gratitude for his cure, was so willing to bestow his gifts. And he is determined that, for his part, he will not allow so good a chance to slip. So he runs after the Syrian captain, and is successful beyond his expectation. He gets two talents of silver through his lying story, instead of one; and soon he has his treasure safe in "the tower," or hiding-place. How he can gloat over it there! But Elisha meets him soon, with a searching glance and the searching question—"Whence, Gehazi?" And as the guilty culprit goes trembling from the prophet's presence, "a leper white as snow," he learns, in bitterness of soul, that it is possible to buy a "success" like his *too dear*!

He was an instance of a very respectable man, living in the best of company, ruined by a very respectable sin. Gehazi was the companion of the prophet of Jehovah; He had picked up religious phrases; He was spending his life outwardly in religious service. But all the while he was really an atheist and idolater; and covetousness, like a canker, was at work within his heart. "Get all you can, and look out for more," says the world: "honestly, if possible, but anyhow get it." "Take heed, and *beware of covetousness*," says Jesus. And again and again He enforces this lesson. Why? For these among other reasons—

(1) Covetousness is so *deceitful*. All sin is; but this sin is specially so. It cloaks itself under fair names and respectable disguises. It calls itself "prudence," or "shrewdness," or "making the most of life." It leads a man on and on by degrees, thinking that he is making money his servant. But lo! the gold has become his master. It is his idol. He is found bowing to the molten calf.

(2) Covetousness is so *unscrupulous*. When it has fairly taken possession of a man, there is hardly anything he will not do to gain his object. Covetousness has led many besides Gehazi to lying and forgery. It has led many besides Judas to treachery and betrayal. There is no sin, from the pettiest meanness to the cruellest murder, to which it has not successfully tempted men.

(3) Covetousness is so *destructive*. It is often destructive of the peace and well-being of others. But it is especially destructive of the covetous man himself. Gehazi "went out from Elisha's presence"—a filthy leper, separated from the society of the noble, and good, and generous—a leper both in body and in soul. So is it always. The covetous man is a miserable, shrivelled, wretched, outcast soul. The covetous, the Bible tells us, "shall not inherit the kingdom of God" (1 Cor. vi. 10).

"*That I may win Christ*" (Phil. iii. 8).

WHAT a world this is for competition ! People on all sides, and in every sphere of life, are pushing and pressing to get in before their neighbours, and to win more than others do. You know something of this already in your schooldays : in your classes, at your matches, and otherwise. And you may be quite sure that, when you go out into the bigger school of the world, you will not find your competitors fewer or less keen.

Here is a man whose great ambition is to get into Parliament. With what assiduity he sets himself to "nurse his constituency"—to win the favour and confidence, that is, of those who have votes to give him. What a number of speeches he is ready to make, into everyone of which he throws all the wit at his command. What an interest he takes in all the charities of the neighbourhood ; and what a willing ear he lends to the whims and grievances of individuals—if they happen to have a vote. He is "hail fellow, well met," with persons whom, in other circumstances, perhaps he would not touch with his finger-tips. He becomes all things to all men, and is sometimes found becoming everything by turns, if only he may win the coveted "seat." He counts as a sheer loss, time and strength which he may have to expend on other objects.

Here is another man, whose crowning desire is to amass a colossal fortune. Nothing short of seven figures will satisfy him : he must be a millionaire. And so he schemes by day, and even dreams by night, about the one thing. His eye is ever on the market, and on the state of the Funds. With mingled caution and daring he carries on his operations. You may get him to speak of other things, but his interest in them is only on the surface. If they cannot be reduced to pounds, shillings, and pence, he counts thought and energy bestowed upon them nothing but loss, except in so far as they afford him recreation for the further and more ardent pursuit of money.

And here is Paul. He, too, has an object on which his heart is set, and to the attainment of which he gives the undivided energies of his life—"that I may win Christ." More of Christ—more of Christ—this for him is the supreme gain, compared with which all other gain is loss.

Who has won? Is it the man of the world, or is it the man of God ? Ask each of them a hundred years after this ; nay, ask them even now ! And if for answer you get the true secret of their hearts, I know well what the conclusion you reach will be.

There are earthly ambitions which you may rightly cherish in their place. But see that you keep them there. The desire to excel is not a wrong thing ; but it must be rightly directed and wisely governed. One kind of gain you may seek without restraint ; for, no matter how much you win, nobody else will be the poorer for it—"that you may win Christ." The man who is in Christ, like Christ, and at length with Christ for ever, is the only man who will at last be counted, by himself or others, to have truly won.

April 12   **Growth and the Secret of it.**

"*I will be as the dew: and he shall grow*" (Hos. xiv. 5, 6).

THERE is nothing that you are more anxious for, than that you should grow. You look forward to the time when you shall have reached full-grown manhood or womanhood with eager hope; and many are the plans you lay, as to what you are to be and to do when that time comes.

Now, it is a great pleasure to those who love you young people, to notice that you are growing. You do not know how lovingly your fathers and mothers have watched over your development, from your earliest days. Especially does a wise parental love delight in any evidence that you are growing in goodness as well as in height. It would set before you no lower ideal than that of the apostle—"till we come unto a perfect man, unto the measure of the stature of the fulness of Christ."

Our passage from Hosea teaches us very beautifully two things—the *nature* of spiritual growth, and the *secret* of it.

"He shall grow *as the lily*." This may remind you of the tender beauty and fragrance which should characterise the Christian life in its development. Everything coarse or indelicate is out of keeping with it. It should be like the refined and modest lily.

"He shall cast forth *his roots like Lebanon.*" This suggests that, though the Christian character is tender, and in the highest sense delicate, it is at the same time strong. Refinement is not weakness. To the tenderness of the modest lily there should be united the strength of the cedar of Lebanon. "And his beauty shall be *as the olive tree.*" This is a beauty of constant freshness and fruitfulness. The olive is evergreen. It finds a place to grow where the lily might be blighted, and where there would not be room enough for the cedar; and though its appearance does not greatly attract the eye, it is covered with berries, and is marvellously fruitful.

But how shall *your* growth be like this—fair as the lily, strong as the cedar, fruitful as the olive tree?

Here is the secret of such growth—"*I will be as the dew unto Israel.*" Of course there must be life first, before there can be growth. But Israel, as here spoken of, has returned in penitence to God, and has entered upon the new life. And what is needed then is, that God's Spirit should continue His gracious influence day by day—silent, copious, refreshing like the dew—seeking in about the roots of the life—and giving every leaf and petal a daily renewed baptism of holy vigour. May that be your experience! Then you shall grow—as trees of the Lord's own planting, that He may be glorified.

Strange Perversity.   April 13

" Ye will not come unto Me, that ye might have life" (John v. 40).

How often in the course of a day you say, "I will," or, "I will not," without thinking that this power of yours, which we call "will," is the greatest power which man can wield. If you examine human history, you will find much that the will of man has been able to accomplish. But the most marvellous thing about the human will is, that (no doubt with the divine consent) it has been able to assert itself against God.

One of the saddest sayings of Jesus is His lament over lost Jerusalem—"How often would I have gathered you, as a hen gathers her chickens under her wings; but ye would not." How strange this is; but also how true! The Saviour is stretching out His arms of love. Would you not expect men thankfully to run into them, that they might find safety, and peace, and satisfying? You would; yet they do not run. They rather observe lying vanities; and so they forsake their own mercies. Jesus calls; but they turn their backs on Him. He invites the weary and heavy laden to cast their burdens at His feet; but they seem to prefer to carry their loads themselves. He invites dying men to come to Him that they may have life—real life, life that will last eternally, and will in every respect be worthy of the name of life—life at its fullest, most happy, most useful, and best. But they will not come.

How slow people are to accept the invitation of the loving Jesus! This may be explained on various grounds. Many do not feel their want; and, thinking they can do without the water of life yet awhile, refuse to be indebted for it, and try in their own strength to go their way. Others think the news too good to be true,—like the crowds who passed the man on London Bridge, as he held out real sovereigns for a whole day, offering them at a shilling, without selling a single one!

In Norway, a few years ago, I had a simple illustration of how different people treat the gospel. We came upon a group of children in a remote place one day, and held out to them—what you are more familiar with—some "sweeties." One, a bigger boy, evidently "didn't want them," and looked half insulted. A little girl would fain have come, but "didn't think we meant it," and held back, doubting. Another came frankly forward, and showed a disposition to come "for more." A fourth—and this is the one to imitate—came and shook hands (which means "thank you!" in that country), and then *brought her little brother*, that he too might have a share. Here you have the true spirit of the gospel—"Come and take!" *And*—"Let him that heareth say, 'Come.'"

April 14   **Work away.**

"I must work while it is day: the night cometh" (John ix. 4).

Jesus is the speaker here. He says that He has been sent into the world to work, and that He knows He must work hard, for He has only a short time to work in. You know who sent him? It was God the Father. And what the work was? The salvation of men. You know how busy He was? He went about, we are told, continually doing good; and, even when a boy, He spoke the deep, earnest words which Mary must have wondered over as she laid them up in her heart—" I must be about My Father's business." You know how short His life on earth was too? Not more than three and thirty years—and yet how much, in doing and suffering, He accomplished in it! And oh, how much brighter the world has ever since been, because of His presence in it!

But now, dear young people, what has this verse to say to *you*? It ought, in the first place, to make you love Jesus very much, for all He has done and been for us; and also love His Father very much, because He so loved the world as to send to it the Saviour. And then it should make you ask, how you are to be like Jesus, in finding some good work to do to-day, and doing it with all your might.

You are not expected to know much about labour yet. But you do know the difference between work and idleness; and you have already learned, I daresay, that there is truth in the saying, that the unhappiest of people is he who "can find nothing to do." The truant from school is never really happy, nor the truant from duty either. The mere idler does not deserve to be, and he is not, happy. And though busy people rightly long for, and really enjoy, a holiday sometimes, the greatest of English poets is right when he says—

"If all the year were playing holidays,
To sport would be as tedious as to work."

Of this you may be quite sure, that in this world there will be plenty always for *you* to do, if you have an open eye, a ready hand, and a willing heart. The advice of a veteran servant of God to a young friend is worth remembering—" Do all the good you can—in all the ways you can—to all the people you can—and just as long as you can."

"*Mine own vineyard have I not kept*" (Song of Sol. 1. 6).

EACH of us, even the youngest, has a garden, or vineyard, which we are to dress and keep for God : some sphere of duty which we are to fill, as in His sight and for His glory.

It is said of some, that their "eyes are in the ends of the earth." They are taken up greatly about things that are far away from them, and about which they have no direct responsibility; but they do not take half enough interest in matters of practical duty, which lie close to their own hand. A little boy, whose clothes were rent, and who had holes in his stockings, was asked by a companion why his mother did not mend them for him. "Oh," he replied, "my mother is so much occupied in sewing for the heathen that she has no time to mend *my* clothes!" That mother acted very foolishly. It is, indeed, a good thing to take an interest in the heathen, and to do all we can to help them. Our sympathies cannot be too wide. But we are not to neglect the duty that lies nearest to us, on the plea that we want to help some good cause that lies beyond.

To say that you were giving a hand in the keeping of some other great garden, will be a poor excuse for allowing the little garden to run to waste which God gave specially to you to keep. There is some sphere of life awaiting every one of you, in which there will be room enough to honour God. May you not have to make, at the last, the sorrowful confession—"Mine own vineyard have I not kept"!

It is told of a great philosopher, that he was always boasting about his garden, and of the delight he had in it. Some of his admirers thought that they would like to see it. When they went, they found that it was just a little patch of ground; and they said —"Is *this* your famous garden?" "Yes," he replied. "It is not very long, you see; and it is not very broad. But—it is wondrous high!" And, so saying, he looked up to the sky, with such a look of thankfulness and joy upon his face. It was the place where he was wont to commune with the Highest.

So, in our garden, wherever and whatever it may be, we may hold communication with high heaven. And if only we realise that Christ is looking down upon us in loving interest, it will encourage us, in joy as well as fidelity, to keep it for Him.

April 16   The Head.

" The Head of the body, the Church" (Col. i. 18).

THE head is not only the noblest and most beautiful and interesting, but the most necessary part of the human frame; and the Church without Christ would be a body without a head. Now—
1. The head is the *centre of life*. All the nerves connect with the brain; and if the head is struck off, the body dies. So is it with the Church. Christ is "our life"; and because He lives, we live also. As Mr. Spurgeon says: "You cannot drown a man while his head is above water; therefore, though he feel below water, he is not drowned, if his head is above the stream. So you cannot destroy the Church while the Head is alive." It seemed once as if the Head had been removed. But it was not so; for Jesus rose the third day from the grave, in the power of an endless life.
2. The head *provides* for all the body. The eyes are there, and the ears—ready to see and hear everything that is either of advantage or of danger to the whole. And not only so: it is the head that thinks, that remembers the past, and plans for the future. So is it with Christ. His eyes are upon His people. His ears are open to their cry. His thoughts are busy for their good. For He is their Head; and as such He can never be taken by surprise, or found without resource. For God hath put *all* things under His feet, and given Him to be the Head over *all* things to the Church, which is His body.

And then (3) it is the head that *governs*. At the bidding of the head the feet walk; the hands do useful work; the tongue speaks; the eyes turn to see; the ears are attentive to listen. All obey the head, which governs. So Christ is the Head of the Church; and being the centre of life, and providing as He does for the entire body, He has the right to govern. But alas! just as we sometimes see in the human body some members beyond control, refusing to obey the head; and some paralysed, and no more able to obey it than if they were dead—so do we see, sometimes, in the Church. Is not that very sad? May we all be true, *living* members of Christ's body! May we all be thankful to be *provided for* by Him! And may we all be ready to *obey* Him at all times, as our wise and gracious Head!

A Rich Legacy.   April 17

"Peace I leave with you, My peace I give unto you" (John xiv. 27).

It would be a great delight, as well as surprise, if somebody came to one of you young people and said, some fine day, "You are no longer to be poor and little thought of, but to be rich, and honoured, and great. For a powerful friend, whom you have not even seen, has made you his heir, and given you a great estate; and now you are to live in a fine house, and to keep a carriage, and to have plenty of servants, and everything at your command that the world can furnish, to make you happy."

You would be inclined to say, "Ah, it is too good news to be true. I have not any rich friend like that; and even if I had, it is not likely that he would care so much for me. If I am ever to be rich, it will be a long time after this, and as the result of a whole lifetime of hard, unceasing labour."

Yet something like what I have mentioned has occurred to people before now. A poor man in a town I know was suddenly left a large fortune, by a relative who had long lived abroad. He stopped working, that he might "live upon his money," and be a great man, and order people about. But money is a poor thing to live upon, and he could not order himself aright. His time began to hang heavy upon his hands. He used his wealth just to pamper himself; and the selfish became a weary life, which sank at last into a drunkard's grave. The rich inheritance, you see, made that man only the poorer: instead of being a blessing, it proved to him a curse.

Now you need not expect that you will hear some day that you have come into a large fortune in that way; and you are not to put on the wishing-cap, in the hope that the fairies may come and tell you of it. But Jesus speaks here of a far richer legacy than any the world could offer you—"My peace." If this were extended to you in one hand, and all the world's wealth in the other, it would be your wisdom to accept this—His own peace. And how may it be yours? He tells you. "Ye believe in God," He says; "believe also in Me." The secret of peace is trust. The secret of perfect peace is perfect trust in Jesus.

April 18. Broken Cisterns.

"They have hewed them out cisterns, broken cisterns, that can hold no water" (Jer. ii. 13).

Suppose you were thirsty, and had your choice—either to go to a clear, bubbling spring near by to quench your thirst, or to get a draught from a cistern not far off, if it should turn out to have water in it—to which, do you think, would you turn? "To the spring, of course," I hear you reply. What a stupid thing it would be in anyone to hesitate for a moment about that! Who does not know that spring water is far more refreshing than cistern water at its best?

Yet there are a great many people committing that very blunder; which is, in their case, more than a blunder, since it is, at the same time, a sin. They are forsaking God, the living fountain; and turning by preference to man-made cisterns instead. This they do because they want to be independent, if they can, of God. They flatter themselves that they have no need of Him, and can find a better way than His to slake their thirst and satisfy their hearts.

But it is a terrible mistake, as well as a cruel slight on God, thus to forsake Him. For those who follow lying vanities forsake their own mercies. What can the cistern at the best do? It can only hold a limited supply at the most; and if it holds it long, it will become brackish and impure. But even the little that the earthly cisterns will hold cannot be counted on for long; because the cisterns are cracked and leaky, so that the water will speedily filter away, in spite of the best efforts to retain it.

The cisterns of pleasure, of wealth, of gaiety, of fame, of fashion can bring no abiding refreshment to man's heart. The cisterns of music and of art will not do it. All who drink of these waters will thirst again. If we have been learning already what it is to thirst again, may none of us know what it is to thirst for ever—except with that thirst which is not a torment, but a joy, because the satisfying Fountain always is at hand.

There is One who calls, as He did on the last, the great, day of the Feast, "If any man thirst, let him come unto Me, and drink." You know His name?

"O Christ! *He* is the fountain,
The deep, sweet well of love."

And with such a living Spring—clear, free, inexhaustible—to drink at, who in his senses would turn to a *cistern*—a *broken* cistern!

"'Jehovah-nissi,' the Lord my Banner" (Ex. xvii. 15).

THE children of Israel were braced to duty at Rephidim. They had perhaps come to expect everything to be done for them by God, who had led them safely through the sea, and had given them manna and quails from heaven, and water out of the flinty rock. But now God permits the Amalekites to fall upon them ; and they have to fight for their lives.

We, too, have our Amalekites, within and without, to contend with, from "generation to generation." And it is sometimes well, still, for God's people to be roused from a fretful and listless humour, to face the stern necessity of conflict, and to grasp a truer conception of the arduous, but high and noble, Christian calling.

The lesson taught to Israel and us at Mount Rephidim is, that on the way to the Promised Land *we have both to struggle and to pray*. Both. We are not to pray without fighting, for God does not promise to do for us what we can do for ourselves. Nor are we to struggle without praying, for that will mean sure defeat, because it will mean fighting in our own strength, which, apart from God, is utter weakness.

A schoolgirl asked her companion how she was always able to say her lessons so well, and got the answer—" I always pray that I may say them well." Next day, the unsuccessful scholar came, after class, to her companion in great chagrin. She had done worse than ever, though she had prayed for success, and she charged the other with deceiving her. "But did you learn well, as well as pray?" No ; she had not thought of doing that. "I understood," she said, "that if I prayed it would be enough." We can all see how foolish this was. Yet how many Christians fail just because, while they profess to pray, they put forth no hearty effort in the direction which their prayer professes to seek.

On the other hand, our effort apart from prayer will not achieve the victory. When the hands of Moses hung down, Israel wavered in the fight. What we have perseveringly to do is, to hold up the rod of God (which for us means the divine promise grasped by faith, and pleaded in the name of Christ), while we use the means at our disposal ; and the God of battles will give the victory. "Prayer and pains," as Dr. Chalmers use to say, "will accomplish anything." And what an encouragement it is, that we have with us in our prayers a Divine Intercessor who never wearies, and before us in our conflicts a Joshua who never knew defeat !

April 20 — **Bringing us to God.**

" He that hath the Son hath life " (1 John v. 12). *" In whom we have boldness and access with confidence "* (Eph. iii. 12).

HAVE you heard the story of the little English boy who was looking wistfully in at the gates of the royal palace one day, and longing for just a peep within the mansion, when a soldier upon guard stepped forward, and, learning what he wished, laughed at his impertinence, and with rough words drove him away? As the child was sadly taking his departure a young gentleman who had witnessed the scene came forward smilingly, and said, " Come with me, my little man, and I will show you all."

There was something so reassuring in his look and manner that the boy felt he could trust him, and trust himself to him. Nor was his confidence misplaced. The dreadful soldier did not point his bayonet at him, did not speak or even frown, but only touched his cap with the military salute as the two passed within. The gentleman, with much apparent zest, led his young companion through the grounds, into the hothouses, and among the beautiful gardens, until at length they entered the great mansion itself.

There was a lady there, whom the gentleman called "mother," and who smiled as he laughingly explained to her about the youthful visitor. And then he kindly led the boy back to the gate; and, as they parted, said that he hoped he would now be satisfied, for he had not only seen the grounds and the palace, but the Queen of all England!

Was it not kind in that prince to do so much for a forlorn and friendless child? But God's Son, the Prince of Life, does more for you and me. He opens the way into the Father's house, and the righteous guards at the gate do not deny an entrance, when we " have the Son." He takes us within the palace, and He shows us all. But He does more than this. He introduces us to the King; and as He calls Him "Father," He calls Him ours as well—" My Father and your Father, My home and your home." He gives us a blood-bought right not only to enter Heaven, but to dwell for ever there. He that hath the Son, hath life. In Him we may have "boldness and access with confidence."

"*His eyes behold, His eyelids try, the children of men*" (Ps. xi. 4).

WHEN I was young, there was a portrait upon a wall in my father's house whose eyes seemed to follow me. No matter to what corner of the room I went, those eyes appeared to look down upon me, and to read my heart.

Now what was true, or what I felt to be true, of that picture, is certainly true of God. His eyes are in every place, beholding the evil and the good. We cannot go anywhere, do anything, or even think any thought—but God sees it.

This consideration might well *deter us from evil*. A man set forth once upon a stealing expedition, taking his son with him. What he wanted to steal was his neighbour's corn. They reached the place; he had his bag all ready to receive the precious grain; and he looked round to see that no one was looking on. His son, seeing him look this way and that way—north, south, east, and west—said, "You have forgotten to look in one direction, father." "Where?" inquired the man excitedly. "You have forgotten to look up, father," said his son. And the two went home again, *without the corn*.

Two boys were passing through an orchard. They were sorely tempted with the fruit. At last one said, "Let us have some of those apples." "Nay," said the other, "for that would be stealing." "Oh," was the reply, "but they belong to Widow Jones; and she is from home, and doesn't count." "But God counts," said the other; *and the apples remained untasted*.

But the same consideration may well be to God's children *a great encouragement*. When Lafayette was in prison, what he felt most irksome and hard to bear was, the knowledge that there was an eye always peering in upon him through a hole in the door of his cell. But what a comfort it is for those who have God for their Father, to know that His eye is always upon them for good. When a little girl was hearing ghost stories in a dark room, and was asked if she was not afraid, she replied—"No; God sees me." And when any of you young people have to bear pain; or, in trying circumstances, to speak the truth; or to suffer reproach; or to work hard, without much on earth perhaps to cheer you—oh, what an encouragement there will be for you in the thought—"God sees me, I must be about my Father's business."

April 22   **Sowing and Reaping.**

"*Whatsoever a man soweth, that shall he also reap*" (Gal. vi. 7).

WHAT would you think of a man who sowed rye and expected to reap wheat, or who sowed barley and hoped by and by to reap beans? You would think such a man very foolish—almost fit for a lunatic asylum. Yet that is just what a great many people are doing. Take care lest you be found among them. They are going on sowing, with the greatest composure, tares; and apparently they expect, either that it will not bear a crop, or that it will somehow grow up wheat. They freely scatter evil thoughts, desires, deeds; and they are under the delusion that they will not reap the appropriate result.

This verse reminds us of three important truths—

1. *We are all sowing.* Perhaps you have seen the husbandman setting forth into the field, with his seed-bin strapped before him, from which, with both hands earnestly, he scatters far and wide into the furrows the living germs of pearly grain? Now, you are just like him. You are always sowing seed of some sort, good or bad. To cease to sow, you must cease to act, to speak, to think. You must needs cease, in that case, to *be* what you are.

2. *All who sow shall reap.* This is not true in outward and ordinary husbandry. The farmer sometimes, after all his activity and patience, has little or no crop for his pains, because of a nipping frost or some other blight which has come upon his field before the time of harvest. But moral seeds—by which we mean thoughts, words, deeds, of various sorts—always bear fruit. What you are sowing in youth will certainly bring you a harvest in later life. From what we sow in time, we shall reap in eternity.

3. *All who reap shall have a harvest like their sowing.* Not to speak of results outside of us from the influences we scatter among others, we should think seriously here of the effect of our sowing upon ourselves, in our own characters and lives. This is seen in the growth of *habit*, to which there is both a dark and a bright side. Every time you do a wrong act or indulge a wrong feeling, the power of evil is strengthened within you. It is easier to do wrong again; and you are a worse boy or girl than before. But the opposite is no less true. Every time you do an unselfish, generous thing, or speak a brave, true word, or cherish a pure and lofty desire, *you* become the better for it, and your character the nobler. Remembering that you are building your character for eternity, pray that God's Spirit may ever dwell within you, and make you both to will and to do of His good pleasure.

" Whosoever shall do the will of My Father, the same is My brother and sister"
(Matt. xii. 50).

In some households the family likeness is very strong. When I see a boy or a girl on the street sometimes, I can at once say—"There is a son, or a daughter, of So-and-so." The features of the face—the eyes, the nose, the mouth, the brow, the chin—reveal their parentage; or perhaps it is, at first, their style of walking, or something of that kind, that suggests who they are.

Now, in God's household the family likeness is well marked. Jesus, the Elder Brother in the family, tells us here how we are to know who they are that belong to it. He says, "Those that do the will of My Father in Heaven are My brothers and sisters." If you see a man or a woman, a boy or a girl, with the love of God in their hearts, and who are showing their love for Him by keeping His commandments, then you are safe to say, "That is a brother, or a sister, of Christ!" Such are far nearer to Him than if they had been merely born into the same family in Nazareth. Jesus did not spurn the ties which bound Him to those who were of His own flesh and blood in the earthly home. But He plainly showed, more than once, that the nearest and dearest of kindred to Him were those whose hearts had been given to God, and who loved to do the Heavenly Father's will. I hope you are among these? If you are—

How close this brings you to God! When Jesus says, not merely "My servants," or "My friends," but "My brothers," what a tender attachment, what frank and intimate fellowship this implies! "My brothers"—"My sisters"—this means oneness of nature as well as of name—one Father, one Inheritance, one Home.

How great a family circle is yours! People sometimes speak proudly of their "connections," and seem to despise those who have not the inestimable privilege of belonging to them. But the Christian need envy no man his pedigree. For he belongs to the seed-royal of Heaven, and the children of God of every nation are his spiritual kindred.

How abiding is your family joy! It is the blessedness of a deathless fellowship. Families on earth get broken up and separated. Your brothers and sisters in the earthly home may be sundered far enough from one another yet, by stormy seas, or by the stream of death. But if you and they are members of God's family, the time of separation will be only for a little season. The brothers and sisters of Christ are all to be gathered into a safe, bright home, from which there will be no more going out, and into which no sorrow will intrude. "He that doeth the will of God abideth for ever."

April 24   **The Way of Life.**

"Thou wilt show me the path of life" (Ps. xvi. 11).

You have sometimes, when walking in the country, come to a point where two ways parted, and you were not sure which of the two to take. It was of importance for you to take the proper road, so as to reach your destination; and how glad you were when a man who knew the country-side well appeared, just in time to point you on the right way.

Now, something very like that happens to you young people, before you have travelled far upon life's journey. You come to the parting of the ways; and everything, under God, depends upon which of the paths you follow. How well it is for you that there is One near who can show you the good way, the right way, for you to walk in! Turning to Jesus, you are invited to say with every confidence—"Thou wilt show me the path of life." And He will not only point you to it, but lead you in it, for His name's sake.

The path of life—Why does the way to heaven get this name in the Bible? Not only because it leads to life—the region of life—the home of the living God, but because it is trodden by the living, and strengthens and gladdens the life of those who walk in it.

See it stretching out before you, young reader, from where you stand this day! It is a narrow and rough-looking path—not very attractive, at first at least. There are few flowers to be seen upon its borders; and only an occasional resting-place beside it. It seems, moreover, always to ascend the mountain to the right; and comparatively few appear to choose that for their way. But do you not notice that the travellers who are in it go onward with more heart as they advance? See how their faces are brightening, and their eyes gleaming with fresh hope even in old age, as they grasp the pilgrim staff of promise and press upward in God's name. For it is the path of life. Life thrives in it, and it leads to the fulness of life and peace in the everlasting habitations of the blessed.

To enter upon it you must yield yourself to Christ. And as an act of self-surrender ushers you upon the way, a course of self-denial is implied in walking in it. But neither here nor hereafter will you have reason to regret entering upon it and keeping in it. The air upon the steeps of holiness is bracing air; and the rest upon the mountain-top, within the Heavenly Zion, will be all the sweeter from the remembrance of the upward struggle thither.

The Path of Death.   April 25

"The way of the wicked seduceth them" (Prov. xii. 26).

THE path spoken of here is just the opposite of the one we were speaking about yesterday. It is a way which seduces people—that is, leads them wrong, alluring them off the proper track, and on to ruin. It is the way, not of life, but of death.

It is a broad and easy way this—very attractive-looking, at least at first. It descends by a pleasant, gradual slope through the rich valley to the left, as you stand at the parting of the ways. The sides of it are bedecked with sweet flowers of pleasure; the birds carol over it songs of delight; and it seems, in its earlier reaches at anyrate, to be thronged by very jovial company.

But do you not notice that the travellers in it appear to grow more feeble as they advance? The eye which sparkled at first gets heavier, the expression spiritless and unsatisfied. The limbs begin to totter; and though at intervals the voice of merriment is heard, it sounds forced, unreal, hollow, more and more,—until, as they enter among the brooding shadows, it echoes back upon the choking air more like a wail of anguish than a shout of mirth.

For this is the way of death. True life cannot be enjoyed in it. And though it is a broad and easy-looking way, it leads to a dismal place, from which there is no retreat, where no sweet flowers of hope can grow, and where sin's promises, which the travellers carried in their hands, are all completely blighted, never to bloom again. It is the way of death!

How are you to get into it? There is no need to ask that question; but rather to ask, How are you to make sure to get out of it? It is the easiest thing in the world to wander down the broad road. You have just to go with the crowd, and to make no effort to resist the natural inclination of your own heart. There is no gateway at all into the way of death, or it is so wide that you may never know of its existence. But what you should be in earnest about, what Christ bids you strive to do, is—to get out of the broad road by entering in at the strait but open gate,—the wicket-gate of faith in Christ—into the narrow, but plain, and safe, and happy way of life.

April 26   **Martyr Stephen.**

"*Thy martyr Stephen*" (Acts xxii. 20).

STEPHEN was a brave man, and a good servant of Jesus Christ—one of the bravest and best. And this was the brightest title he could possibly have won—far better than an earthly princedom—"Martyr Stephen." It just means *witness* Stephen; and though I do not expect you will ever be called to witness in the same way exactly as he did, you should remember that all who belong to Christ are expected to be witnesses for Him.

1. Stephen *worked* for Jesus. He was one of the seven first deacons appointed in the Church; and in that capacity he "served tables," and divided out portions for the poor. It was humble enough work for a man with the powers that Stephen afterwards manifested. But he did it faithfully and well; and in so doing he was witnessing for Christ. He was showing the power that the love of Jesus had over him, and manifesting a love like His for God's poor and "little ones." There is no duty too insignificant to glorify Christ, if it is undertaken in a great spirit and done "for His sake."

> " A servant, with this clause,
>   Makes drudgery divine:
> Who sweeps a room as for Thy laws
>   Makes this and the action fine."

2. Stephen *spoke* for Jesus. It is not given to everybody to be a great preacher, and to witness publicly with the tongue for the Saviour. But this honour was put upon Stephen; and he used the opportunities given to him with eagerness and fidelity. He was enabled to do much in the early days on behalf of the freedom of the gospel. The longest sermon, I daresay, in the Book of Acts, is Stephen's sermon to a very unsympathetic audience—the Jewish Sanhedrim. But they did not sleep under it. It was so faithful and rousing a discourse that they gnashed upon him with their teeth.

3. Stephen *suffered* for Jesus. Yes, he suffered willingly, forgivingly, even unto the death; and it is specially this witnessing, by suffering and death, that has brought him his glorious distinction as the first martyr of the Christian Church. What was the secret of his strength all through—of his humility—his courage—his patience? He had *the example of Jesus before him*; and that example did much doubtless to inspire him, even as his own example was to have a profound effect on the young man Saul, who beheld his martyrdom, and held the clothes of his murderers. But he had not only the example of Jesus before him, but *the Spirit of Jesus within him*; and this is what we need, if we are to do, or speak, or bear anything aright as witnesses for Him. It is an echo from the Cross of Calvary we hear in the expiring words of Stephen—"Lord, lay not this sin to their charge!" And with the peace of God in his heart, even while they battered him with stones, the noble witness fell asleep.

A Good Soldier.

"*A good soldier of Jesus Christ*" (2 Tim. ii. 3).

I HOPE you have enlisted in Christ's army, and that it is your ambition to be not only a soldier, but a *good* soldier of Jesus Christ. What are the qualities of such an one?

1. *Loyalty* to our Leader, and *enthusiasm* for His cause. The success of our British arms in days gone by has been greatly helped by the esteem of our men for their commanders, and their thorough-hearted loyalty. You remember how, in one of Wellington's great battles, a portion of the army was yielding before the foe. But at the critical moment the general rode forward into the midst of his faltering battalions. "There's the Duke! God bless him!" cried one of the men, with enthusiasm. "I'd rather see his face than a whole brigade." The news spread; the troops took courage; and the tide of battle turned. Surely *we* have a Leader in Jesus Christ toward whom we should manifest a like devotion; and a cause that is worthy of our warmest enthusiasm. Ours is a Leader who never knew defeat; ours, with Him, a noble struggle on behalf of all that is pure, and peaceable, and worthy on God's earth.

2. *Obedience* is another characteristic which should always go along with enthusiasm. A band full of zeal, but ignorant of discipline, would be a mob, not an army worthy of the name. Our own Covenanters sometimes found this to their cost. The once victorious cry—"Christ's Crown and Covenant"—did not marshal them to victory, when disorder and disaffection crept into their ranks. Where before they had swept all before them, they now fell like grain before the sickle of the enemy. Prompt, unquestioning obedience is the soldier's part toward a wise and trusty Leader. He does not know, as the Commander does, the plan of the campaign. He has but to do his part, and so contribute to the success of all.

> "His not to reason why,
> His not to make reply,
> His but to do—or die."

3. *Courage*, too, will often be needed in the line of obedience; and the Christian is especially the soldier who, putting on the whole armour of God, and looking to his invincible Leader, may be expected to manifest this quality. It will show itself not only in a brilliant dash in the field, but in the *fortitude* which can endure hardness as well as brave danger,—like our gallant men in the Crimea, who could bear the weary waiting in the trenches, though they felt it a harder thing than to face the cannon's mouth. In *presence of mind*, also, true courage will be revealed; for the good soldier will not be flustered and made useless by every emergency. He is alert, and has his powers in hand, and can rise to the occasion—quick of expedient and ready of resource. And, like every truly brave soul, he will be full of genuine *chivalry*. He does not confound valour with bluster, or self-assertiveness with dignity. He is gentle to the weak, unselfish, and courteous to all. In this, as in other particulars, the best soldier of Jesus Christ is he through whom most clearly the Spirit of his great Commander shines.

April 28. Good Company.

"He that walketh with wise men shall be wise: but a companion of fools shall be destroyed" (Prov. xiii. 20).

Boy or man, girl or woman—all are known by the company they keep. Tell me of what sort your chosen companions are, and I will tell you of what sort you yourself are, or very soon will be.

The text shows us the kind of companions to choose, and the kind to avoid; and it also reminds us of the influence that our friendships, of whatever sort they be, are sure to have upon us. Some of us who are older, looking back upon our life, find traces of early companionship upon us still; and so, by and by, it will be with you. And, remember, there is another side to this. *You* are making your companions either better or worse, by all that you do and say and are, when you are with them. Seek, then, that you may both find *real* friends for yourself and be a real friend to them.

As to the influence companions have upon us, plenty of illustrations might be given, both from the Bible and from common life around us. Don't you think David was a better man for his friendship with the pure and nobly unselfish Jonathan? And was not Rehoboam, on the other hand, ruined by the "bad set" among whom he fell?

Many in our churches are thanking God for what true friendship has been to them, and made them. Many in our jails are cursing their own past, and will give you as the explanation of their evil plight—"bad company." A judge, in passing sentence upon a young man, once said—" Had I listened in early life to certain of my companions instead of to God, I would have been before now, instead of a judge upon the king's bench, a prisoner standing at the bar." How true is it that "evil communications corrupt good manners."

Be it yours, dear reader, to say with one of old, "I am a companion of all them that fear Thee." That will assuredly tell for good upon your character day by day. Above all, may you walk daily with Him who is the best of Friends. His, to the heart that is laid open to it in faith and love, is the most telling, as well as most gracious, of all influences. Others will take knowledge concerning you, that you have been, and are, with Jesus.

A Wise Servant.

"*Who, then, is a wise servant?*" (Matt. xxiv. 45).

It is possible to be a servant, and yet not a wise one. If you are a follower of Christ at all, you are also a servant of His. And if you are a servant at all, surely it should be your ambition to fill your place and do your work as worthily as possible.

If it be asked what constitutes a *wise* servant, I would answer that these four things, at anyrate, are true of such an one :—

1. *He takes an intelligent interest in his work.* He is not a mere "hand," but a being gifted with a head and with a heart, and capable of using these. He is one who knows what he is about—who perceives what he is expected to accomplish—and who can take a sympathetic interest in the scheme to which his own bit of work is meant, along with that of others, to contribute.

2. *He has the good sense to stick to his own post.* It belongs to the Master to give to every man his service and his burden ; and, having had his work assigned to him, he does it with a will, and with all his might. Interest in others, and sympathy with them, cannot divert him away from the fulfilment of personal duty. Still less will he allow himself to envy others, or to meddle with them needlessly in their work. But, having got an answer to the prayer —" Lord, what wilt Thou have me to do ? " he does it, in the same sincere and humble spirit with which he asked to be guided to it.

3. *He not only knows the end he is to seek, but the right means for attaining it.* The wise servant is not shiftless, or without ideas. He has a sense of fitness, and he is a man of resource. He knows how to do the right thing, and to do it at the proper time, and in the most suitable way. This is an important part of his outfit for the practical service of the great Christian cause, which often needs not only a sharp eye but a delicate hand.

4. *He lives in the remembrance that all his work must come under the Master's eye.* He is one who looks for the coming of his Lord ; and he does all his work in view of that event, as something which may occur at any moment. Nay, he conducts himself as if his Master were already and always present. He lives, and labours, "as ever in his great Taskmaster's eye." This is the truest prudence. "Blessed is that servant whom his Master, when He cometh, shall find so doing."

April 30 — Trusting the Pilot.

"I will trust, and not be afraid" (Isa. xii. 2).

In one of his beautiful short pieces, Tennyson speaks of "meeting his Pilot face to face," and of his confidence that He will guide him safely to the haven.

What a blessed thing it is for those who are Christ's, to know that He is with them in the ship, and to be assured that He will guide them in safety through all the varying experiences of the voyage of life, till they cast anchor in the haven of everlasting peace!

If *you* have Jesus with you in the ship, you may well say to your soul, "I will trust, and not be afraid." For He is worthy of your complete confidence, at all times and in all circumstances. In fair weather and in foul, in calm and in storm, on the still bosom of the lake or in the rushing cataract of difficulty and danger, He is equally worthy of your full reliance, and will not be pleased if you withhold it from Him.

You are sailing smoothly, let us say, upon the calm, broad bosom of one of the great American lakes; and you never dream of questioning your pilot's skill. All is going well. You sun yourself upon the deck; you amuse yourself with your book, or in conversation with your fellow-passengers; and, as you pass from port to port along the border of the lake, you view the scenery with interest, and have no disquieting thought of danger.

But by and by the point is reached where the lake disgorges into the river, and the rapids are approached; and as you see the whirling, eddying waters, and feel the tremor of the vessel, as it seems, like a plaything, to be tossed by the seething torrent underneath—you cry out in alarm, and begin to more than question the skill of the pilot to bring you safely through peril so imminent and strange.

He smiles at your fears, as he grasps the helm with well-accustomed hand. He pities your disquiet, and is ready to make every allowance for your inexperience. But he is hardly gratified by your lack of confidence in his practised skill! You should have trusted him in the rapids as well as on the gently rippling waters.

Even so, for the honour of your Heavenly Pilot, as well as for your own comfort and well-being, "Trust in Him *at all times.*"

A Perfect Likeness.

"The Image of the Invisible God" (Col. i. 15).

IF you had an unseen friend, one away in another land, whom you had never set eyes upon, but who, you knew, was interested in you, and bent upon your good,—you would be very anxious to know all about him, would you not? If anybody came from that land who had known him, you would be eager in your questions—"What is *he* like?" "What kind of man is he?" "What do people think of him there?" You would be glad to see a picture of him; and, gazing at his image, you would feel that you knew him better than before. And especially if there came his son, whom people who knew them both spoke of as "just his father's image "—with "*his* very looks and ways "—why, in that living picture you would have the best possible idea of what your unseen friend was like.

So it is, dear young people, with God and you. You have not seen Him. He is "the Invisible God." No eye hath seen Him at any time. But you have beautiful accounts of His character and ways, and many proofs of the love that is in His heart for you. And, best of all, you have, in Jesus, One to look to who is "His Father's very Image." He can say—so like are the two to one another!—"He that hath seen *Me* hath seen the Father."

Look then to Jesus! And, as you see Him, pure and holy, scorning and scathing everything that is mean, abhorring everything that is vile, despising and detesting sin, but loving the sinner's soul, and melting in tenderness over the lost—there, dear young reader, there you behold "the Image of the Invisible God."

May the sight and the love of Jesus purify your heart from every contrary evil affection and desire. May it be yours to say, in answer to the enticements of sin—

> "I have heard the voice of Jesus,
> Tell me not of aught beside:
> I have seen the face of Jesus.
> All my soul is satisfied."

It is one of M'Cheyne's sayings, that "it is not so much great talents that God blesses, as great likeness to Jesus." How earnestly, then, should each of us seek to be, in character and life, "an image of the Image of the Invisible God!"

A Beautiful Vision.

"As the doves to their windows" (Isa. lx. 8

WHAT the prophet sees here is to him a very delightful and beautiful vision. The Zion of the Holy One of Israel has become a universal attraction. The sea is studded with ships, bearing down toward it from every quarter, with their throngs of eager voyagers and their rich freights of abundant merchandise. The land, too, is covered with caravansaries trooping to the same cherished centre—multitudes of camels and dromedaries from Midian and Ephah and Sheba, with their gold and frankincense; and the shepherd-princes of Kedar and Nebaioth leading their willing flocks to the ministry of the House of the Lord. And the city, whose walls are Salvation and her gates Praise, is open continually, to receive the thronging worshippers. Its gates are not shut, day or night; and still they crowd into the Holy City as the place of rest and joy, like doves flying to their windows.

Now, do we see anything going on in our own time which suggests to us the fulfilment of this beautiful vision?

On a Sabbath morning I have seen, on the crowded streets of a Christian city, and, still more suggestively, on the crowded roads of a quiet country-side, something that reminded me of what Isaiah saw. Look at all these people—these eager, sharpened, but often weary-faced dwellers in the city, or these devout and placid-looking country-folk, making their way to their accustomed place of worship; and what do you see? Have you not there some outward token, at anyrate, of a desire—in many a case sincere and deep—for the rest which the dove has in returning to her home?

But, to realise the picture, this outward flocking to the house of God must not be all, thankful as we are to see it in a land which has been favoured, as ours so long has been, with the ordinances of the gospel. There must be the flocking of souls *to Christ.* Not in an outward sanctuary, but in the secret place of the Most High, in the sanctuary of true heart-fellowship with God, must rest be found. And, thank God, Christ's own vision of the future *is* having its fulfilment. He who was lifted up is drawing men of every clime and kindred to Himself, that in Him they may find rest unto their souls.

And then, on the heavenward side, how bright and glorious is the fulfilment of the prophet's vision! From north, south, east, and west the seeking travellers come; and from whatever quarter they come, they find gates open to receive them within the New Jerusalem. There they sit down with Abraham, and Isaac, and Jacob, and rejoice in the union and fellowship of the heavenly feast. But "to be with Christ" is what makes it heaven, the true place of rest, the true home of the soul. Would this mean Home for you?

"The light of the knowledge of the glory of God in the face of Jesus Christ"
(2 Cor. iv. 6).

Do you not sometimes wish that you could have seen His face as He walked this earth of ours in Palestine? The face of Christ! What calm peacefulness must have rested on it—what clear intelligence must have beamed from it—what holy anger sometimes flashed across it—what sacred sorrow sometimes pained it—what wistfulness of divine love must have looked from those eyes, as He went about our world constantly seeking that He might save the lost.

Some have fancied that the face of Jesus was singularly devoid of attraction, and have even been foolish enough to imagine (founding on Isa. lii. 14) that it was actually repulsive. I agree rather with those who love to think of it as a countenance of heavenly beauty, because of the soul which shone through the features,—a face on which was mirrored in some way every heavenly grace. And I do not wonder if you sometimes sing, with special earnestness, the verse which says—

> "I wish that His hands had been placed on my head,
> That His arm had been thrown about me,
> And that I might have seen His kind look, when He said,
> 'Let the little ones come unto Me'!"

Such a look of Him you cannot have on earth. We have not even a portrait of Him, to tell us what He was like as the Man Christ Jesus. Some of the greatest painters of the world have tried to put on canvas their ideal of His face. But none of them completely satisfies the heart. There is always something wanting, something which disappoints. Perhaps it is better so. If we had possessed a true likeness of Jesus, people would have been prone to worship it. And even such a sight of Him as men had on earth might not have done much for us. Many looked into His face, but were not illumined by it; for they looked with darkened minds and blinded hearts.

But we may by *faith* discern something of the glory of God, as it is seen in the face of Christ. If we direct to Him the look of trust and adoring love, the light of His countenance will fall upon us. And even if that light searches us, and so humbles us, in revealing more plainly to us by contrast our own sinfulness, the sight of the Saviour's face will make us glad. For we shall see in it, not only a beautiful face, but a face full of compassion; and while we adore the beauty of holiness that is in it, we shall realise the better what the Psalmist meant by "the help of His countenance."

May 4 — Caught in the Meshes.

"They hunt every man his brother with a net" (Mic. vii. 2).

It is a terrible picture which the prophet here gives of the state of society in his time. "There is none upright among men : they all lie in wait for blood; they hunt every man his brother with a net." Those of whom this could be said were children not of God, but of the devil ; and they were busy doing devil's work.

Among the ancients, as you know, there were frequent contests between gladiators in the arena ; and not infrequently the victory lay with the combatant who seemed least likely to carry the day—namely, with the "retiarius," as he was called, the man who was armed only with *a net* in his hand, and a small sword hanging by his side.

Here is how such a scene has been described :—" The two combatants are seen entering the *campus* at the different sides. How unevenly matched they are ! That slim figure, all unguarded, with nothing in his hand save only a net which he bears at the end of a long pole—*he* can be no fit antagonist for yonder hero, who clanks into the arena in his shining armour, mailed *cap-à-pie*, and wielding haughtily his sword and buckler. But wait ! See how nimbly he with the net eludes the champion's eager onslaught. Time after time he does it. And now, when the warrior is getting weary, forth goes the net ! It has caught on a point of his armour—it is entangled on a spike of his helmet—he strives—he writhes—to tear, to cut it away. In vain ! Worse and worse grows the entanglement. Those meshes will not asunder. He is helpless ; he is ensnared—a slave ! "

Ah, young reader, beware of the man with the net. There are many enemies of our souls lying in wait to deceive and to destroy. Above all, there is the arch-foe Satan, ready, if he can, to entangle you in the meshes of evil habit, that he may lead you captive at his will. Confident in themselves and in their proud defences, the young make bold sometimes to despise this foe. They dare him to do his worst. They even tempt him, mayhap, to the contest. But lo ! a mesh of his net lays hold on them, at one point or another; then another mesh ; unconscious or unheeding, they go on, until the snare is all about them, and they are found lying helpless (and, it may be, what is worse, even willing) victims ! What hope can there be for such, any more ? There is hope for them only in One —in Him who is the great Deliverer, and who came to destroy the works of the devil.

"*Ye belong to Christ*" (Mark ix. 41).

This is as good a description as any of what it means to be a Christian. A Christian is "one who belongs to Christ." And there are various senses in which—besides the right which creation implies—the Christian may be said to belong to his Heavenly Master.

1. He belongs to Christ *by purchase*. The Christian is one of "the redeemed." Do you know what this means? If a person had fallen into debt, and lost his property, and with it the rights of citizenship, and another came and paid his debts for him, and restored him to his place,—that other might be said to have redeemed his rights for him—bought them back again. Or if a person had committed a crime, and had been cast into prison, or, as in some countries, sold into slavery, and another came and bore the penalty, that the imprisoned or enslaved one might go free—that would be redeeming *him*—buying him back from prison and from bondage. Now this is what Jesus has done for His people. Their debts were so heavy that they could never have paid them. But He has purchased forgiveness for them. They were guilty, sold under sin, condemned to a miserable servitude. But He came and bought them—not with corruptible things like silver and gold, but with His precious blood. Therefore they are "not their own, but bought with a price." He who redeemed them is their Owner and Lord. They belong by purchase and of right to their Redeemer—Christ. But, further,

2. The Christian belongs to his Master *by consent*. It is not merely something done for him or outside of him, but something wrought in his heart, which furnishes the secret and explanation of his life. The love that bought the Christian has done more than pay a price for him: it has wrought a conquest in him. And, though the door lies open, he will not sally forth. In Christ's ownership of him, he sees not only Christ's right, but his own joy and privilege. For that which constrains him is the love of Christ; and the law of Christ is for him the law of liberty. "The symbol of redemption," said Rudolph, the first of the Hapsburg line, meaning by that the Cross, "the symbol of redemption is as good as a sceptre"; and with that he laid hold of a cross, for want of a sceptre, at his coronation. "The Cross," says the Christian, "is better than any sceptre. The Cross of Calvary has done more than all the sceptres in the world could have done. It has subdued, and won, and bound to Christ multitudes of rebellious, lost souls—and mine among the rest."

The Character of Isaac.

"And Abraham called the name of his son, Isaac" (Gen. xxi. 3).

THE name of Isaac means "laughter." When he was born, the hearts of Abraham and Sarah were filled with joy, and their mouths with singing; and he continued to be, as every boy and girl should seek to be, a bright and gladdening influence within their home. A good and happy child is like a sunbeam of light in the dwelling. Isaac was a good son. We never hear of him causing pain to either his father or his mother by anything he did. In him they had a loving, dutiful child. So his name was, in a true sense, his proper name.

The character of Isaac was full of gentleness and modesty. He was fond of quietness and meditation. He was not so brilliant a man as either his father Abraham or his son Jacob. But, if not brilliant, he was brave; and he showed this by being able to *bear* a great deal without a murmur. For you must remember that it is not only those who cut a brilliant figure in the eyes of the world who are to be respected for their valour. A poor sick woman on a bed of pain may be every whit as brave as a proud soldier on a battlefield. Though Isaac was gentle, you must not think of him as weak. He was one of those who, as in his contest with the Philistines (ch. xxvi. 17-23), can conquer through patience, which is often a harder and nobler thing than to strike a blow.

We cannot all be brilliant, but we may all be virtuous; and there is something for us all to learn in Isaac's modest goodness. Some of the noblest lives are those least noticed by the world; and his was to be counted among them. In a great emergency of his life, before he was quite grown up, he showed himself capable of a heroic self-sacrifice. And throughout his unconspicuous career he proved himself a true-hearted man—a man of faith and godly fear. There is for such as Isaac an important place and use in God's kingdom. It is not only the great and clever in the world's eyes who may lead a noble life. Let us learn the beauty and the glory of any life that is spent for God, and yielded heartily up to Him.

> "Be good, dear youth, and let who will be clever;
> Do noble things, though lowly, all day long:
> And so make life, death, and that vast for ever
> One grand, sweet song."

True Gratitude.

"What shall I render?" (Ps. cxvi. 12).

In a certain church in Rome there is a bell which is tolled at intervals every day, all the year round, by the appointment, and at the expense, of a man long since dead. I was told that the arrangement was begun in this wise. The man in question had been visiting the Catacombs,—the underground labyrinth of passages and chambers which, in ancient days, furnished a burial-place for the dead, and sometimes a secret refuge from the living,—when, to his horror, he found that he was separated from the rest of the party, and had completely lost his way! Soon the light he had in his hand became exhausted; and if his search for the way out was hopeless before, it was doubly hopeless now, in the dreary darkness. On and on he groped for many weary hours, till, worn with hunger and fatigue, he lay down in the stony path to rest—or perchance to die. He slept; but ere long he awoke again, to pursue his frenzied search—in vain! At length, just as he was sinking into absolute despair, he heard a sound. He listened: it was the muffled and distant tolling of a bell. All his soul for the time was in his ears. He followed where the sound seemed to lead; and soon, to his unspeakable relief, he reached the entrance to the Catacombs, and was rejoicing in the light of heaven again. What had saved him was the ringing of the church-bell; and in gratitude for his deliverance he set apart a sum of money as an endowment, that the bell might be rung several times a day to all generations, for the guidance of any poor, bewildered travellers who might be lost in the Catacombs near by.

Now, that man showed a becoming spirit; and though he might perhaps have found a more useful avenue for it, we respect his gratitude. If the sound of the gospel has been blessed to our salvation, and has led us out of the dark and dreary labyrinth of sin into the glorious light of God—ought not we, too, to find some way of expressing our thankfulness? Should we not be anxious that other poor wanderers, now lost and in despair, should hear the joyful sound and hail the joyful light? He is indeed an ungrateful and unworthy Christian who is not often asking himself—"What shall I render?" What is there that I can do or give, to show my thankfulness to God, and my desire that others may be blessed?

May 8

A Lesson from Sinai.

"I the Lord thy God am a jealous God" (Ex. xx. 5).

IF you look at a map of the Red Sea, you will notice that it divides at the north end into two horns, between which there is a peninsula or neck of land. In the centre of that peninsula there is a cluster of mountain heights, largely of granite formation, one of which, still called the Jebel Mûsa, or mountain of Moses, is believed to be Mount Sinai.

The district is very bare and lonely; but once it was peopled by the great pilgrim-nation of the Hebrews, who encamped here for about eleven months, on their way to the Promised Land. And, sternly impressive as Jebel Mûsa still appears, it was once the scene of terrors such as the most imaginative of travellers to the spot cannot possibly realise. For here it was that He who is the God of nature and the Lord of man "came down upon the top of the mount in fire"; and, amid the smoke and tempest, and the quaking of the earth, made known to the awe-struck children of Israel His holy law. So terrible was the sight that even the heroic Moses said, "I do exceedingly fear and quake."

Perhaps your conscience has sometimes made you feel, in some small measure at least, like these Israelites when they perceived how near God was, and how unfit they were to stand in His immediate presence. It is told of a poor Hottentot girl, called Jejana, that the first time she was in church she heard the minister preach from the words—"I know thy works." And, in her ignorance, supposing the preacher to be God, she attempted to hide from him behind a pillar. All her false words and evil deeds seemed to rush to her remembrance, when she fancied herself standing in the immediate presence of God. That was Sinai speaking to her, and saying, "I am a jealous God."

The law of Sinai—the Ten Commandments, which you have no doubt learned by heart—sums up for us what God requires of us as His moral creatures, capable of knowing right from wrong, and bound to do the right when we know it. These commandments endure from age to age. They have been likened to Sinai itself, as the granite foundation on which the whole world of men, all human society, must rest—duty to God and duty to our neighbour. They may also be compared to a spotless mirror, into which we are called to look, that we may see what sort of persons we really are. Alas, how many flaws such a look reveals in character and life! No wonder that we are fain to hide our faces from God, and to ask—"Whither shall we flee from His pure presence?" But while God is jealous about His glory being given to another, and is angry when the love and obedience due to Him are not rendered by us—His jealousy is the other side of His love. He willeth not that any should perish, but that all should come to repentance. And for the penitent there is acceptance with Him, through a better Mediator than Moses was at Sinai.

Grieving our Best Friend. May 9

"Grieve not the Holy Spirit of God" (Eph. iv. 30).

NEVER forget that the Third Person in the Godhead, the Holy Spirit, is a Person; and One who is interested in your highest good. This is just as true of Him as it is of the Father and of the Son, though we often fail to take it in, or are unmindful of it. When we speak of the Holy Spirit, we should speak not of "it," but of "Him." For He lives, and loves us. He is not indifferent to our character and conduct. We can cause Him grief; or we can give Him joy.

When Jesus was leaving His disciples, and about to go from earth, He promised to send them Another Comforter—namely, the Holy Ghost. When He came they would not be like orphans, without anyone to care for them. For He would console them; He would give them light, and bring them peace; He would guide them into all truth; He would be their constant Helper, cheering them in duty, supporting them in trial, aiding them in every holy purpose and good endeavour. And that promise Jesus has fulfilled, not only for His first disciples, but for all His followers. How good a Friend He has sent to us, in sending to us the Holy Spirit, we may know when He says, in all love and sincerity, "It is well for you that I go away; for if I go not away, the Comforter will not come unto you; but if I depart, I will send Him unto you."

Now, if the Holy Spirit is so good a Friend to us, must it not be very wrong to grieve Him? and would it not be very hurtful to ourselves to grieve Him away?

You understand what is meant by *grieving* a person,—such as your father who loves you. It means wounding him to the heart; and it is just because he loves you that you are able to do that. You can annoy and anger another, even an enemy; but it takes one to love you before you can grieve him. And oh, dear young people, just because the Holy Spirit loves you dearly, you can grieve Him easily and sorely. If you want to know what grieves Him, just ask—"What would grieve Jesus?" For their hearts beat together, and whatever grieves Jesus grieves the Spirit too. Not only gross outward sins, but evil thoughts, bad words, bitter feelings grieve Him, because He loves you, and desires to see and to make you holy.

I knew a young man once who not only grieved, but grieved away his best earthly friend—his kind and tender-hearted father. He fell into habits of intemperance, and though everything was tried to reclaim him, and to encourage him in the good way, he continued to be a perfect heart-break to his parents; and at length, as the old man sorrowfully told me, they had actually to change their address from time to time, and conceal it from their own son. His father provided him with the bare necessities of life, till he died. But he could not possibly "dwell with him." He had grieved his parents away. That was sad. But it is unspeakably more sad to grieve away, or to quench, the Holy Spirit!

May 10

For Christ's Sake.

"God for Christ's sake hath forgiven you" (Eph. iv. 32). *"I take pleasure in distresses for Christ's sake"* (2 Cor. xii. 10).

This is a beautiful motto for the Christian life—"For Christ's sake." There are two ways in which we may regard the words, as suggested by these two texts.

(1) *For Christ's sake* sums up for us all that the Bible has to tell us of the mercy of God to sinners. There are a great many things mentioned in the Old Testament that God is ready to do "for His name's sake"—to spare, guide, forgive, sanctify. And there are many things God is asked, in the Psalms and elsewhere, to do "for His mercies' sake" to them who seek Him. Now, all this we learn, in the New Testament, to connect with the person, and work, and name of His dear Son. Here all the rays of divine light converge as in a focus; and Jesus Himself says—"Whatsoever ye shall ask the Father *in My name*, He will give it you."

Here, then, we have *our great argument with God*—"for Christ's sake." Surely we may rejoice to plead it. Not—because of fifty, thirty, twenty, ten good days in a year, or good deeds in a life, receive and bless me; but, "for Christ's sake"! That is a plea which never fails. Do not merely repeat it, as a thing of rote, at the end of your prayers, but *use* it every day. It is like a bank cheque left for you to fill in; and, with His signature at it, it will never be dishonoured at the bank of heavenly grace.

(2) *For Christ's sake* sums up for us something else, however,—namely, all that the Christian life should be, and will be, in so far as it is true to its ideal. It is a life lived "for Christ's sake." Here is the key to much in it which the world, on its own maxims, cannot understand. So was it with Paul. "For Christ's sake" he was willing to serve, to suffer, and to die. And he was seen to "take pleasure" for His sake in what was altogether unwelcome to ordinary men—in infirmities, reproaches, distresses, and the like. And so should it be with us. But alas! how very little there often is in the character and life of those who bear the name of Christ which the world cannot perfectly comprehend.

Hence we have here *God's great argument with us*—"for Christ's sake"—as He sends us forth to duty. Think of what Christ has been, and done, and suffered for you; and whenever, in the path of obedience, you are called to be, or do, or suffer anything for Him, let the watchword "for Christ's sake" ring in your ears, and plead with you to be worthy of Him and of yourselves. "All this for thee; what hast thou done for Me?"

What she could.   May 11

"She hath done what she could" (Matt. xiv. 8).

THIS was high praise, given by Jesus to the woman who brought the alabaster box of ointment and poured it on His head. It was not a very great thing she did. But the deed proceeded from a great heart, a heart very full of love to Jesus; and such kind deeds never die. The fragrance of that ointment has filled not the room only, but the world; for, wherever the gospel is preached, and in whatever language,—in India, Africa, China, and the far-off islands of the sea,—it is gratefully told, by the Lord's own appointment, what that poor woman did out of love for Him.

The question is, not how big a thing you are able to do, but what is the motive of it—out of how much love do you do it?

It is told of a powerful king, that he resolved to build a mighty church or temple to God; and so anxious was he to have full credit for it, that he strictly enjoined all his subjects that they were to have no part whatever in bearing the cost of it. Everything done by anybody towards the erection of it was to be paid from the king's own treasury. A great staff of workmen were employed, under the direction of the most skilful architect in the realm; and, by and by, the large and beautiful pile was finished, and all the work paid for. Then the king had a ceremony at the opening of it; and the assembly saw, printed up on one of the walls in shining letters—"Erected to the Glory of God by the King."

When night came, the king dreamt a dream that troubled him. He fancied that his own name was blotted from this inscription, and that the name of a poor widow, who lived near the palace gate, was blazoned in its stead. For two succeeding nights he dreamt the same thing; and, summoning the trembling woman before him, he sternly asked her—"Have you taken any part in the building of this temple, contrary to the king's command?" "None, your majesty." "Think again," the king said: "None whatever?" "None, O king, unless it be that, out of pity for God's creatures, I sometimes gave a wisp of hay to the poor horses struggling past my door with their heavy loads." The mystery was solved; and the king, conscience-stricken, had his own name removed, and the poor woman's printed in its stead. He had done a big thing for his own glory; she, a little thing for the glory of God, and the good of some of His creatures. She had done "what she could."

May 12   **The Father Himself.**

"The Father Himself loveth you" (John xvi. 27).

WE cannot be too thankful for the love of God the Son. But we must not fall into the mistake that some people commit—of making little of the love of God the Father. This is the last thing that Jesus would like any of us to do. He says, "He that hath seen Me, hath seen the Father." So that, if we see love in Him, we may be sure that there is love in the heart of the Father toward us also. God so loved the world that He gave His only-begotten Son. "The Father Himself loveth you."

It is strange what perverted notions people often have about the divine love. There are some who do not feel quite sure about the love even of the Son of God Himself, who died for sinners; and they turn to the Virgin Mary, asking her to plead with her Son on their behalf. I remember seeing in Sicily, upon the walls of a church, a picture which made me sad. It represented a poor man, in the horrors of death, stretching out his hands in agony for help. At the top of the picture there was a representation of Christ, looking away with something very like indifference upon His face. But between Him and the dying man was the Virgin Mary, with pity on her face, pleading for the sufferer who had sought her help.

What a shame, you say, to represent a woman as more compassionate than the Saviour, and to direct the faith of the poor Roman Catholics to the Virgin, rather than to the Son of God! Yes; but we Protestants must not make a similar mistake, in representing God the Son only as pitiful, and God the Father as harsh and severe. Another continental picture will illustrate what I mean. It pictures God the Father showering down His arrows, with a vengeful countenance, upon the miserable sinners on earth, but His own Son interposing between, and catching the arrows in His own body, before they can reach their earthly victims.

To set God the Father thus in contrast with God the Son is not only an error, but a sin. Both are equally righteous, and both are equally loving. Neither of them could allow sin to go unpunished. But the love of both is equally seen in the sacrifice of Calvary. "The Father Himself loveth you."

Looking up.

"Jesus lifted up His eyes to heaven" (John xvii. 1).

WHEN Jesus was addressing His Father, He lifted up His eyes to heaven. Where heaven exactly is we do not know. There is some part of the universe where the throne of the Almighty God and King is set, in the midst of the heavenly palace. It is far beyond the sky that we can see. But it is natural for us, when we think of heaven,—as, we see, it was for Jesus Himself,—to look up. Heaven for Him was, where His Father was. And heaven for us is, where He is with the Father.

It is a great encouragement and help for us, day by day, to be permitted to look up. The troubles of earth, the loads we have to carry, do not seem so great or so wearisome when we look up. And if we have a good desire in our hearts, we are encouraged to hope for its fulfilment when we look up. Because, not only are there bright and glorious things above, which God has invited us to set our hearts upon, but Christ is there, "at God's right hand." And, since He is there, in the place of power, we know that the good things God bids us seek will be bestowed on us by Him.

You remember how Stephen, in the hour of his agony, looking up, saw Jesus "standing on the right hand of God," as if He had risen from His throne, in eager interest, to look down upon His suffering martyr. And when the servant's eyes met the Master's, he was strengthened. You are not likely to have to suffer martyrdom. But you will have your difficulties and dangers to go through. May you have faith to see Jesus looking down upon you with the eye of interest and love!

A boy applying for a place upon a ship was asked, "Can you climb?" Soon after leaving land he was required, in a storm, to prove his powers by going to the top of the mast. As he rose higher and higher on the rigging, his head grew dizzy, and, looking down at the waves, he cried in terror, "I shall fall!" "Look up!" shouted the captain; and he did, soon reaching the mast head. Keep you looking up, not into the empty blue, but into the face of Christ; and it will be your safety, your comfort, and your strength.

May 14 — A Free Salvation.

" What shall I do that I may inherit eternal life ? " (Mark x. 17).

THE question put to Jesus by this young man seems to have been perfectly sincere. He wished to know what he had *to do* in order to earn eternal life, and he fancied that he was ready to do anything that might be necessary in order to secure it. Taking him even on his own ground, Jesus, in revealing to him more than he had known of his own heart, showed him how unable he was to earn a place in heaven. When it became a question between God and gold, he turned his back sorrowfully upon Christ. And Christ, too, was sorry to see him go away.

The young man was, however, on quite a wrong track. The Bible order is not, *Do* in order to receive; but, *Receive*, and then do whatever gratitude may dictate. Salvation is a free gift; and if it is to be yours, you must be humble enough to take it for nothing. You can neither pay for it nor work for it. You have only to receive it.

How slow people are to believe in the generosity of God! This is so cold and selfish a world that "Nothing for nothing" is a common proverb; and "Salvation for nothing" means to many that salvation either can't be worth the having, or that, if it is a great boon, it simply can't be true that it is to be had without paying for it.

"Herrings for nothing! Herrings for nothing!" cried a Christian man for hours on the streets of London one day, as he passed along with a well-stored barrow. Many refused to heed him; some smiled and passed on, thinking he was weak; some stopped long enough to fling a jibe at him and his advertising trick: not a single one had simple faith enough to take him at his word. Yet he was neither silly nor insincere. He was quietly putting the passers-by to the test. He was quite prepared to give the fish for nothing to any who sought them. But the freeness of the offer was so like God's way that men did not believe it; and even the inhabitants of the poorest streets, to whom the herrings would have been a boon, allowed the opportunity to slip.

That was a small matter, you say? Yes; but it is not a small matter to neglect in like manner the great salvation. When God says—"Without money and without price," He means it. You are not to wait till, by your good deeds, or your patient sufferings, or your pious feelings, you can earn salvation. You are simply to take Him at His word, and to hold out the hand of emptiness, that you may receive it.

How to be in a Majority. May 15

"There be more with us than with him . . . with us is the Lord our God"
(2 Chron. xxxii. 7, 8).

THESE were among the comfortable words with which good King Hezekiah strengthened the hearts of the men of Jerusalem, when the great Sennacherib, King of Assyria, came up against the city to destroy it. Nor was his confidence misplaced. Since the Lord of Hosts was with them, Hezekiah and his people were more than all they who could be against them. And the victory lay, not with the proud Assyrian king and his mighty men of valour, but with the poor Hebrew people, whom they had despised.

And here we may still learn how to be in a majority, as regards true power and genuine success. Some people are so anxious to be always on the winning side that they will follow the multitude in whatever direction it may go. But the first question with us should be, "What is *right*? Which is the side that Christ would take?" If we are enabled to settle that, and to take our stand along with Him, then we are sure to be on the winning side at last. For He must reign, until He hath put all His enemies under His feet. If the Lord of Hosts is with us, the victory is secure. If you are in the right, then you are on the side of Christ; and if you are on the side of Christ, all will come right at last.

It is told of a little boy that he came to his father with a very earnest face one day, and asked—"Father, is Satan bigger than I am?" "Yes, my boy." "Is he bigger than you, father?" the little fellow continued. "Oh, yes," was the answer; "Satan is bigger than your father." The boy looked surprised and disappointed; but, after thinking for a moment, he further asked, "Is he bigger than Jesus?" "No, my boy," said the father; "Jesus is bigger than he is." And the little fellow, with a smile of relief and satisfaction, said—"Then I am not afraid of him."

Christ's followers are sometimes apt to be discouraged when they think of the odds that are against them in their struggle with error, sin, and wrong. But it is foolish and even sinful for them to be down-hearted. When Antigonus, the great commander, came in sight of the enemy's fleet, the pilot cried—"Alas! we are outnumbered." "What?" said the conqueror; "but how many do you count *me* for?" And he swept the sea. Even so, Christ may well ask His dispirited followers—"Against how many do you value Me?" If the Captain of Salvation is on our side, He will make us more than conquerors.

May 16

Two Lovely Sisters.

"Mary and her sister Martha" (John xi. 1).

In the Bible there is quite a number of pairs of names, the mention of either of which is sure to suggest the other. Such are Cain and Abel, Moses and Aaron, Jonathan and David, Peter and John, Barnabas and Paul, and many others which will readily occur to you. And so it is with Martha and Mary. The name of the one sister at once suggests the other, and the mention of either summons up the peaceful home in Bethany to which the Lord used to resort, and on which our minds still love to dwell.

1. The sisters were very different, as often happens in the same family among those who gather by the same hearth, and are brought up amid the same surroundings; *but Jesus loved them both.* " Now Jesus loved Martha and her sister" (verse 5). What a blessing it is that He does not love only persons of one particular type! Our hearts are narrow. We might have had such a distinct preference for either Mary or Martha that there would have been no place, or hardly any place, left in our affection for the other. But people of all sorts of natural disposition are the objects of Christ's love. You may be very different from your brother or your sister; and yet, as with Mary and Martha, the heart of Jesus is big enough to love you both.

2. The sisters were very different; *but both loved Jesus.* This is a very remarkable thing about our Lord, that He draws and keeps the affection, the deepest and most constant love, of persons who in many, and perhaps in most, other things, are quite different from one another. Is not this a blessing? It would have been a sad world for many of us, if the drawing power of Jesus had been capable of reaching only one class of minds and hearts. Let us be very thankful when we have reason to believe that someone else, no matter how different otherwise from us, really loves Jesus; and for His sake let us love such too.

3. The sisters were very different; *but we should learn from both.* Mary showed her love for Jesus by sitting at His feet, and drinking in His spirit, as she listened to His voice and enjoyed heart-fellowship with Him. Martha showed her love by bustling actively through the house, and seeking to give her very best service to her Lord. We should learn from Mary to sit often at Christ's feet, that we may learn of Him, and enjoy communion with Him. We should learn from Martha to seek to serve our Master and His cause where, and as, and how He may direct us. That would be indeed a lovely Christian character that combined in itself the outstanding qualities of both the gracious sisters of Bethany!

The Proper Standard.

"Lord, what wilt Thou have me to do?" (Acts ix. 6).

It is said that men measured their cloth in England long ago by a yard measure of their own, so that there was great diversity in different places, and even in the shops of the same town. But King Edward I., seeing this, took a stick and measured with it his own arm, which became thenceforward a fixed standard for the yard. This was a great boon. Before, all was uncertainty; but now there was something to go by, and a yard meant really a yard.

Now, if we Christians wish to go by the proper standard, we must take it from the King. We read of a time in Israelitish history when "there was no king in Israel, but every man did that which was right in his own eyes." This, of course, meant anarchy and confusion. But if such a state of things prevails to any extent among us, it is not because there is no King, or because He has left us in any sort of doubt as to the rule by which we ought to live. Christ's will is to be our standard; and if at any time we are perplexed about how we are to apply it, we are to go to Him with our difficulty—"Lord what wilt *Thou* have me to do?"

There are many people content to live by a false standard—which means for them, in the longrun, a misshapen character and a distorted life.

1. Some set before them no higher standard than *their own inclination.* They follow their own sweet will. But though it may be sweet for a time, such find it bitter in the end. Our own wishes are no safe guide to follow. The prodigal son wished to be "lord of himself"; and it proved a "heritage of woe." The self-willed man is sure, sooner or later, to come to grief.

2. Some set before them no higher standard than *public opinion, and the general practice of those around them.* "What will others expect of me?" they ask: and "What are others wont to do?" If they can gain the praise of men they are content; and if they do like So-and-so, they think they do very well. They may even lay claim to a false humility, on the score that they "don't set up to be better than their neighbours."

3. The one true and safe standard to live by is *the will of Christ,* as revealed in the book of His Word and the book of your own Conscience. Accept His will heartily as yours. Then, and not till then, will it be safe for you to follow your own inclination. Seek to raise public opinion, not slavishly to bow before it. You *are* to seek to be better than the best of your neighbours; for you are to seek to be like Christ—and the best of them come far short of Him. But it will fill you, not with conceit, but with deep humility, to be ever asking—"Lord, what wilt *Thou* have me to do?"

May 18 — Pleasing God.

"Without faith it is impossible to please Him" (Heb. xi. 6).

THERE is nothing that displeases an honest, thoroughly trustworthy person more than to know that he or she is not being trusted. This is a slight upon the character, and it cuts such to the heart. So is it with God. You may profess anything you choose, and do anything else you like; but if you are not trusting Him, you cannot be pleasing Him.

On the other hand, there is nothing that gratifies a trustworthy person so much as to enjoy entire confidence. And so it is with God. By faith it is possible to please Him. And if this is possible, surely you would like to do it—to please God.

What, then, is faith? It is just taking God at His word, and trusting Him, trusting yourself to Him. People sometimes mystify themselves about the meaning of "faith." But God, in His Word, has made its meaning as plain as language can make it.

Not only the *tongue* which expresses faith by words, but the *hand*, the *foot*, the *ear*, and the *eye* are referred to, that we may the better understand what faith means. We "lay hold" on God, or "touch" at least the hem of Christ's garment, by faith. We "come" to Him in obedience to the urgent gospel invitation. We give response by the ear to His call, "Hear, and your soul shall live." And one of the simplest expressions for faith is, "looking" to Jesus (Isa. xlv. 22), as the dying Israelites looked to the brazen serpent that was lifted up.

A little boy lay dying; and when he seemed afraid, his brother told him to trust in Jesus. He asked what that meant—what he was to do? "Pray to Him," he answered. "I'm too weak; I'm not able to pray." "Then," said his brother, "just you hold up your hand—*Jesus will see it, and know what it means.*" Up went the thin, wasted little hand. And that was faith! Jesus knew what it meant.

The Name above every Name.

"Thou shalt call His name Jesus" (Matt. i. 21).

This was a common name among the Jews, its Old Testament form being *Joshua*, who is called "Jesus" in the Book of Acts.

But it was an uncommon name in Him who was called "Jesus of Nazareth." When He took it up it became the name above every name, at which every knee will yet require to bow. It was given to Him, as Matthew tells us, not because it was a family name, but because of its meaning—"He shall *save* His people from their sins." And His whole life, but especially His death on Calvary, showed how worthy He was of this precious name of *Jesus*,—as the Saviour who came to deliver us, not only from punishment and misery, but from our sins—to save us from *bad hearts*.

It is told of a famous general that he used to take his boy in his arms and speak to him about Jesus. The little fellow was greatly pleased; the "old, old Story" seemed always new to him. One day his father said to him, "Would my little son like to go to heaven?" "Yes, father," was the answer. "But how can you go to heaven? Your heart is full of sin," the father said. "All are sinners, papa," the boy answered, deep in thought. "But only the pure in heart are to see God; and how can my little boy hope to be among them?" The child's face grew for a little while unspeakably sad. Perhaps he was for the first time realising his *own* sinfulness. But, after a few moments, with full heart and tearful eye he sobbed forth, as he laid his head upon his father's breast, these words of penitence and hope, "Papa, *Jesus can save me!*"

That little boy was right; and not only his father, but Jesus Himself was glad to hear him so speak. He is the "Mighty to save." Can *you* call Him, "Jesus, *my* Saviour?"

"He did not come to judge the world; He did not come to blame;
He did not only come to seek,—it was to save He came;
And when we call Him *Saviour*, then we call Him by His name."

A Noble Aim in Life.

" Who went about doing good" (Acts x. 38).

THE following touching entry was found in the small pocket-book of the late Emperor Frederick of Germany. It was pencilled by him as he rode in state through London, on Queen Victoria's Jubilee Day:—"The ambulance arrangements—the drinking-troughs for horses and dogs—the cabmen's shelters in streets of London." These, and not the pageants, were the sights that day for "Frederick the Noble." The welfare of his people lay ever on his heart; and because he had a great pity for the poor, ay and for the dumb creation, his ruling passion found, even on a day like that, its opportunities.

As that Prince loved and sought to serve his country, the Christian should love, and seek how best to serve, the kingdom of his Lord. In constant thoughtfulness and devotion on its behalf, he should look higher for his pattern than to any earthly model—even to Him who, though He was the Lord of all, became the servant of all, and ever " went about doing good."

How true as well as beautiful a description this is of the life of our Redeemer upon earth! He was unwearied in His endeavours to do good to others—healing the sick, comforting the sad, guiding the perplexed, bringing hope to the despairing and peace to the sin-troubled heart. Unwearied! No, not always; but even when wearied *in* the work, He never wearied *of* it. Look at Him by the well of Samaria, where, " being wearied with His journey, He sate thus on the well." His heart so yearns over the lost that even these tired moments are not given to repose, but to the seeking and saving of a poor wandering soul.

Wherever Jesus went He carried blessing in His train. Every company He mingled with, every person He spoke to, was, or might have been, the better for meeting with Him. In our own place and measure, the same should be true of us, if we are Christ's. This at anyrate should be our desire—to be in the world even as He was in the world. There are those of whom it is sadly true, as the summing up of their biography—"They went about doing evil." Let your life rather be a reproduction, as close as grace will enable you to make it, of the life of Jesus. As you have opportunity—and remember that you are not only to accept, but to seek for opportunities— do good unto all men.

Something to be sure about.   May 21

"Be sure your sin will find you out" (Num. xxxii. 23).

Sin may be hidden for a while from man's sight. But all things are "naked and open" to the eyes of God; and a day is coming which will declare every secret thing, whether it be good or bad.

Every now and again society is startled by the discovery of some crime, coolly planned and carefully concealed, to which some very little thing gave an unexpected clue. Some drops of blood on the pavement led to the tracking of a robber in Edinburgh, who had cut his finger in breaking through the window of a house he had plundered. A shoe, fitting a shoe-print at a certain place, has sometimes helped to the conviction of a murderer. A finger on the sealing-wax, when compared with the lines upon the finger of a high and trusted official on an American railway, led to the discovery that it was he who had opened certain bags, and taken from them valuable papers; and this in spite of the fact that he had carefully sealed the bags, and taken means to direct suspicion to other people. Thus, even on earth there are many significant reminders that sin is sure to find men out. And these are but hints of the complete and universal disclosure to be made by and by.

(1) You should *pray that you may have as little the desire as the power to hide anything from God*. When the search was being made for the Achan in the camp,—as the circle was narrowed, from the tribe of Judah to the clan of the Zarhites, to the house of Zabdi, to the family of Carmi, till at length the wretched, guilty, trembling man was pointed out by God's unerring finger, and dragged into the light,—how happy were those Israelites, amid the growing interest and excitement, who felt, on that searching day, that *they* had nothing to hide from God's eye! May there be no concealment between you and your Heavenly Father!

(2) And instead of waiting for your sin to find *you* out,—vainly hoping, like Judas at the Last Supper, that you may somehow escape among the crowd,—you should *rather find out your sin*, and go with it to Him who died upon the Cross to take our sins away. We must all appear, and everything about us shall appear, at the Judgment Seat of Christ. How well for us if we then see in our Judge our Saviour, from whose lips we have heard long before the words of free and full forgiveness! Frankly confess, and He will freely pardon. "If we confess our sins, He is faithful and just to forgive us our sins, and to cleanse us from all unrighteousness."

A Free Pardon.

"He will abundantly pardon" (Isa. lv. 7).

JOE was a deserter. There was no denying that. He had been in the Queen's service, but had left his regiment in a hurry. And though he had imagined that nobody in London knew of his history, he was horrified one day to hear one of the fellow-clerks in his office hiss into his ear—"I know your secret, young man; it's worth your while to make it worth my while to keep silence; for you're a craven, cowardly deserter." Let me briefly tell you the rest of his story, as I found it, at much greater length, in a paper which came into my hands the other day.

Joe was miserable. He went about through life with a load upon his heart which nothing could throw off.

But the Queen's jubilee year arrived; and one day, in a post office, a placard caught his eye which seemed to be of little interest to others, but at once arrested Joe. It was a proclamation by the Queen, "for extending pardons to soldiers who may have deserted from our Land Forces." With beating heart he drew near and read its terms. It declared that all men who had been absent through desertion for more than five years would not be called upon to join again for service, but would be granted protecting certificates, *if they reported themselves within two months.* The warning was added —"Every offender who shall not avail himself of the penalty we now graciously offer shall be held amenable to all pains and penalties provided under the Army Act.— Given at our Court at Windsor, the 17th day of June 1887, in the fiftieth year of our reign."

For a time Joe could not bring himself to believe that such good news was true. He feared to run himself into a trap. He could not get the offer out of his head, but put off for several wretched weeks without doing anything to avail himself of its terms. At last he grew so excited that he felt he must do something to test the matter. And so one day he wrote a letter to the commanding officer, full of explanations and excuses, about the regiment "having been ordered abroad when he was ill," and the like; but craving the Queen's protecting certificate.

Nervously he waited the answer, which was a curt note, saying that "the commanding officer had nothing to do with his case: his business was solely with deserters." It ended in Joe, after a sore struggle with himself, having to put aside his unbelief. "I'll trust the proclamation," he cried; "and if the Queen won't pardon me, it's all up." With what tremor he opened the next reply—"On Her Majesty's Service"; and with what thankfulness he read out his certificate for a free pardon.

Does any deserter from the service of Christ the King read this? Let him not foolishly seek to evade justice. But let him avail himself of the proffered amnesty. "Let him return unto the Lord,—and He will have mercy upon him; and to our God, for He will abundantly pardon."

"*The disciple whom Jesus loved*" (John xxi. 20).

THIS is the name the writer of the Fourth Gospel gives to himself. Perhaps he adopted it from some of the other disciples or early believers, who spoke of him so. And we may be sure that there was no description of him that John—for we know that it was he—would glory in so much as this—"the disciple whom Jesus loved." He was the disciple who was honoured by the closest intimacy with Jesus. To him Jesus revealed most of His heart; and we get the benefit of that in John's Gospel, which, more than any of the others, discloses to us the heart of Christ. It was he to whom the place of greatest nearness was given in the Upper Room, where he leaned upon the Saviour's breast at supper. And it was to him that the Lord, when He was hanging on the Cross of Calvary, committed her who was the dearest to Him on earth—his mother. To whom could He entrust her so fittingly as to the loving John? "He saith unto him, Behold thy mother!" How truly this disciple must have been a brother to Jesus, when He could speak of him so at such a moment, and confide to him such a charge!

John was the youngest of the disciples; and on that account you may take a special interest in him. But he lived to be a very old man, and he was privileged to suffer much for Christ in Patmos. God gave him a wonderful reward at that time, in the sight He gave him into heaven; and a yet greater reward when afterwards —through martyrdom, it is believed — He summoned him into heaven itself.

You remember the story of aged John at Ephesus being carried among the congregation, over whom he could now only repeat the words—"Little children, love one another"? By that time he was mildness, and gentleness, and lovingness itself. And it is in that light we are wont to regard him. But there are two things I want you to notice.

Two boys especially may learn a lesson from John. The first is, the boy who *is struggling to overcome a bad temper*. John was not always so loving and lovable as, through grace, he became. He was naturally fiery and revengeful (Luke ix. 54), and there was at one time a selfishness in his ambition (Mark x. 35), which was the reverse of amiable. But the more he was with Jesus, the better he was enabled to overcome evil, in himself and others, with good. The second is, the boy who *thinks that love means weakness*. This is a great mistake. John could, to the end, hate and denounce everything false and mean with the greatest force. His was not the mildness of mere softness. "If we say we have fellowship with Him and walk in darkness, *we lie.*" "He that hateth his brother is *a murderer.*" "He that committeth sin is of *the devil.*" John did not mince matters. He called a spade a spade. Fellowship with his Master only made his love a purer and stronger love, and his hatred a purer and stronger hatred.

May 24   The New Heart.

"A new heart also I will give you" (Ezek. xxxvi. 26).

THIS is a very remarkable promise. There may, as it has been suggested, be an allusion in the words to the hope cherished by at least one ancient nation, the Egyptians, with whom Israel had much to do. The Egyptians, as you know, used to preserve the bodies of their dead by embalming them as mummies. In doing this, they had to take out the heart and other organs; and in their place they put what are called "amulets,"—small stone tablets, with some words of hope on them, pointing to the day when the body would be revived again. For the Egyptians believed in the resurrection, and expected that the heart of stone, for instance, would be taken away, and a heart of flesh put in its place once more.

God here promises to Israel that He will do this for them in a spiritual sense. He will remove the hard, rebellious, stony heart from their breast, and give them, instead of it, the soft, submissive, loving heart,—the possession of which will lead to the life of true obedience and real happiness. You young people are fond of getting new things—new clothes, new books, new playthings. See that you do not miss this best of all new things—the new heart. Ask God for it. He only can give it. But He is willing, as well as able. Take Him at His word.

A little girl was trying, in an awkward waste corner of ground, to make a garden for herself. She used the hoe and rake diligently, but made little way. The tools always struck on something. She spread some earth, and planted a few roots as best she might. But a single night of rain swept away the soil, and with it most of her labour. When the gardener came, he smiled; and, in spite of her entreaties, he took his big pick-axe, and struck right into the heart of her little plot, scattering the roots on every side. She thought that her garden was for ever ruined now. But soon he removed the great stone from beneath, and smoothed the soil again, and planted the roots anew, and promised her more, that she might dress and keep them in her little garden.

That is just what God has to do for us, if we are to have fair flowers blooming in the garden of the soul. The hard and stony heart has to be broken and taken away; and He has to give us the new heart, and to put the right spirit within us.

"*Within and without*" (Ex. xxv. 11).

This is part of the description of the ark, which was ordered to be made according to the pattern shown to Moses on the Mount—"And thou shalt overlay it with pure gold, *within and without* shalt thou overlay it."

The work God asks from His servants is thorough work. Some people nowadays would have said—"Why overlay the ark within, as well as without, with gold? What a waste of money and of trouble, since nobody will see the inside!" But not so God. The ark of His Covenant was not to have a mere outside veneer of gold; it was to be as well finished within as it was without.

There is a lesson here for us, as regards the commonest tasks we do from day to day. They ought to be conscientiously performed; they should be done as well as we can possibly do them. One of the great complaints of our time is, that so much of the work that is done is hurried and shoddy work. Houses are built to look well, rather than to last; the woodwork soon shows ugly seams, if the walls themselves do not begin to crack. Drains are badly laid; some careless workman omits a tile here and there, or does not join the pipes properly. He says, "What does it matter? It is underground, and nobody will see." But fever breaks out, and perhaps a whole family sickens and dies in consequence. And this kind of thing is done in many different professions and walks of life. Remember you that God condemns it. He says—"within and without."

It is told of the great sculptor Phidias, that a visitor to his studio remarked with surprise one day—"Why do you polish that statue so carefully on the back? Nobody will see it." He paused for a moment, and answered seriously—"The gods will see it." Here was one great secret of his pre-eminence. He did his work as in the sight of God, and for eternity. Many a professing Christian might learn from that heathen artist how to do his work.

And do not let us forget the lesson there is for us here, regarding *our character* as well as our work. We are not to be content with a mere appearance of goodness. It is a very false and misleading counsel given by one of Shakespeare's characters—"Assume a virtue, if you have it not." This is the very thing the Pharisees did, whose hypocrisy Christ scorned and scathed. Not only the outside of the cup and the platter should be clean, but the inside too. We may deceive men, at least for a time; but God looks into the heart. And His demand as regards goodness is—"within and without."

May 26 — Crossing the Jordan.

"Ye have not passed this way heretofore" (Josh. iii. 4).

THE river Jordan had to be crossed by the children of Israel, coming, as they did, from Moab. They might, perhaps, have waded the fords at certain places, or have gone over upon rafts. But God led them across on dry land. Just as, with Moses at their head, and with the cloudy pillar betokening God's presence, they had crossed the Red Sea on foot,—so now, with Joshua at their head, and with the ark of the Covenant among them, as the symbol of the Lord's presence, they passed over the river in safety and in comfort. It was an unwonted way for them to travel; but He would show them where to go. What they had to do was, to "sanctify themselves"—to give themselves anew to God, as a people holy unto Him—and just to follow trustfully where their captain, Joshua, led. Whenever the feet of the priests touched the river-brink, the waters stood up in a heap, like a wall, instead of flowing on. Then the priests carried the ark into the midst of the river-bed, and stood there. And though perhaps some of the boys and girls, and grown-up people too, may have been rather afraid, when they looked up at the great wall of water, "all the Israelites passed over on dry ground, until all the people were passed clean over Jordan."

Now, by "Jordan" we sometimes mean another stream which has to be crossed—*the river of death*; and, from the experience of the Israelites, we may gather some lessons about the crossing of that river too.

1. It will be *an unaccustomed path*. The way of death is for us an untrodden way; therefore a path for faith in Him, who leads the blind by a way that they have not known.

2. *A path on which the Lord of the Covenant goes before us.* Jesus has Himself stepped into the river of death; but its waters did not prevail against Him. "Thanks be to God, who giveth us the victory!"

3. *A path to be prepared for by holiness.* "Sanctify yourselves." Without holiness no man shall see the Lord or enter into His rest. Those to whom He says, "I will be a Father unto you," are expected to put away from them all filthiness of flesh and spirit.

4. *A path of safety for all God's children.* Jesus is a greater Captain of Salvation than Joshua; and He is also the Great High Priest. If He is with us in Jordan, He will stay the waters; and even Mr. Fearing will pass over dry-shod to the large inheritance beyond, in the Better Land.

Weighed in God's Balances.   May 27

"Thou art weighed in the balances, and found wanting" (Dan. v. 27).

This was part of the handwriting upon the wall which filled King Belshazzar with such dismay, as he sat feasting with his gay courtiers in the palace at Babylon. It told him that, though men held him in high honour, and though he had everything that earthly rank and riches could provide, his life was, according to a truer test, a sorry failure. For, weighed in God's balances, he was found wanting. And swift sentence, as we know, followed on the divine condemnation.

The balances of God are wonderful things.

1. How *great* they are! Nothing is so big that He cannot take and weigh it. He has "weighed the mountains in scales, and the hills in a balance"; and He "takes up the isles"—such an island as this Great Britain of ours—"as a very little thing." The whole of the world of matter has been created by Him, and He can handle it with the greatest ease. No person, either, is so great that he can avoid being put into the balances of God. The kings and mighty ones of earth, however great they are in their own sight, and in the sight of other men, have their exact weight taken by God. Even the nations are counted as the small dust of the balance, so little does it weary *Him* to hold the scales! And no individual, therefore, will seem very heavy to God. The question is, as to whether his weight is what it might be, and what God has a right to expect it to be. This will certainly be clear to Him. For

2. How *minute* God's balances are! As nothing is too big to be weighed in them, so nothing is too small to be weighed in them. He that weighs the mountains knows also the weight of a single grain of sand or of a dust-mote in the air. And, more wonderful still, "the Lord weigheth the spirits" (Prov. xvi. 2), and "by Him actions are weighed" (1 Sam. ii. 3). God not only weighs bodies, but spirits: actions as well as things.

There is in the Bank a machine for weighing gold; and when a sovereign or half sovereign is at all lighter than it should be, it throws it on one side. With far more accuracy than any machine, our Maker and Judge weighs our spirits and our actions. May He not have to throw any of *us* aside with the word—"Tekel; Thou art weighed in the balances, and found wanting"!

May 28   Rebuked by an Ass

" The dumb ass speaking with man's voice forbad the madness of the prophet" (2 Pet. ii. 16).

THIS is said of Balaam, who was "rebuked for his iniquity" by one of the lower creatures, in his foolish eagerness to secure "the wages of unrighteousness."

It was a very humbling thing this—for a man to be rebuked by an ass. When Balaam was determined to get his gold, and to take his own way rather than God's, a warning was given to him, even through the beast he rode. God opened the eyes of his ass to see an angel in the way with a drawn sword. Balaam beat her when she swerved aside. Soon they came to a narrow place, where the angel blocked the way. The poor ass fell down; and when Balaam mercilessly smote her with his staff, the Lord, who before had opened her eyes, now opened her mouth to reason with him about his sin. She reminded him that she had always been obedient to *his* will, when it was right and possible : why was he so cruel and reckless now? How humiliating to be rebuked by such a tongue!

The words might have made Balaam ask—"Have I been as obedient to the will of Him who is over me? Have I done my part, as man, as well as this poor creature has done an ass's part?" It was a miracle, the speaking of the ass; but many of the lower creatures, as men call them, and *ought* to have the right to call them, are a rebuke to men.

Some time ago, in Edinburgh, a blind man (blind it would seem, in every sense) might have been seen on the Mound, in the neighbourhood of Princes Street, with a dog which he was holding by a string. The dog was pulling toward home. The owner was pulling and stumbling in another direction. The man was drunk! It is an unkindness the animals do not deserve, to call such a being as he a "dog" or an "ass."

God says : "The ox knoweth his owner, and the ass his master's crib; but Israel doth not know, My people doth not consider." Surely, if we consider, there can be only one answer to the question—Ought not a man to be better than an ass?

The Eleventh Commandment.   May 29

"*A new commandment I give unto you, That ye love one another*" (John xiii. 34).

It is told of a high dignitary of the Church of England that on one occasion, when travelling in the North of Ireland, he lost his way. Night came on; and, as the region was a lonely one, it was with difficulty that he found his way at last to a cottage inhabited by a solitary woman. He knocked for admittance; but she was afraid to let an utter stranger in at such an hour. After listening to the traveller's story, the good woman thought she would test his Bible knowledge, if not his character, by putting the question—"How many commandments are there?" "Eleven," was the prompt reply, which made the woman wonder, and made her also thankful that she had not too hastily opened the door. But she was quickly reassured when the stranger continued—"Eleven; for Jesus said, 'A new commandment I give unto you, that ye love one another.'" Acting on this commandment, she then undid the bolt, and let the stranger in.

The spirit of love is one of the plainest marks of a true Christian. If any one's heart is destitute of love to others, he has reason to fear that he has not been born of God; because the Bible tells us that "love to the brethren" is found in those who are truly God's children, and that it is vain for one to say that he loves God unless he shows a loving spirit to his brother also.

Do everything you can, then, to promote the spirit of true love everywhere. Some children were startled by their father telling them one day—"I want to bring two bears into the nursery." "Oh, father, how dreadful!" the children cried. "Not at all," the father answered; "the one is *bear* and the other is *forbear*, and you would all be much the happier for their presence."

"As I have loved you," Jesus says. When *can* we love one another as He has loved us! But we might love one another more than we do, and so call forth and strengthen one another's love. For "kind words wake kind echoes."

May 30. Shadows.

"Till the day break, and the shadows flee away" (Song of Sol. ii. 17).

A "shadow" is something which can exist only where there is more or less of darkness. It is called, in the dictionary, "a faint appearance," or "something only in appearance." The time is coming when, in God's light, we shall see light. Then the shadows will flee away. But in the meantime we must reckon with them in our life on earth.

(1) Some people are *saddened* by shadows. You have sometimes passed from the bright sunshine into a thick wood, or under some heavy cliff, where the sun was hid from view; and, in spite of yourself, your spirits fell. For the time, you had come under a shadow. So is it often in life. People in the midst of prosperity and joy are suddenly called to share a different experience. A bank breaks, and their money is lost. Disease lays hold of them, and they are laid upon a bed of weariness and pain. Or death takes from them some loved one. There may be blessing mingled for them with the pain, even in experiences like these. But they are, at anyrate, shadows. They bring some measure of darkness and chill upon the life. And those upon whom they fall are saddened by them, until God's own light appears.

(2) Some people are *frightened* by shadows. There are persons silly enough to be alarmed at "ghosts." I read lately of a man who was scared, almost to distraction, by what turned out to be nothing more nor less than the shadow cast by a lense like that of a magic lantern. There is one shadow, dreadful enough to the Christless, which even believers sometimes greatly fear, though they need not. It is the shadow under which they have to pass in the Valley which we call Death. Yet a shadow, though it may fright, cannot hurt. And very often God's children who feared death most beforehand, pass through the shadow with least alarm, and over the river almost dry-shod.

(3) And, worst of all, some people are *in pursuit of* shadows. You may have noticed a kitten doing this—chasing a shadow upon the floor; and you have laughed. But what is amusing in a kitten may be the opposite in a being with an immortal soul. And yet many people are chasing after riches, rank, fame, gaiety, with all their might; which are mere shadows in comparison with the heavenly realities they forget to seek. Edmund Burke said : "What shadows we are, and what shadows we pursue ! " He was wrong in the first part. *We* are not shadows : we shall endure for ever. But what flimsy shadows (as unsubstantial as an air bubble) we often chase !

After many Days.   May 31

"Thou shalt find it after many days" (Eccles. xi. 1).

THE farmer casts the seed into the furrows, in the faith that it is not lost, but will be more than found again, after many days. The man of business scatters his capital in various trade enterprises in the same belief—that by and by he will get his own, with interest. What this text from Ecclesiastes urges is, that we are to be no less free-handed and trustful in our gifts and efforts in order to the good of others. There may be an allusion to the scattering of the seed "upon the waters" in such a country as Egypt, where the furrows are flooded by the Nile. At anyrate, the lesson is plain. What the preacher counsels is—to sow the seed of good deeds and generous endeavours with liberal hand, even in circumstances so seeming adverse as to leave little apparent ground for hope; and sooner or later, he says, a blessed result will come.

There is a special encouragement here for the servants of Christ. The striking instances in which the text has been verified in their experience would fill whole volumes.

A minister dropped two tracts near a group of young women, who were standing beside a schoolhouse in the country, as he was driving past one day. Some time after, he was conversing with a young person about her spiritual state, and found that she was rejoicing in the Saviour. She traced her religious impressions to a tract dropped by a traveller, which he recognised as one of his own. A while after, he was called to the deathbed of another woman. She was awaiting the solemn change in great composure, because a saving change had been wrought in her heart some time before. She proved to be the cousin of the other young woman; and to her the other tract had been blessed. She had kept it as a treasure; and when she drew it from beneath the pillow and showed it to the minister, he saw his own pencil marks upon it.

A French soldier, bound for the Crimea, was offered a New Testament by a good man who was distributing books among the troops. He sneeringly said to his companion, "Oh, this will do to light my pipe with"; and the gentleman felt rather sorry he had given his last copy of the Testament to such a man. Nearly two years later, he stopped for a night at a roadside inn in the south of France. The landlady's eldest son had just died, and she was speaking warmly of his goodness and of his happy deathbed. "And, sir," she said, "all his happiness was got from a little book given to him some time ago." She showed the little book afterwards to the guest, who recognised it as the French Testament he had given to the soldier so long before. The first few pages were torn out, probably for the lighting of his pipe. But on the fly-leaf these words were written—"Given to me at Toulon, on—: first despised, then read, and finally blessed to the saving of my soul."

June 1   **The Lessons of the Rainbow.**

" The bow shall be seen in the cloud, and I will remember My covenant"
(Gen. ix. 14, 15).

You have seen a beautiful rainbow spanning the sky after or amidst a shower. Could anything be more lovely? What a splendid arch! And how these rich and varied colours—"all the colours of the rainbow"—melt into one another! It is a picture that could be painted only by the hand of God. Yes; *but have you ever thought of the rainbow's meaning?* For it *has* a meaning, given to it by God Himself.

The Flood has ceased. Noah has offered his sacrifice,—in token of his unworthiness, his thankfulness, his desire that the world, now getting a fresh start, might be devoted to God; his confidence, too, that the Lord's mercy would be continued from generation to generation. The sacrifice has been accepted; and God has given His promise that He will not repeat the judgment He had sent, but will maintain the revolving seasons in their course.

And then came in the rainbow, which God calls "the token of a covenant between Me and the earth." It is as if a king pardoned you for some offence, and took you out of prison, and gave you a signet-ring, and said, "Now, I am not to imprison you again. You have a free pardon. Every time you look at that ring you may feel yourself secure of this." Even so, God, pointing Noah and us all to the bow in the cloud, said, " Look at that; every time you see the rainbow, remember My promise. Every time you see it you may be sure that I too see it, and that I shall not forget or be untrue to what I have spoken."

Let us not merely admire the rainbow, then, but regard it as a radiant token of the merciful covenant God has made with the earth. And let it remind us that there are other covenants (cf. Ex. xii. 13; Heb. xii. 24) into which God has graciously entered with man, the appropriate token of which is the blood of the Innocent, which has been shed in the room of the guilty.

There is always a bow in the cloud for God's people. However dark the sky, God gives them a token for good.

God is always true to His promises. There has never been a Flood again. None of Israel's first-born were destroyed in Egypt. None who have believed in Jesus were ever lost.

God looks upon the bow; and so should we. He says, "I will look upon it, that I may remember." He does not need to be reminded, but He speaks in language we can understand, to comfort and reassure our hearts. Let us, too, look upon the bow, that we may remember, and assure our hearts before Him.

From the Throne of Judgment at last, there proceed "lightnings and thunderings and voices." But the face of Him who sits upon the Throne is brighter than the sun; and round about the Throne a beauteous rainbow encircles His people (Rev. iv. 3.)—fit sign of the perpetual safety and peace of all who dwell beneath it.

" Yet doth He devise means, that His banished be not expelled from Him."
(2 Sam. xiv. 14).

It would be a dreadful thing, would it not, if you were to be banished from home and country? There are persons who have had that sad experience. They have been sent off to Botany Bay, or elsewhere, and never allowed to set foot again on the soil of their native land. But the worst of all banishment—did we but realise it—is banishment from God. That is what Sin has brought; and oh, it is a dreadful thing for a human soul to be shut out from Him who is Love, in whose presence is the fulness of joy, apart from whose favour no true peace or happiness can possibly be found.

Now, God might justly and reasonably have kept us sinners for ever far away from Him. He might have said, "They shall never darken the threshold of My Palace Home; they shall never speak with Me, or look upon My face for ever." But He does not thus put an absolute gulf between Himself and us. "Yet doth He devise means, that His banished be not outcast from Him." He has made a complete reconciliation possible; and He gives us the heartiest invitation, to leave the life of banishment, and come back to Him. David's reconciliation with Absalom was at first only a partial thing. He allowed him to return to Jerusalem; but he kept him for years without seeing the king's face. But with God it is not so. Not only is the way to the Heavenly Jerusalem laid open to His banished ones; but He is willing to take them, if they are sorry for their sin, and sighing for His love, to His very heart again.

You know how the way back has been prepared. There was a great gulf between man and God, which had to be filled on the heavenward road, before any of earth's children could be led home to the Father. How was it to be done?

It is one of the suggestive stories of ancient Rome, that a great chasm appeared long ago in the Roman Forum, which, according to the soothsayers, could only be filled by throwing into it Rome's greatest treasure. Mettus Curtius, a noble youth, heard of this. He mounted his steed in full armour; and, declaring that Rome had no greater treasure than a gallant citizen, rode forward and leaped into the gulf—upon which, the tradition runs, the earth closed over him.

Into the dark, impassable abyss of condemnation, wrought through sin, God's own Son, the Captain of Salvation, leapt, in the ardour of more than a patriot's love. And now there is a highway and a way, by which His ransomed may be brought back with singing.

The Exile Home.

"To be absent from the body, and to be present with the Lord" (2 Cor. v. 8).

Some of you young people have perhaps lived away from home, at boarding-school. No matter how kind your teachers have been, or how comfortable they have made you in your place of sojourn, your thoughts have often wandered back to the old fireside and the loved family circle; and as the time approached for the vacation, you have taken your almanac and scored off each day as it has passed, with unconcealed thankfulness, so eager was your delight in the prospect of "getting home." That may help you to understand faintly what Paul felt when he spoke, as here, about being willing, and more than willing, to be absent from the body, and *"at home* with the Lord." He has much to be thankful for on earth, he acknowledges; and he would not shun duty, or get away from school a day sooner than the proper time. But a strong desire does come over his heart now and then, for which home-sickness is the most expressive name.

Home—what is home? "Where mother is," said a child, with a love-gleam in his eye; and that meant home for him, for it was for him the centre of affection and the place of rest—"where mother is." Home—what was home to the Apostle Paul? "Where Christ is"—that was home to him. "To depart and to be with Christ, which is far better."

"Heaven our home"—why can we speak of heaven so? Because Jesus is there, and has taught us Himself so to think and speak of it. He calls it the Father's house of many mansions, where He Himself has gone to prepare a place for each of His disciples. Every one of them will find that he has been expected, and that everything is ready to receive him, to full comfort and a joy that is unspeakable and full of glory. What love Jesus has for His people! It is He that opens the gate of heaven to them, having prepared for their life of blessedness through His death of shame. And what confidence He has in their love for Him! He takes it for granted that He can hold out no brighter prospect to them than this—"that where I am, there ye may be also." And rightly so; for "where Jesus is" is heaven to His people, and heaven is home. It is not so much the pearly gates and streets of gold they think of, as to be "for ever with the Lord."

> "*He maketh His sun to rise on the evil and on the good*" (Matt. v. 45).
> "*The Lord God is a Sun*" (Ps. lxxxiv. 11).

How very good God is to everybody! The Lord is good to all and His tender mercies are over all His works. The very commonness of God's gifts, instead of making us more grateful for them, sometimes leads us to make light of them, and to take them as a thing of course. But if the sun some morning were to come under a total eclipse, and to remain so all day, it might make us appreciate more fully the great and constant beneficence of God, "who maketh His sun to rise upon the evil and upon the good." And so with many another blessing. Only an interruption in the bestowal of it would be needed, to awaken us very emphatically to a sense of its importance.

But now, there is a wrong effect of another kind that the general goodness of God, in the bestowal of His common mercies, has on some. It not only makes them thankless toward Him, but indifferent and careless as to what sort of persons they themselves are. God is a Being unseen; and they manage, with wonderful ease, to forget about Him and their obligations to Him. They come to regard the universe as a great machine, swayed by self-acting laws; and they vainly imagine that, since the sun rises upon the evil and the good, and the rain falls upon the just and the unjust, it really does not matter what sort of people we are. But this is a great mistake. For all these common mercies, and the effect they have had upon us, we must yet give an account. And, besides, the man who is receiving these in the spirit just described, is forgetful of the far richer blessings which God is willing to give him, and which others, alongside of him, day by day are receiving at His hand.

"You are a saint, and I am a sinner," said a careless scoffer to a Christian once; "but what advantage have you in life over the like of me? Does not the God you profess to serve make the sun to rise upon us both alike, as your own Bible tells you?" "Yes," replied the other quietly; "but He makes two suns to shine on me—the one on my body, and the other on my soul." The right effect of God's common goodness is, to lead us to repentance, because we are so unworthy of the least of His mercies; and to lead us upward in faith and love toward Himself, that we may be made sharers in those better blessings, those best gifts, which He asks us most to covet and which He loves most to bestow.

A Fearless Confidence.

"The Lord is my light and my salvation; whom shall I fear?" (Ps. xxvii. 1).

You must often have been struck with the number of times the word "faith" occurs in the New Testament. I wonder if you have asked yourself what it means, and whether you yourself have any of it, or as much of it as you ought to have.

"Faith," said a little girl in a Sunday school, "means taking God at His word." This was a beautiful answer. Faith is just this —believing whatever God has said, and *acting upon the belief.*

You may have heard the story of the common soldier who sprang from the ranks and seized the bridle of Napoleon's runaway horse. "Thank you, *Captain*," said the Emperor; and the man, making his salute, returned—but not to his place among the privates any more. "What is that fellow doing among the officers?" some said. But he replied—"Fellow! *Captain,* if you please." And when they would have laughed him to scorn, his simple answer, with a dignified motion of the hand toward the monarch, was, "*He* said it." That was faith; and it was not misplaced, for that very day the appointment was confirmed. Do we believe our God as that man believed his Emperor?

It must be noted, however, that by "faith," in the Bible sense, is meant more than merely taking God's word on trust. It means trusting *ourselves* to God—"lippening ourselves" to Him, to use an old Scotch word, which was a favourite with Dr. Chalmers. It means depending upon Him for everything—for protection and provision every day, as well as for eternal salvation through His Son, Jesus Christ.

You have seen a little boy let himself drop from a high wall into his big brother's arms. You have read of the young Highlander who was willing to go down the face of the cliff to the eagle's nest, "if father held the rope." You have heard of the poor children who comforted their mother with the words—"God always hears, mother, when it comes to the scrapings of the barrel." Ask yourself, Have I the faith which trusts self and everything to God? If you have it not, you are in that proportion weak, and when the hour of trial comes you will discover this. But if you have it, the Lord will prove, in time of darkness, your light and your salvation; and, with the Psalmist, you may sing, in the confidence of victory, "Whom shall I fear? Of what shall I be afraid?"

"*King*" (Matt. II. 1, 2).

In these two verses you have two very different kings mentioned—King Herod and King Jesus. The one, a wicked, untrue, selfish tyrant; the other, a holy, just, and gracious Governor. I do not need to ask you which *seemed* the more powerful of the two. It was not the Babe in the manger, but the monarch on the throne. Yet that Babe was King of the whole earth, though the world knew Him not—King of kings and Lord of lords; and of His government, unlike poor Herod's, there would be no end.

Have you ever seen a king? If not, you may have been in Edinburgh Castle, and have seen the regalia, or "royal things"—the throne, the crown, the sceptre. Well, King Jesus has all these. He has *two* thrones—heaven and the believer's heart. He has *two* crowns—the crown of thorns and the crown of glory. He has *two* sceptres—or rather one sceptre with two ends—truth and grace.

And as our own monarch is said to have three kingdoms, King Jesus has three far greater kingdoms subject to His sway. They are the kingdom of nature, the kingdom of grace, and the kingdom of glory. I wonder if you can answer this question—Who is the one man we read of in Scripture as having been a subject of each of these three kingdoms in the course of a single day? See Luke xxiii. 43.

But then there is a much more important question for you to be able to answer aright, and it is this—Have I taken Christ to be *my* King? Am I one of His true and loyal subjects?

It is related of the King of Prussia, that, passing through a pretty country village once, he stopped to visit the village school. Taking up an orange, he said to the children, "To what kingdom does this belong?" "To the vegetable kingdom," answered a little girl. "And this?" continued the king, holding out a gold coin which he had taken from his pocket. "To the mineral kingdom," was the answer. "And to what kingdom do I belong?" he said, expecting that the little girl would straightway answer, with her former promptitude, "To the animal kingdom." But, after a pause and many blushes, she replied, "To God's kingdom, sire." Whereupon the king, greatly moved, with a tear in his eye, and much solemnity in his tone, responded, "God grant, my child, that I may be counted worthy of that kingdom!"

A Living Way.

"A new and living way" (Heb. x. 20).

THE Mohammedans have a strange parody of what is meant by "a living way" in one of their ceremonials, which it was my lot to witness a number of years ago at Cairo. It was called the "Doseh," and it was certainly a sad token of the essential cruelty and folly of Moslem superstition. The birthday of Mohammed was in course of celebration; and on this, the great day of the feast, a welcome was given to a sheikh supposed to be descended from him, by preparing for him and his sacred white horse a living way to tread upon. A pavement of flesh and blood it was, with three Saadiyeh dervishes, wedged in, to the yard; and there, for a considerable time, the poor wretched men lay, with their faces downwards, till the great man arrived, and rode over their prostrate bodies!

The very horse, a noble animal, seemed to know something of what pity meant, and vainly tried to pass tenderly over; but the holy rider was all unmoved, as, with long beard and prodigious turban, he kept swaying his body listlessly to and fro, and looking for all the world as though he were drunk—with something else than religious transport. The dervishes try to maintain that nobody is hurt by the terrible ordeal. All who are able spring, accordingly, to their feet, whenever the horse is past, and the others are carried, as hastily as may be, out of the public sight. In many cases, however, the injury would not hide. Some yelled vigorously with pain; others, with fractured spines, perhaps, had their limbs stretched rigid, and were to all appearance dead. Alas! poor people, that they should expect in this way to commend themselves to Allah, and enrich their Paradise!

The living way to which the Bible introduces us is of a different kind. It, too, is a way of agony, and tears, and blood, but not for us who now are invited into it. It is a way which has been prepared for sinners, even the chief, to walk in—a way besprinkled with the atoning blood of God's own Son—and it leads them onward, without let or hindrance to those who by faith enter and advance upon it, into the Holiest of all. The way is ever new or fresh; for the marks of consecration on it never are effaced. And it is a living way, both because it leads to the enjoyment of life in its fulness, and because the very walking in it promotes the life of those who go in it on the road to God. Thank God that we live in a land, not of dark superstition, but of gospel light and liberty—where the Dayspring from on high has visited us, to guide our feet into this way of peace!

A New Song.

"And He hath put a new song in my mouth" (Ps. xl. 3).

GLANCING down the newspaper columns, I sometimes see advertised —*A New Song*. And the publisher pronounces it "a distinct success," and "sure to be a favourite." One wonders with how many it will really become a favourite, and how long its success will last. Perhaps there will not be very many, after all, who will take the trouble to learn it; and, even if it is popular for a time, there may be nobody singing it before the year is out.

But it is otherwise with the song that is mentioned in our verse. The marvel about it is, that it is a very old song now, and yet that it is always new. Many, many centuries have passed since it was first rehearsed on earth, and first sung in perfection in the courts of heaven. For it is the song that Abel was honoured first to sing there—the song of a soul that has been redeemed by Christ, and must needs pour forth its gratitude to Him. And since the day when its keynote first was struck, and the angels listened to it first as something new in heaven, there have been multitudes whose hearts and voices have been given to the singing of it; and yet it is a song that never tires.

One thing that keeps it always new is just this—that there are constantly fresh voices added to the choir who sing it in earth and heaven. They are those whose hearts the Lord has touched; and, as their thankfulness wells forth in spiritual melody, the song is delightsome and new to them. Nor does it seem to pall or to grow old with use in the singing of it; for its theme, even praise to our God, has in it a perennial freshness, and those who dwell upon the redeeming love of God find ever new matter for their song.

To the Lord, too, the song is always new. He never wearies of the singing of it. Every ransomed sinner, whose feet have been taken from the miry clay and set upon the rock, has a fresh experience of his own to tell, in his own peculiar cadence, which adds an element to the richness of the harmony that the ear of the Redeemer does not fail to catch. The ever-enlarging living flood of melody is grateful to the Lord, whose love has awakened it, and whose sacrifice it celebrates. To Him it always is the new song—sweeter far than even the songs of the angels who never fell, and who, in the long ages before man was made, joyfully sang from a pure heart their Creator's praise.

June 9 — The Lion, yet the Lamb.

"The Lion of the Tribe of Judah . . . a Lamb as it had been slain"
(Rev. v. 5, 6).

THE lion and the lamb are two very different animals. The noble lion is the strong, majestic, fierce king of the forest. The humble lamb is the tenderest, most submissive, and kindliest of creatures. But both names are given to Christ, as showing diff'erent sides of His character.

He is the Lion of Judah—the Mighty Conqueror, who can sweep before Him all His foes. In presence of sin and hypocrisy, He burns with righteous indignation. If you would see how fierce He can be, read, for example, the 23rd of Matthew—"Woe unto you, scribes and Pharisees, hypocrites! . . . Ye fools, and blind! . . . Ye serpents, ye generation of vipers, how can ye escape the damnation of hell?" In reading such passages, one is reminded of the prophetic psalm, which speaks of the coming King, of irresistible might, who is to break His enemies with a rod of iron, and dash them in pieces like a potter's vessel. And the wisdom appears of not paltering with sin and rebellion, but of giving in an unfeigned submission, "lest He be angry, and we perish from the way, when His wrath is kindled but a little."

But Christ is also a Lamb. In that same 23rd chapter of Matthew, how tenderly He weeps over lost Jerusalem! How gentle He is! "He is led as a lamb to the slaughter." How pure and innocent He is! "A Lamb without blemish and without spot." And how precious He is! He is "the Lamb of God." What does that name tell us? It reminds us of God's fondness for Him. A father takes his son into his arms, and fondly says, "My lamb"; and that is what God the Father says of the well-beloved Son. But the name also tells us, that Jesus is the Lamb of sacrifice, which God provided and accepted for our sin. God has, in Him, provided Himself a Lamb, as Abraham said He would, to take away the sin of the world.

And now, young people, do you know what is the most terrible thing in the Bible? It is *"the wrath of the Lamb"* (Rev. vi. 16). I pray that you may not encounter it. And if you can sing from the heart, as you have often sung in words—

"I lay my sins on Jesus,
The spotless Lamb of God,"

you never shall. Ah! what a terrible thing, even to hear the anguished cry of others, echoed back from the mountains and rocks, "Fall on us, and hide us from the face of Him that sitteth upon the throne, and from the wrath of the Lamb; for the great day of His wrath is come, and who shall be able to stand?"

"*It doth not yet appear what we shall be: but we know*" (1 John iii. 2).

HERE is a tiny rill, trickling down its mossy bed upon the hillside. It is swelling a little in volume; it is leaping now from crag to crag; it is seeking its way somewhere. Where is it going? What is to become of it? What is it to be? You will have to trace it far upon its future course before you can, as a matter of experience, give an answer to that question.

Here is a tender shoot, just appearing above the ground. If you penetrate below the surface a little way, you will see the seed from which it sprang. Bending down, you can detect a fresh green leaf or two. Whereunto is the plant to grow? Is there to be a glory yet of foliage, fruit, and flower? To answer that, you will have to wait awhile. "First the blade, then the ear, then the full corn in the ear." It doth not yet appear what it shall be.

Here is the foundation of some structure laid. As you pass along the road, it has caught your eye. It promises to be a noteworthy edifice. You can fancy that you see it rising in majesty and grace—a very poem wrought in stone. But you have not the details of masonry before you; nor has the architect made you the confidant of his design. You see the foundation. You have a glimmering that a great plan is afoot, and will be wrought out in due time. But to see what it shall be, you must wait.

Here is a statue, which a noted artist has permitted you to look at in his studio. It is not very long since he blocked it out. His work, he tells you, is only in the rough. As you look over his shoulder and admire his deft and patient use of hammer and chisel, you begin to see the features taking shape a little. You think you can discern some outline now of what may be a noble form. But the artist carries his own ideal meanwhile in his brain. Stroke by stroke he will work it out; touch by touch it will reveal itself. But it doth not yet appear what it shall be.

And here is a Christian. His future is not all mapped plainly out before us either. It is a future full of promise, bright with hope, and big with safe anticipation of large coming good. But the rill is only at the opening of its course; the shoot just recently sprung above the ground; the foundation of the building little more than laid; the rough-hewing only of the statue done. The Christian was but lately born again. Yet, since he is a Christian, a child of God, *we know*, without being able to foresee every step in the process, that he shall at length be *like Him*,—the Redeemer and Elder Brother,—the attainment of whose likeness will alone satisfy the heart.

June 11   Honour to and from God.

"Them that honour me, I will honour" (1 Sam. ii. 30).

ELI honoured his sons before God. He was more mindful of their will than of Jehovah's; so he let them "have their own way," instead of teaching them to bow to the authority of God. And both he and his sons had their reward. They passed to an early and dishonoured grave; and their father died a broken-hearted old man. He had a high position in Israel, and might have exercised a noble influence on Israelitish history. But he is "lightly esteemed"; and, though in some respects an amiable character, Eli can never be counted among the heroes of Old Testament story. How different from Samuel! He honoured God throughout a long and faithful life; and God greatly honoured him. There is no name, excepting that of Moses, in the Old Testament that comes in still for equal honour.

Is it your desire, then, to honour God? How is it possible for us to do this? It seems strange to think that One so great and mighty should speak of being honoured by the like of us. And yet so it is. We may either honour or dishonour God, in our hearts and in our lives.

We honour God by cherishing right thoughts about Him, and right feelings toward Him. You must never think meanly of God. You must not live as though there were some things He did not know, or as if He might be prepared to wink at sin; but you should seek to have high and holy thoughts of Him, and to reverence and love His name.

We honour God, also, by letting others see, in our conduct from day to day, that it is our supreme desire to please Him. It is not enough to worship God in our hearts. We should pay to Him the homage of our lives. We should make it plain that it is He, and not the world, that is our God; and that it is His will, and not the will of men, that we are most anxious to consult and to obey.

A Scotch boy called Jamie, who had determined to go to sea, gave the promise to his mother that every night and morning he would kneel down and pray to God. On the voyage out to India all went well, because there were some godly sailors on board. But on the way home some new hands were employed; and one of these, a wicked sailor, seeing Jamie kneel, ran forward and gave him a sound blow on the ear, exclaiming, "None of that here, sir!" A friendly seaman, indignant at this, challenged the bully to a fight, and fairly thrashed him. The next night Jamie thought he would make no disturbance, but would quietly say his prayers in his hammock; and, with that purpose, he crept into bed. But no sooner had he lain down than his friendly protector taught him a lesson he never forgot. Coming forward, he dragged him out on the floor, exclaiming, "Kneel down at once, sir! Am I going to fight for you, and you not say your prayers, you young rascal?"

Years passed. Jamie continued consistently to honour God, both in heart and life. And by and by, when the Atlantic cable was laid, the commander of the *Great Eastern*, which carried it, was no other than he. Only, by the grace of Her Majesty the Queen, his name was changed. He was no longer Jamie, but Sir James Anderson, *Knight*.

Even in this life you will not be a loser by honouring God.

"And Moses went up to the mountain of Nebo, to the top of Pisgah"
(Deut. xxxiv. 1).

By Pisgah is probably to be understood the whole of the range of high lands on the east of the lower Jordan; and this range apparently reached its height, or head, in the Mount Nebo. The latter it has not been found easy to identify; and opinion is still divided as to which of the points on the mountain-wall of Moab opposite Jericho it was, on which Moses took farewell of earth and entered upon immortality. Thus it is not only true that "No man knoweth of his sepulchre unto this day," but even the summit on which his grave lies cannot apparently be quite determined now. But God knows where He put the dust of His great servant Moses to rest; and though the precise spot has been screened from the possibility of idolatrous worship on the part of the Hebrew people, Mount Nebo—somewhere in these Pisgah Highlands beyond Jordan —must always have tender and suggestive associations for the Christian, no less than for the Jewish heart.

Pisgah makes us think, among other things, of—

1. *The God-kept graves of all believers.* It is true of all of them, as of Moses, that their death is precious in God's sight. The timing of it, and the arranging of all its circumstances, are in His hand. Their grave, too, is in His keeping. Their very dust to Him is dear. "God knows every grave—the little child's few inches of sod, and the old man's last resting-place, and the sweet mother's, without whom the world would have been a waste. It is enough. These regions are not in our keeping, except in some cases as to their surfaces. The key is in heaven; and as to the time when the door will open, we know not: enough to know where the key is, and to know that it cannot be lost."

2. *The outlook beyond.* There is a noble painting, which some of you may have seen, of Moses sweeping, with his keen, undimmed eye, the earthly land of promise he was not to enter. Who knows what great prophetic thoughts then stirred his soul, or what a panorama of events as well as scenes was laid open to his spiritual vision? One thing we may be sure of, that no distrust or gloom would settle on his spirit. Earth, with its one unsatisfied desire, was now beneath his feet. And as his eye dimmed in death and his natural force abated, the eye of his soul took in more clearly the Pisgah view of the Heavenly Land, fairer than the land of Palestine. The Spirit of God made Nebo the Mount of Transfiguration for his spirit, and gently ushered him into the august but joyous presence, where faith at length received the recompense of the reward. Call that not death, but life and rest. The eternal God was his refuge; and underneath, the everlasting arms.

What a comfort for many a saint in his last hours on earth it has been, to have a Pisgah view of the far-off land, and, what is even better, a sight of the King in His beauty who will bring him safely thither, though Jordan lies between. For while the man of God led Israel only to the borders of the earthly Canaan, the God-Man leads His people in, to full and everlasting possession.

June 13   A Stern Opponent, yet a Real Friend.

"Mercy and truth are met together; righteousness and peace have kissed"
(Ps. lxxxv. 10).

IT is told of a judge that he had brought before him, as a culprit at the bar one day, the son of his dearest friend. The offence with which he was charged was a very serious one; and as the judge thought of the youth's dead father, his heart bled when he looked upon him. But justice demanded either imprisonment or a very heavy money penalty for such a crime; and those in the court who knew of the lad's parentage were thrilled when they heard the severity of the sentence which was meted out. They pitied the lad as, in grief and despair, he buried his face in his hands; and some of them thought, "How harsh a judge, to impose so severe a penalty on his old friend's wayward son!"

But their feelings altogether changed when, the trial being over, they saw the judge lay aside his ermine and descend from the bench to where the young man stood, before he could be taken to his cell, and heard him address the culprit thus—"Young man, it is my part, as judge, not to make or alter, but to administer the law; and I could not in justice have pronounced on you a milder sentence. But, for your father's sake, I desire that you should have a fresh opportunity in life. You shall not therefore go to prison. I myself will pay your fine." He thereupon wrote out a cheque for the amount, which the prisoner could not himself otherwise, by any possibility, have found; and the young man went free.

That was a beautiful instance of mercy and truth meeting together, of righteousness and peace embracing one another. Should it not make us think, and think lovingly, of God? He cannot allow sin to go unpunished. Were the righteousness of God to be in the least departed from in His government of the world, the universe would go to wreck and ruin. But He will never deny Himself: He will stand true to the law, whose sentence of wrath is revealed from heaven against all unrighteousness of men. God's justice is inflexible.

But there is a great pity in His heart. Think not, I pray you, hard thoughts of God. See Him, in the person of His Son, leave the throne of glory, to take His place beside the sinner—nay, to suffer and even to die in the sinner's room! Truth *must* have its way; but so will mercy. And in the Cross of Calvary the claims of both are fully met. They seemed to be irreconcilable foes; but they were not so. And now you find them conspiring for the well-being, full and everlasting, of the repentant and forgiven sinner. But for this, he never could have known true peace. But the peace which is kissed by righteousness is a peace which abides and satisfies for ever.

A Way of Escape.   June 14

"God will, with the temptation, also make a way to escape" (1 Cor. x. 13).

It is a terrible thing to be hemmed in by enemies, *without* having a way of escape. Some time ago, when Britain was at war with the Matebele tribe in Africa, the savages were put to rout by our soldiers, who pressed on, in the hope of capturing King Lobengula, and so putting a speedy end to the campaign. A handful of brave men, headed by a gallant young leader, Major Wilson, pushed ahead of the rest of the British forces; and, crossing a river by a ford, they camped for the night in the immediate neighbourhood of the fleeing Matebeles. It was expected that they would be supported next day by additions to their force. But a terrible storm came on; the river was soon in heavy flood; the rest of the army knew the danger the little band were in, but could not help them; and Major Wilson and his companions could not retrace their steps, so as to rejoin the main body of the English troops. Then the savages, discovering how few they were, and that they were hemmed in between them and the swollen river, came down upon them in overwhelming numbers, and put every one of them to death. How terrible must have been the feelings of even these brave fellows when they looked before, and behind, and on every side, and saw no way of escape!

Now, we are beset in this world with spiritual foes. Difficulties and temptations sometimes seem to hem us completely in; our breasts are exposed to the poisoned spear, and the only alternative may seem a leap back into the dreary swollen river of despair. But God invites us to trust in Him, and to seek in Him our refuge. If, when we are tempted, we cry to Him, then, perhaps in the very moment when we are most hardly pressed, He will make a way to escape.

Have you ever seen a house on fire? It is a terrible sight. Away up on the highest storey yonder there is a mother sleeping with her child. The flames have taken hold, long before she is awakened. But at length she is aroused to her danger. She clasps her infant to her breast, and makes for the stairway. To her horror, she finds it already enveloped in the belching flames. As she stands for a moment, bewildered at the prospect of almost certain death, hesitating to commit herself and the one she loves better than herself to the crackling staircase, a fireman rushes in, and, seizing her by the arm, cries, "Come with me!" And soon he is conducting her, with her babe in his strong arms, down the ladder which has been slung up to the window; and she is thanking God, who, with the danger and alarm, has made "a way to escape."

Our First Home.

"And the Lord God took the man, and put him into the garden of Eden"
(Gen. ii. 15).

THE beginning of the Bible story brings out, very strikingly, God's wonderful goodness to man—the last and greatest of His works, the crown of creation,—into whom He had breathed His own "breath of life," a higher life than any of the other creatures knew.

1. He gave him *a beautiful home*. The whole earth might be called man's dwelling-place. But, besides that great Estate, he had a spot which he could call his Home. Its name was Eden—a very Paradise of beauty—watered by fine streams, adorned by charming trees and shrubs bearing all kind of delicious fruit, and enlivened by all sorts of beautiful and playful birds and beasts.

2. He gave him *plenty of pleasant work.* God did not mean man to be idle. He gave him something to do. Otherwise he might have tired even of Eden, as you yourselves may know—for what active boy or girl would be content to snooze life away in a perpetually idle holiday? God put man into Eden "to dress it and keep it," just as He gives every one of *us* some sphere of duty to fill, some garden or other to keep for Him.

3. He gave him *the place of power*. One of man's Godlike qualities was, that he was able to rule; and he was made "Lord of Creation." He had the naming of the beasts, and the right to govern them. But man was expected to rule in kindness; and, in being allowed to govern, he was taught to obey. To do wrong to God's creatures, we should still remember, is to displease Him.

4. He gave him *the happiest of company.* You can easily see how lonely it would have been for Adam, to have lived always by himself, even in the fairest Paradise, with nobody to talk to, and none to share with him his joy. You know something, I hope, about the value of a real companion and friend. And so God gave him "an helpmeet," one taken from his side, to live thenceforth by his side, his equal. Now Adam fully knew what "sympathy" is: it was the first wedding of true hearts.

And so our first parents lived on together, each counting the other "the better part," and both dwelling in mutual love and joyful converse about God, as well as in peaceful enjoyment of the beauties of the earth. For God Himself was better to them than all His gifts; and the best thing He gave them has yet to be mentioned—fellowship with Himself, "walking in the garden in the cool of the day." How bright a place was man's first home!

Hiding from God. June 16

"Adam and his wife hid themselves from the presence of the Lord God"
(Gen. iii. 8).

THAT is, they tried to hide themselves. But they could not. The trees of the garden could not screen them from His sight. They could not get beyond the reach of His voice—that voice which before was sweetest music, but which sounded to them in their hiding-place like the knell of doom.

What a contrast between to-day and yesterday! *Then* all was bright and fair; not a cloud upon the sky. Adam and Eve rejoicing in the love they bore to one another, and to God, the Giver of all good. *Now* everything is changed. A small cloud has appeared, no bigger at first than a man's hand; and ere long the sky is darkened, and gloom has settled on man's life, and joy has gone out of his heart.

What did it all? Why, it was Sin that did it. The tempter had been at his unholy work; and man had yielded. The step was no doubt prepared for, but it seemed sudden enough when it came; and man had "fallen" from his holy and happy place, as utterly and helplessly as a traveller, by one wrong step, may fall over a precipice into a dark and dismal morass below, from which he is quite unable to extricate himself.

Sin often, as at the first, is made to look attractive; but it is the blackest of all things. It looks very small and simple often; but it is the strongest of all powers, save only one—the grace of God. A little sin brings a world of woe. That is a lesson which our first parents learned, and which some of their descendants are learning every day.

Just as a single drop of poison in a cup may make its contents deadly, so man's first act of disobedience, instead of adding anything to his happiness, poisoned the cup of joy which had been so sweet and full. Ah, how much a single false step has cost the world! And how much a single wilful step may cost some of you boys and girls yet!

From the outskirts of Eden, the voice still echoes down to us—Beware of temptation! A youth was once tempted by some companions, when his father was away from home, to go to a place which his father had forbidden him to visit. "Your father will never know," they said. "But I would know," he quietly, but firmly answered, "and *I could never look my father in the face again.*"

June 17   Our Last Home.

"*Through the gates into the City*" (Rev. xxii. 14).

THE City—of what sort is it, the Heavenly Jerusalem?
(1) It is an *abiding* City. So the earthly Jerusalem seemed to be. Its patriots gloried in its strength, and proudly dreamt that, like its surrounding hills, it would abide for ever. Yet the hour of trial came, and its enemies razed it to the ground. But this is a City which hath foundations, whose builder and maker is God. It has a wall great and high; on its twelve encompassing courses of stones, precious and durable, are the names of the twelve apostles; and they all rest on the everlasting Rock.

(2) It is a *fair* City. So the old Jerusalem, and not without reason, was deemed—"beautiful for situation, the joy of the whole earth," as it seemed to the pious Jew. But this is a City lovelier far than Oriental imagination could conceive. Its glory is not that of domes and minarets, glistering in the Eastern sun; but it is radiant with the beauty of God Himself. The Lamb is the light thereof.

(3) It is a *holy* City. So the Jerusalem of earth was called. It was the centre of Israel's worship, the place of God's holy habitation; and the Hebrew exile, even when far away, felt his bosom glow as with a sacred fire, as he turned in thought to the sacred temple. Yet the reality which corresponded to his vision was at times grim and dark enough, with its scenes of squalor, vice, and wretchedness. But the Jerusalem above is pure "as a bride adorned for her husband." It is a holy City; for it is the City of the Holy God; and a City for holy men.

(4) It is a *happy* City. So the earthly Zion was supposed to be. It was named "Jerusalem," the vision of peace. But alas! for it peace was but a vision. How often, through the passions of its inhabitants and the assaults of its foes, were its streets seen running with blood, and seething with iniquity. But the sound of strife is never heard on the streets of this Jerusalem; the wail of sorrow never rises from its homes; the pinch of poverty burdens no heart; the blight of impurity or drunkenness rests upon no life there; deceit, envy, backbiting, the rivalries of selfishness—black shadows of the earth —have passed away. Purity, plenty, peace reign—unity of language, thought, and feeling—concord of the heart.

(5) It is a *commodious* City. So the old Jerusalem was held to be. Thither the tribes went up; and millions of pilgrims found place sometimes, we are told, within and around the walls, at the feasts when the nation assembled to give thanks unto the name of the Lord. But into this City is poured, from every side, a troop of pilgrim-worshippers whom no man can number, out of all nations and kindreds; and there is room for all. Foursquare it stands with three gates on every side, ready to receive the countless travellers whom the King is gathering in from north, south, east, and west; and *yet there is room*. It is a commodious City; with many mansions—with room for all and a suitable abode for each. But, remember, there is an entrance through the gates only for those who "have washed their robes," and who do the King's commandments.

Lazarus of Bethany.

"Our friend Lazarus" (John xi. 11).

WHAT a multitude of people this "our" includes! Every believing reader of the gospel story, every true friend of Jesus, feels that he has a friend in Lazarus, and a kind of personal share in the sorrow and the joy of the home circle in Bethany. There are few better-known names in the Bible than that of Lazarus; and though there is not very much recorded of him, we seem to know him well.

(1) His *position* was just that of a humble villager. He dwelt in a small hamlet, over the shoulder of Olivet, not far from Jerusalem; and probably few in the great capital knew so much as his name, until Jesus made it for ever illustrious. He was, all the same, a member of one of the noblest families of earth. They were not rich, indeed; they did not even keep a servant. But theirs was the true nobility of kind hearts, which are "more than coronets," and of simple faith, which is better than the most ancient blood. It was a loving family circle, that of Bethany, with room in it always for Jesus; and if Martha and Mary and Lazarus were alive, what Christian would not rather visit their humble dwelling, than the richest palace in the world?

(2) His *character* is clearly set before us, in at least two important particulars. He was a *good brother*, and had greatly endeared himself to those who knew him best. Oh, how his sisters loved and missed him! Do those who see most of us love us best, and will they greatly miss us when we are gone? And then Lazarus was a *friend of Christ*. The Lord loved him, and he loved the Lord. Between him and the Saviour there was the bond of a true affection. "Now Jesus loved Martha and her sister, *and Lazarus*," and the sorrow of their hearts in the hour of bereavement was also His. Behold how He loved him—"Jesus wept"!

(3) His *history* was for the most part an uneventful one. It was not usually a life of much incident or variety, the life at Bethany. But at length one day Lazarus fell sick; and that mortal illness brought him into everlasting fame. For, amid circumstances which you well remember, the "strong Son of God, immortal Love," even while grief filled His eyes with tears, spoke the word of power which raised Lazarus from the dead. His death thus became a means of blessing to others: "by reason of him, many of the Jews went away and believed on Jesus."

Of the after history of Lazarus, nothing certain is known. He has not told the world any of the secrets of the unseen world, which he had visited for four days. As Tennyson says of him, "something sealed the lips of that evangelist." But perhaps, driven from the neighbourhood of Jerusalem by the hostility of the chief priests, he may have done a better thing—preached the gospel of his Lord. The tradition is, that he went to Cyprus, where I was shown, some years ago, his reputed grave—the "last resting-place" for his dust, in view of the general resurrection. How interesting to think that it may have been the preaching of Lazarus that spread the gospel in Cyprus, and won to Jesus, among others, Barnabas, the friend and comrade of the Apostle Paul.

Not.

"That walketh not in the counsel of the ungodly" (Ps. i. 1).

THE little word *not* is a very important word here; and it is a very important word for many a life. The great difference between different classes of persons in this world lies just here—in the use they make of this small word. Some say *not* to God; others say *not* to sin. Some say *not* to others, but forget to say it to themselves.

In this first psalm you find suggested two very different characters, whose course of life and whose end are set in the strongest contrast.

The one is a man, or a youth, who begins by *walking* in the counsel of the ungodly. He crosses their path oftener than he need do, or should do; and he even consults with them sometimes, and has their maxims lodged within his mind. By and by we find him *standing* in the way of sinners. Their evil spell is more upon him now. He has less power, and less desire, to break away from them. He has got into their way, and he is standing in it. And at length we see him *sitting* in the seat of the scornful; quite at home among those who not only are bad in their counsels and ways themselves, but who make a mock at religion, and scoff at what is good.

The other is one who begins by saying *no* to others, and to himself, when he is tempted to evil; and, since he refuses to walk in the counsel of the ungodly, we do not find him standing in the way of sinners, or sitting in the seat of the scornful. For he knows a truer delight than theirs. He has found the secret of true happiness. His heart is God's; and his constant aim, therefore, is to do, and not to do, whatever God's law requires. Not only happiness,—a thing of "hap,"—but blessedness is his.

Have you then learned to say *no* when you are tempted to do evil? "When sinners entice thee, consent thou not." It may be hard to take a stand for what is right, in the midst of your companions, sometimes. But God will strengthen you, and God will reward you. Remember the three Hebrew youths: how, in the most trying circumstances, they braved the wrath of King Nebuchadnezzar—"Be it known unto thee, O King, that we will *not* serve thy gods, nor worship the golden image which thou hast set up." God did not allow them to be losers in the end because of their loyalty to Him. They were afterwards promoted to high honour; but their highest honour was, that they had taught all Babylon a lesson in the reality and strength of religious principle. Theirs were not lives like the chaff driven before the wind, but like the fruitful tree by the living stream.

" A mighty man in valour : but he was a leper" (2 Kings v. 1).
" No man stood with me . . . but (R.V.) *the Lord stood with me"*
(2 Tim. iv. 16, 17).

HERE we have another very important little word—"but." You see, on the one hand, how important it was in the life of Naaman ; and, on the other, how important it was in the experience of the Apostle Paul.

This little word "but" suggests, that there is always (1) *some great drawback in the most successful worldly life.* Naaman was captain of the victorious host of Syria. He was a great man with his master —the right-hand man of the king. He was honoured by the people, too, because of his past achievements. And he was a mighty man of valour—not only a paper leader, but a hero in the field, accustomed to lead his troops to victory or death. Who would not envy Naaman—the king's favourite, the people's hero, the army's idol, the man of sterling virtue, the leader born not made ? "But, but— he was a leper." Ah, who *would* envy him now ? Who would take the gorgeous trappings, along with the leprous skin beneath ? Who would choose the varied honours, with the sickness gnawing at the heart ? The victories, with the constant sense of defeat from an enemy that could not be shaken off ? How that one "but" must have dashed all the pleasure of the great captain's life, and made the best that the world had to offer him seem an unreal and fleeting shadow !

So, in every worldly life there is some jarring note that mars the music ; some fly that spoils the fragrance of the ointment ; something or other in disposition or fortune, or surroundings, that makes full satisfaction here impossible. Haman has his Mordecai at the gate ; Ahab has his Naboth's vineyard, which he *must* get, to square his royal property ; in the fullest earthly cup there is a "but"—a dash of bitter in the sweet.

But we are further reminded by this little word of (2) *one great advantage in every godly life, however tried.* Over against the trials there is set what is called a "compensation"—something put into the other scale—which makes the trials light. This is, the presence and sympathy of Christ. Paul had often occasion to feel this, after he became a Christian ; and he felt it to the end. Near the close of his life, when he is old and the time of his departure is at hand, he has to tell how, when he was brought before the bloody Nero, all men forsook him. "*But*," he adds, "the Lord stood with me, and strengthened me ; and I was delivered out of the mouth of the lion." This "but" made all the difference. It made the absence of others of comparatively little moment. And what Paul felt, many a tried believer has felt before and since his day.

June 21. Laying Past.

"So is he that layeth up treasure for himself" (Luke xii. 21).

THE lesson here turns on the little word "so." There are other important "so's" in the Bible. "Let your light *so* shine before men," "*So* run that ye may obtain." And especially that unfathomable "*so*" in John iii. 16—"God *so* loved the world."

To understand the "so" in the text, you need to read the story that goes before, of the rich but poor man, who lived only for himself, and made such a miserable failure of his life. He was what is counted a shrewd man; but he did not look very far ahead. He dwelt on his estate as if it were his home, his true abiding-place, and he made his plans for many years. But what he lived in was only the house of his pilgrimage. He was but a guest at a wayside inn. And in his plans he was counting without his Host. For God suddenly called him away, and of all the goods he had laid past he could carry nothing with him. His selfishness defeated itself. When death came, it stripped him of all that he had counted precious.

Hence the "so" means, that whoever is worldly and selfish—whether it is money or not that his heart is most set upon—is just like that foolish man. He is not shrewd—he is not wise in the real sense. However eager he has been in laying past, he has not been laying past the true and abiding riches.

Jesus again and again insists that what one *is*, is far more important than what one *has*. It is not the girl with most dolls or the finest dresses, it is not the boy with the most tops and kites and marbles and pocket-money, that is to be most admired and envied; but it is the girl or the boy with the most pure, and true, and loving nature—the boy or the girl with the richest *heart*.

Seek, then, that your heart may be made rich. Lay claim by faith to the unsearchable riches of Christ. He will give you, not only pardon, and peace, and joy, but those inward graces of character, by the blessing of His Spirit, which will be a kind of riches that you will carry with you into the next world, when death summons you to enter upon the inheritance of the saints in light.

"Abba," Father.

" Ye have received the Spirit of Adoption, whereby we cry, 'Abba,' Father"
(Rom. viii. 15).

You young people have your own ideas about God. Sometimes you think of Him as a great Being, who made the world, and governs it; and who lives high above us, in a heavenly palace, with angels and archangels to sing His praise. But sometimes you think of Him—and does it not bring you comfort?—as "our Heavenly Father."

This is a beautiful name for God. It is a name which Jesus taught us. How often He spoke about God as His Father! Did you ever notice that the first recorded sayings of Jesus makes mention of His Heavenly Father (Luke ii. 49), and that His last saying upon the Cross (Luke xxiii. 46) makes mention of Him too? And not at the beginning only, and at the end, but all through His life, the thought of His Father was constantly in His mind. "The Father," He said, "is always with Me."

You, as well as Jesus, are permitted to use this name in speaking about God. And you are allowed to use it in speaking to God. He loves to hear you saying to Him, day by day—"Abba," Father.

But, remember, in order to use it aright you will need the right spirit—what the Bible calls "the Spirit of Adoption." You know what is meant by a person "adopting" a child? It means, taking a child into the family, and treating it as a member of it. But how sad when, after this is done, the child does not show the proper spirit, and has to be turned away again!

A lady once adopted a child in this way, a little outcast whom she washed, and dressed, and fed, and was prepared in every way to treat as her own daughter. But the little one had been already so steeped in evil, and was so utterly bad as well as ungrateful, that the lady felt constrained to part with her. She would be kind to her still, and pay for her board and education, but she could not have her in her home and call her "my child."

But when God adopts, He gives the Spirit of Adoption, to fit us for a place in His family. May that be seen in you—the same mind which was in Christ Jesus! For "the Spirit of Adoption" just means "the Spirit of Christ."

June 23 **Looking unto Jesus.**

"Looking unto Jesus, the author and finisher of faith" (Heb. xii. 2).

A DROWNING man may be said to be saved the moment he steps into the lifeboat. But it is also true that he is saved only as he continues in the lifeboat. So a single look at the Crucified One may be truly said to bring salvation. But it is no less true that, in order to be saved, we must keep looking unto Jesus.

The Christian life, in the passage where the text occurs, is regarded as a race, in which "staying-power" is needed; and the secret of having and manifesting this is here indicated—"looking unto Jesus." What chiefly gives encouragement and strength to the runners is, not the fact that others are running with them, and that there is a great cloud of witnesses, but the privilege they have of looking continually in the face of Christ—who, having traversed the path before them, amid discouragements far greater than any they have to meet, is standing at the goal, with His face beaming on them in loving interest, and His arms stretched out over them in blessing. It is as we keep looking to Him, and have His Spirit imparted to us, that we shall make genuine and steady progress, and at length obtain the prize. Here, then, is a suitable life-motto for you young people who have already given the first look of saving faith to the Lord Jesus. Continue as you have begun. Be thankful that He has led you to begin the race at all. Be yet more thankful that He is able and willing to enable you to finish it with victory. He is not only the beginner, but the perfecter of faith. Keep "looking unto Jesus."

Surely He may expect you to continue giving Him the look of *confidence*. There is nothing which one who is thoroughly trustworthy values more than to be thoroughly and always trusted. Do not hurt Jesus, and injure yourself, by denying Him the tribute of your full and constant trust.

And surely you will not disappoint Him, as He looks to see in your face the answering look, the habitual look of loving *aspiration*. "Like Thee, Lord, and with Thee—that is what I fain would be!" If Jesus sees this longing in your face, as you turn it, and keep it turned towards Himself, He will know how to lead you onward to its fulfilment. Join in the ringing watchword, "Excelsior"—Higher, ever Higher,—Upward unto Him! But, whether in the valley or upon the height,—in moments of discouragement as well as of exultation,—this gentler voice will be your main support—"Looking unto Jesus."

"*I love my Master; I will not go out free*" (Ex. xxi. 5).

THE case supposed is that of a Hebrew who has fallen into debt, or committed some offence unworthy of a freeman. According to the law, he has forfeited the rights of free citizenship; and he may, in such circumstances, be sold to a brother Israelite, and have labour exacted from him in payment of the debt, or in expiation of his crime. But his servitude is not always to last. The trumpet of Jubilee, if it sounds, will proclaim his freedom; and, in any case, he must be allowed, when the seventh year comes, "to go out free for nothing." Only, if he has formed such an attachment, meanwhile, to the household of which he has been, during these years, a humble member, and is unwilling to go out, he may still secure a place in it, by freely giving up his freedom. His master, in that case, will take an awl, and bore his ear through against the doorpost, in token that he is never to be parted from the home circle within. For him, henceforth, there will be no more going out. He will serve his master for ever, but as a freeman at heart—less a bondman than a son.

Now, no doubt it would require a very strong inducement to bring a man thus to lay his freedom at another's feet. A servant would not readily enter into such a permanent agreement with any earthly master. But, in the case supposed, the sufficient motive is not wanting. So thoroughly engaged are the affections of the servant, that, so far from shrinking from a life-engagement, he would feel it the sorest of all compulsion for him to have to go away.

It is the power within the heart that makes all the difference. You remember the story of the sirens, who used to lure passing mariners to destruction with their beauty and their music. One distinguished voyager, Ulysses, managed to pass them undestroyed, by putting wax into the ears of his sailors, and tying himself with thongs to the mast. But another band of voyagers sailed bravely past the sirens, all unmoved by their most tempting strains. These were the Argonauts; and the secret of it was, that they had Orpheus with his lute on board, so that they had ears for none beside.

May you have Jesus with you in the ship! Then the sirens of carnal pleasure will not allure you to death with their most tempting strains. Christ's love, with its sweet constraint, will break the world's spell. As His voice keeps speaking to the heart, you will say to the world's temptations—"I will not go out free."

June 25

Weakness in Strength.

"Then shall I be weak, and be as another man" (Judg. xvi. 7).

SAMSON'S boyhood was apparently a bright one. He was born into a pious home : the one thing wanting for the complete happiness of which seemed to have been given, when this little boy was sent by God to Manoah and his wife. Before, there was no nursery in their dwelling : the laugh and prattle of childhood was not heard within its walls. This, if to any, was a great trial to an Israelitish woman, who, if she had a child, might hope to be the ancestress, if not the mother, of the Promised Seed. But the boy's coming shed such a brightness within their home that his parents called him Samson, "The Sunny One." And now, Manoah feels that his own name—"My Rewarder, the Lord"—is more fitting than ever ; for God has been very kind. It is with pious thankfulness that they observe the growth of the child, and the evidence that he gives in youth that the Spirit of the Lord is stirring within his breast. For a time there is illustrated in him the secret of true progress—"The child grew, and the Lord blessed him."

But Samson the young man out in the world is not the same as Samson the child nestling under the pious parents' roof. He soon shows, in the matter of his marriage and otherwise, a self-will and selfishness that portend mischief. His is, indeed, "a strange, eventful history." He proves himself to be the most curious compound of strength and weakness. Though, as a Nazarite, he is separated from the world, there is in him much of the earth, earthy ; and, all through his life, we seem to see two powers striving for the mastery —the power of the Spirit and that of the flesh. Is it not the same with every one of us ? May there not be a battle carried forward in some boy or girl's breast (cf. Rom. vii. 21-25) which is more important for him or her than a Waterloo ?

As we follow Samson's feats of prowess, we cannot but admire the unfailing courage and cheerfulness that shone through him, even when he was left to fight his battle single-handed. So long as the Lord was with him, he found that "one could chase a thousand" ; and the news of his early exploits made hope dawn again in the nation's breast. But he was not, alas ! to be the Deliverer of Israel. Samson is a sad disappointment after all. Though enormously strong in body, he is not strong in mind, and has not a fixed and lofty purpose in his heart. He is full of whims ; and, even when assailing the Philistines, he attacks them less as a patriot than as a man who wants to avenge some personal slight. And then, when the great giant sinks into the lap of Delilah, and trifles with his vow, and the Lord is departed from him, the secret of his weakness is speedily discovered by his foes. He becomes an easy prey, and is soon a blind slave grinding in the prison-house—a wreck, a splendid failure ! A great soul is better than a strong body. As Isaac Watts sang—

> "Were I so tall as reach the Pole,
> Or grasp the ocean in my span,
> I must be measured by my *soul* ;
> The mind's the standard of the man."

Strength in Weakness. June 26

"Strengthen me, I pray thee, only this once, O God" (Judg. xvi. 28).

SAMSON'S strength, as we noted yesterday, made him only a splendid failure. He was not careful to use his gifts for the glory of God, but squandered them on selfish uses. He could not say *no* to himself. He yielded to his besetting sin—a snare of the flesh. He sought it again and again, like the silly moth attracted by the flame; and he was sadly scorched by it at last. He grieved away the Spirit; and though he was insensible for a time (verse 20) of the evil change that had come over him, we soon see what sin made him, and what sin makes the strongest and proudest of men, when it has its way—a blind slave grinding in a prison-house!

But now the bottom of "the down-grade" has been reached for Samson. He begins to rise again: and at last (verse 30) he is a genuine hero. There had all along been good in him, with much alloy. As the gold must be tried in the fire, so his heart had to be purged with pain. Sweet are the uses of adversity. He gets nearer to God in the prison than he has been in days that seemed more prosperous. His hair begins to grow again, and with it his spirit of devotion, his courage, his might. The Philistines, looking at their blind captive, make sport of him on a great feast-day to Dagon, their "fish god." But they can look only on the outward appearance: they do not read what is passing in the heart.

In that crowded heathen temple, Samson feels, amid their revelry, that it has come at last to a direct and public trial between the religion of Israel and of Philistia. He is a different Samson—poor, blind, groping man!—from what he once was. Yes, a different, but a better Samson. For, in penitence he has found pardon; through affliction he has been purged of pride; and in his weakness he is to find true strength. See! his lips move—not in defiance of his enemies, or in helpless scorn, but in prayer. Then, with his hands on the pillars of the house, he bows himself with all his might. The answer comes. The temple is a ruin; and Samson has fallen with his foes. But he has died for God's honour. The pride of Philistia is laid low. The Nazarite has risen at last to the full meaning of his vow. Given over utterly to God, Samson in death has triumphed by the power of prayer.

May we not see in Samson's death a faint picture of another? Of the people there were none with him; but in his death he accomplished, by his self-surrender, what in his life he could not have achieved. So was it with Jesus. He trod the winepress alone; but, in His sacrifice of Himself in the room of His people, He glorified God, vanquished our foes, and wrought our complete deliverance. What a friend we have in Jesus! "He gives us rest by His sorrow, and life by His death."

June 27 Christ's Feast and Banner.

"He brought me to the banqueting house, and His banner over me was Love"
(Song of Sol. ii. 4).

THE feast Christ gives His people is a better feast than the world's feast at its best. Is has more satisfying fare—food which satisfies the hunger of the heart; and the peace which He gives His people is a peace which the world cannot give and cannot take away.

It is told of Dionysius, the tyrant of Syracuse, that one of his courtiers, Damocles by name, having spoken in a flattering and envious way of the happiness of kings, he prepared a rich feast, and set Damocles in the seat of honour at the royal board. For a time, the sycophant counted himself supremely happy. Amid the palatial furnishings, and in the enjoyment of the costly viands, he felt "as happy as a king." But, chancing to look up, he saw what put a sudden end to all his mirth. For lo! there hung right above his head a keen and glittering sword, suspended by a single horse-hair! And he learned from this practical device on the part of Dionysius, how insecure is the tenure of mere earthly happiness, and how foolish it is to envy the luxury of earthly princes.

But at the banquet of Christ there is no such element of insecurity and danger. His beloved, on looking up, sees not a naked drawn sword, but a banner. And on its rich folds there is a legend inwrought, which is full both of comfort and of inspiration. It consists of a single word—*Love*.

Now, young reader, if you have a place beneath Christ's banner, it means, first of all, that you have been *conquered by Love*. Your heart has been subdued by the love expressed on Calvary. The Cross has conquered. Christ has won your heart. You are not an unwilling captive, dragged at His chariot wheel; but He has made you willing, in the day of His power, to abide under His banner as a trophy of His grace.

And then it means that you are now *a soldier of Love*. Christ's banner is also yours. Your presence beneath it implies, not only that you desire to love all who are beneath it already, but to win by love, to the allegiance of your Heavenly King, those who as yet are among His enemies. "My love to you!"—"My love to you!" was all that a missionary, landing upon a barbarous island in the South Seas, was able to say, in their strange language, to the natives drawn up in line, with their clubs and spears, to receive him. But his face told them that he meant it; and the few words were enough. The clubs and spears were set aside; and soon the missionary and the savages were the best of friends. There is no weapon to compare with Love.

Every One from his Place.

"Men shall worship Him, every one from his place" (Zeph. ii. 11).

HAVE you ever heard of the Dancing Dervishes? It was my good fortune to see them once in Constantinople, and to witness their strange and interesting religious service. It consisted in a remarkable dance, long sustained, with the most extraordinary ease and regularity—each of the Dervishes, with arms outspread, and head leaning on his shoulder, spinning round as on his own axis, and at the same time moving round the hall, and through among his companion-worshippers, in a series of twinings so rapidly and dexterously carried through as to be almost difficult for the eye to follow. There were no collisions: every man kept in his place toward his neighbours. And why? Because they were each and all keeping in right relation toward an imaginary central sun. Their worship was, I believe, an earthly imitation of the praise which is silently rendered to God by the serene and steady motions of the well-balanced planets of the sky.

It is a great New Testament privilege, to be permitted to worship God "every one from his place." Neither in Jerusalem now, nor in Mount Gerizim, are men specially called to pay their homage to the Most High ; but wherever the Father is worshipped in spirit and in truth, the worship is acceptable to Him. Let us see to it, then, that we daily worship Him from our place, and serve Him in our place with true and loving heart.

There is a lesson for Christians from the poor superstitious Dervishes of whom I have spoken. If our service is to be beautiful, and harmonious, and effective—and, if we are to sustain becoming and helpful relations to each other in it—it must be by each one of us seeing to it that we are, and that we keep, in due relation to Him who is our Central Sun.

Then will our worship and service be on earth "as it is in heaven." Not only, as in the material heavens, where all the planets move in their appointed courses, and—though "there is no speech nor language, and their voice is not heard"—sing the Great Creator's praise ; but as in the holy Heaven, beyond them and unseen to mortal view, where ransomed sinners, in the company of unfallen angels, serve Christ, and see His face, and have His name written upon their foreheads! There is no dead uniformity there, any more than there is on earth. There are many posts on high, and servants differently qualified to fill them. "Each in his office waits" ; and there is perfect harmony among themselves, because they are all the while waiting upon Him.

June 29. Holy Anger.

"And the Lord said, I will destroy man" (Gen. vi. 7).

AFTER Abel's death, a little brother, Seth, was born to fill his place on earth. And so, we read, the world went on : good people and bad people both increasing. There were many wandering, like Cain, from God—forgetting, despising, hating Him. There were others who "called upon the name of the Lord"—trusting Him, and seeking to serve Him. The two kinds appear for a time to have kept apart. But by and by they got mingled together; and the taint of wickedness got more and more clearly the upper hand. There were plenty of *great* men in the world—"giants," mighty in stature, very strong, and clever, and famous—"men of renown." But *good* men, of the type of Enoch, more precious than great ones, were exceeding scarce ; and, for one obeying God's Spirit, there were multitudes serving sin.

And the Lord, who has no pleasure in greatness apart from goodness, was "grieved at His heart" by the wickedness of men. He grew weary of striving by His Spirit in their hearts ; and so bad did the world at last become, that God determined to destroy it. But you will observe of what sort was this wrath of God, which so deservedly went forth against sin. It was not the anger which is sometimes seen in men, and was seen, for example, in Cain. It was not a blind fury like that of an enraged wild beast, only bent on sweeping all before it. No; it was *a holy anger*, which did not forget the difference between good and bad. "In the midst of wrath, God remembered mercy." In righteous indignation, mingled with sorrow, Jehovah said—"I will destroy man, whom I have created." "But," it is added,—one of many important "buts" in the Bible—"But Noah found grace in the eyes of the Lord." And God gave him directions for the building of the Ark to the saving of his house.

Should we not be taught by this early passage in the history of our human race, God is slow to wrath ; but what an awful thing God's anger is, when it is stirred? It brings death. The most dreadful of all wrath is the wrath of the Lamb. And what a fearful thing it is, when the Spirit of the Lord ceases to strive with men, when conscience even is hushed and stifled, and they are left to the doom of sin ! How blessed and safe a thing it is, on the other hand, to "walk with God," like Noah ; and how condescending it is in God to invite us to walk not only after Him or before Him, but with Him, as His friends and children ! And how can we be thankful enough that there is an Ark of Safety for our souls provided by God Himself? You have not to toil long years in making it ; but simply to step into it and be safe. Commit yourself to Jesus. Come thou into the Ark !

"*Look every man also on the things of others*" (Phil. ii. 4).

THERE is nothing more contrary to the spirit of the gospel than the sin of selfishness; and there is no duty more plainly taught in the Bible, than the duty to consider others and to seek their good. It is very certain that, by what we are and what we do, we are either helping or hindering others day by day; and, of the responsibility which thus is ours and which cannot be shaken off, we should bethink us oftener and more earnestly than we do.

The ancients had a parable to illustrate the truth that no man can do evil without others suffering too; and it was intended to teach how very thoughtless, as well as selfish, evil-doers often are. A vessel—so the story ran—put out to sea with a passenger on board who was found cutting a hole beneath his berth, through the ship's side. The others remonstrated with him—"What doest thou, O miserable man?" But, continuing at his perilous freak, he coolly answered—"What matters it to you? The hole I have made lies under my own berth." This man had evident reason to be taught, that none of us liveth to himself. So is it with many others. It is sometimes said, as a judgment of charity upon a wrong-doer —"He is his own worst enemy." But none can be an enemy to himself without being an injury to a great many besides. It was a lifelong grief to John Newton, after his conversion, that, in his unregenerate days, he had by his example and influence led so many others astray. The thought of a young midshipman of the *Harwich*, in particular, lay heavy on his heart. Newton's example had led him into sin; but when, changed himself, Newton afterwards tried to reclaim him, it was in vain. The midshipman at length threw himself into a malignant fever through his misdeeds, and died a miserable death, without a symptom of hope in God.

But there is a brighter side to the truth we are now considering. Every true, honourable character, every good and honest piece of work, is telling and shall tell for good, in quarters and in circumstances little thought of at the time. The old smith who wrought with such pains and thoroughness at the big chain in his grimy shop, was laughed at—as we read—by the smart ones who looked in, for his excessive trouble. But *he* would not scamp his work, and the last link was forged as carefully as the first. When, long years after, the storm-tossed ship was drifting on the rocks, and anchor after anchor was lost, till at last the great sheet-anchor with the heavy old chain was flung out, and they breathlessly watched to see if *it* would abide the strain—there was no derision, but deep thankfulness in the breasts of crew and passengers, when they saw that the anchor held, and kept the vessel riding safe through the storm. The old smith might be gone; but the good he had done lived after him. His plain but honest work had been the means of saving the lives of others.

The God of Hope.

"The God of Hope fill you with all joy and peace in believing" (Rom. xv. 13).

Is not this a beautiful name for God—"the God of Hope!" He has many precious names in the Bible; but this is one for young people, like you, very specially to treasure—"the God of Hope."

Why is God spoken of so? For different reasons, I think. For one thing, it was God alone who could have cherished hope for fallen man, when sin entered Eden and wrought his ruin. All was dark in that terrible hour for man, and there seemed to be nothing left for him but despair. But, just then, like a wedge of golden sunshine in a black and cloudy sky, God's word of promise came. He spoke to our first parents of the coming Deliverer: spoke to them a word of hope, which lifted them from despair and utter desolation. And all down the Old Testament centuries, Jehovah was still the God of Hope, pointing His chosen people forward to a greater blessedness than they yet had known, which was to be ushered in by the Coming One.

And now we especially see, in "our Lord Jesus, who is our Hope" (1 Tim. i. 1), how worthy God is of this bright and inspiring name. It is in God's own Son, who came in the fulness of time, that the fondest expectations awakened by that first gospel in Eden, and all the gospel promises which succeeded it, have been realised. It would be still a dark, despairing world, and a black outlook, if no Saviour had visited our earth; but He whose Son was sent to redeem us is indeed the God of Hope.

And are you not prepared, from your own experience, to give God this beautiful name? Has He not by His Spirit awakened bright hopes within your breast? Is it not He who keeps the best hope alive there, even when the cloudy weather threatens utterly to overshadow you? What *is* your most glorious hope, which stretches out beyond the attainment, or the missing, of all other objects, however dear? Is it not this—that you will one day have an entrance into heaven, and be made fit to enter there? And, when sin and failure oppress you, and your heart is ready to sink within you, what keeps you from giving up even the aspiration after better things? What nerves you to press onward and upward again, in the narrow way, in the patient energy of reawakened hope? What but this, that you have the God of Hope to fall back upon, who, having begun His good work in you, will not leave the work half done!

"*What will Thou have me to do?*" (Acts ix. 6).

IF you belong to Christ, you may depend upon it that He has something for you to do. You are perhaps inclined to ask, "What is there for me, for one so young, to do for Him?" It is a good question. It is the very question that Saul asked Jesus, when he met Him on the Damascus road; and it is a question which the Master loves to hear from anyone, if only it is honestly asked.

If you really want to do some good in Christ's name this week, or this very day, you have only *to look about and try.* This is an advice which a teacher, as he tells, once gave to his class with good result. The boys smiled as though they did not believe that they could be useful. But he got them to promise that they would try; and they agreed to tell him the following Sabbath how they had succeeded. They parted; and when the teacher met with them next, each of the five had a smile upon his face, which showed that he had something to tell.

"I thought of going to the well in the morning," one said, "to save my mother trouble; and she looked so pleased, I mean to keep on carrying the pitcher every morning." "And I," said another, "thought of a poor old woman, too blind to read, and I now go every day, and read to her a chapter from the Bible." "And I," said the next, "was going along, wondering how *I* could be of any use, when a gentleman asked me to hold his horse. I did it; and here is the sixpence he gave to me. I have brought it for the missionary box." "And I," said the next, "saw a little fellow crying bitterly because he had lost some pennies, and, when I found them for him in the gutter, he dried his tears and ran off quite happy on his message." "I knew mother was very sick and tired one day," said the last, "and baby was very cross. So I asked mother to put him in my go-cart, and gave him a grand ride in the garden. And how much cheerier mother looked, when I carried him in again!"

All these five scholars found it possible, you see, to make the world somewhat brighter for their presence. "I would have run His errands for Him"—was the answer of a little fellow who, having expressed the wish that he had been on earth while Jesus lived, was asked the reason. That was the answer of a loving heart. But if you feel like him, you must remember that Jesus still lives, and has still some errands for you.

A Rich Inheritance.

"God hath given to us eternal life" (1 John v. 11).

THIS is a great inheritance. It is a priceless possession—*eternal life*. You know something of what *life* means, though you cannot explain it. You know it as the opposite of death; and what death is, at least in the shadow of it, some of you have sadly learned to know, beside the coffin of a loved father or mother, or little brother or sister. Now, *life eternal* is a life that never ends. But it is far more than this, the inheritance of which we speak. It is a life of perfect peace, and purity, and blessedness; untouched by sorrow, or want, or care; in that beautiful city which has no need of the sun, because Christ the Lamb is there, and the glory of God shines in it.

Read, in the two last chapters of the Bible, the description of the blessed unending life in God's bright home, and say—Would you like to be a sharer in that inheritance? Or rather, let me ask —Has it not been secured to you already?

The Apostle John says that is already *his*, though he has not entered on the full enjoyment of it; and he names others with himself, saying, " God hath given to *us* eternal life." Who are the *us* here? They are God's children. And who are God's children? Those who believe in Jesus as their Saviour. In the first verse of this chapter we read—"Whosoever believeth that Jesus is the Christ is born of God." Have you believed in Him—trusted Him as your Saviour? Then God *has* given to you "a place among the children"; and, since Christ is yours, all things are yours in Him.

But if you count yourself a child of God, I hope there is some likeness of your Heavenly Father and the Divine Elder Brother appearing in you. It is told of the Roman censors, that they were so shocked by the dissipated son of the great general Africanus, and the contrast he presented to his dead father, that they refused to allow him to wear a ring with his father's likeness engraved upon it. " One so unlike the father's person," they said, " was not worthy to wear the father's picture." We may be sure of this, that one unlike the Heavenly Father could not possibly enjoy Heaven's happiness, and that it is only those who are like Christ, through grace, that shall be joint-heirs with Him for ever.

The Master.

"The Master is come, and calleth for thee" (John xi. 28).

This is one of the most endearing names of Christ, though at first sight you might not think so. There is no name which in itself has less sweetness in it, and yet there is no name which falls more sweetly on Christian ears than this—"the Master." At no time, to those who truly know and love Him, is there anything of harshness in it. "The Master is come, and calleth for thee," it was said to Mary, sitting in almost prostrate grief about her brother. And as soon as she heard that, she arose quickly and came to Him—not in obedience to a harsh necessity, which disturbed the sacredness of sorrow, but as lovingly drawn to the feet of Him who was indeed "the Master"—sin's Master, death's Master, hell's Master, but first to Mary the Master of her heart. "The Master!" There was to the Bethany sisters no sweeter name for Christ; and if only we can put as much love into the name, there will be no sweeter name to us.

Now, young people, the Master has come and called for you. Have you gone to Him at His call, and yielded up yourself to Him as His disciple, for whom it is the greatest privilege to be taught and ruled by Him?

The name "Master" makes you think of just these two things—*teaching* and *ruling*. To you who are at school, "the master" means your *teacher*. To many of those about you, who are older, the master means the person whom they *serve*. I hope that you all love your teacher just now, and try to learn as much as you can from him; and that, when you boys go out into the world for situations, you will find a good master, whom you will obey with pleasure. But what I am specially anxious for is, that you would take Jesus, now and for ever, as your Master in both senses,—to teach you and to govern you,—and that you would seek to learn from Him as much as you possibly can, and to obey Him always.

Happy are they who enter young the school and service of Christ! Happy are they who early give their hearts to Him, and grow up to be, like Mnason, "old disciples" in His school, becoming grey in the service of their Lord!

July 5

A Walk on Olivet.

" The mount called the Mount of Olives" (Luke xix. 29).

If you were to visit Jerusalem, I am very sure that one of the first things you would like to do would be, to climb the Mount of Olives. In the city itself, many so-called "holy places" are exhibited to the traveller which have really little or no connection with Bible history; and we know that the streets on which Jesus walked are buried many feet beneath the level of the modern streets. But on the Mount of Olives you feel that you are on sure ground. From its slopes you look on the same landscape on which Jesus often looked; and, standing there, your mind and heart are filled with thoughts of Him. What are some of the things the Mount of Olives makes us think of?

(1) The Redeemer's *prayers*. For here it was that He so often found a mountain sanctuary, a quiet retreat out of the bustle of the noisy neighbouring city, where He might pour out His heart in the presence of His Father. On one occasion we are told (John vii. 53 and viii. 1) that—after a day of preaching to the people, and of discussion with their rulers in Jerusalem—"every man went unto his own house: Jesus went unto the Mount of Olives." He had no home of His own to go to; but He sought a home-shelter on the hillside, where He could hold strengthening communion with the Unseen. And though, no doubt, He might have found a lodging that night in the city, or a welcome at Bethany at anyrate near by, He preferred, as often, to spend the night in prayer for the world He came to save.

(2) The Redeemer's *tears*. The Gospels tell us of two occasions only, apart from Gethsemane (Heb. v. 7), in which tears fell from the Saviour's eyes. Once, when He shed those tears of brotherly sympathy with the bereaved at the grave of Lazarus; and the other time, when He shed tears of divine compassion over doomed Jerusalem. As we look across the valley of Jehoshaphat to the city, from the path leading toward it over the shoulder of Olivet, we recall the significant scene when, amid the hosannas of the multitude, "Jesus beheld the city, and wept over it." And it gives us solemn thoughts of the Redeemer's tears over lost souls.

(3) The Redeemer's *agony* and *glory*. Both of these are associated in our minds with Olivet. In the garden at its base—the place called Gethsemane—"He began to be sorrowful" with a sorrow that we can never measure, so that His sweat was, as it were, great drops of blood falling down to the ground; He found there a refuge in prayer, and, in resignation, won the victory. And it was from the slope of Olivet overlooking Bethany (Luke xxiv. 50), that He ascended to the right hand of the Father. What a depth the Son of God had stooped to, in His agony for sinners! What a height He has risen to now, in entering again on the excellent glory above! But as we stand on Olivet we may remember that He is still the same Jesus who, when His disciples saw Him last, was stretching out His hands over them in heavenly benediction; and that, according to His promise, He will come again to receive them to Himself.

"As for me and my house, we will serve the Lord" (Josh. xxiv. 15).

THIS was a noble resolve on the part of Joshua; and we know how true and valiant a servant of the Lord he himself was. In the choice he here avows, and the determination he announces, his family are included with himself; and one wonders in how far *they* stood faithful to the resolution of their noble father. In so far as the example and influence of the head of the household could influence the members, we may be very sure that Joshua's would be a God-fearing family and a pious home. But his hope and ambition for his household could only, after all, be realised through each separate member of the family making the father's choice and resolve his own. That Joshua's home might be all that he wished it to be, it was needful that each of his children should yield his own heart and devote his own life to his father's God.

So is it still. It is not enough for any of my young readers to know that his or her parents are true Christians, and to reckon that all will be well because *they* are serving God. Religion has to be, in every case, a personal matter—an affair of the individual heart. It is a very possible thing for your father and mother to go to heaven, and you to be left without. But what a blessed thing it is when an entire household, parents and children together, are "one in Christ"! What a joy to a Christian father it is to be able to say, from what he sees and knows of his boys and girls—speaking for them as well as for himself—"As for me *and my house*, we will serve the Lord."

Whom have *you* chosen, then, to serve? Young as you are, God has already, by His Spirit, been calling you to decision. See that your choice is the right one. Seek first the Kingdom of God and His righteousness; and you will have every reason, both in this life and the next, to be satisfied with the choice that you have made. A London gentleman who did quaint things, took a curious way once of impressing this truth upon his servants. He called them in, one by one, and asked them to choose between a Bible and a five-pound note. The groom said he could not read well, and he would take the money. The gardener said he had trouble at home, and the five pounds would be very useful. The cook, with visions of a new dress, made the same choice. At last the errand-boy was called, and he said—"I remember how my dear mother used to say, 'Thy Word is better unto me than thousands of gold and silver.' I'll take the Bible, sir!" "God bless you, my boy!" said his kind master. "You will never have reason to regret your choice! May God add to you riches, and honour, and long life!" And as the boy took the Bible reverently in his hand, he found, in the place where it opened, a five-pound note between the leaves. This was a first, though unlooked-for, lesson to him, that sooner or later it will appear that God will not suffer them to be losers who have made Him their choice.

A Hard Life.

"The way of transgressors is hard" (Prov. xiii. 15).

ON the evening of 14th February 1894, the body of a man was found on the railway near Redhill, in England, and in the pocket of his coat the following pathetic communication:—"My name is Robert ——, of ——, Essex. I am now about to finish a revolting, cruel, and wicked existence by an act of my own. I have broken every law of God and man, and can only hope that my memory will rot in the minds of all who once knew me. Drink has brought me to this fearful end. I am dying hopeless, friendless, penniless, and an outcast. And it might have been so different."

Yet that poor fellow was once, no doubt, some fond mother's pride. As she treasured him in her arms as a babe, or watched his growth in early youth, she little thought where his path was yet to lead him. "And it might have been so different!" Different indeed it might and would have been, had he chosen the good way, and walked therein. But the way of transgressors—how often have we seen it!—is hard.

A life such as is pictured in the above melancholy lines is sometimes called a *fast* life. And so it is. For it quickly runs its course; and, however jovial it may appear for a little while, its gaiety becomes more and more forced and unreal: there is all the while a sickness at its heart; and the end of these things is death.

Such a life is certainly, also, a *hard* life. There is a good deal of hardship endured on earth, often, by the well-behaved and well-deserving. But hardship, in such cases, may be turned into a blessing, as part of the discipline whereby they are being prepared for a noble destiny. The worst of all hardship is that which the sinner inflicts upon himself; and the bitterest element of the cup of misery he has to drink is this—"And it might have been so different!"

The narrow way of life, though it may seem steep and difficult at first, is found, by those who walk in it, the way of true pleasantness and peace. It is the way of transgressors that turns out—however broad and easy it appears at the beginning—terribly, unspeakably, hard.

"*Not of works, lest any man should boast*" (Eph. ii. 9).

It is a very natural, and a very common inquiry—"What good thing shall I do, that I may inherit eternal life?" There is something in the human heart which leads people, even when they have been brought to feel their need of salvation, to ask, what good thing they may themselves do in order to deserve it.

Some time ago, I was in Rome; and, among other objects of interest, I saw there a famous staircase. It is called Pilate's Staircase, because of a tradition that it was once the staircase of the Judgment Hall of Pilate in Jersualem—the staircase on which Jesus descended, when the Roman governor, looking upon Him, said—"Behold the man!" When I saw it, there were a number of poor devotees struggling up the staircase upon their knees, without venturing to touch the steps with their hands; and on each step they were muttering a prayer. What was the meaning of this? It just meant, that, by this act of penance, they hoped to commend themselves to God, and to do something thereby to earn eternal life.

Yet this was the very staircase upon which, as he climbed it, divine light visited the soul of Martin Luther. As he was laboriously making his way up the *Scala Santa*, uttering an incantation on each step, he seemed to hear a voice sounding in his ear—"The just shall live by faith." Rising to his feet, he made his way back to Germany. It was no human voice that had spoken in his ear, but the voice of the living Spirit of the living God. And soon he was proclaiming in trumpet tones, which compelled the attention of Germany and of the world, the grand central doctrine of the Reformation—justification by faith alone.

"Not of works, lest any man should boast." You would like, no doubt, to have a share in the merit of your salvation. But it must be all of grace. You must accept salvation as God's free gift, purchased with the precious blood of His well-beloved Son. "Not of works, lest any man should boast."

Faithful in Little and in Much.

"Who is a faithful servant?" (Matt. xxiv. 45).

IT is a pleasant sight, to see a good servant in the employment of a good master, whom he has served so long and faithfully that his master feels and knows that he can be trusted with anything. One such rises now before my mind's eye, though he is dead long ago. He had been fifty years in the employment of the same firm. His employers, at the end of that time, gave him a Jubilee celebration, with a crown-piece for every year of service; so that a witty minister who was present said—"Queen Victoria has one crown; but John has fifty crowns!"

"Who then *is* a faithful servant?" I would answer—

1. He is *one whose heart is wholly in his Master's work*. It is a rule which knows no exceptions, that where a servant's heart is divided, he is found faulty. If anyone is trying to serve both God and Mammon—Christ and the world—he will be doing his best for neither. And, certainly, such an one is not a faithful servant in the sight of God. He expects His people to serve Him with the whole heart.

2. He is *one who is as careful of his Master's interests as if they were his own*. This, indeed, follows from what has been said already. If there is the single heart, and that entirely yielded to the Lord, there will be the single eye as well, to the advancement of the Master's plan. I like to hear a workman speak, not of "their concern," but of "our concern"—not of "their firm," but of "our firm"; and to see him working for his employers as eagerly as if he were "on his own account." And so should it be with the Christian. There should be no thought of "mine" as against "thine" between him and his Lord.

3. He is *one who is observant of details of duty*. He is not content to do well on the whole, but is bent on doing wholly well. And so he is attentive to little things. Society everywhere is suffering from negligence about matters of detail; and so is the Christian Church. The faithful servant is one who not merely is "interested in everything that is good"; but who is so interested in his own particular piece of work that he is resolved to do *it*, at anyrate, thoroughly well. The little sins, little failings, little errors, little opportunities, little duties are not overlooked by "the faithful servant."

3. He is *especially one in whom the fear of God is mingled with regard for man*. A servant-girl was asked what difference her conversion had made in her character and conduct. Her reply was— "I always sweep below the mats now, sir." Nobody likes, even in the petty affairs of life, to have to do with people whom we can trust no farther than we can see them. But when a person lives "in singleness of heart, fearing God," he can be trusted, in things great or small. In the Church, or out in the world, such an one may be safely relied upon as "a faithful servant."

"Acquaint now thyself with Him, and be at peace" (Job xxii. 21).

PEACE is a boon which all men crave ; and here we are taught the true way of attaining it.

The very word peace is pleasant to our ears ; and at this season of the year the eye loves to rest upon the quiet scenes of nature, such as some of you will be visiting in the holidays. The summer landscape, with its waving fields, and its cattle browsing on the sunny mead, near the tranquil homestead, over which the smoke wreathes lazily to heaven ; or the still evening scene, by the peaceful hamlet, near the river or the lake, on whose gently rippling waters dances the fair moon's silvery sheen—which of us does not love to dwell upon scenes like these, just because they speak to the heart as well as the eye, as visions of peace ?

But what men long for is, a deeper peace than any which Nature has to offer : a peace which can only be found in God.

The conscience is ill at ease because of sin, which is the great disturber in God's universe. The heart is troubled with doubts and questionings for which earth has no satisfying answer. The life is vexed with petty cares and trivial annoyances, from which, even if heavy trial be absent, a haven of retreat is sighed for. And he who longs for a refuge, and asks where peace of conscience, heart, and life is to be found—must find his answer here—" Acquaint thyself with God." Not in a place, but in a Person : a living, loving One, into whose ear we may pour our penitence, and our trouble, and our inner conflict—to whom we may bring our petty vexations, as well as our weightier burdens—in such an One as God must we seek relief. And if only we are rightly acquainted with God, we shall be comforted in drawing near to Him, just as your little burdened heart was often comforted in early childhood, and perhaps since then, as you found a refuge in your mother's lap.

The knowledge of God which brings peace, is that knowledge of Himself to which His Spirit leads us, through what He has been graciously pleased to reveal in His Word, and especially in the person and work of Him who could say, "He that hath seen Me hath seen the Father." And it is not a mere laying-hold with the head of certain truths about Him. It is the kind of acquaintance which can only be obtained by living with a person—walking with Him, as Enoch walked with God, and holding daily personal converse with Him. To this acquaintanceship with Him, God in Christ most lovingly invites you. You are guilty ; but He is the guilty sinner's Peace. You are perplexed ; but He is made of God unto us wisdom, and you may commit your way tranquilly to Him. You are perturbed and vexed in spirit. Draw near, John-like, to Jesus, and pillow your head upon His breast ; and the peace of God which passes understanding will fill your soul. What a Friend we have in Jesus !

July 11   A Lie in the Right Hand.

"He cannot deliver his soul, nor say, 'Is there not a lie in my right hand.'"
(Isa. xliv. 20).

THIS is the sad position of the idolater, as he is described in this chapter. Though he has taken a bit of the very wood with which he has cooked his dinner, and made an idol of it, before which he has fallen down in worship, crying, "Deliver me, for thou art my god," and though the stock of a tree can certainly bring him no sympathy or succour, he goes on in his delusion. He is far too much debased, and too utterly blinded by his idolatry, to arouse himself to the perception that his heart has been deceived, and that what he has been mainly resting upon is nothing better than a sham. If divine light, the knowledge of the true God, do not visit him, he will go down to death "with a lie in his right hand."

So is it still with multitudes. There are comparatively few who are, like Ananias and Sapphira, smitten down by death in the very act of uttering falsehood. But how many there are who pass into the unseen world, leaning, not upon the strong and infallible support of the divine promise, but upon some frail earthly reed, which will not bear their weight at all amid the dark and deep defiles of the Valley of Death, but will fail them in the hour when they need it most, and pierce them to the heart!

How different is the experience of those who advance to meet the shadows with the truth of God in their right hand—knowing that they have *that* to lean all their weight upon which will infinitely more than bear, in any emergency, whatever strain they may require to put upon it!

So was it, very literally, with a young missionary, named Cotter, who set off with other three Englishmen, in 1890, to carry the gospel to the poor heathen in the heart of Africa. Hardly had they landed on the African coast when young Cotter fell sick and died; and they buried him with something in his right hand that he counted very precious. What do you think it was? It was a little bit of paper merely, containing the message he had gone out to Africa to tell to the poor benighted people there: "The blood of Jesus Christ, His Son, cleanseth us from all sin." On his deathbed, far away, he kept that little slip of paper in his hand; and, when death approached, he asked that it might never be taken from him. And so, we are told, it still lies in that dead hand in that distant land! He died with *the* truth in his hand, and, still better, in his heart, in the strength of which death may be met without danger and without fear—that in Jesus Christ, God's Son, we have an all-sufficient Saviour.

"She loved much: but to whom little is forgiven, the same loveth little"
(Luke vii. 47.)

THERE is one thing which Jesus does look for in those whom He has blessed; and that is, the love of a grateful heart. It is indeed true that what He has done for us was not done for a recompense. Nothing is more certain than that the love and sacrifice of Jesus never can be recompensed by mortal man. But "the coin of the heart," as the Irishman called his gratitude, will surely be freely given to Him by those who are partakers of His benefits. This He has shown us that He values; and He more than hints that, where there is no desire to express it to Him, the reason must just be, that His blessing has not been really sought and accepted at all.

The woman in this touching Gospel story did not earn forgiveness by her loving words and deeds; but by these she showed that she had been consciously forgiven much, and felt deeply thankful for the blessing she had received from Jesus in her soul. The formal, cold-hearted Pharisee, again, too plainly showed that he did not feel that he had anything to be thankful for to Jesus. The truth was, that he had not seen himself to be a sinner yet, and that the last thing he would have thought of in his pride was, to come with his sin to the Nazarene and ask forgiveness at His hands. The Lord brings all of us to a searching touchstone when He asks, "Lovest thou Me?"

The mate of an Atlantic liner thus describes the thankfulness of a passenger who had fallen overboard on a rough but moonlit night, and whose life the mate and two sailors had saved at the peril of their own. Drawn helpless into the boat, and at length brought in safety to the deck, the poor man was too exhausted to be able either to walk or to speak. "He clasped our feet, and began to kiss them. We disengaged ourselves from his embrace. He then crawled after us, and, as we stepped back to avoid him, he followed us—looking up at one moment with smiles and tears; and then, patting our wet footprints with his hand, he kissed them with eager fondness. I never saw such a scene in my life. During the rest of the voyage he showed the deepest gratitude, and, when he reached the port, loaded us with presents."

Was not this very like the woman who washed the feet of Jesus with her tears, and found a ready towel in her flowing hair, and who kissed his feet, and anointed them with the ointment? Who would not be grateful to a sailor who rescued him from drowning? Who would not be grateful to a Saviour who has saved his soul from death?

July 13

Sad Ignorance.

" Thou knewest not the time of thy visitation " (Luke xix. 44).

THE case of the Jews was surely a very sad one. They professed to be looking for the Messiah, and some of them at least were eagerly longing for Him. Yet, when Christ came, they did not receive Him. They were looking for Him of whom the prophets spake. And, lo, He was among them. But they knew it not.

There is a story of an old Irishwoman, told by James Gilmour the missionary, which illustrates what sometimes happens still under the gospel. The poor old body was grieving her heart out because her son in America had not sent her money for the payment of her debts. Yet, all the while, there was the post-office order in her hand, which his letter had enclosed ! To her, it seemed a valueless piece of paper. She did not appreciate its worth, though it was more than she needed for the purpose on which her heart was so much set !

An anxious sinner sometimes goes on sighing for deliverance, crying out for a Saviour, when all the while the Saviour is just at hand, and the promissory-note is his, if he will use it—" Believe in the Lord Jesus Christ, and thou shalt be saved." And sometimes an anxious-minded saint allows his peace to be needlessly disturbed by sad forebodings, and his heart oppressed by unnecessary burdens, through failing to appreciate the literal truth of the assurance— "The Lord will provide"; and to obey in all circumstances the invitation—" Cast thy burden on the Lord, and He shall sustain thee . . . Cast *all* your care upon Him, for He careth for you ! "

You may, perhaps, have heard the story of the vessel which had wandered out of her course so long and far, that the supply of water was quite exhausted. The crew were in great distress. Coming in sight of another ship, they signalled her. On getting within hailing distance, they told their trouble. Back came the answer, in trumpet tones of wonderful cheer—" You are in the mouth of the Amazon. Dip and drink ! " Down went the buckets into what had seemed to them the briny deep; and up came the welcome supply of fresh river-water, to slake their burning thirst. They had been well-nigh perishing for lack of what was all around them, and was freely theirs for the taking ! Even so, there are souls dying of thirst while the water of life is within their offer, and within their reach, if they will but "stoop, and drink, and live."

"Concerning faith have made shipwreck" (1 Tim. i. 19).

In early life you are at the outset of a voyage on a great ocean. How long the voyage is to last you cannot tell, or how stormy the weather you have to encounter may be. But I hope you do know what port you are making for, and that you have taken right precaution, and made due provision, for reaching it in God's good time?

The port of everlasting safety and unspeakable blessedness is Heaven. Everybody starts with some vague expectation of getting there. But multitudes never arrive at that haven, because they have not a proper pilot on board their vessel; they do not sail by the proper chart; they do not have in store the necessary provision for their souls' life; and they are not minded to attend to the ship's duties, which are so incumbent on those who are to make a safe and successful voyage.

It is terribly possible to make shipwreck of the life. Be not high minded, but fear. There are many rudderless wrecks, broken and dismantled, floating keel upward on the ocean of society, and which, though they started on the voyage in gay security, are now the sport of wind and tide. God save you from such a doom! May He in mercy grant, that under no stress of stormy weather—on no reef of subtle temptation, or quicksand of unsettling doubt—through no leak of evil habit—by no sub-current of bad influence, you may suffer shipwreck! There is a little prayer, which the fishermen of Brittany are said to utter as they launch out into the deep, which is very suitable for you to use—"Keep me, my God; my boat is small, and the ocean wide."

See that you have Christ with you in the ship. Trust Him as your Pilot, and obey Him as your Captain. Be thankful to be always guided in accordance with the dictates of God's Word—that true chart which never misleads. Do not forget the prayer—"Keep me; my boat is small, and the ocean wide." And, while you pray, use under Christ's direction all the means appointed for safety. Then, even in the darkest night, God will cheer you with a star of hope; and whatever experience you have to go through in the interval, your vessel will not fail to reach the harbour. You will come in, not as a dismantled hulk, but with sails set and colours flying; and an abundant entrance will be administered to you within the Heavenly Kingdom.

Becoming Stars.

"*As the stars for ever and ever*" (Dan. xii. 3).

PEOPLE often seek to be "stars" among men—to get credit for brilliance, to shine among others, for this or that which they have been or done. Thus, one man gets to be reckoned a great soldier, and he becomes a "star"; a great singer, and he is a "star"; a great orator, and they call him a "star." You boys sometimes wonder, "What shall I be?" and you hope to be and to do great things some day. You girls, too, have your own quieter ambitions. You also hope to "shine."

But, remember, the brightest earthly lustre fades. Its brilliancy dies away, and is soon lost sight of, if not quite forgotten. "Seek not great things for thyself." Do not covet honour from men, but that which cometh from God only. Aspire to a place among *His* stars. Then your light will never go out in darkness. You will shine in enduring splendour.

It is those "who turn many to righteousness" who are to shine "as the stars for ever and ever." And do you not think that this is the kind of achievement most deserving of everlasting honour? Is not this the noblest kind of life—if we have found the true wisdom and righteousness ourselves, to seek that others may be led to Jesus too? The Lord charges the disciples, *so* to shine that they may glorify our Father who is in heaven. To shine merely for the sake of shining, or in order to self-glorification, is a poor thing. But it is a great thing, to shine so that others may be helped, and the name of Jesus glorified.

In the sky, at night, there are some stars that shine more brightly than others. One star differs from another star in glory. So, there are some saints who shall be more radiant in heaven than others—who shall reflect, that is, more of the glory of Christ, than others who have merely obtained, through grace, a place in the bright land for themselves. They shall be singled out for honour—not because they were great, or wise, or mighty in the world's esteem, but because they were wise in the sight of God, and earnest in leading wandered ones to Him. Good Matthew Henry said: "I would rather win one soul for Christ than mountains of gold and silver for myself." And, doubtless, he is "a bright particular star" in the heavenly firmament. Are you to be another?

A Lesson from Mount Moriah.

"By faith Abraham, when he was tried, offered up Isaac" (Heb. xi. 17).

ISAAC was a type of Jesus. It is a great thing to be able to say of him, but it is true, that his name, more than almost any other name in the Old Testament, makes us think of Jesus. This is the case, not merely because there was in Isaac so much of the meekness and gentleness of Christ, but because, in being offered on Mount Moriah, he points us so directly to "the Lamb of God, which taketh away the sin of the world."

It is a beautiful story. You remember how God "tempted," that is *tried*, Abraham in the tenderest place—put him to the proof, by asking him to part with what was dearest to him—"his son, his only son Isaac, whom he loved." Abraham was asked, not only to give him up, but to put him to death with his own hand, in sacrifice to God. Then you remember how he rose up early in the morning and journeyed for three long sad days with his darling son; and how, as they climbed the slopes of Moriah, Isaac innocently put a question which must have stabbed his father to the heart, and got an answer back the full meaning of which Abraham himself did not know—"God will provide Himself a Lamb." Then, how the altar was made, and the wood set in order, and Isaac (though a big lad and well able to resist) laid and willingly bound upon the altar; and how, just as Abraham was about to plunge the knife into the heart of his son, God stayed his hand, and told him rather to offer a ram, which he would see caught in the thicket near by, in the stead of his son.

What a touching tale! It should make us *wonder at the faith and obedience of Father Abraham*, and ask, whether we would be willing to give up what is dearest to us at at God's bidding, assured that He would make it turn out for the best? It should make us also *admire Isaac's submission*, in freely yielding himself to death, because God asked it and his father said it would be right, though neither of them could understand it. But it should especially make us *adore the love of God*, who, though He spared Abraham's son, did not spare His own, His only-begotten Son, but "delivered Him up for us all"; and *the love of that Son Himself*, our Saviour, Jesus, who loved us and gave Himself for us, and died for our sins on the cruel cross of Calvary.

Living to Purpose.

"Let us not be weary in well-doing" (Gal. vi. 9).

I HOPE you are living to purpose, and to a good purpose. An aimless life is not a life worthy of an immortal being; and the proper aim for such an one is, to live so as best to promote the glory of God and the good of men.

No doubt one who has this great end before his eyes will have a good deal to dishearten him from time to time. But he must be true to his purpose, and never suffer his energies to flag; for perseverance will certainly, by God's blessing, have its reward.

There is a French proverb—"One may go far after he is tired"; and an old English one, which we used to write in our copy-books at school—"Patience and perseverance surmount all obstacles."

A little boy, after a snow-storm, was trying to cut a path through a great bank of snow that stood before his grandmother's door. He had only a little shovel and a little strength. But he gave a good and brave answer to the passer-by who cried—"How do you expect to get through that great drift?" The little fellow, without slacking his work, replied—"By keeping *at it.*"

These words of Sir Thomas Fowell Buxton are well worthy of being learned off by heart: "The longer I live, the more I am certain that the great difference between men, between the feeble and the powerful, the great and the insignificant, is *energy—invincible determination*—a purpose once fixed, and then death or victory. That quality will do anything that can be done in this world; and no talents, no circumstances, no opportunities, will make a two-legged creature *a man* without it."

There is great truth in these words; and whatever you are to be, you should remember and act upon them. Do not forget them in the religious life. God invites you there to be of good courage and of strong determination. He does not promise harvests to the idler, or to the fitful and half-hearted. But He does assure those who trust in Christ, and seek in His strength to do their duty, that the harvest will come. "In due season we shall reap, if we faint not."

"He shall be called a Nazarene" (Matt. ii. 23).

This name was no doubt given to Jesus in contempt, and it became a nickname afterwards for His followers, who were scornfully called "the sect of the Nazarenes." But, so far as Jesus was concerned, the name brought Him no dishonour—rather the reverse.

Nazareth, it is true, was a very *humble* place. There is no mention of it in the Old Testament, and there were no great events in its history. But it was just like our lowly Saviour to be counted among the obscure villagers there. He not only stooped to earth, but became a member of the subject Jewish race; and not a citizen of the great Jerusalem, but a Galilean countryman, and a dweller in one of the smallest and most despised towns in Galilee. And even in Nazareth He was not a child in one of the rich families in it, but was known in the place as "the carpenter's son," working for daily bread in the shop of "His father Joseph."

Nazareth, moreover, was a very *wicked* place. Perhaps this is what Nathanael refers to when he says, "Can any good thing come out of Nazareth?" The people there seem to have been specially hardened. It was in itself a quiet nook, up among the hills; but it was close upon the great caravan route between Egypt and Syria, and it is thought that many bad people may have stopped there, and corrupted the morals of the town. Yet it was this bad place that was honoured, for nearly thirty years, by the presence in it of the one perfectly pure and holy life which the world has seen outside of Eden.

For you, young people, the name "Nazarene" must have special interest, because it makes us think of our Saviour's early days. May you be like the holy child Jesus, who "waxed strong in spirit, filled with wisdom; and the grace of God was upon Him." How happy would your homes as well as your own lives be, if you were as pure, and loving, and diligent, and obedient as He was, who, though the Son of God, was not ashamed to be "called a Nazarene."

July 19

As Lights in the World.

"Among whom ye shine as lights in the world" (Phil. ii. 15).

A poor fisherman was out in his little boat one night, and was overtaken by a storm. The darkness deepened. He was driven near the shore—so near that the great beetling cliffs could be dimly seen almost hanging over him. But he dared not make for shore; for there was only one safe but narrow pathway to the land on all that coast, and he could not find it for the darkness. Suddenly, as he drifted on, his eye caught sight of a light upon the shore. He turned the prow landward, and pulled with all his might. Soon he was in the place of shelter. And, as he thankfully moored his boat and clambered up the beach, he found that the light had come from his own cottage window, where his loving child had set a lamp, trembling for her father tossed upon the sea.

Was he thankful for his safety? Yes. As the great rough fisherman clasped his motherless daughter to his breast, he lifted his heart in praise to God, who had put it into *her* heart to guide him on that dark night "into the way of peace." But he did more. His gratitude was not spent in words. He vowed, and kept true to his resolve, that *every dark night* there would shine from his humble dwelling a light for those at sea.

This is the true spirit of the gospel. That is a poor soul who is careful only for himself. As we have opportunity, we should seek to do good to all men. If we have ourselves received the true light of the gospel, we should transmit it to others. What a blessed thing, to turn even one sinner from the error of his way, and to save one soul from death!

The apostle here reminds believers in Christ, that they ought to shine for Christ. This is a sin-darkened world; and each of them should be like the lighthouse, sending a bright gleam outward upon the gloomy waters. There are two ways in which they are to shine as lights in the world. The first is—by what they are, by their *character*: as "blameless and harmless, the sons of God, without rebuke." The second is—by what they do and speak: "holding forth the word of life." Even you boys and girls can commend the gospel, if the same mind is seen in you as was also in Christ Jesus. You may not be called to speak much for Jesus; but a humble, loving, obedient, self-giving spirit, like His own, will speak better for Him than many words.

"*I have found a ransom*" (Job xxxiii. 24).

The word "ransom" is just another form of the word *redemption*; and it literally means, "a buying back"—very often in order to release from captivity.

Every now and again we read in the newspapers of the brigands in Sicily, or in Greece, laying hold of some rich citizen, and carrying him off to their mountain fastnesses, where they keep him in concealment, and refuse to give him up, except on the payment of a large sum of money. It might be possible to overpower the brigands by superior force; but they usually threaten that, if this is attempted, their captive will certainly be put to death. And very often the friends of the latter are glad to make terms, by paying down the sum demanded for their friend's release. This money, which is the price of his liberty, is called a "ransom."

Now, in order to deliver the souls of men from the captivity of sin, a great redemption-price was needed. All the money in the world would not suffice to set even one soul free. But God is able to say—" I have found a Ransom." Surely this should be welcome news to the captive and oppressed—" There is a prospect of liberty for you; for a Ransom has been found!"

You know what the ransom-price has been—the life of God's own Son! This was the very purpose for which He came to earth—" not to be ministered unto, but to minister, and to give His life a ransom for many." We were held in righteous bondage, under the condemning law; but Jesus has borne the penalty for us, that we might be set free. He was sent, and gladly came, that even through His blood He might set at liberty them that were bound.

You have heard of Joan of Arc, the peasant-maiden of the Vosges, in France, whose pious and patriotic enthusiasm aroused her countrymen to beat back the invading English foe. It is told of her that, when asked what reward she would have for the remarkable service she had rendered, at the peril of her life, to her country, she sought nothing for herself, but asked, "that the inhabitants of her native village of Domremy should be relieved of all their taxes." And accordingly, for hundreds of years afterwards, the taxes of the villages there were cancelled in the Government books, for the sake of Joan, the Maid of Orleans. But what is this compared to the benefits secured to His people for ever, by Him who gave His life as the price of their redemption! There is everlasting joy upon the heads of "the ransomed of the Lord."

July 21 — Our Duty.

"We have done that which was our duty to do" (Luke xvii. 10).

"DUTY" means that which is *due* from us to God and man—that which we are bound to do, or to refrain from doing, if we would be worthy of ourselves and of the place we fill in this world of God's.

Jesus here teaches His disciples, that when, in any particular case, they have given obedience to their Master's will, it is nothing to be specially proud of, because this was their duty, and nothing more. It is a bad sign of anyone if he is disposed to boast in such a case, or to imagine that he has established any sort of claim upon God. But it is a good characteristic of anyone, to be found ever anxious to do his duty, while humbly conscious that, at the best, he is but an unprofitable servant of the Lord.

A man once excused himself to his superior, who was reproving him for repeated misconduct, by saying, that "at anyrate he never misbehaved when he was *on duty*." "On duty?" was the answer; "and when may a man, and a professing Christian man, be said to be *off* duty?" It is a profound mistake for anyone, whatever his sphere may be, to suppose that he can divest himself of duty at certain times and in certain places, just as a policeman may throw off his uniform. Particular *duties* may be discharged, and then we are done with them. But *duty* always abides—what is due from us to God and man; and it is as vain for us to try, as it is wrong for us to wish, to rid ourselves of that.

We should seek to cherish a large and lofty conception of what duty means; and, accepting implicitly the teaching of conscience and the Bible upon the point, we should strive to do our duty well. For us, duty may be summed up in this—*obeying in all things the will of Christ.*

There have been many inspiring examples of devotion, not only among the confessors and martyrs of the Church, but among men who have served God and country in different departments of life. We are all familiar with Nelson's signal to the Fleet at Trafalgar—"England expects that every man will do his duty." Wellington, too, had a saying—"There is little in this life worth living for; but we can all of us go straight forward and do our duty." And that was a worthy spirit manifested by the Connecticut Senator last century, during a total eclispe of the sun which impressed many in the House with the belief that the Day of Judgment was at hand. It was moved that the Legislative Council should adjourn. "I move, rather," said Colonel Davenport, "that candles be brought. Either the Day of Judgment is come, or it is not. If it is not, there is no cause for adjournment. If it is, I choose to be found doing my duty."

God Understands You.

"Thou understandest my thought afar off" (Ps. cxxxix. 2).

SOME people complain that they are always being misunderstood. But none has reason to make this complaint against God. He understands our very thoughts afar off. He looks, not upon the outward appearance, which is often a poor thing to judge by, but upon the heart; and He can read and thoroughly interpret everything which is transpiring there.

This is a truth of *great comfort to God's children.* It is said of Him in one of the psalms, that He "hears the desires" of the humble; as though His ear were so acute and so attentive that He hears even desires as they pass through the heart, without their being put into language by His needy children. When Moses held up the rod of God upon Mount Rephidim, supported by the hands of Aaron and Hur, it did not need words to tell God what he meant. He could interpret his meaning well. That was a mute but eloquent appeal to the God of battles, to give the victory to Israel over their wily and malignant foes.

And so none of us need be discouraged if we feel ourselves unable to express to God our meaning as we would, when we draw near to Him in prayer. He can interpret our desires, and meet all our wants. For He is our Father, our Heavenly Father, with infinite love in His heart, and infinite wealth at His command. He loves to be asked for blessings by His children : "for this will I be inquired of," He says, "by the house of Israel, to do it for them." And He delights to show that, where others may fail to apprehend their meaning, He understands them, and takes in fully all they have to tell.

This comforting truth has been beautifully brought out in these lines, which appeared once in the *Spectator* :—

> "I pray so ill, I am ashamed to pray;
> And marvel oft,—Can He who reigns on high
> Give heed to my poor inarticulate cry,
> Who, stammering, would my childish wants convey,
> Yet know not what to wish, nor how to say?
> They seem such little selfish things that I
> Most care to ask of God's great Majesty.
> And, sighing thus, I went upon my way.
>
> "Then, in a friend's house came his little boy
> And prattled to me, full of eager joy.
> But I, to construe baby-tongue unskilled,
> The father's face with questioning glances scanned.
> Then, smiling on his child with eyes love-filled,
> The father said, 'But *I* can understand!'"

A Man of Progress.

"A man of the Pharisees, named Nicodemus" (John iii. 1).

IT was seldom indeed that a man of the Pharisees could be called a man of progress; but Nicodemus certainly was one. Not "a man of progress" in the smug, modern sense, which often points to a progress really backward—but a man of progress which was true, inward, manifest, and heavenward.

The history of Nicodemus is a very interesting one. We have only three glimpses of him, all afforded to us in the Gospel of John; but they enable us to discern very clearly the course he took; and they mark very distinctly three stages on his upward way. We see in him—

1. *An eager learner* (John iii. 1), at the feet of the Best of Teachers. One dark night, at the close of a busy day, when Jesus has gone into retirement, a knock comes to the door, which bespeaks a late, if not a stealthy visitor—a knock, an appeal comes, too, to the Saviour's heart, for this is a genuine seeker after Him. It is Nicodemus, a ruler of the Jews, a man of rank, one of the great ones of the city. And he is welcome to Jesus, not because he is all this, but because he is *a man*—"a man of the Pharisees"—with deep questions rising in his breast, which only the Christ of God can answer. Immediately the two are closeted together in frank, earnest, confiding converse; and Nicodemus is taught the two most important of all lessons—the need of salvation, and the way of salvation: "Ye must be born again"—"the Son of Man must be lifted up." Next we behold—

2. *A brave, though a naturally shrinking man* (John vii. 50). Jesus, in parting with Nicodemus, had said to him, as he passed out into the concealing shadows of the night, "He that doeth truth cometh to the light." Time passed, and the day arrived when Nicodemus, "he that came to Jesus by night," felt that he could no longer be a true man and hide himself in the darkness. It is a meeting of the Sanhedrim, and his brother Pharisees are scoffing at Jesus, and deriding the officers whom they had vainly sent to take him—"Are ye also deceived? Have any of the rulers or of the Pharisees believed on Him?" It is a direct challenge, whose full force is felt in a quarter they are not thinking of. And Nicodemus gets courage to put in at least a word for Jesus, which brings him under the suspicion of his fellows, but shows in what direction his heart is turned. And then, at last, when the time of trial comes, and Jesus has actually been crucified, Nicodemus comes forth as—

3. *A true friend and open confessor of his Lord* (John xix. 39). In a way that cannot be mistaken, he avows his attachment to the Saviour. Others, who were with Jesus in the daytime,—the day of prosperity and gladness,—have forsaken Him and fled. But this once timid inquirer stands forward in the hour of extremity, with Joseph of Arimathea, to give the King of his heart a royal burial. The Cross has conquered. The perfect love of Christ has wrought in Nicodemus the perfected love which casts out fear. If he was once a coward, he is now a hero. And if it be not such an one as this, who *is* "the man of progress"?

Mount Zion.   July 24

"Ye are come unto Mount Zion" (Heb. xii. 22).

By Mount Zion, geographically, is meant the highest of the elevations on which the city of Jerusalem stood; that, namely, to the south, on which the towers and palaces of what was distinctively called the City of David rose. It was a name, however, which came to include a good deal more than it did at first. By Zion, by and by, was understood the whole city; and the Church, whose centre was in Jerusalem. And, as we shall see, it has now a yet wider meaning.

If we trace the use of the name from the commencement, we find that Zion was originally—

1. *A heathen fortress.* It was a stronghold that had long been held against all comers by the Jebusites. And when David, the newly-appointed King of all Israel, standing at the head of his great army, turned to his men, and said—"Ye are come unto Mount Zion. Who among you will conquer it for me?" he was confronting them, as he and they well knew, with the sternest piece of work they had to do in the whole of Palestine. But the doughty captain Joab led the attack, and wrested "the Castle of Zion" from the proud and scoffing men of Jebus. So the heathen stronghold became the seat of David's government, and the resting-place of the Ark of God. Then Zion was—

2. *A religious centre for Israel, and all the world.* In the 87th Psalm, for example, it is represented as the spiritual capital or metropolis of the whole earth. In other psalms, the Holy Hill of Zion, where God dwells, is spoken of with an almost adoring affection. For there it was that the Shechinah of the divine glory rested; and the pious Jew said of this sacred mount—"the joy of the whole earth is Mount Zion." How much more true is this of the Church of Christ, which we sometimes speak of still as the Zion of our God! Conquered from among the heathen, the Church is the abode of Christ; and as the glory of His presence and influence shines forth from her, she is the joy of every land. And thus, Zion is—

3. *A name for the glorified Church in Heaven.* All the brightest hopes that pious Israel could connect with the name of Zion, have their ample fulfilment above. It must have been an impressive scene when the pilgrim hosts, having pressed on from strength to strength (as the 84th Psalm describes them), appeared at length before God in Zion, and joined heart and voice, with the multitude of fellow-worshippers from all parts of Palestine, in the praises of the sanctuary. But St. John in the Revelation (ch. xiv. 1) discloses to the eye of faith a more glorious scene by far, when, as he looked, "lo, a Lamb stood on the Mount Zion," surrounded by the throng of the redeemed, who sang a new song before the Throne.

There Zion has in it no trace of the old heathen fortress. It is the citadel of perfect safety, and purity, and peace, for the ransomed of the Lord. And on that holy hill of Zion the Holy One of Israel shall for ever dwell among them. Will you be there, and I?

July 25. Prisoners of Hope.

"Turn you to the stronghold, ye prisoners of hope" (Zech. ix. 12).

It is related of King Richard of England that, on the way to the Holy Land, he was thrown into an unknown dungeon. His friends were anxious to discover him, but for a time could find no trace. But a favourite minstrel hit upon a device which had the desired result. He wandered from place to place, playing an air familiar to his royal master, until at length, one day, as he stood without a prison, his music had an answer from the king within. Then help was brought; and thus was King Richard restored to his kingdom and his throne in peace.

Even so are those who, under the gospel, are longing for a Deliverer from the bondage of sin, "prisoners of hope." They are not consigned to despair. They are invited to be of good courage. They are called to listen for the voice of Him who has been anointed, and sent, to set at liberty them that are bruised.

And, when Jesus comes and speaks to such, and wins for Himself a divine response within them, not only does His voice sound to them like the sweetest music. It opens for them the prison doors, and it awakens within them a new life of hope, and energy, and high resolve. It brings them out of the prison, and into the stronghold, where, no longer prisoners but willing subjects of the Captain of Salvation, they are changed into soldiers of hope, honoured to strive beneath the banner of their King for the deliverance of others whom Satan has enthralled.

Have *you* yet heard the voice of Jesus, who says to the prisoners, "Come forth," and to them who are in darkness, "Show yourselves"? Did not the first notes of His voice, which you truly heard and recognised, stir within your breast the beginnings of a new and blessed experience? And, if you have obeyed as well as heard His call, and come forth at His bidding to the freedom wherewith He makes His people free,—shall it not be yours, as a prisoner of hope who has tasted the sweets of a Christ-given liberty, to quit you valiantly beneath the Saviour's standard, as a soldier of hope for the emancipation of the world?

Try it for yourself!

"I have trusted also in the Lord" (Ps. xxvi. 1).

"WILL the raft bear?" "Yes; I am sure it will. But try it for yourself!"

You have gone down to the seashore, let us suppose, with your father, in the summer time. He takes you out with him among the rocks, while the tide is back, until you reach a ledge to which a raft is tied. He tells you what it is, and that it is possible to float upon it with safety, because he has been upon it, and knows how well it bears. You quite accept what he says; for you have never known your father to tell you what is false. But the subject gives you little concern; and you are soon far more interested in gathering your weeds and shells, while he sits down and is buried in his book.

Suddenly your father is startled by a cry from you—a wild cry of alarm. He looks up, and sees, not that you are hurt, but that the tide, unobserved by you both, has risen and cut you off from the land. It still is rising, and threatens wholly to submerge the shelving promontory on which you stand. But your father does not share your panic. For he knows that there is help at hand. He points you to the raft; he leads you to it; he bids you step aboard, and he will bring you in safety to the shore. You hesitate for a moment as you survey its timbers, but only for a moment. A single glance at your surroundings, and you step upon it—and, in that step, even if it be a trembling one, what was merely *belief* before has passed into personal *trust*. You have now committed yourself to the raft; and your trust grows more calm and radiant as it bears you, under your loving father's guidance, nearer and nearer to the land. Now you know that it will bear, not because you have been told so merely, but because you yourself have proved it.

Can *you* say—"*I* have trusted also in the Lord"? There is a mighty difference between believing *about* Christ with the head and trusting *in* Him with the heart. The gospel summons you, if you have not done so, to step into the Lifeboat—to try it for yourself. Then you will assuredly find, that it will bear you safely onward, amid the storms of this sin-troubled world, to the haven of everlasting peace.

The Great Leveller.

"Thy pomp is brought down to the grave" (Isa. xiv. 11).

DEATH is no respecter of persons. He will not, to suit the proudest earthly monarch, stay his approach, for millions of money, by so much as one moment of time. Death comes with equal foot to the palace of the rich and the hovel of the poor; and, though one may be buried in an oaken coffin and another in a pauper's shell, the humiliation of death and dissolution is in its main features the common lot of all.

I remember standing near the pyramids of Sakkara, on the site of the once great city of Memphis, which, in accordance with Bible prediction, is now little more than a graveyard and a name. All around were the traces of ancient tombs: some of them places where kings and other mighty dead were laid, others places of humbler sepulture. In the excavations which were then going on, at every turn of the spade, as I stood at the grave-mouth, bones and other relics of the long-departed were disclosed to view. Whose skull was that? A king's? Perhaps. Whose thigh-bone, this? A labourer's? It may have been. What matters it? These thousands of years agone, that was a king's—this, a labourer's. Where are *they* now? These were *a man's*. That is the important thing. Let the bones crumble; let the dust mingle. The great and solemn consideration is, that when these bodies were committed to the earth it meant that, for the immortal beings to whom they had belonged, the earthly term of life had closed, and a new phase of life begun.

That death is the great leveller of worldly distinctions is quaintly taught, through an old ceremony, at the burial of members of the Imperial House of Austria, in the Capuchin Chapel at Vienna. The master of ceremonies knocks with his official staff at the door, and, in answer to the question, "Who is there?" replies—"His Majesty the Emperor." "I know him not," answers a voice from within. The knock is repeated, and so is the inquiry—"Who is there?" "It is the Emperor." "I do not know him," is still the firm reply. Another knock is given; and this time, in answer to the demand, "Who is there?" the master of ceremonies gives the meek rejoinder, "Our brother Francis." And then the chapel door is opened, and the body, without special mark of distinction, is committed to the tomb.

Filial Love.

"Honour thy father and mother; which is the first commandment with promise" (Eph. vi. 2).

It has been remarked that among Eastern races the mother, if her husband died, became subject to her son, but that in the Bible the son is enjoined to honour his mother no less than his father. This is surely as it ought to be. A true mother is one of the richest blessings given by God; and both father and mother are to be honoured by us, if we would do His will, be worthy of ourselves, and promote our true advantage. A youth whose great ambition it is to cut as early and completely "loose from leading-strings" as possible, that he may become "lord of himself, that heritage of woe," may think himself very manly. But he is not likely, along such a line, to come to much good; and, unless his spirit changes, he is likely to continue something less than man.

It is a good sign of a boy to show a loving deference to the wishes of his parents, even where these run counter to his own desires; and God will not permit him to be a loser thereby. A notable instance of this was George Washington, who afterwards became one of the great men of history. It was his eager ambition to go to sea as a midshipman, and his mother had at last reluctantly agreed that he should go. He was of course delighted at the prospect. But when the morning of his departure came, and his trunk had been lifted by the servant to the door, he went in to bid farewell to his mother, and found her in a state of distress, which, with all her efforts, she could not conceal. His resolve was at once taken. "Bring back my trunk," he cried to the servant; "I will not go away. It cannot please me to break my mother's heart." "George," exclaimed his mother, when she heard this, "God has promised to bless those who honour their parents; and I believe He will bless you." We all know how amply, in his case, the promise was fulfilled.

The great example here, as in all else, is the Lord Jesus Himself. It is a short but beautiful account of His early life which is given by Luke—that He went down with Joseph and His mother to Nazareth, and "was subject unto them"; increasing in wisdom, and stature, and favour all the time. The boy is father to the man. Seek to be, in youth, like Him—

> "A Son that never did amiss,
> That never shamed a mother's kiss,
> Nor crossed her fondest prayer";

and, in manhood, you will not fail of the divine reward.

July 29. Not much Time.

"Brethren, the time is short" (1 Cor. vii. 29).

To you young people, the time you have in store seems very long. But to us who are older, the time we have to look back upon seems very short; and each year appears to speed more quickly by than that which went before it. We are all accustomed to look at the past, and at the future, with different ends of the telescope. We see the past as with the small end of the glass next to it, which belittles what we see. We view the future as with the telescope's great end, which magnifies the prospect. But we may believe that the Bible is right when, having regard to the whole of a lifetime upon earth, it impartially declares—"the time is short."

In the museum at Berlin, you see the cradle and the death-chair of Frederick the Great standing side by side. It is to teach the lesson that life's day is brief, and that the cradle and the grave are separated by no great interval. But it also teaches, that it is possible to accomplish much in the time that lies between; and it enforces the lesson, that every one of us should seek to make the most of life's opportunities while they last.

"I have only one candle," said a poor seamstress in a London garret, to an idle visitor one night, "and it will soon be done. I must make the most of it, to finish the work I have in hand." We have only one life on earth, and it will soon be done. Let us see to it that its days and hours are well occupied, in doing the work of Him that sent us—in finishing the work He has given us to do.

If this is the spirit in which we live and strive, in the strength and for the glory of God, we shall not have lived in vain. We cannot tell whether your life on earth is to be, comparatively speaking, a long or a short one. There are small graves, as well as large in the cemetery. But, in such a case, a broken column will be no meet emblem of your life. You will have lived much, if not long. And, short as time is, it will have been a worthy prelude to the great eternity.

The Only Begotten.

"*He gave His only-begotten Son*" (John iii. 16).

If you have only *one* of anything, dear young people, you know how much you prize it. If you had only one piece or money, you would be loath to part with it; and you remember the man with the one ewe lamb, how sorry he was to give it up. But God gave up for sinners a priceless treasure, which money could never buy. He gave for them a Lamb which was His only one—His only-begotten Son. Should it not melt the hardest heart to think—"God had only one Son, His well-beloved, and He gave Him up to die for me!" There is a word in this verse so short and simple that the youngest of you have learned it long ago; but here it has a meaning which the oldest of us can never fathom. It is the little word "so."

Think of that word "so"; and the longer you think of it, the more you will wonder at it. Nor will it only surprise you: it will also rebuke you. The thought that God so loved you will lead you to ask—How much have I loved God? He has given His only-begotten Son for me. What is there that I hold precious that I have ever given for Him?

It is told of Zinzendorf—and the story, though familar, is worth repeating—that, when a young man, he saw in a country inn a picture which greatly affected him. It was a representation of the Crucifixion: in itself a poor enough daub; but underneath it were the words—"All this for thee. What hast thou done for Me?" From that moment the thought of God's love to him in Christ filled his soul as never before. He became a prince among missionaries—the leader of the noble band of Moravian brethren. Perhaps some boy among my readers may, in thinking of God's love, resolve to become a missionary too; and even his mother may not grudge him to the work of spreading the gospel among the heathen, when she remembers that "God gave *His* only-begotten Son, that whosoever believeth in Him should not perish, but have everlasting life."

July 31. Constant Protection.

"The Lord is thy Keeper" (Ps. cxxi. 5).

EVERY man, it is said, is immortal till his work is done. And no doubt it is true, that none die until God's time comes. But the Bible teaches us, that the Lord's own people are under His special protection. "He knows the way of the righteous," through looking constantly upon them, and following, with the peculiar interest of love, their track in life; and though they are not warranted to dispense with any available means of self-preservation in the midst of danger, the Lord often shows, in an unmistakable way, how truly He is their Keeper.

"Twine them about the hill, O Lord, and cast the lap of Thy cloak over puir Saunders and these puir things!" cried the leader of a little band of exhausted Covenanters, fleeing from the persecuting troopers, but almost ready to sink from utter weariness upon the mountain-side. Hardly had he prayed when the mist rose about the hill, and wrapped the fugitives as within the cloak he cried for. Their enemies grew bewildered, and, while they vainly sought to find them, an order came which took the troopers on another errand, in a wholly different quarter.

Similarly, in Reformation times in Germany, a worthy man suffered persecution, because he preached the gospel; but God marvellously protected him. Learning that his life was in danger, he left his own house, and lived in an attic in another part of the town. The soldiers searched a whole fortnight for him, but in vain. The remarkable thing was, that every day during this fortnight a hen came and laid an egg close by the spot where he was concealed, and that, on the very day the soldiers left the town, the hen ceased to come!

We are not to court unnecessary difficulty, or to run into needless danger, and then to expect God to shield and help us. But, when we are in the path of duty, He is surety for our defence. By night as well as by day, in our going out and coming in, we are beneath His unslumbering watchfulness. What a comprehensive promise this is—"He will preserve thee from all evil." He can change what would otherwise be a mischief into a good, and make even death itself, if need be, "ours."

How complete is the security of him who has Omnipotence for his defence, and can find a refuge in the secret place of the Most High!

A Happy Holiday.

August 1

"And the streets of the city shall be full of boys and girls playing"
(Zech. viii. 5).

This is part of the prophet's description of restored Jerusalem. It is to be a *holy* city, for the Lord is to dwell in the midst of it (verse 3), and to make His presence felt. Yet it is to be a *happy* city—a true Jerusalem (" vision of peace "), healthful and tranquil, where people live long enough to be very old; but where, by their side, the young generation of boys and girls is to be seen growing up, in all the brightness and buoyancy of early youth.

It is a great mistake, which some people make, to suppose that religion brings gloom. It is really the want of true religion that is at the root of all the gloom and sorrow in the world. In the New Jerusalem the presence of Jehovah, and the presence of the old people—the good old men and women whom neither war nor disease has been permitted to cut off—do not prevent the boys and girls from having a good time. No; they know that God loves to see them happy, and so do all who are like Him. And so we find them playing upon the streets, which is a very natural and beautiful touch in the picture of that bright and glorious home. You see the old and the young side by side—enjoying God's presence and God's peace together. It is a pleasant sight: an old age, sedate but serene and joyous, encircled with the innocent merriment of gladsome youth, not rudely boisterous, though unrestrained in happiness— the secret of joy for both being, the knowledge that the Heavenly Father is near, and is looking on with interest and love.

May your playtime be full of a gladness such as this. Let it be no mere "vacation," a time when you vacate the school, and are set free from work. But let it be a "holiday" in the best sense—a time in which you realise something of the holy presence and favour of God, as One who loves you and seeks your good. Then it will be a season, not only of rest for the body, but of "recreation" for the spirit, such as only the true children of God can enjoy who are born of the Spirit, and have the Spirit of Adoption in their hearts.

And then, if you thus are kept near to God all the time, whether at work or at play, old age, if you are spared to see it, will be still a time of happiness and peace. Even as an old man, leaning on a staff " for multitude of days," you will in your heart know something of the joy of a perpetual youth, in the presence of the Eternal Father, to whom even then you will be but as a child.

August 2 — Leaving our Mark.

"For David thy father's sake" (1 Kings xi. 12). *"Jeroboam, the son of Nebat, who made Israel to sin"* (2 Kings xiii. 2).

BOTH of these phrases are a frequent refrain in the record of Israelitish history. Long after David and Jeroboam were dead their influence was being felt. Each of them, in his day, had left his mark—the one for good, the other for evil—upon society; and the effects were seen not only in their own time, but afterwards.

You would like to leave your mark, wouldn't you? Some young folks seek a very transient immortality by carving their names on wooden benches in the Park, or upon the wall of some famous building of public interest and resort. Boys have been known to endanger their lives, in the attempt to have their names cut higher than those of their comrades, upon the face of a steep and dangerous cliff. And a more laudable ambition has been, to get the name engraved, in golden letters, on the board of honour for the Duxes in the school to which they have belonged. But what I want you now to observe is this, that, whether for good or for evil, every one of you is sure to make, and to leave, his mark somehow. It may be only a little splash that the stone makes; but it goes circling over the pond. And our life may not make any great noise, but it will have its influence all the same. God's eye may be able to detect the circles of movement we have set agoing, for good or evil, long after we ourselves have left this earth.

It is told of a Japanese workman, that, more than sixty years ago, he determined to make his mark by doing something for his country. He had no wealth, and no conspicuous talent. But "where there's a will, there's a way." Round the town of Tokio, in which he lived, there was a great unsheltered common, on which the sun beat scorchingly in summer, to the great discomfort of weary wayfarers. He determined to provide a shade for these, though he himself might not live to enjoy it. And so he did. Day by day he planted pine cones all round the city, in his leisure time. And now the city is noted for the beauty of the trees around it, and the tired traveller finds rest beneath their shade.

Thomas Carlyle is right in counting among the heroic souls all that ever did a piece of honest work in their day and their degree—"all the men that ever cut a thistle, drained a puddle out of England, contrived a wise scheme in England, did or said a true and valiant thing in England." May it thus be yours, in some true way, however humble, to make your mark!

Who will miss you?

"And he departed without being desired" (2 Chron. xxi. 20).

COULD you imagine a more miserable epitaph? How would you like a sentence like this to be put upon your tombstone, or, worse still, to be recorded of you in God's own book? The words are spoken of a young king, Jehoram. He was the son of a good man and monarch, good King Jehoshaphat; and he had enjoyed splendid opportunities. But he made such a poor use of these, and showed himself so unlovable, that nobody seems to have missed him or mourned for him when he was gone. "He departed without being desired." His country, and even his own relatives, seem, with too much reason, to have been positively glad to be rid of him.

It should be your desire and aim to live so as to be missed. Not that the mere fact of being missed is the thing you are to live for; but because, if you are not missed by somebody when you are gone, it will very plainly show that you have not lived as you should have done.

You do not require to fill a prominent sphere in order to be greatly missed. Some of those whose loss is most sincerely lamented, and whose place it is most difficult to fill, have occupied a lowly enough place. But they have so lived as to make a real blank for others, when they were taken. Their friends have felt the world poorer by their removal from it; and someone has even felt, perhaps, as if most of the sunshine had gone from life along with them, beneath the horizon.

How deeply mourned, as well as loudly lamented, a humble, loving woman like Dorcas was! She achieved a nobler immortality than that of the great ones of her time. The most practised and numerous band of hired mourners could not have "got up" a scene of grief like that which followed on her death. "Here is the coat," said one, "on my little boy, which Dorcas brought him on his last birthday as a glad surprise." "These garments which you see on me and my two girls," another poor widow would answer, "were given to us, oh so quietly and kindly, by Dorcas, at the sad, sad time when their father died." And another and another would tell what a friend they had lost in her, and show that, in speaking of her gifts, they were thinking far more of herself. How much better to be the humble woman, who was loved and missed, than the lofty prince, who "departed without being desired."

A True Obedience.

"If ye will obey My voice indeed, ye shall be a treasure unto Me"
(Ex. xix. 5).

SOME people, like ancient Israel, are very ready to promise obedience to God, but very prone to forget the promise when the temptation to disobedience comes. Yet the path of obedience is the way of real happiness as well as of safety; and God shows the value He sets upon the "obedient indeed," by declaring such to be a treasure unto Him. Just as a fond mother sometimes says of her little girl, "Mary is a good child; and so obedient. She is a perfect treasure"—God says of those disposed in heart to render to Him a proper obedience, "They are a peculiar treasure."

Now, wherein does a proper obedience consist?

(1) *In doing the very thing demanded at the time by God.* It is not enough that the thing you do is not in itself a bad but a good thing; but are you doing the thing God bids you? When Saul was offering a rich oblation to God, he was told that "to obey is better than sacrifice." Mr. Spurgeon, in illustrating this to some soldiers, said—" Suppose one of you gets an order to keep guard at such and such a door. All of a sudden, he thinks to himself, 'I am very fond of our commander, and I should like to do something for him.' He puts his musket against the wall, and sets off to procure a bunch of flowers. He is missed from his post. When he comes back, he says, 'Here is the bunch of flowers I went to get.' But I hear his officer say, 'To obey is better than that; we cannot allow you to run off at every whim of yours, and neglect your duty.' And he would be taught proper military discipline."

(2) *In doing all things commanded you by God.* We are not to pick and choose, and do only some agreeable things, leaving others undone. "Obedient in all things" must be our motto: both in what we are to do and to refrain from doing—in the face, it may be, of strong contrary inducement. It may sometimes have to be "the obedience of faith," as with a girl in a public school in New York, during a panic caused by an alarm of fire. There was a terrible rush to the doors and windows. Many of her companions were hurt; one, who jumped from a window, was killed. But she was safe; for, though her cheek was pale, and her lip quivering, she had kept her place. When order was restored, she gave this explanation —" My father is a fireman, and he told me that, if ever there was an alarm of fire in the school, I must just sit still."

Other characteristics of a true obedience might be named. But do not, at any rate, forget these two—to do *the* thing, and *all* things, commanded you of God.

Idols in the Heart.

"*Little children, keep yourselves from idols*" (1 John v. 21).

HAVE you ever seen a heathen idol? If not, perhaps you may see one some day at a missionary meeting; or some of you may go out to India or China for yourselves yet, and there you will see idols in abundance. How sad it is to think, that men and women are foolish enough to bow down to sticks and stones and ugly images, and worship them as gods! Are *you* not thankful that you know better than to do that? And are you not glad to be able to do something, through the missionary box, toward teaching the poor heathen children about "the only true God, and Jesus Christ whom He has sent."

But it is not only heathen people who have been known to worship idols. The Bible tells us that even the children of Israel, to whom God had made Himself known, and for whom He had done so much, were guilty of this folly. Moses has been called up to the mountain-top; and, day after day, the people look for him, but he does not return. They are impatient, and anxious to push on from Sinai. At last they persuade themselves that he will not come back at all; and, in their folly, they think that they will do without "this Moses," and make a god of their own to worship and follow. Aaron, in his weakness, humours them. Their earrings and golden ornaments are freely given; and soon they are dancing round a golden calf, before which they offer sacrifices, and hold a merry "religious" feast. Alas! what better were they than the Egyptians, whom they used to see worshipping the reeking ox! "They—made—a calf—in Horeb" (Ps. cvi. 19). Every word in this phrase of the Psalmist, if you pause over it, will bring out more terribly their folly and sin.

But, coming nearer home, it is certain that many boys and girls need the Bible warning—"Keep yourselves from idols!" You may be under no temptation to bow before a calf of gold; but what if you worship money, or what money can purchase, in your heart? Dress, praise of others, a toy—anything or anybody that is loved more than God is an idol. These idols of the heart are very alluring; and their worship is all the more ensnaring, that it can be so secretly and respectably carried on. But we should earnestly seek to be idol-breakers to our own hearts. They are intended to be temples only for the living God; and this should be our sincere and earnest prayer—

"The dearest idol I have known,
  Whate'er that idol be,
Help me to tear it from Thy throne
  And worship only Thee."

A Lesson from Mount Hor.

"And Moses stripped Aaron of his garments . . . and Aaron died there"
(Num. xx. 28).

THE Jebel-Nebi-Harûm, "the mountain of the Prophet Aaron," as it is called, stands close by the rock-city of Petra, on the border of the land of Edom. There is little room for doubt that it is the Mount Hor where Aaron died, during the encampment of Israel at Kadesh.

It must have been a solemn day in the experience of Israel when, at the command of Jehovah, Moses, Aaron, and Eleazar climbed this mountain "in the eyes of all the congregation," and only Moses and Eleazar came down again. Strange, sad thoughts must have filled their hearts when they saw that Aaron was missing, and the news went round that the High Priest was dead.

He who for forty years had transacted for them with Jehovah, whose entrance within the Holy Place they had witnessed with awe, whose lips so often had spoken over them the words of blessing, was dead. They would see his face no more; they would never hear again the accents of his voice. If you have known what it is to lose a venerable minister, who baptized you perhaps, and has taught you from childhood, and prayed over you, and been to you like a father, you may understand a little of how Israel felt that day. How much of the comfort and peace of life, as they had known it, must have seemed to be dead and buried with Aaron in the grave. And must there not have stirred within them a longing for One who would have an unchangeable priesthood?

The event at Hor had its lessons, too, for us. As Scripture enables us to see the venerable High Priest stripped of his official robes, before he passes from this world, it may well remind us of two things:—

1. That the time is coming when *we shall all be stripped of mere earthly distinctions*. The robes of position, honour, dignity, in the world and in the Church, will be taken off us; and, as we came naked into the world, we shall not be able to carry any of these things with us into the presence of Him before whom we must all *appear* for judgment. And—

2. That our only hope for acceptance, in that day, is *in the sacrifice and intercession of that great High Priest*, of whom Aaron was only the imperfect type. He, too, has had his anointing, for He is God's Christ. He, too, has His robe of beauty, His girdle, His breastplate, and His crown. Above all, His one offering is a sacrifice in which we may for ever trust. Could Aaron's voice reach you from the top of Hor across the centuries, what would be his dying message, think you, as they strip him of his robes, and he sinks in death into the everlasting arms of God? What but this—"Behold the Priest and Lamb of God!" May it be yours and mine to say, with Augustine—"I rest in the Man who has no successor"!

Bible Addition.

"All these things shall be added unto you" (Matt. vi. 33).

IF you were to purchase something in a grocer's shop, the man from whom you bought it would not lay any great stress on the paper needed to tie up your parcel, and would never think of charging you for the string wrapped around it. Even so, according to an old writer, is it with "these things" which men are so anxious about securing. They are, in God's sight, "no more than the paper and pack-thread," which are thrown into the bargain, for the man who makes Christ and the great Salvation his own. They are hardly worth reckoning, in comparison with the Infinite Possession which such can claim; and, certainly, God will not grudge, to any such, any gift whatever which will be for their true good. If only we seek first the kingdom of God and His righteousness, all these things shall be added unto us.

The trouble is, that so many people, in their seeking, begin at the wrong end. They make "these things"—the paper and pack-thread—their principal object, as if these were their chief good. And so bent are they on acquiring the inferior blessings, that they have apparently no thought or caring at all for the highest blessing of all. This is very sad. A poor man in a lunatic asylum kept on continually crying—"Oh, what a fool I've been! Oh, what a fool I've been!" It is to be feared that this will be the weary refrain of many a worldly heart throughout eternity.

You have heard of the Disruption of the Scottish Church in 1843. The smoke of battle has now disappeared; and we can all admire the action of the noble ministers, who gave up their churches and manses and glebes, rather than wound their consciences, or do anything which they counted disloyalty to the "Crown rights" of the Redeemer. One of these Disruption Fathers tells, that after his family had been sent away from the manse, and the last cart of furniture was nearly ready to go, he entered his dismantled study for the last time. "On looking around me," he narrates, "with feelings which I shall not attempt to describe, I saw lying on the mantelpiece one of the little printed tickets which I was in the habit of using in the Sabbath school. Impressed with the idea that the texts it contained might be charged with a message suited to the solemn occasion, I lifted it, and read the following verses:—'But seek ye first the kingdom of God and His righteousness; and all these things shall be added unto you' (Matt. vi. 33). 'But my God shall supply all your need, according to His riches in glory by Christ Jesus' (Phil. iv. 19). The words came on my heart like a voice from heaven." How many besides these "Disruption Worthies" have had the fulfilment of the promise of our text!

August 8

A Bountiful Harvest.

"In due season we shall reap, if we faint not" (Gal. vi. 9).

It is a beautiful sight, at this season of the year, to see the reapers gathering in the harvest. There is nothing you enjoy more than to visit the harvest-field, or to sit upon the top of the cart that is bringing home the sheaves. And it is indeed a time for thankfulness, when, through man's labour and God's favour, there is a bountiful harvest gathered in.

The lesson I want you to learn to-day is, that while it is only God who can give the increase, He does not give harvests to the idler. We must not weary in well-doing, or be sparing of our efforts, if we wish to reap a worthy and bountiful crop. As Dr. Chalmers used to put it, *prayer* should be accompanied by *pains*. These two together will accomplish almost anything.

Two husbandmen went forth to sow their several fields. But the one, observing the wind and the gathering storm, bethought him—"My family is large, and my store of seed is small. I must hold it mostly in my granary; for I dare sow but a little of it in this cloudy weather. It may be that God will prosper the little that I sow; and, in another season, I shall sow the more, if brighter days be given." So saying, he sprinkled a few niggard handfuls, and gat him home again to his wife and hungry children. The months rolled by, and autumn brought him but a sparse return; and, ere another season had come round, that husbandman was dead.

His neighbour, too, went forth to sow, and carried with him all his store, save only what was needed for the frugal but sufficient support of his well-appointed household. He was a man of high hopes and generous endeavours; and in his heart there was a great living trust toward God. He, too, saw the wind and the gathering storm; but he feared it not, and said—"I must work while it is to-day, and look to God, who gives to all without upbraiding." And so, with faithful heart and liberal hand, he cast his seed into the dark furrows, and dressed the soil with all needed diligence. Then, when the time for resting came, he waited with long patience for the early and the latter rain. And when the time for reaping came, there was a glad home-bringing of the sheaves; and the poorer neighbours freely shared the goodly gleanings.

Which of these two professing servants of Christ are you to be? The last, I hope: who prayed and trusted, but laboured too. Let your labours, like his, be themselves unspoken prayers; and God will give a divinely bountiful response.

Guided with God's Eye.   August 9

"I will guide thee with Mine eye" (Ps. xxxii. 8).

Two members of a family may be so different in disposition, that the same father may require to control and guide them in very different ways. One boy may have to be taken by the collar and dragged to duty, or kept back from evil. Another needs no more than a look from his parent. He sees the glance of his father's eye. And that look is enough. He at once springs to his feet, to do the thing he sees his father wishes to be done; or, without a moment's hesitation, he puts from him what he perceives his father wishes him to set aside.

Now, this last is the sort of obedience our Heavenly Father looks for in His children. He does not like what has been called "rope-end obedience." The kind of control and guidance He enjoys having His children under, is the guidance of the eye. He has no pleasure in the punishment of offenders. To speak after the manner of men, it is a sore thing to the heart of God to have to mete out sore chastisement, or what looks like harsh treatment, to any member of His family. He would much rather draw us than drive us. Instead of dragging us as with a halter, He greatly prefers to lead us with a glance of His loving eye.

And surely, if this is more agreeable to God, it should be the welcome course for us. A look from God should be enough. When a mule needs to be torn and dragged by what is a really kind and wise master, before it will obey his will, we may find some excuse for it, because it is of "no understanding." But its mulishness is really hurtful to itself, as well as displeasing to its owner. And, certainly, "mulishness" in a boy or a girl is a very unworthy, as well as hurtful, trait of character.

Pray that you may clearly discern the loving eye of God looking down upon you every day, and that you may be kept sensitive to His will,—reading at a glance what He desires of you, and at once obeying every look He gives. This is the only *way to be really happy.* If you are skulking from your Father's sight, you and true happiness must needs be strangers. It is the true *safeguard also against temptation,* to live ever as beneath God's eye. "Johnny," said a customer, with a wink, to a draper's assistant one day, "you must give me good measure. Your master is not in, you know!" But Johnny was a Christian youth. And, looking straight in the man's face, he answered solemnly—"*My Master is always in.*"

August 10. Onesimus of Colosse.

"I beseech thee for my son Onesimus, whom I have begotten in my bonds"
(Philem. 10).

THE story of this Onesimus is a deeply interesting and a very suggestive one. He had formerly been a servant in a family at Colosse, in Asia Minor. It was a Christian family, for his master Philemon was one whom Paul could address as "our dearly beloved and fellow-labourer," referring also to "the Church in his house." But such a pious household was not, at that time, to the liking of young Onesimus. Possibly he was dishonest (verse 18), and felt both rebuked and bored by the atmosphere he had to breathe there. At anyrate, he got somehow discontented with his surroundings; and, anxious possibly to see the world, he makes off one day, gets into a coasting vessel, probably at Smyrna, and makes his way to Rome.

But now, in the sequel, observe—

1. *The wonderful providence* of God. Here was this poor slave-boy, adrift in the great, seething capital of the Empire. It would not have been wonderful if he had sunk into sin, or at anyrate into utter oblivion,—remembered even by his old master only as an ingrate, who had ill-requited all the kindness shown to him, and had proved himself unworthy of the comforts of such a home as he had left. But God's eye is upon Onesimus. There is perhaps only one man in Rome who knew him in earlier days. It is Paul, the preacher, whom he has seen at his master's table, but who is now a prisoner in the capital. And, under the superintending providence of God, Onesimus meets with that man again.

2. *The power of true religion in the heart* is now illustrated in Onesimus. Paul speaks of him as a genuine convert, a changed man in every way, through the blessing of God upon his dealing with him. He speaks of him affectionately, as his son in the gospel, and tells his master that, if in time past he had been unprofitable, he is now certain to be a profitable servant. Onesimus has evidently confessed his misdoings; he is willing to go back to Philemon, and do what he can to make amends for the past. And Paul can now trust him with his letter to the Colossians too.

3. *The love of true Christianity* is beautifully exhibited, also—is it not?—in the attitude of Paul to Onesimus. We see the apostle stretching out a hand even to the wretched runaway. It might have been easy to drive him away from all good influence, into the dark haunts of vice and wretchedness in the great city. But Paul meets him, with something of the love of Him who came to seek and to save the lost. He extends the same love to Onesimus the slave, when he becomes a Christian, as he had cherished for Philemon the master. He counts and calls him "a brother beloved" (verse 16), and he confidently expects that Philemon will do the same.

'Her hap was to light on a part of the field belonging unto Boaz' (Ruth ii. 3).

RUTH went away that morning, hardly knowing whither she went. It mattered little, she thought, if only her feet carried her where the gleaning privilege might not be denied her. But she went forth in the spirit of one acknowledging God in everything. And so "her hap was" to light on the very best field in all the world for her. It happened—by what people call accident—to be the field of Boaz, the kinsman of Naomi. And this "accident" was to change the whole current of her life. Not only so; but her "happening" on that field was to affect not her own future only, but, through David, the dynasty of Israel's throne, and, through Jesus, the destiny of all the world.

But was it, then, an accident? Yes, in the sense that she may hardly have been aware of what instinct or impulse it was that seemed to lead her thither. But not in the sense of happening by "mere chance." For it was the God of Providence that was guiding her feet that day, by a way she knew not, to a field of plenty, to a home of peace, and to a notable place in the world's history.

A blind man on one of the bridges in London was reading aloud from an embossed Bible, in the hearing of a few persons who had, in curiosity, gathered round him. A gentleman who happened to be passing stopped for a moment to listen; and, just at that moment, the poor man lost his place, and, in trying to find it again with his finger, kept on repeating the last clause he had read from the fourth chapter of the Acts—" None other name, none other name." Some others smiled at his embarrassment; but the gentleman went away in deepest thought. He had been vainly trying to find peace of conscience and of heart apart from Jesus. These words exactly fitted his state of mind that day. They kept ringing in his ears, as the true answer to his soul's inquiries—" None other name! None other name!" And ere long he found the rest he sought, in the only Saviour. Was *that* "mere chance"?

You often hardly know why you choose a certain road rather than another—why you speak a certain word at a particular time, and are silent at another. You forget how it was, exactly, that you came to make the acquaintance of someone, who has largely influenced you since first you met. But God knows all these things; and while you act freely, you act beneath His providence. He can give the right balance even to feelings and purposes within the heart. Do not believe that anything comes to you by "mere chance." Acknowledge God in all your ways, and He will direct you in the right path. He makes all things work together for good to them who love Him.

August 12 ### The Brazen Serpent.

"Every one that is bitten, when he looketh upon it, shall live" (Num. xxi. 8).

WE know that when a boy or a girl is out of temper, everything seems to be out of joint. They are apt to be dissatisfied with food, books, clothes, companions—everything. So was it with the Israelites in the wilderness; and so peevish and discontented were they, that God sent fiery serpents which bit the people, so that many of them died. Oh, what a dreadful scene it was—multitudes writhing in death throughout the camp—helpless, hopeless, with nothing in the desert there to stop the plague or check the poison in their blood—turning their glazed eyes wistfully to heaven—in vain!

Misery is sure to follow upon sin. It is well when sorrow for sin follows upon misery: then the hour of forgiveness and rescue is not far away. The stricken Hebrews did the best thing possible, indeed the only thing to bring them help, when they turned to God. And, in answer to their cry and that of Moses, the Lord graciously offered them a cure.

At the divine bidding, Moses stood in the midst of the camp, and lifted high upon a pole, that every one might see it, a brazen image of the venomous brood which had done such deadly mischief among the people. And, as Jehovah's herald, he cried in trumpet tones—"Look to this, and you will live!" And "it came to pass that, if a serpent had bitten any man, when he beheld the serpent of brass he lived."

And thus the plague was stayed. If they were foolish enough to refuse to look, they quickly died. But don't you think that most of the miserable sufferers would be only too glad to turn even the eye almost closed in death to where God told them—if haply even for them there might be hope? And if they looked, *they lived!*

Now, is not sin a terrible scorpion, poisoning the life-blood? Unbelief, presumption, ingratitude, rebellion, were unseen serpents that had wrought much spiritual havoc in the Israelitish camp before the fiery serpents came. Are there any hidden snakes of this kind in *your* bosom?

Not only some, but all of us are stricken. *You* are suffering from the serpent's bite. And none of us can cure himself. None of us can cure his neighbour. Even a Moses could only point us to the Lord's Salvation. There is help only in God. But there *is* help in Him.

"Look, and live" is still God's call. As the brazen serpent was raised upon the pole, so Christ, the Son of Man, "made *sin* for us," in "the *likeness* of sinful flesh," has been lifted up upon the cross, that He might draw our eyes and hearts to Himself. "There is life for a look at the Crucified One."

Therefore. August 13

"*Ye shall keep the Sabbath, therefore*" (Ex. xxxi. 14).

"THEREFORE." Why? Because he who does not keep the Sabbath is both a fool and a thief, and will by and by discover that he is no better than a slave. These are strong names; but the Bible shows us that they are true.

1. The Sabbath-breaker is *a fool*. According to Scripture, the fool is one who says in his heart—"No God"; and who tries to persuade himself that there is "no eternity." Now the Sabbath is given to us that we may be wise unto salvation, that we may get near to God, and be made ready for a future life. It is one of God's three best gifts for men, which are these—His Son, His Book, His Day. If you despise the Sabbath, then, and are taken up only with the sticks and straws of earth, forgetful of the heavenly crown—the Bible's name for you is a short but emphatic one—"a fool."

2. The Sabbath-breaker is *a thief*. Although God has given us this day, He has given it to us for a particular purpose. It is "holy to Him." It is "a rest of deep rest, holy to the Lord." He has appointed it for our good, but also for His glory. It is still the Lord's Day. The Son of Man is Lord of the Sabbath; and we have no right to put it to any use of which He does not approve. Now, if anything is given you for a special purpose by your kind father or mother, you would think very meanly of yourself if you went away and applied it to something quite different from what they had intended. If you received a sixpence, for instance, to give to a poor starving woman and her family, or to put into the missionary box, and if you went off to the confectioner's and spent it on your own shortlived pleasure, your conscience would surely speak. And for those who misapply the Lord's Day so, it is not too strong a name, the name of *thief*.

3. The Sabbath-breaker is *a slave*. He may think himself very free and very clever. But all the time he is bound in the fetters of a miserable earthliness. He only is free on the Sabbath who is free to rise in soul toward God. It is said that if the mules in a coal mine are kept constantly below, and are not brought into the sunlight at least once a week, they grow quite blind. So it is with those who are buried in the world's engagements constantly, and get no Sabbath uplook toward heaven. They are poor slaves; like the blind mules in a coal mine. Philip Henry used to meet his children on the Sabbath morning with the words, "The Lord is risen!" And they answered, "The Lord is risen indeed!" So should the Sabbath be in all our homes—a day of sacred joy and liberty with Christ.

August 14   **Retribution.**

" The wicked is snared in the work of his own hands" (Ps. ix. 16).

By retribution is meant what, in popular phrase, is called "being paid back in your own coin." Perhaps it is a token that there is a great deal of malice in the world, that the word, which literally means merely a "paying-back," is never used now to express reward, but only punishment.

There are a great many instances, in history, of people being "paid back in their own coin"—evil which they had planned for others recoiling on their own heads. A malicious attempt to injure others is very often like the Australian boomerang—a weapon which, flung violently to a considerable distance, has a way of bounding back to the spot from which it was thrown. Or it is like a gun which explodes in the hands of him who fires it, and blows his own head away.

If we turn to the Bible, we see the wicked Prime Minister Haman strung up on the gallows which he had craftily prepared for the innocent Mordecai. Something very like that occurred at the time of the great French Revolution. The Queen, Marie Antoinette, as you know, was cruelly put to death by the guillotine. But what happened less than a year after? It is recorded that "everyone implicated in her untimely end, her accusers, the judges, the jury, the prosecutors, the witnesses, all—everyone at least whose fate is known—perished by the same instrument as their innocent victim." Verily there is a God that judgeth in the earth. "The Lord is known by the judgment that He executeth."

You doubtless remember the story of Ralph the Rover, who, hoping for plunder, cut away the bell from the Inchcape Rock, to which the Aberbrothock monks had attached it, to warn unwary mariners away from the sunken reef. Some time after, the pirate, as Southey vividly describes him, struck during a storm on that very rock, and perished, amid curses of self-reproach and wild despair. And, indeed, you may often see in the newspapers of the day, illustrations of the very same thing. Not long ago, a miscreant was making for one of the public buildings in London with a bomb; but, before he reached it, the dynamite exploded in his pocket and shattered him in pieces.

There is an eternal fulfilment of the same law of "retribution" on the wicked and impenitent too awful to think of. Their darling sins and unclean appetites are made the whips to torment them. They are "sunk down in the pit that they made."

Bible Multiplication.

"There is that scattereth, and yet increaseth" (Prov. xi. 24).

This is the Bible rule of multiplication—Give, in order to get; scatter, if you would accumulate.

Nature itself enforces the lesson here. There are two ways in which you might try to increase your heap of corn. You might keep it carefully hoarded in the granary, and be always on the outlook for additional handfuls, here and there, which you might add to it. But that would be a very slow way of increasing it. It would be a long time before, with all your scraping, you would see very much difference on your pile; and, very possibly, by that time it might be fusty and half useless with age and damp. The other way would be, to take your corn-heap out to the field prepared to receive it, and boldly and generously to scatter the precious grain over the dark upturned furrows. This faith and freehandedness will not, by God's blessing, go without its reward. Every seed, by the harvest-time, will have multiplied itself many times. Your granary will be filled to overflowing; and, if this process were repeated another year, it would need other barns to hold the increase.

Now, what is true of seed is true of other things besides. It is true, for instance, of *money*, when wisely scattered, that this is the best way to multiply it. *Wisely* scattered, I say; for, of course, nobody would expect a crop from seed cast among rocks or upon the sand, and nobody need expect a return from money squandered without sense anywhere. But everybody knows, that to lay out money well is a far more effectual way of increasing it than to hoard it up in the proverbial old-wife's stocking. And it has been proved in the experience of many, that, even with regard to earthly increase, one of the best possible ways to secure it is, to "lend it to the Lord."

But the text holds good of higher things than money—it is true of *light*, and *warmth*, and *music*, and *joy*, and *love*. A candle is no poorer by lighting other candles, or the gas jets round the room; but the room is vastly the brighter for it. A warm coal grows warmer and more glowing, by communicating its warmth to those around it. The music in your heart is richer, if you sing and give others the benefit of it. Your own joy is intensified, if you bring others to share it with you. Your love grows in degree and quality —it becomes liker to Christ's own—as, in a spirit of sacrifice, it expends itself on others. But the music, the joy, the love will die, if you attempt to hoard them for yourself. The selfish policy will be found in the end to be the most unkind even to self.

August 16   Christ the Prophet.

"A Prophet: Him shall ye hear in all things" (Acts iii. 22).

By "a prophet" you generally understand "one who foretells the future." And Jesus was this, as truly as Isaiah or Daniel, or any of the rest. He was often speaking, for instance, of His coming death, and of what was to follow on it, so that men had afterwards, and still have, to own His miracles of knowledge as well as of power.

But "prophet" means more than a "foreteller": it means "one who *speaks for another.*" In this sense, it is used of Aaron. God says to Moses, you remember, when he has been complaining of his stammering tongue, "And Aaron, thy brother, shall be thy prophet." That is, "Aaron shall *speak for thee.*" And so, Jesus is the great Prophet, who *speaks to men for God.*

Now, you know *what*, as Prophet, He tells. He tells us what God, in whose bosom He dwelt from eternity, is. He tells us, also, how different we are from God, and from what God would have us to be. But He likewise shows us the way to the Father—the way back into a yet brighter home than Eden, by an approach at which no stern cherubs stand, with flaming sword, to bar the way, but only the gentle messengers of Light and Truth, to lead us and bring us near to God.

You also know *how* Christ, as our Prophet, teaches us. He does it, in His Word and by His Spirit. You and I do not see Him going about in our midst, as He did among the men of Jerusalem and Galilee; and we do not hear Him with the bodily ear. But we have His message of salvation in the written Word; and He is Himself present with us by the Holy Spirit, who was promised to lead us into all truth.

What Christ as our Prophet, then, has a right to expect is, that we carefully read and think about all that the Bible tells us of Him, and of the way of life and peace; and that we earnestly pray for His Holy Spirit, not only to open the Scriptures to us, but to open our hearts to receive the Word. We are to hear Christ "in *all* things, *whatsoever* He shall say unto us"—not taking only what is welcome to us in His teaching, but hearing and acting upon it all. If Moses or Elijah were to appear again upon the earth, or if an angel were to speak to you, it is difficult for you to imagine yourself despising him. But what if any boy or girl is doing a more daring and foolish thing than this? If God in these last days has spoken to us by *His Son*, how shall we escape if we neglect so great salvation?

One of God's Forget-me-nots.

"*Fear not ; thou art Mine : I will be with thee*" (Isa. xliii. 1, 2).

A GOOD Christian lady of my acquaintance called the "Fear nots" of the Bible "God's forget-me-nots." You will find quite a number of these, if you look through the pages of Scripture for them. This is one of them, and one of the most precious. He who said to Abraham, "Fear not": and to Hagar, and to Isaac, and to Jacob, and to the Hebrew people at the Red Sea, and to Gideon, and to many more: says here to His Israel, "Fear not." And He gives two reasons—first, that they belong to Him, as His redeemed, whom He has bought and greatly values; and, second, that He is present with them to keep them safe. "Thou art Mine: I will be with thee."

How like this is to the "Fear not" of the Good Shepherd to His "little flock." He valued them so much that He gave His life for the sheep. His hold on them is so sure that He can say: "None shall be able to pluck you out of My hand." And, whatever may lie before them, He gives them cheer : "Fear not; little flock, it is My Father's good-pleasure to give you the kingdom." And when, at length, His bodily presence is about to be withdrawn, He leaves with His Church this word of strong consolation, in giving them the commission to win the world for Him—"*Lo, I am with you all the days, even unto the end of the world.*"

This is a promise, you will observe, intended not only for the Church as a whole, but for every believer in it—even the youngest and feeblest. Perhaps some of you are as yet like Nelson when he was a boy. One asked him if he knew what fear was, and he said, "What like a creature is it? I have never seen it." Some of you may not know what fear is yet; and I would be the last to darken your young hearts needlessly with it. But others of you know too well, I daresay, what fear means; or, at anyrate, you yet may know, and it will be well for you, when called to enter the dark cave of adversity, to know where to lay hold of a precious candle-light of promise such as this—"Fear not: I will be with thee."

Give yourself wholly into Christ's keeping; and then, knowing that you are His and that He is with you, you will have as much right as any to carry in your bosom, for your comfort, the Forget-me-not of God.

August 18 — **Love in Anger.**

"And Moses' anger waxed hot" (Ex. xxxii. 19).

ISRAEL at this time have sinned *a great sin*, in circumstances of great aggravation. God, who has given them the manna, and the quails, and the clear springing water, has also defended them against their enemies, the Amalekites. And at this very Sinai, where they are encamped, He has further shown His interest in them by declaring to them His will, and entering into covenant with them; while the people, on their part, have answered together, "All that the Lord hath spoken we will do." Yet it was here —where they had been apparently so impressed that they could never possibly forget what they had seen, heard, and promised— it was here that they fell into the grievous and miserable sin of worshipping the golden calf.

Need we wonder that we hear next of *a stern punishment?* God tells Moses that it is time to go down among the people, because "they have turned aside quickly," after all their fair promises of obedience, so that God proposes to sweep them away. Moses puts in an earnest word that they may be spared, but hastens down the mountain-side. When he comes in sight of the camp, he is himself filled with such horror that he dashes from him the tables of the law—springs into the camp—seizes the idol, and burns it— grinds the molten mass to powder—and, scattering the dust of it upon the water, makes the idolaters drink their god. Nor is this all. The sons of Levi, at his bidding, go through the camp sword in hand, and do not stop the work of vengeance till three thousand of the worst of the idolaters are stretched dead upon the ground. "This from Moses, who had put in a plea for the people on the top of the mount! Is he not very hard-hearted since coming down?" Do not judge until you see what follows!

We now hear the accents of *an agonising prayer.* It is from the lips of Moses, who has returned to the Lord to plead that Israel even yet may not be cast off. He does not hide their sin from themselves (verse 30), and he does not try to hide it from God. But his heart, which had been filled with righteous indignation, is overflowing with the sorrow of disappointed and outraged love. And, though he does not know very well what to say, he bursts into the cry—"Yet now, if Thou will forgive their sin"—and then he stops; but he begins again—"And if not, blot me, I pray Thee, out of the book which Thou hast written!"

Ah, who will speak of harshness in Moses now, when we see his heart melted thus in the presence of God? Do you not know that anger—the anger of parent or of teacher—is often only the other side of love? The love of Moses here makes one think of Paul's (Rom. ix. 3). Nay, it is wonderfully like a yet greater love than any other—the love of God for sinful men.

Bible Subtraction.

" Whosoever hath not, from him shall be taken even that which he seemeth to have" (Luke viii. 18).

You know why the blacksmith's arm is so brawny and muscular? Because he is constantly using it. If you don't use your muscles, your arm will grow limp and flabby, and even the little strength you had to begin with will disappear. I know a man who lay down in bed, thinking himself very feeble, though the doctors considered that he was able to go about; and he lay so many months and years in bed that he actually lost the power to rise. So, too, in the Kentucky Cave, which I once visited, there are fishes in the underground river that have no eyes, or which, at anyrate, cannot see. What is the reason of this? Just this, that, in the darkness there, the fishes found no use for eyesight, and hence did not use their eyes,—the consequence being, that, in course of time, the power to see vanished, so that the little fishes there are born blind.

This is a rule that holds good in the moral sphere as well. When God gives us any special opportunity, if we do not take advantage of it, it will be taken from us; if He bestows any particular gift upon us, that gift, if unused, will vanish.

Bible subtraction applies to (1) *Good impressions.* The immediate reference in the text is to hearing God's Word. If we make a good use of the light we receive, we are assured that we shall have more light. But if we put the light under a shade, or if we do not accept God's message as for ourselves, but hand it on to somebody else, we shall get no lasting benefit from it. The good impression which it may for a moment have made upon us will vanish. It may leave us even more unenlightened, and careless, and frivolous than we were before. (2) *Gracious opportunities.* If we do not employ these as we should, they are very likely to be taken from us altogether. There are places that once had the gospel preached to them that are now in heathen darkness. The candlestick of most of the Seven Churches of Asia has been taken away. The Church of Rome, which had so promising a beginning in Paul's day, is now a centre of dark superstition and idolatry. There are lands of Europe which did not use the Lord's Day as God intended; and now they cannot be said to have a Sabbath at all. Where it is not given to toilsome labour, it is a day of restless gaiety. (3) *Spiritual faculties.* These, not employed, are like the bodily faculties: they sink into decay. The eye of the soul, if not used, ceases to see. The energies of mind and heart, if not devoted earnestly to worthy ends, shrivel up and vanish. A man I know had the musical faculty in his youth. He was taught, when a boy, to play the piano. But he was too lazy to keep himself in practice. And now he can hardly play at all. Beware lest not only the music, but the usefulness of your life, come thus under the Bible law of subtraction, through your not exercising the spiritual faculties with which God has endowed you. Let us have a care, lest God take from us even that which we seem to have.

August 20

Noah's Sermon.

" Noah, a preacher of righteousness" (2 Pet. ii. 5).

By the time Noah's Ark was ready, he was a very old man—600 years of age. His grandfather, Methuselah, was not long dead, however; and *his* life went back to the time of father Adam. Thus Noah knew well all the past history of the human family; for what his grandfather could not tell him of his own knowledge, he could report as having heard it from Adam. And of one thing Noah was quite sure, namely, that no Flood such as God had foretold had ever occurred before, in the days of mortal flesh. Yet he did not sagely shake his head, and say it was impossible, and do nothing. He was a truly wise old man, and did not set up his own experience against God's Word. He believed, and obeyed; and, unmoved by the scoffers, he went on preparing his Ark for the saving of his house.

For about 120 years the work went on; and the world was as merry and as heedless in its wickedness as ever. If people thought of Noah and his Ark at all, in their constant round of gaiety— eating, and drinking, and marrying, as though to-morrow would be only more abundant than to-day—it would be to laugh at the old man's craze, and to make fun of his queer, lumbering, useless piece of work. Some of them may have helped at the making of it for day's wages, and have laughed all the same. But there is an old proverb which says, " Let *him* laugh that wins."

Meanwhile, Noah went on preaching to them. This is the point I wish you specially to note to-day. I do not mean that he made sermons. Perhaps he did speak out *in words* God's warning, as something for them, as well as for him. But, at anyrate, he was "a preacher of righteousness"; and his 120 years' patient work, in obedience to God's hint, was a noble sermon. It showed *his* deep sense of the righteousness of God, and his earnest desire to be saved in the day of trial. So far as his neighbours were concerned, Noah's preaching went for nothing; but he had delivered his soul of their blood (Ezek. iii. 19). And it turned out, as it has often done, that *the one* was right, and *the many* were wrong. The Flood came, and destroyed them all; but Noah and his house were safe.

Now, remember this. *Every boy and girl of you is also preaching every day* in life and conduct. Is it truth or error, wisdom or folly, holiness or wickedness you preach?

The Secret of Safety.   August 21

"Preserve me, O God: for in Thee do I put my trust" (Ps. xvi. 1).

A SHIP was sailing to the West Indies, when she encountered one of the worst of Atlantic storms. A gentleman, who managed to hold a place on the deck, though the vessel was being tossed like a plaything on the surge, witnessed an incident which he never afterwards forgot. The mate, looking up, saw that, to the danger of all on board, the rigging on the top of the mainmast had got out of proper gear. Calling a boy from the forecastle, he cried, "Climb to the royals, and right that rigging!" It was a summons that might have tried a more experienced nerve; and the boy was not unconscious of the peril. He bolted back to the forecastle, and disappeared for a minute or two. But it was not to try to shun his dangerous task, for he was speedily on the deck again; and, without the least apparent hesitation, he climbed the mast, adjusted the rigging, notwithstanding the terrible pitching of the vessel, and then came down again, rewarded by the consciousness that he had done his duty.

At this point, the gentleman stepped forward to him, and asked why he had taken time to go down below, when the mate ordered him to go quickly up. "I thought," was the answer, "that it would do no harm to stay long enough to ask God to take care of me; and that was what I did for a minute down below." "Who told you to do that?" inquired the gentleman. "My mother; she said it would be no lost time to pray to God." "I thought," continued the gentleman, "that I saw something in your pocket?" "Yes, my Bible, sir; if tossed into the sea, I wanted to have my Bible with me. But I felt no fear, since I could pray to God."

Now, that boy had learned the true secret of safety, which the Psalmist also knew. He had put himself into God's hands, and thus he felt that he was safe whatever might betide. We are not, of course, to court unnecessary danger, to run needless risks, and then expect God to take care of us. That is presumption, which the Bible often rebukes, and Providence often punishes. But when, at the call of duty, we have to meet difficulty and to face danger, this is a suitable prayer for us: it is a prayer of faith, which puts God, so to speak, upon His honour, and which He will not disregard —"Preserve me, O Lord: for in Thee have I found refuge."

August 22. Christ the Priest.

"A great High Priest, passed into the heavens" ... *"Not an High Priest who cannot be touched"* (Heb. iv. 14, 15).

IN Jesus we have not only a Prophet, but a Priest; and we require this in Him, if He is to be our Saviour. For not only do we, in our blindness and ignorance, need One to speak to us from God; but, in our guilt, we need One to speak to God from us,—One who, having made a sufficient sacrifice, can plead with God on our behalf, and secure our acceptance with Him. When "God drove out the man," there was no way back to Paradise but one way—the blood-besprinkled way. And that is the way which Jesus, as our Priest, has prepared and opened for us.

In the Old Testament, the High Priest went into the Holy of Holies to plead for Israel. But was this all he did? No. It would have been of no use for him to plead, unless he had first offered sacrifice, and carried the blood of the lamb or bullock with Him into the Holy Place. For this was his argument; and, in making such an offering first, he was obeying the divine requirement.

Even so, when Jesus, our great High Priest, passed into the heavens, His going there to plead that sinners might be pardoned, and cleansed, and received to glory too, would have availed nothing, if He had not first made that offering to which all the sacrifices of the Old Testament had pointed forward—the offering of Himself, upon the tree of Calvary. This had to be His argument—His own precious blood shed in the sinner's room! And this plea He can and does present within the veil; for He was Lamb as well as Priest; and it is as the Lamb that once was slain that He has gone "to appear in the presence of God for us."

It is related in Greek story, that an offender against the State, having been tried, was sentenced to death. All that he himself could say, or that the advocates could urge on his behalf, could not save him. But, just as the dread sentence was about to be executed, his brother, Amyntas, stepped forward, and, without saying anything, held up before the judges the withered stump of the arm he had lost, in the successful defence of his country in a moment of greatest peril. And, touched by the remembrance of the service and sacrifice of Amyntas, they spared his guilty brother *for his sake.*

Our Saviour and Brother can deliver us from condemnation when no other can, and secure all needed blessing for us, as, with perfect sympathy, He pleads our cause on high. He ever liveth to intercede; and, even apart from spoken utterance, how must His very appearance before God for us, with the marks of Calvary still upon Him, appeal to the Father's heart!

Submit!

"Submit yourselves, therefore, to God" (Jas. iv. 7).

To *submit* ourselves to God, in the sense intended here, implies that we have first been enabled to *conquer* ourselves. For there are two ways of submitting. You may yield to your father, for instance, because he is stronger than you, and can compel you to obey. Or you may yield to his wishes because you know he is wiser than you, and because you are sure that he loves you, and that, though your foolish heart may be half inclined to rebel, it is right for you to submit. Now, God can exact submission by force from all the creatures He has made. But what He desires is, the willing surrender of a heart that loves Him, and is prepared to trust Him, even where it cannot understand the wisdom or the love of His requirements.

It is a great thing to be able to say to God from the heart—"Not my will, but Thine be done!" It is far from being easy always to say it, as young people, when they gain any real acquaintance with their own hearts, soon come to know.

A little girl who was wont, very glibly and blithely, to repeat the Lord's Prayer at her mother's knee, faltered one night in the middle of it, and broke down, amid sobs and tears. The petition she had stuck at was—"Thy will be done on earth, as it is in heaven." And the explanation soon came—"O, mamma, I can't say that, since God took away my pet canary to-day!" As people grow older, they have their pet canaries too, and other treasures, which the Heavenly Father sometimes sees meet to take from them. Then is the time to bow submissively before Him, and to seek really to count His choice for us the best.

It is only through prayer that the spirit of ready submission and cheerful patience can be made ours. But it will be given in answer to sincere and humble prayer. This was beautifully illustrated in another little girl of whom I have read. Some rude boys were flinging stones on the street, and one of them struck her in the eye. She was carried home, and the surgeon sent for. He said she must submit to a serious operation. Her father comforted her upon his knee, and asked if she was ready. "Not quite, father," she answered; "I wish to pray to God first." And here was her simple prayer—"O God, forgive the boy who hurt me, and help me to bear the pain well; and may Jesus be with me. Amen." She immediately added —"Father, I'm ready now." And so courageously, and even cheerfully, did she bear what she had to pass through, that the grace of God was manifested in her to all around.

August 24 — Vulgar Fractions.

"After these things do the Gentiles seek" (Matt. vi. 32).

WHY fractions are called vulgar, I do not altogether understand. Vulgar means, originally, "belonging to the people" (Latin, *Vulgus*, as you boys know). Then it means common; and from that it has come to mean contemptible,—though it would be a great mistake to suppose that everything which is common is to be despised.

Perhaps fractions were first called vulgar, by some high and mighty people who professed to think them "not worth bothering about." And then it may have become fashionable to speak of them like that, and to show a contempt for them.

This contempt may be carried too far. Dr. Chalmers used rightly to dwell upon the value and the power of littles. A penny is only a fraction of a shilling, and a yet smaller fraction of a pound. But that great man, in putting his Sustentation Scheme, as he called it, into operation for the support of the Scottish ministers, did not forget that pennies, if gathered frequently and regularly enough, will soon amount to a good deal; and that it only needs a sufficient number of such fractions to make a great many shillings and even pounds.

On the other hand, it is possible to deal too much in fractions. Some people seem never to get beyond them. In their *giving*, they delight in fractions. They won't give a pound, if they can get off with a shilling, however good and needy the cause may be; and perhaps, instead of the shilling, they will bestow a penny, or even a halfpenny—their only regret being that they have not a farthing handy for the purpose. This is mean. From the very poor, the widow's mite is of great acceptance with God. But the widow's mite from those who are not widows, is an insult in His sight.

It is, however, to those who, in their *getting*, are content to be always dealing with vulgar fractions, that our text points. There are people whose great concern and constant thought is—"What shall we eat? What shall we drink? Wherewithal shall we be clothed?" These, says Christ, are very far from being the chief thing to live for and care about. After these the Gentiles seek. But one who has the Bible in his hand, and lives under gospel light, should be better than a heathen.

What would you think of one whose devotion to the gathering up of pence and halfpence was such that he quite overlooked or refused to receive a pearl of great price? What do you think of one whose heart is absorbingly given to the mere vulgar fractions of existence? Is he not well represented by Bunyan's picture of the Miserable Man with the Muck-rake, who is so intent on scraping together the straws, and small sticks, and dust of the floor, that he neither looks up, nor regards Him who stands over his head, with a celestial crown, which He proffers him for his muck-rake? Alas, how true it is that "earthly things, when they are with power upon men's minds, quite carry their hearts away from God"! Well may we say, with Christiana, "Oh, deliver me from this muck-rake!"

Christ the Prince.

'The Prince of Life" (Acts iii. 15) . . . *" A Prince and a Saviour "* (Acts v. 31).

SAMUEL was a prophet and a priest. David was a prophet (Acts ii. 30) and a prince. Melchizedek was a priest and a prince. But Jesus is all the three.

We are ignorant : Jesus is our Prophet ; we should hear Him. We are guilty : Jesus is our Priest ; we should trust Him. We are enthralled : Jesus is our Prince ; we should follow and obey Him, that we may be free. He is our Prophet, Priest, and Prince-Redeemer.

There are two views that we may take of the princedom of Christ Jesus. He is Lord of the Universe, with a crown of glory on His head, with a rod of strength in His hand, and seated upon a throne of majesty. But He is also the Lord of His people's hearts, the King of saints : on His brow, a crown of thorns ; in His hand, the sceptre of His grace ; and the throne He sits upon, the Mercy Seat. Under the one aspect, He is a Potentate with unlimited control, with all power in His arm to crush His enemies beneath His feet, and to show them what is meant when it is said that " the Lord is a man of war." Viewed on the other side, He is the Prince of Peace, who subdues, by His gentle Spirit, the tumult in His people's breasts, and leads them on to victory—over themselves and all their spiritual foes.

Now, remember, if you are calling Jesus your Saviour, you ought constantly to be owning Him as your Prince. You must not suffer rebels to rise up against Him in your own heart. Unbelief and disloyalty must be cast out ; self-will, and rebellion, and pride, and discontent must be put down ; you must seek that every thought, and feeling, and desire, and purpose within you may be brought into captivity and willing submission to the law of Christ. Thus, fighting the good fight in your own heart and life, and warring the good warfare in the great campaign beyond, in which Jesus invites every true follower of His to have a share, you will be made "more than conqueror through Him that loved you."

When Martin Luther listened to Christ the Prophet, speaking to him in the old Bible which he found in the monastery at Erfurt, he was led to Christ as his only Priest. Then, when Satan said to him, " Thou art a great sinner, Martin ; therefore thou art lost," he could answer, " Nay, not lost, for the blood of Jesus Christ, God's Son, who is a great High Priest, cleanseth from all sin." And, hearing Christ as his Prophet, and trusting Him as His Priest, he had courage imparted to obey Him implicitly and fearlessly, as the Prince of his heart and life. He was ready to meet as many devils in Worms as there were tiles upon the house-top, when he went there at his Master's bidding. " Poor monk, poor monk," said the gallant old warrior Freundsberg, "thou art going to make a greater stand than I in the bloodiest of our battles." But Luther quailed not, For Christ was his Prince, and Rome's hierarchs were as nothing in comparison with Him. " Here I stand," he firmly said ; " I cannot otherwise : so help me God."

And the man who had so wholly yielded himself to the authority and care of his unseen Lord, was the instrument of subduing nations to the acknowledging of the truth as it is in Jesus.

August 26   Christ our Surety.

"Be surety for Thy servant for good" (Ps. cxix. 122).

By a "surety" is meant one who becomes bound for another—one who undertakes, in certain circumstances to do, or to give, or to bear something in another's stead. It is a common enough thing, for instance, for a man to put his name to a document, declaring that if, at a certain date, his friend is not able to pay a certain debt, he will meet the claims of his creditors for him. In that case, he becomes "security" for his friend,—a position not to be rashly entered upon, since, as Solomon reminds us, the surety often has to "smart for it," and is sometimes involved in ruin, without really helping him for whom he stands.

There is a touching instance in the Old Testament of one brother becoming security for another, by yielding himself up to prison in his stead. I refer, of course, to Judah, who, in pleading with his aged father to allow Benjamin to go down with the rest of his brethren to Egypt, said—"Send the lad with me: *I will be surety for him.*" When Joseph, in assumed sternness, was for detaining Benjamin as a bond-servant, because of the cup that had been found in his sack, Judah pleaded most earnestly with him to be allowed to suffer in his stead—"For thy servant became surety for the lad unto my father, saying, 'If I bring him not unto thee, then shall I bear the blame unto my father for ever.' Now, therefore, I pray thee, let thy servant abide instead of the lad, a bondman to my lord; and let the lad go up with his brethren."

This was nobly said, and nobly done; and Judah was here unconsciously foreshadowing Jesus, the Elder Brother and Divine Surety for His people. Dear young reader, have you found in Him *your* Surety? He is called, in the Epistle to the Hebrews, "the Surety of a better Covenant": a Covenant better than any other, both because of the greatness of the blessings it provides, and because of the absolute security that they shall be bestowed on all who, by trusting in Jesus, come within the Covenant.

The following lines, written upon a bank-note, convey their own lesson, and are worth remembering:—

> "This piece of paper in your hand
> Declares to you, that on demand
> You twenty shillings shall receive.
> This simple promise you believe;
> It puts your mind as much at rest,
> As if the silver you possessed.
>
> "So Christ who died, but now doth live,
> Doth unto you this promise give,
> That, if you on His name believe,
> You shall eternal life receive.
> Upon the first you calmly rest.
> Which is the surest, and the best?
> The bank may break; Heaven never can.
> 'Tis safer trusting God than man."

Phœbe.

"I commend unto you Phœbe, our sister, a servant of the Church"
(Rom. xvi. 1).

This is the only mention we have of Phœbe; but the little that Paul tells of her gives us a good deal of insight into her character. It would be well if every girl were in certain respects like Phœbe.

The apostle calls her (1) "*our sister.*" How his sister? Because she was God's child; and so Paul and she had the same Father, and the same Elder Brother, and were brother and sister to one another, and to all the brothers and sisters of Jesus. And who are these? Jesus Himself has told us—"Whoso doeth the will of My Father which is in heaven, the same is My brother and sister." And what *is* His will? Again the Bible answers—"This is His commandment: that we believe in the Lord Jesus Christ, and love one another." It is a great family of whom this is true—part of it on earth, and part in heaven; and it is always being added to. Are we among those who trust in Jesus, and love one another? Then Phœbe is "our sister" too.

Paul next describes her as (2) "*a servant of the Church at Cenchrea.*" Perhaps you need to revise your geography to be able to tell where that place was? It was the port of Corinth, on the Saronic Gulf. Paul had formerly visited the town; and, by the time he wrote this letter, there was a church or congregation there, in which Phœbe had shown herself abundantly useful. Some think she was a deaconess; perhaps she was a Christian nurse, or what we would call a Bible-woman. Anyway, she found plenty of good to do—for she was "a succourer of many," relieving them in distress, soothing them in anxiety, bringing hope and joy to those around her, by telling them about Jesus and His love.

(3) "*A succourer of many, and of myself also,*" Paul continues. He acknowledges the help and encouragement he himself had received from Phœbe. How often the weak in this world have to support and help the strong! You remember Æsop's story of the mouse bringing deliverance to the lion? Phœbe, especially in those days, might be looked down upon, as "only a woman." Yet we see how she had succoured the great strong-minded Apostle of the Gentiles, and how thankful he is for it. No wonder he commends her to the Christians in Rome, showing a beautiful confidence both in Phœbe and in the strength of the bond which, uniting them to Jesus, would join them to her, and make them interested in her. "That ye receive her *in the Lord*, as becometh saints, and assist her in whatsoever business she hath need of you."

Now, if any little girl has love to Jesus in her heart, she will find some way of serving His cause. You may do much to brighten the world around you, and benefit people bigger, and in some respects wiser, and stronger, and more influential, than yourself. Will you not try?

August 28   A Witness to be relied upon.

"God is my witness" (Rom. i. 9).

IF you are making a very solemn statement, or a very important claim, it is a great matter to be able to appeal to someone else, as a thoroughly reliable witness on your behalf. And such is the Witness to whom the believer can appeal.

A witness is just "one who wots," or knows; and who tells what he knows. The Greek word for it is "martyr," a name now commonly reserved for those who not only give their testimony, but seal it with their blood—men like Stephen, and James, and Antipas, and multitudes of others whose names the world has forgotten, but who loved Jesus so much that they were ready to die for Him. And, though "martyr" simply means witness, it may remind us that every witness ought to be "of martyr stuff"—ready to die rather than sacrifice the truth.

Now, when Paul makes certain declarations about himself, and when John (1 John v. 11), and Paul, and others come forward and lay claim to the rich inheritance of eternal life—the question at once arises, "Where is the proof? What is your evidence?" And it is well for these claimants that they are able to answer, "We have the best of all evidence. If we receive the witness of men, the witness of God is greater; and *God is our Witness*. To Him we make appeal."

But you have not heard God speak? No; but He *has* borne witness on our behalf; and what He has said is written down where all may read it. What a witness tells is called his "evidence"; and when this is noted down, it is called the "record" in the case. And so, what the Divine Witness has said has been put on record; and "this is the record, that God hath given to us eternal life, and this life is in His Son."

Need I tell you where this record is to be found? It is in the Bible, in God's own book, where He reveals the provision He has made for us, and tells of the good He has laid up in store for them that love Him. In the Bible, which is both God's word and man's word, you have God speaking to us, through a great variety of holy men, in the Old Testament and in the New, whom He chose, and fitted, to make His declarations. Above all, you have One to whom God Himself points, as a nobler Witness still—One who came, not only to tell of eternal life, but to bestow it. "This is My beloved Son: hear ye Him." And, if ye listen, what do you hear Him say? "Verily, verily, I say unto you, He that heareth My word, and believeth on Him that sent Me, *hath* everlasting life." It is already His secure possession.

"For there is no difference; for all have sinned" (Rom. iii. 23).

THE Duke of Wellington deservedly stood high in the regard of his nation, and in the admiration of the world. But, though a man of a lofty spirit and unbending will in presence of his fellow-men, he manifested a becoming humility before God. Thus, one Sunday, when he had remained behind to take the Sacrament at the parish church which he attended, he administered a memorable rebuke to some who seemed to forget that God is no respecter of persons.

A poor old man, who had passed up the other aisle, reached the communion table at the same time as the duke, and knelt close by his side, to receive the bread and wine from the minister's hand, according to the custom of the Church of England. Some of those near by seemed to think this an impropriety; and one of them actually came forward and tapped the poor man on the shoulder, motioning him to move farther away, or to wait till the duke had first received the Sacrament. But the great commander at once took in the situation. He grasped the hand of his humble neighbour, to keep him where he was, and said, with subdued but emphatic reverence, "Do not move : we are all equal here."

By that action, the duke showed that he had appreciated, better than some of those around him, Paul's meaning when he says, "There is no difference." There are differences between men and men, to whose importance, in their own place, he, with the apostle, was very fully alive. But when it was a question of appearing before God for acceptance and spiritual blessing, Wellington rightly recognised that the place appropriate for him was just the place appropriate to the lowliest sinner.

It is a sad delusion for any to suppose that, because they belong to a particular nation, their persons will be accepted of God. The Jews were very prone to imagine this, and received many a rebuke for it, through St. Paul and others. And it is an equally foolish and hurtful snare, when any of us thinks that, because he belongs to a respectable church-going family, and can point to a good outward life, he may, on these and kindred grounds, lay claim to the divine favour, and expect an entrance into heaven. Nay; for all have sinned, and all are guilty before God. And though there is a difference between people, in character as well as condition, and will be a difference in future awards to the guilty, some having "few stripes" in comparison with others, there is no difference as regards a righteousness that can commend us to God. There is only one way of salvation, for Jew and Gentile, high and low, rich and poor. There is only one way into heaven—the way of faith, which leads by the Cross of Calvary.

August 30

The Sprinkled Blood.

"When I see the blood, I will pass over you" (Ex. xii. 13).

IT was a terrible piece of news that Moses had to tell both Pharaoh and his own countrymen in Egypt, when he announced to them that, on a certain night, the destroying angel was to pass through the land, and that, before morning, the air would be filled with the wailing cry of multitudes, mourning for a first-born. Even to the Israelites it was solemn news, fitted to fill every man, and woman, and child among them with strange thoughts—"The messenger of death is to go from door to door to-night!"

But, in the case of the Israelites, there went along with the tidings *a blessed promise of safety*. Moses told them, in God's name, that *their* homes would be perfectly safe, if they did a very simple thing that He commanded them. "Take a spotless male lamb," he said, "of a year old, in every family, and slay it. Then take some of the blood, and sprinkle it on the lintel and the side-posts of your door, and you will be quite safe to hold a feast within, on the slain lamb. The destroying angel, when he sees the blood, will *pass over* your houses, and your eldest-born will be spared."

The Israelites did as they were told; and they, as well as the Egyptians, found that *God is true*. For though there was a great cry throughout Egypt next morning—every father and mother wailing, "Alas, my eldest son is dead!" and every boy and girl crying, "Oh, my eldest brother is gone!" there was nothing but "the melody of joy and health" among the Israelites. Death had not entered *their* homes. They were ready to start on their journey to Canaan—and the Egyptians were as ready to send them—before the day had fairly dawned.

And then, year after year, by God's appointment, a feast was held by Israel, called the *Passover* feast, to recall the ever-memorable night when the destroying angel *passed over* the homes of the Israelites, while the houses of the Egyptians were entered by death and sorrow. The feast at the same time pointed forward to the greater deliverance upon Calvary—through Jesus, the Lamb of God, slain for His people's sins.

How perfectly safe God can keep His own amid surrounding danger! And how very simple the way of salvation is—so simple that people sometimes make a mock at it. "Believe in the Lord Jesus Christ, and thou shalt be saved." "But what good," say some, "will believing do?" Heed them not; but listen to the voice of God! If an Israelitish father, that awful night, had said, "What good will it do to sprinkle a little blood upon our door-post?" he would have regretted it in the morning. And a sinner who despises God's way of salvation will regret it in eternity.

Balance.   August 31

"What shall it profit?" (Mark viii. 36).

In every well-regulated business of considerable size there is a certain time in the year which is called "the balance-time." The books are then carefully examined, and the results of the past transactions computed, in order that the balance may be taken between the profit and the loss. It is called the "balance" (from a French word meaning "two scales"), because the gains and the losses are, so to speak, put into opposite scales, and weighed against each other, and then the outcome of the comparison is put down on "the balance-sheet."

Now, it is very important that this process should be gone through systematically from time to time. A man who stumbles on without it, "does not know where he stands"; and his business cannot be expected to come to any good. And, of course, it is important that the balance should be truthfully and accurately taken; otherwise, the balance-sheet will be quite erroneous and misleading. Some years ago, the country was startled by the discovery that the directors of a great public bank had allowed its affairs to get into hopeless confusion. They had been bringing out balance-sheets, year by year, which showed a considerable profit. But the balance-sheets had been "cooked," as it was called. The losses had not been all put in; the figures had been altered to suit a purpose: so it was easy to bring out *on paper* an apparent gain—while, all the time, it was a case of utter ruin, not only for the directors themselves, but for the homes of thousands besides.

The case suggested by the question of Jesus in the text, is that of a man who imagines he has been doing well for himself, but who, at balance-time, has his eyes opened, and gets a terrible shock. He has had some gains of a sort, on which his heart has been gloating. But he has effected one terrible loss, of which, till now, he has thought little or nothing. For he has squandered *his life* in securing these petty gains: he has lost *his own soul*. And what compensation would he have for such loss, even if he had acquired all the world besides?

The soul—*your* soul—how unspeakable is its value, in the eyes of Christ! Have *you* been taught at all its worth? Perhaps you have been treating it as thoughtlessly as a boy did a stone, which a passing traveller saw him fling, with some other stones, for amusement, at a settler's door in South Africa one day. The stranger picked it up,—when "something made his heart beat fast. It was a diamond. The child was playing with it as a common stone; the peasant's foot had spurned it; the cart-wheel had crushed it—till the man who knew saw it, and recognised its value" (*Imago Christi*). And this incident, it is said, led on to the discovery of a whole diamond-field.

May you value most what Jesus sets the highest price upon! May you never know the sinking of heart *that* man must feel who, striking his balance in eternity's clear light, is aroused to the discovery, that, with all his getting, he has been an immeasurable loser—because he has lost his own soul.

September 1   **Spiritual Photography.**

"Changed into the same image" (2 Cor. iii. 18).

THE great aim of the Christian is, to become like to Christ. What he most desires, or ought most to desire, is, that Christ's likeness should be reproduced in himself.

Now, in this verse we are told how this is to be brought about. Two things are needful. The one is, that you should keep looking to Jesus, in faith and love, "with open face." The other thing is, that "the Lord, the Spirit," should exert His gracious influence upon you all the while from above. "We all, *with open face*, beholding as in a glass the glory of the Lord, are changed into the same image, from glory to glory, even as *by the Spirit* of the Lord."

This is what I have called spiritual photography. Some of you who have a camera, or who have a friend that owns one, will know what I mean.

Suppose you turn your camera, at noonday, to a beautiful landscape,—no matter what other steps you had taken in order to the result, if you forgot to uncover the eye of the camera you could hope for no picture on your glass.

Suppose, on the other hand, you turn your camera to the landscape, before the sunrise. You may have prepared the plates with every care; you may have burnished carefully the lenses; you may have uncovered them, in full view of the scene you wished to reproduce. But although you have kept the camera looking long with open face, I see no picture on the plate. And why? Because the sun is not shining in the heavens; and the twinkling starlights mock your purpose with their feebleness.

You must both keep looking unto Jesus, and pray for the gracious influence of the Holy Spirit, if you would have the fair image of the Saviour reproduced upon the tablet of your heart.

The Living and Life-giving One. September 2

"The first Adam, a living soul; the last Adam, a quickening Spirit"
(1 Cor. xv. 45).

THE name *Adam* means "Man"; and the two most important of all the men who have ever lived are these two—the "first Adam," of Eden, and the "last Adam," of Bethlehem and Calvary. But, as the text shows, the second of these is far nobler than the first.

Taking the first Adam at his best, he was a "living soul." And that means much; for it means, that he was able to know, and love, and have fellowship with God. But, alas! he fell, and became a dead soul. So, then, there was needed the second Man, who should be not only a living soul, but a life-giving Spirit. And this the Saviour was.

Even before He became man at all, life proceeded from Him; for He was the Creator (see John i. 3) who breathed into Adam's nostrils the breath of life. And the same life-giving power was continually shown by "the Lord from heaven" when he dwelt as man upon the earth. It was seen in raising the dead body from the grasp of death, and even of the grave. It shone forth by the couch of the daughter of Jairus, when, at a word, He restored the damsel to her stricken father's side; at Nain, too, when Jesus said to the dead youth upon the bier, "Young man, I say unto thee, arise," and brought joy again to his mother's bleeding heart; and, again, at the grave of Lazarus, when, at the voice of Jesus, the dead man came forth, with the grave-clothes on him, from the corruption of the tomb. But especially was it shown then, and has been often shown since, in His power to quicken (that is, to make *quick* or alive) the dead soul.

Ah, young friend, what *is* a dead soul? I will tell you. It is a soul that never hears, or sees, or speaks to God—that never tastes the preciousness of His truth, or knows the comfort of His good Spirit—a soul that is quite *dead* to God. Such an one is beyond all human help, as much as the body which lies mouldering in the grave. But Christ can say even to a soul like that, "Arise from the dead!" and, immediately, it is filled with a new life. Before, it was dead in trespasses and sins; but now, new thoughts, new feelings, new desires, new purposes, give constant proof that the living and life-giving One has breathed into it the breath of a new, and fruitful, and abiding life.

September 3 **Not Ashamed to Pray.**

" Daniel kneeled upon his knees, three times a day, and prayed as he did aforetime" (Dan. vi. 10).

THE command of King Darius had only served to put Daniel upon his mettle. No earthly power would be allowed to come in between him and God. He would rather face the den of lions than be untrue to his religious convictions, or turn his back upon the sacred privilege of holding fellowship with God in prayer. Nor would he even seem to fall in with the tyrannical decree, by conducting his devotions henceforth in secrecy. Let the consequences be what they might, Daniel went into his house, and, the windows being open in his chamber toward Jerusalem, kneeled down, and prayed, and gave thanks before his God, *as he did aforetime.*

The counsel given by the head of an ancient school to his followers was—"Think, on every occasion, *I am a philosopher.*" He meant by that to fill them with a high conception of what was expected of them, as those who had been under training such as his, and to inspire them to meet the demands of life, at all times and in all circumstances, in a way worthy of themselves. How much more ennobling and strengthening a consideration ought it ever to be, to the follower of Christ, "I am a Christian; let me seek to live worthily of the name I bear, and of the profession it implies."

Now, there is nothing more characteristic of a true Christian than this—that he is one who prays. It was the mark of a new life in Saul of Tarsus, when it could be said of him—"Behold, he prayeth." No doubt he had often "said his prayers" before; but that was the first time he had really prayed out of a humble and contrite heart.

What you are to seek is, *sincerity* in prayer, and *courage* to pray. You are not merely to mutter over a certain form of words every day, but to give true expression to the desire of your heart. And, wherever you may go, you are not to be ashamed to go down upon your knees, morning and evening, to pour out your heart in supplication before God. You may not find this easy in the midst of careless companions, as I well know from the remembrance of early experience in a boarding-house. Pillows and shoes, and jibes more hard to bear, may be flung at you. But never mind. If you persevere, your example will tell for good; and you will be respected, even by those who at first had tried to laugh you to scorn. And you yourself will be strengthened through prayer. "These men kneel for mercy," said King Edward to De Bohun, as the Scots, before joining battle, bowed themselves in prayer. "Yes, sire," was the answer, "but not from you!" And, by God's blessing on their arms, they drove the strong invader from the land.

Giving up for God.   September 4

"Make me thereof a little cake first" (1 Kings xvii. 13).

It is told of Richard Cecil, the well-known minister of the Church of England, that he put his little daughter's confidence in him to a severe test one day. She was playing with some beads, and was greatly delighted with them, when, to her dismay, her father suddenly said —"You have some pretty beads there. I wish you to throw them behind the fire." The tears started into the little maiden's eyes; but, after looking earnestly at him, she nerved herself for the sore sacrifice, and, with heaving breast, dashed the beads into the fire. Some days after, her father brought home far larger beads and finer toys, and set them before her as her own. The child's tears this time were tears of joy. "These, my daughter," said he, "are yours, because you trusted me. Your obedience has brought you this treasure. My desire, in what I asked, was to teach you the meaning of faith. Put the same confidence in God. Whether you understand Him or not, have faith in Him, that He means your good."

It was something very like this that God did with Abraham, when He asked him, without giving explanation of His purpose, to give up his only son. And it was something very like this, too, when the prophet Elijah, the representative of the God of Israel, asked the poor widow of Zarephath, who had only a handful of meal altogether, and was just on the brink of starvation, to make a cake for him first, and then to think of herself and her son. He accompanied the request, it is true, with a rich promise of larger good. But it was no small test of the widow's faith and generosity. Nature, no doubt, bade her hold by what she could see and handle, as a means of subsistence, however slight, for herself and her little one. What faith called her to was, to give this up, without any outward guarantee that he would be able to make it more.

Faith triumphed. She did not argue—"Let me see you increase the meal and oil beforehand, and then I'll commit myself to you." She did not wait to see, before she would trust. She trusted, that she might see. And faith had its reward. "There is that scattereth and yet increaseth." In yielding up a day's bread to God, she got daily bread from Him. "The barrel of meal wasted not, neither did the cruse of oil fail." None is ever a loser from taking God at His word, and putting himself and his personal interests entirely at God's disposal. The promise of Christ is—"There is no man that hath left house, or brethren . . . or lands for My sake and the Gospel's, but he shall receive an hundredfold now in this time . . . and in the world to come eternal life."

September 5 — The Atonement.

"We joy in God, through our Lord Jesus Christ, by whom we have now received the atonement" (Rom. v. 11).

THE Greek word here for "atonement" means *change* or *exchange*. Our English word explains it very well. Atonement (or "at-one-ment") signifies *reconciliation*, the bringing together as one of those who had been at variance. It indicates the change, from distance and hostility to nearness and friendship, between us and God; and it implies, on the part of the reconciled sinner, the exchange of the cold, hard, estranged heart, for a heart filled with confidence, love, and joy. And, as our verse reminds us, all this is brought about through our Lord Jesus Christ, who is our Peace, and has brought us nigh by His blood.

The word Atonement sends us back to the Old Testament time, and especially to the observance of the Great Day of Atonement, which occurred in the early autumn, five days before the Feast of Tabernacles began. It was appointed in order to bear in upon the hearts of the people, before they entered upon the season of feasting and thankfulness, a deep sense of their own sinfulness and unworthiness in the sight of the Holy God; and, at the same time, to prepare them for the time of rejoicing, by bringing vividly before their minds the truth, that there is forgiveness with God and plenteous redemption.

You will find the celebration described in the 16th chapter of Leviticus. It was a day on which no manner of work was to be done; on which the entire congregation were to fast and humble themselves before God; and especially a day on which certain offerings were to be made by the High Priest—of which the most interesting and suggestive was the offering of two goats for the sins of the people.

After the High Priest had offered a bullock for his own sins, he brought the two goats before the door of the tabernacle, and drew lots upon them—the one "for Jehovah," and the other "for Azazel" (which means "complete sending away"). The first goat was slain, and its blood sprinkled before the Mercy Seat; the other, after the people's sins had been confessed over its head, was sent away by a fit man to the wilderness, or, as it is called, "the land of forgetfulness."

What a beautiful twofold type we have of Jesus here, as One who died, yet lives—as One who bare our sins in His own body on the tree, and bare away His people's sins to the land of forgetfulness, as far as the east is distant from the west! What wonder that Christians "joy in God" through such a Saviour! The modern Jew, alas! has no preparation for joy in the celebration of the Day of Atonement, which takes place about this time of year. And why? Just because he has found no real atonement yet. Even the old types have been done away. Certain passages of Scripture are read, and there are many prayers and lamentations. But the Jews have now no temple, altar, priest, or sacrifice; and their own penitence and fasting, and reconciliation among themselves, are their only atonement. Will you not pray that they may be led to look on Him whom they have pierced; that they may mourn because of Him, and have their mourning turned to sacred joy?

The Valley of Achor.

"I will give her the Valley of Achor for a door of hope" (Hos. ii. 15).

THE Valley of Achor, or "Trouble," once witnessed a terrible scene. God had just been teaching Israel that, if they were true to Him, there was no blessing too great for Him to give them. In the fall of Jericho, He had shown them how easy it would be for Him to make them more than conquerors. But now He has to give Israel a different lesson. He has to burn into their hearts a sense of His abhorrence of sin, and to teach them that, if faith and obedience bring strength and triumph, sin and disloyalty bring weakness and defeat.

Little Ai with its few inhabitants, to the dismay of Joshua, puts Israel's army to rout. What could be the reason? God lets him into the secret. *Israel has sinned.* And both the brave commander and all his host have to be unmistakably taught, first of all, that *sin brings weakness.* This is a lesson for us still. Every time you willingly sin, your soul is the weaker for it, in presence of the enemy. Nor is the accompanying lesson to be forgotten by us, which God at this time engraved upon the memory of His ancient people—that *sin brings trouble.* Not only does it, sooner or later, bring misery to the sinner, but it often brings distress to all connected with him.

And what God now tells Joshua is something for us, too, to lay to heart. He tells him, that, if he wishes the trouble to be removed, *he must search out* its cause, *and put away "the accursed thing"* from the midst of Israel. He also shows Joshua how to set about this: and the leader, himself so true-hearted, rises to obey.

You remember the result. The wretched Achan—"*the troubler*," as he was well called—*is found out.* Joshua gives him the opportunity to confess; and, with faltering voice, he acknowledges that, in an evil hour, he had stolen of the spoil of Jericho, in defiance of God's command, a fine robe, and 200 shekels of silver, and a fifty-shekel wedge of gold, and buried them below his tent. Miserable man! What pleasures had these stolen treasures brought him, even when they seemed to be hidden safely in the earth? And now the sentence goes forth that Achan must die. He has occasioned the death of thirty-six Israelites; and, as his family have shared his guilt (at least it is likely they must have known of the hidden spoil), they too suffer with him. And in their death an awfully memorable lesson is given to all Israel, that, if they are to prosper, they must be a true-hearted and holy people to Jehovah.

Then, when the "accursed thing" has been put away, and sentence executed upon the evil-doers, a new era of victory begins for Israel. The Valley of Achor is itself made a door of hope, and the scene of judgment becomes "a place for flocks to lie down in." May God, in His great mercy, change the Valley of Trouble-through-sin, into a Door of Hope for us. May He lead us to search out, confess, and put away our sin. And though we are guilty and deserve to die, may He point our faith to Him who is the sinner's Hope—that Saviour who has died that even the guiltiest sinner might have life through His name.

September 7   Thankfulness.

" And be ye thankful" (Col. iii. 15).

We should be thankful to anyone who has shown us any kindness; and we should find some way of expressing our thankfulness.

(1) We have much to be thankful for *to those who have gone before us*. Perhaps you young people are more forgetful of this than you ought to be. A poor old man was planting young apple-trees one day, when a passer-by, rather roughly, addressed him—" Why do *you* plant trees, who cannot hope to eat the fruit of them?" Resting for a moment upon his spade, he answered, with a grateful gleam in his age-dimmed eye—" Someone planted trees for me before I was born, and I have eaten the fruit. I now plant for others, that the memorial of my gratitude may exist when I am dead and gone."

(2) We have much to be thankful for *to many who still are with us*. I am afraid that young people, like others, are often least grateful to the very persons to whom they owe the most. You are ready to make much of a chance gift from a comparative stranger, who, sharing the bounty of your father's house, perhaps gives you a shilling or a book at parting; and it is right that you appreciate such passing kindness. But how often and how much you are receiving from your father himself, without once saying "Thank you" for it; and how often, even when you use the *words*, there is little of the feeling of gratitude within the heart! Be thankful to the loving ones who are with you,—father, mother, brother, sister, teacher,—and show your thankfulness while you have them near. They may not look for gratitude; but, if you have not cherished and expressed it, it may be to your regret after they are gone.

(3) We have much, especially, to be thankful for *to God*. The kindness of the best of other friends is only a little rill from the great full fountain of the loving-kindness of our Heavenly Father. Let us be thankful to Him for *our common mercies*. Their common-ness often hides from us their value; and we take them as a thing of course. It should rather increase our thankfulness; as we are sometimes taught, when food, or water, or sleep is even for a short time denied to us. Let us, above all, be thankful to Him for *the great gift of salvation through His Son*. "Oh, sir, every drop of my blood thanks you, for you have had mercy on every drop of it! Wherever you go, I will be yours." So cried a condemned criminal, as he threw himself at the feet of Dr. Doddridge, who had obtained a pardon for him. Should not we show a like gratitude to Christ? "Be ye thankful." Let your whole life, as the word means, be a song or a feast of gratitude to Him.

Quartus, a Brother. September 8

"Erastus, the chamberlain, saluteth you, and Quartus, a brother" (Rom. xvi. 23).

The name Quartus does not tell us much about its possessor: it simply means, "the Fourth." But there is another part of his name we can supply, "the Christian." For this is how he comes to be spoken of here as "a brother." This letter is addressed "to all that be in Rome, beloved of God, called to be saints." And, though Quartus was a Roman, that was not the closest bond uniting him to those to whom the epistle was addressed. He was not only a brother Roman: he was a brother Christian—one of the great family of God, named in Him of whom the whole family both in heaven and earth is named.

"A brother." Precious name! It is used *of* Jesus, who is "the Brother born for adversity," whose sympathy, in time of trial, has sweetened many a bitter cup. Used also *by* Jesus, who calls His disciples not servants only, or even friends alone, but brethren— "My brothers"—and is willing to admit them to all the intimacy of loving fellowship which that tender name suggests. And what a precious name this was to Paul. Never, never would he let go the sweet memory of the time it was first applied to himself, when Ananias put his hand upon him (Oh that touch of sympathy!) and said—" Brother Saul, the Lord, even Jesus, that appeared unto thee in the way as thou camest, hath sent me, that thou mightest receive thy sight, and be filled with the Holy Ghost."

Have you sought and found a place in the great Christian brotherhood who believe in Jesus, and are seeking to do the Heavenly Father's will? Then, this unknown Roman, Quartus, may be claimed by you, as well as by Paul, as a brother in Christ. And the spirit of brotherhood that was in him,—and that is in him still, purer and warmer than before,—salutes *you*, too, down the centuries.

When Quartus sent his friendly message to the Christians away in Rome, he little thought that this would perpetuate his name on earth to all generations. Yet so it is. It is this, and nothing but this, that introduces him to every Christian who reads the New Testament from age to age. Learn from him to cultivate the spirit of kindliness toward all, which looks for no reward but answering love. And also learn, that every pure, and generous, and loving thought as well as deed, every Christlike desire, is noted down by God.

September 9   The Test of Faithfulness.

"Ye shall not eat of it, neither shall ye touch it, lest ye die" (Gen. iii. 3).

It ought to have been very easy for our first parents, one might think, to obey this command of God. It was a little thing to ask of them, since they had their full freedom in the rest of the garden, not to take the fruit of one particular tree, which God did not wish them to touch. But the Tempter came in between them and their best Friend. He threw into their minds doubt about God's threat of punishment; and he played upon their ambition, and tried to stir pride in their hearts, and jealousy. "God didn't really mean it, when He said they would die. He knew better: He knew that, if they ate of that tree, they would be as wise as Himself." And so the power of resistance gave way. Eve's eye rested on the fruit, till she put out her hand to pluck; and then she ate, and gave to Adam with her, and he did eat.

This is the sad story of the Fall; and there are some practical lessons which we should learn from it.

(1) *The importance of little things.* It was a little test, not to eat of the fruit of a single tree. But how attractive the forbidden often is! He that is faithful in little is faithful also in much; and he that is faithless about a little thing cannot be trusted about a great. It is as possible to commit a big sin with a knot of sugar or a marble, as with a bank-note or a box of diamonds.

(2) *Beware, therefore, of the Tempter's voice.* When enticed to do wrong, say *no* at once. "He that hesitates is lost." If you stand talking with the Tempter, if you argue with him, if you even quietly listen, he will be more than a match for you. Oppose the beginnings of temptation within the heart. "Resist the devil, and he will flee from you"—cunning and strong though he is. But how may you resist him with success? Take the other half of the advice (Jas. iv. 7, 8)—"Draw nigh to God; and He will draw nigh to you."

(3) *Guard very specially against sins of the eye.* What a wonderful thing the eye is! How much of our knowledge, how much of our delight, comes to us through it. But how often a course of deep, black sin begins with the eye. Evil curiosity sometimes leads to wrong knowledge and wicked delight. As at the first, the lust of the eye still often excites the lust of the flesh and the pride of life—bad desires and unholy ambition. And what God meant to instruct and gladden us is made an instrument of sin.

Thank God that the Second Adam stood (Matt. iv. 1–11), where the first Adam fell; and that all of us who believe in Him shall be "more than conquerors" too.

Come with us! September 10

"Come thou with us, and we will do thee good; for the Lord hath spoken good concerning Israel" (Num. x. 29).

A GENTLEMAN, sitting in a summer-house, observed an ant running across the table. He placed a small lump of loaf-sugar in its way; and, as he expected, it soon found it out, and began to enjoy it. But, greatly to his surprise, it almost immediately disappeared down the side of the rustic table—only, however, to return with some hundreds of its companions, which it had apparently wished to share its delight!

The ant acted, you may say, from instinct. If so, it was a beautiful instinct, which it would be well to see reproduced in every Christian. Those who have tasted of the joy of salvation, and have learned something of the preciousness of Christ, should desire to bring others, also, to taste and see that the Lord is good.

It was in this spirit that Moses gave his loving and urgent invitation to Hobab, to join the onward march of Israel to the Promised Land. Moses felt how good a thing it was, to be allied with Jehovah and His people; and he wished his young relative—for Hobab was his brother-in-law—to share the blessing. It would be good for him, he tells Hobab, to cast in his lot with Israel. He will be in the midst of good surroundings, by joining them—"we will do thee good." And he will have a share in a bright future by so doing, and be a partaker in a rich inheritance; "for the Lord hath spoken good concerning Israel." Moreover, he tells him, he will not only get good, but do good, by joining the Israelitish camp. Moses acts upon the young man's ambition, while touching on his self-interest. He reminds him how useful his knowledge of the desert may be to the pilgrim people—"Thou shalt be to us instead of eyes."

Young reader, have you obeyed the personal urgent invitation of Christ's Church to identify yourself with the cause of the great Captain of Salvation and His people? If not, do it *now*! The Christian society, with all its faults, is the best you will find on the sin-stricken earth. As a whole, it is the most intelligent, kindly, sympathetic, hopeful, healthful, and truly progressive fellowship on earth. And it will afford you full scope for the outlay of your noblest powers of head and heart. You will both get good and do good by joining the host of the Lord. Need I add—does not your own heart tell you—that if you yourself *do* belong to the company of Christ, it should be your cherished desire and earnest endeavour to bring as many others as you can, to share the joy and advantage of the same blessed fellowship?

September 11   **Fire from Heaven.**

"The Lord rained upon Sodom and Gomorrah brimstone and fire from heaven" (Gen. xix. 21).

THERE is something beautiful even yet about the Dead Sea, as you descend upon it from the Judean heights, and see it embosomed at the foot of the mountains of Moab, and shimmering, as I saw it some years ago, in the glowing light of the Eastern sun. But, as you draw nearer, your mind is more filled with the weirdness than with the beauty of the scene; for the surroundings of the lake are bleak and barren; the water is salt and briny, with no fish in it and no birds singing blythely over it; and, above all, the thought is ever present, that in its depths a secret lies hidden—the site of the Cities of the Plain. For here was witnessed one of the most terrible events the world has ever seen—the destruction by fire and brimstone, for their wickedness, of Sodom and Gomorrah.

If you read and ponder the Bible story, you will find in it the following, among other, impressive lessons:—

1. *The wages of sin is death.* So God has said, and proved. Death overtook the men of Sodom. Through sin they incurred death in every sense—the death which consists in the separation of the soul from the body, and the worse death, that consists in the separation of the soul from God.

2. *The most glaring sin of these cities was their impurity.* The plain at that time was very fertile, and the neighbourhood exceeding fair. But it is not *where men live* that makes true well-being. The people of Sodom and Gomorrah were, moreover, very rich, and their cities full of luxury. But it is not *what men have* that makes success. They were vile, bad people; and it was according to *what they were* that God judged them. Abhor that which is evil; shun evil-doers. When sinners entice thee, consent thou not. Come out and be separate, and touch not the unclean thing. Flee from the City of Destruction, if you would not share its doom.

3. *God has many instruments for His purposes,* whether of mercy or of judgment. Before, He had used a Flood; now He uses fire. "The waters of the sea obey Him." He also makes "the flaming fire His minister." How many useful ends water is accomplishing in the world, and how much service fire has done for the earth. Let us admire the wisdom and majesty of Him who so has used such servants.

4. *The sinner, in his security, is often taken unawares.* Perhaps the men of Sodom were presuming on God's promise, that there would never be a Flood again, and thought that they might be as wicked as they chose. But death may come in many ways. A man escapes cholera, and is careless—he is struck down by lightning. Another escapes shipwreck, and is careless—he is run over by a cab, or a fever enters his home, and he dies. The men of Sodom were safe from a Flood; but they were overtaken in the fire, like the heedlessly wicked men of Pompeii long after. The only real security for the sinner is in Christ.

At once!
September 12

"And straightway they forsook their nets, and followed Him" (Mark i. 18).

THE word "straightway" is a very favourite one with Mark. You will find several instances of its occurrence in this same chapter, and quite a number more throughout the rest of this most brief, but most graphic, of the Gospels.

It is a good word for you boys and girls to lay to heart, with reference to your own religious life and duty.

If you have not obeyed Christ's call to follow Him, be like these Galilean fishermen, and do it *straightway*! You remember the familiar hymn, "Come to the Saviour, make no delay." If you put off obeying the loving Saviour's invitation, you may never come at all. How dreadful that would be! And if you do come later in life, as no doubt you think you may do, it will assuredly be a sore regret with you, that you did not come to Him *straightway*,—when first He called you, through His word and by the tender appeal of His Spirit within your heart.

An old man besought a child to give his young heart to Christ, though he himself did not profess to be a Christian. And when the child asked him why he did not himself seek God, the old man mournfully answered, "I would, child; but my heart is hard, my heart is *hard*!" Too many there are who look back regretfully to early impressions that have vanished, to drawings of the Divine Spirit which they successfully resisted in their youth; and there is a deep sadness in their hearts as they sigh over "what might have been." May you not live to share that experience, but obey Christ's call at once.

And not less for those who *have* given themselves to Christ, is there a valuable, lifelong admonition in this word, *straightway*. If the Master bids us do anything, it is right to obey Him promptly, without staying to raise difficulties or ask unnecessary questions. This is the course of safety as well as of happiness.

A pointsman in Prussia, as he went forward to "switch" an approaching train to another track, in order to prevent a collision with a train that was coming up in the opposite direction, saw his little son playing on the line, just before the advancing engine. What was he to do? To spring forward and rescue his child might cost hundreds of other lives. He could not neglect his duty. So, with bounding heart, he called to the boy, "Lie down!" and, as he turned the train on its proper track, he saw that his boy had at once obeyed. Oh the feelings of that parent, as the heavy train thundered over the prostrate child! But what was his thankful relief, when the last carriage had passed, to raise to his bosom not a mangled corpse, but his living son, all safe and sound! He had obeyed *straightway*; and this was the secret of his safety. If he had stayed to answer and to discuss, it would have meant disaster and death. And, more than earthly parent or master, does Christ deserve of us a prompt obedience. We should gladly render that to *Him*, both for His sake and our own.

September 13 — Counting our Steps.

"Doth not He see my ways, and count all my steps?" (Job xxxi. 4).

DID you ever try to count your own steps? If you did, I am very sure that you soon found it rather a wearisome business, and that, before very long, you gave it up. After a while, you may have tried it again—but with a like result. Yet it is true of God, as Job reminds us here, that God has been doing always, what we have taken the trouble to do only once or twice in our lifetime. He has been "counting all our steps."

Does not this give us, (1) in the first place, a remarkable view of *the constant and minute interest that God takes in every child of earth?* None of them ever gets so lost in the crowd, that His eye does not follow him. None of them ever takes a single step that He does not take note of, and record. Who but God could take such a warm and abiding interest in men,—caring as He does to do for them what they do not care to do even for themselves?

Is there not here (2) *great comfort for God's own children?* They are the objects of His special care. He knoweth the way that each of them takes, every step of it. And He is not only looking down upon them, but He is near at hand to give them His guidance and His aid. You have difficult heights to climb? He will cheer you on. You have waters of trial to pass through? He will have stepping-stones ready for you in the midst of the stream, that you may pass safely over. For He counts all your steps.

But should we not be reminded also (3) *of our responsibility to God?* It is not without a purpose that He counts our steps, and not without a reason that He regards them as worth counting. We shall have to speak with Him yet about them all. You cannot easily remember all the steps you have taken, even for a single week past. Not only is it impossible for you to count them now, but you can hardly recall the directions even in which they led you, and all the different spots you visited. But God will help you to remember them, not for a week only, but for a lifetime; for He has counted every right step and every wrong step,—every step taken with glad alacrity in obedience to His will, and every slow and sullen or rash and wilful step in obedience to His call. Let us be very willing, then, to be ever led by Him, that there may be few sinful and wrong steps to grieve us, when in His presence we review and recount the past.

The Lord Reigneth.

September 14

"*The Lord reigneth, let the earth rejoice*" (Ps. xcvii. 1).

EVEN some good Christian people seem to read this, "The devil reigneth, let the earth be sad." And they hang their heads mournfully and in despair, as though the world were hopelessly and irreclaimably given over to the sway of the great enemy of God and man. Now, no doubt there are many evils abroad, the sight of which is fitted to fill the hearts of God's children with sorrow. There is too much evidence everywhere of the baneful influence of the great Usurper. But God is not dethroned by the devil, and never shall be. The Lord reigneth; the victory lies with Him; therefore let the earth be glad.

It is well for each of us, who is a child of God, to remember for our personal comfort, amid the difficulties we have to meet and the perils we have to pass through, that He who is seated upon Heaven's throne is our Father, and that He will take care of us. We may often be helpless enough, and feel ourselves at our wits' end. But He is never taken at an unawares. The Lord will provide.

Some people are, in spite of themselves, almost paralysed with affright in the presence of any danger. And, when there is no real danger, they may imagine that there is; and this for them will be just as bad as if it were really there. They fancy that everything is going wrong, that there are rocks ahead on which they are sure to founder in wreck and ruin; and they are miserable.

If anybody should be brave in presence of real dangers, and ashamed to cower before imaginary ones, the child of God should be. A little boy was at sea with his father, who was a skipper, when a terrible tempest arose. Almost every other face was pale with fear; but the little fellow looked as unconcerned as if he had been sitting by the hearth at home. When they spoke to him of the danger of the ship going down, and asked him if he were not afraid, he said— "No! *father's at the helm*." What that boy said, with such confidence in his earthly parent, the Christian has far better ground for saying about his Heavenly Father. The storm-clouds may gather, and the tempest begin to roar, and the vessel of his life may seem to be the plaything of wind and tide. But the Lord reigneth. "Father's at the helm!"

September 15 — Robbing God.

" Will a man rob God ?" (Mal. iii. 8).

HE must be a very bad man who would do that, you say. *I* never rob anybody; and certainly God is the very last being that I would attempt to rob!

Not so fast, young reader! It is very possible not only for a man, and a particularly bad man, to rob God, but for a youth of good enough general repute to do the same. You rob another, not merely when you slip your hand into his pocket, or break into his house in order to carry off what belongs to him, but when, in any way, you keep from him, or deprive him of, what is his due.

Now, the love of your heart and the devotion of your life are God's due; so that, when these are withheld from Him, you are robbing God. If your father and mother have bestowed their affection, and lavished their gifts upon you from your earliest days, and if you, when you grow up, show yourself quite indifferent to them—will you not be robbing them? Yes; far more seriously than if a thief were to steal in, and to abstract the valuables from your father's desk or your mother's wardrobe! In not requiting their love with an answering love, you will be robbing them of much of their proper joy. But what is the love of an earthly parent compared with the love of the Heavenly Father, who created us, and sent His Son to redeem us? And is it not a cruel shame for any of us to rob *Him* of the reverence, and love, and service which are His due?

It was to robbing God of the tithes, of the money-offerings that belonged to Him, that Malachi referred when he told the Israelites —" *Ye* have robbed God." And, even in this respect, the youngest of us cannot be too careful to deal honestly and honourably with God. A mother gave her boy two bright pennies one day. He was asked what he meant to do with them. "I am to buy something with one of them, and to put the other in the missionary box," he said. At his play afterwards, he lost one of the pennies. "Which of the two have you lost, dear ?" said his parent. "The missionary penny, mother!" he replied very promptly.

Not only that little boy, but older people too, are often well content to let God's cause have a very secondary place, in comparison with self. In the disposal of our time, means, energy, let us beware of the sin and folly of attempting to rob God. We ourselves, in robbing Him, will be the greatest losers.

Christ the Rock.

"*That Rock was Christ*" (1 Cor. x. 4).

The Saviour is a *Rock* for His people—because—

(1) He is *the sure Foundation*. On Him the Church of God is built (Matt. xvi. 18). As the beautiful hymn says—

> "The Church's one foundation
> Is Jesus Christ, her Lord."

And on Him every secure life, every safe hope, must rest. "Other foundation can no man lay" that is worth calling a foundation; for all else is "shifting sand," and you have only to turn to Matt. vii. 27, to see how a building resting upon that will meet the storm.

(2) He is *the safe Refuge*. To dwell high up in "the clefts of the rocks," is to be safe from the assaults of the prowling enemies beneath. The birds securely nestle there. And the Lord is the Rock and Fortress of His people. Flee to the Stronghold, ye prisoners of hope. Cry,—"Hide me, O my Saviour, hide"; and He will hide you, till all calamities are overpast.

(2) He is *the Shadow* or shelter of His people. In the hour of strength and joy, indeed, He is the sunshine of their life. But, in the varying experiences of life, He can meet them and be to them everything they need. And so, in the time of weariness, He is a shelter for them from the world's hot glare—like the shadow of a spreading tree for the tired pilgrim, or of "a great Rock in a weary land."

(4) He is—and this is what the text chiefly points to—*the Refreshing* of His people. Like the rock which Moses, at God's bidding, smote, and from which water flowed, to slake the burning thirst of the desert travellers to Canaan, Christ, stricken by divine appointment upon Calvary, is the *Smitten Rock*,—from whom there flows the living water, which, in the soul of Him who drinks of it, rises up to life eternal.

Here are words you know well. When you sing them next, think of their meaning and make them a prayer:—

> "Rock of Ages, cleft for me,
> Let me hide myself in Thee;
> Let the water and the blood
> From Thy riven side which flowed
> Be of sin the double cure,
> Cleanse me from its guilt and power."

September 17 The Testimony of the Dust.

"Shake off the very dust from your feet, for a testimony against them"
(Luke ix. 5).

THE people of the East are wont to express a great deal by their gestures. Very often they say by some significant action what we would utter in words; and even so humble a thing as the dust can be made, in various ways, an eloquent symbol by a demonstrative Oriental.

When Joshua and the elders of Israel, after the defeat of Ai, put dust upon their heads in the presence of Jehovah, it was in witness of their humiliation. It meant, that they cast themselves, in shame, and weakness, and unworthiness, upon His mercy and help. When Shimei, in cursing David, "cast dust"; and when the Jews, seething around Paul, as he spoke to them from the Castle stairs in Jerusalem about God's message of mercy to the Gentiles, threw dust into the air,—it was not a mere meaningless outburst of senseless rage. Shimei wished David, and the Jews wished Paul, to understand, that this was what he would be reduced to if the spirit of vengeance he had excited had its way. David and his royal hopes, Paul and his grand missionary projects, would be ground to powder, and be no better than a handful of dust cast into the air!

But the shaking of the dust from the clothes or from the feet, was perhaps the most striking symbol employed in this connection. Paul did it, again and again (Acts xiii. 51, xviii. 6); and, as we see, it was a practice which, in certain circumstances, had the sanction of our Lord Himself.

What did it mean? The Jews, when they returned to the Holy Land from heathen countries, were wont to shake off the dust from their feet at the frontier, in token of their severance from all share in the idolatries and defilements of the Gentile world. And, no doubt, when the disciples of Jesus shook the dust from their feet, as they quitted a city that had refused to receive them as messengers of peace, it meant that they left the inhabitants to themselves, and could have no fellowship with them. But it meant more. It significantly said, "Your blood is upon your own head. We have come to you with the Gospel of grace; but you have rejected it. Beware, lest this very dust which we shake from our feet should be preserved by God, in witness of our visit, as a testimony against you in the judgment to come."

A striking instance of the testimony of the dust occurred some time ago in Germany. A box of treasure was found to have been opened and emptied on the railway, and then filled with rubbish. Who had done it? Some sand sticking to the box was scrutinised by an expert man of science with his microscope. He pronounced it a sort of sand which was to be found only at one particular station on the line. This led to the discovery and punishment of the plunderer. When he took the box from the train and set it down in a quiet corner to open it, he little thought that the dust under his feet would give testimony against him!

Double-mindedness. September 18

"The double-minded man is unstable in all his ways" (Jas. i. 8).
"Unstable as water, thou shalt not excel" (Gen. xlix. 4).

WHAT is meant by "unstable"? You have seen a poor drunkard going along the street. What a miserable, weak, tottering creature he is—going first to one side, and then to the other, and ready to fall at every step! Such an one is not to be laughed at, but to be pitied and prayed for. Well, that is a case of being unstable. And Reuben was that, not because he was a drunkard, but because he was a double-minded man. His father had cherished high hopes concerning him. He was "his first-born, his might, the beginning of his strength, the excellency of dignity, and the excellency of power." Yet Reuben became a sad disappointment to his father. For, though he was kindly, and in some sense promising, he was earthly and self-indulgent. His heart was only half given to what was right. Therefore, he did not come to any real good; but he early fell into grievous sin, and came under a dark cloud which never lifted from his life.

Now there are many double-minded, and therefore unstable, people to be found, besides Reuben. Their heart is divided, so that they are found faulty. They are half given to God, and half devoted to the world—half given to holiness, and half yielded to lust and sinful pleasure. They look as if they had *two minds*, pulling in different directions.

About such people, it is safe to say several things.

1. They are *unreliable*. That is, you cannot depend on them, or know when you really have them. They seem to be good among the good. But they are careless among the careless; and, perhaps, if you met with them among scoffers even, you might find them in the scorner's chair. They are like the fabled chameleon, which was said to take on changing colours,—red, brown, blue, yellow,—just according to its surroundings.

2. They are *unhappy*. Sin is never happy. Half-heartedness is never happy. An unstable, double-minded man, when he is trying to serve God, is thinking about how much of the world's good he is missing. When he is serving the world, he is uneasy lest his soul be lost, and is troubled by the thought of what he may be missing for eternity. In trying to get, in a wrong way, the good of both worlds, he is getting the good of neither.

3. They are *undistinguished*. Reuben himself did not excel. Neither did his tribe. No great deed, no great name, of prophet or warrior, is associated with the tribe of Reuben. The double-minded man lacks a high ambition, and does not, in a settled, persistent way, give himself to any one pursuit. Like Penelope with her web, he is apt to undo with one hand what he has wrought with the other, and, having said a thing one moment, to unsay it the next. He has not the characteristics which make for distinction and genuine success.

Beware, then, of double-mindedness. Do not be found among the Reubens. Ask God to give you understanding, that you may know His law; and let it be your consistent resolve, God helping you, to keep it *with the whole heart.*

September 19 — Christ with us in the Ship.

"Why are ye fearful, O ye of little faith?" (Matt. viii. 26).

The storm on the lake was terrible. The fierce wind, rushing down the narrow defiles that border on the Sea of Galilee, had lashed the waves into such sudden and awful fury, that even experienced sailors like Simon Peter, and the sons of Zebedee, and their brethren, were in great alarm. The ship was covered with the waves, and it seemed that any moment might be their last. But there was One who, all the while, was tranquilly asleep, with His head resting on the wooden settle of the boat for a pillow. This was their Master, the wearied Son of Man, who was also the Son of God. And when, in their affright, they rouse Him from His slumber with the cry, "Lord, save us; we perish," He rebukes the winds and the sea, so that, forthwith, there is a great calm. And, at the same time, He gives a gentle rebuke to His disciples for their lack of faith and of the courage that faith imparts.

The meaning of it was, that they should have known that, since He was with them, they were safe. It is told of Cæsar, that, being on one occasion in a boat when a furious storm arose that completely unnerved the ferryman, he confidently addressed him thus—"Fear not, boatman; you carry Cæsar and his fortunes." That man of proud, imperial spirit was so convinced of the importance of the place he had to fill and the work he had to do, that he could not imagine the gods allowing him and his fortunes to perish at such a time; and he sought to impart his own confidence to the boatman too. Such an assurance might not, in his case, have proved well founded. But, if we are in the ship that carries Jesus and the interests of His Kingdom, we are safe. If He be with us as our Saviour, we cannot perish. We may well trust, and not be afraid.

There is a saying, that "every man is immortal till his work is done"; and we may be sure that Christ will keep His servants safe at the post of duty till His end through them is accomplished. If they can serve Him better by giving up life for Him, even in that case all will be well for them, and they may be at peace. When Queen Elizabeth, in a fit of rage, threatened to cast Mendoza, the ambassador of Philip II. of Spain, into prison, he boldly replied, "I have a master who will protect me as his *subject*, not to speak of my being his ambassador." And, with a better confidence, Samuel Rutherford, who suffered much from the enemies of the good cause, said, "I lay my head to rest upon the bosom of Omnipotence."

Loving back again.

"Because He first loved us" (1 John iv. 19).

A LITTLE girl, tired of petting and playing with her doll while her mother was busy writing, ran, the moment the letters were finished, and, nestling close to her mother's heart, exclaimed—"I'm so glad; I wanted to love *you* so much, mamma." "But you and Dolly were having a happy time together?" "Yes," said the child, "but I got tired of loving *her*, because she never loves me back." "That is why you love me, then, darling?" "One *why*, mamma; but not the first or best." "And what is that?" "Because you loved me, *when I was too little to love you back*."

Even so, the Christian may well love God, who, when we were sinners, in rebellion and enmity against Him,—not only too little, but too wicked to love Him,—loved us, and gave His Son to die for us. If He had not loved us, we would never have loved Him. When love wells up in our heart toward Jesus, it is just seeking to rise to its source again.

An eminent servant of Christ has said, that "of all the things that will surprise us in the other world, this perhaps will surprise us most, that we Christians did not love Christ more before we died." Should we not remember more constantly how Christ is thirsting for our love? Should we not think oftener of His beauty, that we may desire Him? Should we not remind ourselves more frequently of the great love wherewith He hath loved us, even when we were dead in sins?

"Why do you make so much ado about Christ, man?" said a careless English traveller to a North American Indian convert, who had been speaking warmly of the name of Jesus: "What has this Christ done for you?" The Indian did not speak, but picked up a crawling worm, which he laid upon a bare spot of ground, and hemmed it in with a small circle of moss and withered leaves. He then put a lighted match to the leaves and moss, and soon the flame rose in scorching power. The worm, in agony, sought escape in vain, and then coiled itself up, to die despairingly in the centre of the circle. At that moment, the Indian put forth his hand, and took the worm, and laid it tenderly on his bosom. And then he spoke—"Stranger, you see that worm. I was that helpless creature, on the brink of everlasting fire. But Jesus rescued me. He took me, a poor sinful worm, and brought me near to His loving heart. Can you wonder that I so love Him, and like to speak about Him, who has loved me so, and is my precious Saviour?"

September 21

Your Name, Sir?

"*What is thy name?*" (Gen. xxxii. 27).

THIS is one of the first things you wish to know about a new acquaintance. If a lady comes on a visit to the house, bringing her son or daughter with her, and you and the young visitor are left to play together, it is a very natural question for you to put—"What is your name?" Perhaps, also, you go on to ask—"What name do you *like* to be called?"—and, "What is your *full* name?" The *ordinary* name may be different from the *pet* name, and both very different from the *full* name.

A well-known American writer, who died so recently as the autumn of 1894,—Dr. Oliver Wendell Holmes,—has said, among other witty things, that when John and Thomas speak together there are really six persons conversing; because there is John's John, Thomas's John, and the real John,—and there is Thomas's Thomas, John's Thomas, and the real Thomas. He means to bring out that our opinion of ourselves, the world's view of us, and God's judgment upon us, may be, and usually are, very different from one another.

Now, in asking for your name to-day, I would ask—

(1) What is *the name others give thee*? The answer to this, if you are able to give it, will bring into view the impression you have left of yourself on the minds of those around you. Depend upon it, they have formed some picture of you in their minds. Your young companions are very quick to notice traits of character, and to read the meaning of this and that other bit of conduct. And when your name—Bertie, or Charlie, or Mary, or Lottie So-and-so—is mentioned, it not only suggests to others your face and outward form, but the thought of what sort of boy or girl you are—true or deceitful, brave or cowardly, generous or selfish.

(2) What is *thy name for thyself*? In other words, what kind of a character do you give yourself? No doubt it is in some respects different from the picture others have of you. We know things about ourselves that others cannot know. There may be good motives in our hearts which they do not give us credit for. On the other hand, we may have evil motives sometimes, and bad thoughts and feelings, which they do not suspect. The picture we have of ourselves *ought* to be truer than the picture formed of us by the world. But—

(3) What is *God's name for thee*? This is the decisive question—when *He* mentions our name, what does it mean? God's judgment of us and description of us are absolutely correct. This is a picture true to life, as regards both light and shade. Others may think too well or too ill of us. We are very likely to flatter and to think too well of ourselves. But God does not flatter, and He never makes mistakes. He does not merely think or imagine, but He *knows*. And He will give each of us openly our name—not our common name, or our pet name, but our full and proper name—in the Day of Judgment. Should we not all ask Him to make us really, in heart and life, what He would have us to be? Then we shall not be ashamed before Christ at His coming, and when we have to appear, and everything about us to appear, at His judgment seat.

Sympathy. September 22

"Bear ye one another's burdens, and so fulfil the law of Christ" (Gal. vi. 2).

By sympathy we mean, suffering along with others, feeling for them and with them—putting ourselves in their place, so far as we can, that we may understand how they feel, and that we may do something to lighten their burden for them. Some people are born with far more of this quality in them than others. They have a rich, sympathetic nature to begin with. But all of us may do much to cultivate the spirit of sympathy in ourselves; and we ought to do it. If we do not, then, though we may be upright and exemplary persons in some other respects, we are not fulfilling the law of Christ, or walking after Christ's example. The whole story of our Saviour's life on earth is an inspiring exhibition of his sympathy.

"It isn't *your* child; don't fret yourself"— cried a heartless man to a woman, who had in agony called upon him to stop a runaway horse, that was making straight, with a lumbering cart, to the spot where a little child was lying. "No," she gasped, "but it's *somebody's* child." For she had a mother's heart; and, in these words, there spoke out the spirit of sympathy, which puts itself in another's place.

Even a kind word spoken in season from a loving heart, how good it is! It may change the trickling tear of disappointment into one of gratitude. It may change vexation into joy. It may ease the crushing load on the sorrowful spirit. It may soothe away tempestuous anger. It may bring hope again to the despairing. Let not the fit and needed word, then, remain unspoken!

But true sympathy will by no means confine itself to words alone. It will be ready, when occasion requires, to express itself in deeds as well. If you see a lad laboriously toiling up a steep ascent with a big load upon a barrow, which he is hardly able to push along, your sympathy won't do him much good if you merely say—"Poor lad! how he is sweating with his burden—I am really sorry for him!" But if you go forward, and add your strength to his, and make the barrow spin along till it reaches the top, he will thank you for your sympathy then.

Two gentlemen were discussing, in presence of some others, the sad circumstances of a distressed family, who, through bereavement, had fallen into straits. One of them did most of the talking, and was very profuse in his expressions of pity for the sufferers. The other was a man of few words, but of a truly kind heart. So, when the other had finished, he quietly said—"It *is* a sad case. I sympathise £10. How much do you sympathise?" The talker, though the richer of the two, was silent now. He could only mutter something about "considering it"; and his considering never came to anything practical. It did nothing to lighten his own purse, or his poor neighbour's burden. I do not need to tell you which of these two kinds of sympathy "fulfilled the law of Christ."

September 23   **Self-help.**

"Every man shall bear his own burden" (Gal. vi. 5).

You remember Addison's allegory about the Mountain of Miseries. All men who thought themselves more burdened than their neighbours were invited to come and cast down their loads in a heap, from which each might then select some other burden in place of his own. From east, west, north, and south they gathered, piling up all sorts of afflictions, till the Mountain of Miseries rose high up to heaven. Then each, with eagerness, chose what he thought a desirable exchange for his own trouble; and off he went with it to his home. But ere one short month was past, he was groaning, and moaning, and worrying, and sighing, to get back his old load again. It was, however, too late; and each man of the malcontent multitude was left in bitterness to realise, that it was worse with him at the latter end than at the beginning.

The lesson is,—bear any burden you cannot be rid of, in brave contentment! It is a miserable thing, to be always contrasting our own lot with that of others, whom we may suppose to be better off than ourselves. We were speaking yesterday about sympathy; and it is often of great importance for us to get it as well as to give it. But we are not to go whining for sympathy about burdens which God means us to carry, and which society has a right to expect us patiently, if not cheerfully, to carry, in the strength which He imparts. "Every man shall bear his own burden."

You do not know much yet of the burdens of life. In time enough, you will know more about them. But there is one burden which the youngest is required to carry, and which no other can really carry for you,—the burden of your own personal duty.

"I wish I had some good friends to help me on in life," yawned an idle youth, stretching himself on the sofa, and looking up at the roof. "Good friends? Why, you have ten," was the answer. "I wish I had even half as many," he said; "any I do have are too poor to help me." "Count your fingers, my boy," his mentor retorted. And as the lad looked at his big strong hands, he felt a bit ashamed of himself.

Self-Help is the name of a very good book, by Samuel Smiles, which you ought to read. Self-help is a very good principle, to carry with you and act upon through life. As Aaron appointed to each of the Levites his service and his burden, so God gives to every one of us our work to do; and He expects us to do it. He is no harsh, unreasonable Master, demanding of us bricks without providing us with straw. He furnishes us with talents and opportunities, and He teaches us, in the honest discharge of personal duty, how true it is, that "God helps those that help themselves."

Support.   September 24

"Cast thy burden on the Lord, and He shall sustain thee" (Ps. lv. 22).

THE spirit of independence, as we saw yesterday, is a commendable spirit. We are not to lean upon others, and expect them to lift and bear a burden which we ought, and are able, to carry for ourselves. It is well to buckle bravely to life's tasks, and to feel that, if difficulties meet us, they are there to be surmounted. A courageous, self-reliant spirit has often wrought wonders in the world.

But independence of spirit may sometimes be carried too far. It may be carried too far towards our fellow-men. We have no right to refuse the sympathy and aid of others, where these are needed, and will enable us better to fulfil the end of life. And independence is certainly not to be admired, but blamed, when it is exercised by a frail mortal towards God. In that case, it is only another name for unbelief and sinful pride.

Sooner or later, the most haughty and self-reliant are brought to feel that they cannot possibly be independent of God; and what puts strength and comfort into the Christian's heart is just this— that he does depend upon God, and that, in depending upon Him, he depends upon One whose sympathy and resources can never fail. He hath said, "I will never leave thee nor forsake thee." Therefore *we* may boldly say, "The Lord is my Helper, I will not fear."

Now, notice what is the picture suggested by the text. It is that of a little child, struggling along the road with a load in its arms, small in itself but heavy for it. The child is weary, and almost ready to sink upon the ground. But it meets its father, and cries to him for help. And the strong man not only takes the burden, but lifts the little one, load and all, in his arms, and carries it in his bosom.

"He will sustain *thee*," the promise says. When the sympathising Jesus calls to the labouring and heavy-laden ones, "Come unto Me, and I will give you rest," He expresses His readiness to carry them and their burdens too.

It is told of a traveller that, having asked and obtained a "lift" from a man who was driving past, he still clung to the burden he had been carrying on his shoulder along the dusty road. The kind friend, observing this, suggested that he should lay the bundle in the bottom of the cart. But he answered—"Oh, sir, it was very good of you to take *me* up like this; but it would be too much to expect you to carry my burden too." This was plainly absurd; but not more so than the conduct of some Christians, who have given themselves to the Saviour to carry, yet vainly think they must needs go on supporting their burden themselves.

September 25 — Son, Remember!

"I will remember" (Ps. lxxvii. 11).

MEMORY is a wonderful gift. Without it, life would be scarce worth living; for all knowledge, virtue, progress of every kind would then be impossible. A person utterly devoid of memory would be reduced, in some respects, lower than an idiot, or than the beasts which perish. It is by the help of memory and its hold upon the past that we even know who we ourselves are; and, if it were taken away, we would cease to be able to think.

The powers of memory are of two kinds. There is, first, the power which keeps things in our minds, stored up somewhere, in spite of ourselves. And then there is the special power we have of recollecting, calling to mind by an act of will, the things of the past which it is desirable for us to recall.

All of us have the first of these powers of memory, far more fully than we are ourselves aware. There is an immense amount of good and of evil from the past laid up in store within us; so that we are sometimes startled, by words, or events, or scenes coming up to us again which appeared, for long years, to have passed into oblivion. It makes one stand in awe, to think how much may be written upon the tablets of memory that God may yet make us read off, to ourselves if not to others—"Son, remember!"

A servant-girl, in fever, surprised the doctor and others by constantly repeating long passages of what proved to be very good Hebrew. On inquiry being made, it turned out that in early years she had been in the service of an old pastor, a man of much learning, who had a habit of pacing up and down, in his room and in the lobby, repeating passages of Hebrew aloud. These, without her knowing it, had been imprinted on the girl's memory. So, too, a man, saved from drowning after a wreck, seemed to hear, as he was sinking into death, words spoken by his mother thirty years before, and not recollected by him for twenty years at least—"Johnny, did you take your poor sister's grapes?"

Let us pray and strive that our memories may have as few blots upon them as possible, so that there may be little to bring the blush of shame to our cheek when God, in the light of eternity, brings from our memory's storehouse all that it contains. And let us hear Him, even now, saying to us, "Son, remember!" that, remembering Him, and His words, and His works, in the days of youth, there may be comfort laid up in store for us against the dying hour. The *storing* power of memory is specially keen and active in early years. See that you use it wisely and well. Fill the treasure-house, not with rubbish, still less with filth, but with real treasure. Occupy the mind, not with what you may vainly wish afterwards to forget, but with what you will be glad to remember for ever!

"*By their fruits ye shall know them*" (Matt vii. 20).

IF you saw grapes growing on a branch, you would not suppose it belonged to a thorn-bush. Or if, on the other hand, you saw thistles growing, you would never imagine that they sprang from a fig-tree. By the fruit you may easily determine the kind and character of the plant which brings it forth.

Jesus is warning His disciples that this is a test which must be applied, not only to plants, but to people. There may be a great deal of profession, but no good outcome from it in the life—as with the leafy fig-tree to which Jesus came for fruit and found none. And there may be fair talk about God and religion, while the character and life are positively bad. "By their fruits ye shall know them."

"Harry is a good boy, I think, and you should make a companion of him more," said the Sabbath-school superintendent to his son ; "he is regular at school, and seems to know and like his lessons well." But Tom hung his head, and said nothing. At last it came out that "the best of the fellows didn't think much of Harry." For, though he might repeat his lessons well enough, he didn't live up to them a bit. He was by no means very truthful, and his language was not very clean. In short, his religion, such as it was, he kept for the Sunday, and showed nothing of Christ's spirit day by day. When he knew this of Harry, Tom's father was *not* anxious that he should make a companion of him.

It is not merely *saying*, but *doing* and *being*, that our Lord lays stress upon. If we say that we are trusting Christ and following Him, let us see that we do it. If we profess to be sorry for our sin, let us bring forth fruits meet for repentance.

You know the hymn—"Lo, He comes, with clouds descending"; and perhaps that other hymn—"The God of Abraham praise"? Well, the author of these, Thomas Olivers by name, was at one time a very bad, dishonest man. His character was such that there could be no mistaking his badness. The evil tree brought forth evil fruit. But divine grace took possession of his heart, and he became a changed man. Providentially, about that very time, some property was left to him ; and what did he do? "He bought a horse," we are told, "visited every person whom he had defrauded, paid every farthing he owed, with interest, and asked pardon of all whom he had wronged." He took a long journey to pay a sixpence ; and he had to sell horse and saddle and bridle before he could pay the last of his debts. Thus when the nature of the tree was changed, the fruit too was changed ; and, from the different kind of fruit, people could see how very real and deep the change had been.

September 27 — Led to Destruction.

"Taken captive by the devil at his will" (2 Tim. ii. 26).

THERE are many on the road to destruction, whom Satan is not driving, but leading there. No doubt there are also those whom, having obtained complete mastery over them, he is openly hurrying onward to the pit. But in the case of multitudes he works by guile. His purpose is concealed under the guise of friendliness; and so he lures them to their death.

That quaint old preacher, Rowland Hill, began his sermon one day thus—"My friends, the other day I was going down the street, and I saw a drove of pigs following a man. This aroused my curiosity; so I watched them, till, to my surprise, he led them right into the slaughter-house. I said to the man, 'My friend, how did you manage to induce these pigs to follow you here?' The answer was, 'I had a basket of beans under my arm, and I dropped a few as I came along, and so they followed me.' So has Satan a basket of beans under his arm; and what multitudes he induces to follow him to the slaughter-house!"

There is great truth in that illustration; and though it is fitted to make one smile, it conveys a solemn lesson, which it will be well for you who are entering upon your life-course to keep in mind.

Satan is sure to be trying to lure you onward with his beans. He cannot *drive* you, as yet, successfully, with the knotted cords and sharp whips of confirmed evil habit. But He will try to secure his purpose, in another and more subtle way. He will strew before you attractive temptations, in the hope that you may thus be induced to follow where he leads.

He has different kinds of beans, which he suits to the different tastes of his intended captives. Very many are taken with the *bean of worldly pleasure*. Through indulging, by strong drink and otherwise, their bodily appetites, they are led step by step to ruin. The *bean of worldly wealth* is another great attraction, in exchange for which multitudes are induced to turn their backs on the unsearchable riches of Christ. The *bean of worldly greatness* becomes, to others, the absorbing object of interest and pursuit. If they can but rise higher in the scale of society, and take rank with the men of great reputed learning and widely-acknowledged power, they are pleased—at least for the time. Their ambition does not rise to the higher things which are at God's right hand.

May Christ, who came to deliver men from the snare of the devil, preserve you from the wiles of the great enemy! May the Divine Spirit open your eyes, and turn you from darkness to light, and from the power of Satan unto God! May loftier interests than those of earth have such a hold upon your hearts, that the pleasures, riches, prizes of time shall have no more than their proper place in your esteem! May the attractions of Christ, and the fruits of holiness, far outweigh with you the devil's beans!

The Finding of Moses.

"And, behold, the babe wept" (Ex. ii. 6).

This is one of many remarkable instances in the Bible, and in general history, of the importance of little things.

The tender mother has done her best for her babe. She saw that he was "a goodly child." What mother does not think this of her little one? But she had special reason to think it in this case. And, for three anxious months, she has succeeded in hiding him from the Egyptian tyrant. Miriam and little Aaron have been growing fonder and fonder of the dear baby; and home would hardly seem home to them now without him. He dare not be longer kept, however; else he may be discovered and rudely killed, and the family punished. So the mother resolves that she will put him into the Nile,—as the king had ordered,—but, in a basket of bulrushes that will keep the water out. And all that her anxious heart can now do is, to hope and pray that his life, somehow yet, may be preserved.

Next, we see the loving sister Miriam, standing afar off, watching the basket that contained their treasure. She is a bright, musical, quick-witted girl; but she must have been sad enough that day, as she looked and longed for the safety of her little brother. Perhaps some of you young people have an older sister like Miriam? If so, you should be thankful to God for her. And now, there is an eager look on the girl's face. She seems to be "all eyes." Why is this? Somebody is coming to the riverside. It is no other than the daughter of King Pharaoh, with her maids of honour, coming down to bathe. And straight on they go, just to where the little ark of bulrushes lies. How Miriam's heart beats, as she watches what is to become of her brother! How she longs to rush forward, and tell the princess that he is the best baby in the world, and beseech her to protect him! But, for his sake and her own, she dare not. Mother and sister can do little for him now.

But the babe is in God's protecting hand. Spying the basket, the kind-hearted princess asks it to be brought, that they may see what is in it. Imagine her astonishment, when, on opening it, she sees—a little baby boy! And not only sees him, but hears him too! For, just at the right moment, "the babe wept"; and the infant's cry goes to the great lady's heart. She is a woman as well as a princess; and, though she sees that the child is of the despised Hebrew race, she has not the heart to throw him into the river.

We know the rest: how Moses became an adopted prince, with his own mother for a nurse, and grew up to be the deliverer of Israel and one of the greatest men the world has seen. Let us learn from the story, what a blessing is mother-love, and how much a loving and active little girl may do as a comfort to her mother and a blessing to those younger than herself. Let us especially admire the wonderful preserving care of God, who had little Moses in His own everlasting arms, and turned such a little thing as a baby's cry into an influence largely felt, not upon two nations only, but upon the history of the world for all time.

September 29   A Cheerful Giver.

"Freely ye have received; freely give" (Matt. x. 8).

GOD Himself is a free and bountiful Giver. He giveth to all liberally, and upbraideth not. If He dealt out His gifts in proportion to our merit, or our thankfulness, we should be poor indeed. Or, if He uttered a rebuke for every time that even His own children receive precious gifts thanklessly at His hand, the air would be ever full of reproaches. He is never weary of giving, and He grudges no gift, however great, for the benefit of any of His needy people.

That is a beautiful declaration by St. Paul in Philippians—"My God shall supply all your need, *according to His riches in glory* by Christ Jesus." He will give, as a King. You are not to limit your requests or expectations by what you know that you deserve, but to extend them in accordance with what you know that He is able and willing to bestow. Alexander the Great once told a needy philosopher at his Court, that he would receive from the royal treasurer whatever he might ask. He forthwith gave an order for £10,000. The treasurer was taken aback at the largeness of the demand, and declined at first to pay it. But the king said—"By all means let the money be paid. It pleases me to know, from the largeness of his request, how high an estimate the philosopher has, not only of my wealth, but of my disposition to give." So we should honour God, and benefit ourselves, by large requests at the throne of grace.

But do not let us forget that there is another side to this. God desires to bring us into sympathy with Himself, in this matter of giving. Jesus meant it, when He said, "It is more blessed to give than to receive"—the only words of His, spoken during His earthly ministry, which are recorded not in either of the Four Gospels, but in another book of the New Testament. He Himself knew this blessedness well; for He gave Himself for us; and, though He was rich, yet for our sakes He became poor. And He wishes us to share this blessedness too. When there is in us the disposition to share it, He draws us near His heart. He *loveth* a cheerful giver.

It is told of John Wesley, that his liberality knew no limit except an empty pocket. When his own simple wants were provided for, all the rest was bestowed on others. When he had £30 a year, he lived on £28, and gave away £2. Receiving £60 the next year, he still lived on £28, and gave away £32. Having £90 the third year, he gave away £62; and so on. It is believed that in fifty years he gave away more than £30,000. He was indeed, as the word means, "a *hilarious* giver." There may not be many in a position to give away so large a proportion of their income as Wesley did. But you should early begin to give in a systematic way to the cause of Christ; and you should seek to give, not only honestly but cheerfully, a due proportion of your means to religious and charitable objects. What that due proportion is, we should consider in the light not only of God's providential goodness, but of the cross of Calvary.

Fitly Spoken.

"*A word fitly spoken is like apples of gold in pictures of silver*"
(Prov. xxv. 11).

THAT is, it is something very beautiful and appropriate,—like one of those exquisite works of art, brought to the palace of Solomon, by the matchless artists of Hiram, King of Tyre.

The use we make of the gift of speech is a matter of far greater importance than we sometimes are apt to remember. The word "conversation" in the Bible—as, for instance, when St. Peter speaks of "a good conversation" alongside of "a good conscience"—means much more than it now means with us. It comes from the Latin *versari*, to go up and down; and "conversation" originally meant the whole of one's going out and in among his fellows—in short, all his moral conduct. That it is now restricted in meaning to the use we make of our tongues, just shows how very important this is, as regards the character we manifest and the influence we exert among others.

Boys and girls, like older people, need to be reminded of this; for sins of the lips are, I am afraid, very prevalent among the young. You cannot be too earnest in shunning bad habits of speech, and in cultivating good ones.

There are some words, I need hardly tell you, which are not fit to be spoken by you at all. Untrue words, impure words, profane words, are degrading to him who utters them, and very hurtful often to others as well as himself. And the habit of profane swearing, which some boys seem to think is manly, is not only a wicked, but a senseless habit. It does not even appear to bring any good result along with it. As an old writer says, "The profane swearer bites the bare, barbed hook of the wrath of God." He is like a senseless, silly fish devouring a hook without any bait on it.

But even words that are good in themselves, and fit to be spoken, are not always fitly spoken. You may say a true thing in a very harsh, unfeeling *way*. You may speak a work of commendation in such a *tone* as shows you do not really mean it, and that your heart does not go along with it. You may say, at the wrong *time*, something which, if said in other circumstances, would have done great good, but which, as spoken by you, does only harm.

Oh what wisdom we need from above, to speak always the right word, at the right time, and in the right spirit! We ought to seek it from God. May He imprint the law of truth, and tact, and Christian kindness on our lips, that, whether we are called to praise or to blame, to rebuke the erring, or to comfort the sad and cheer the weary, ours may be words fitly spoken! Then, if the right habit is formed in us, and if Jesus has His proper place in our hearts, the fit word will sometimes be fitly spoken by us, when we are hardly conscious of its special fitness. The Syrian maid's loving heart led her to speak a very blessed word for the great Naaman; and your words too may be used for noble purposes by God. A word fitly spoken, how good it is! "The good, the joy which it may bring, eternity shall tell."

October 1 — **A Welcome to the King.**

"Lift up your heads, O ye gates; and the King of Glory shall come in"
(Ps. xxiv. 7).

WHO is the King of Glory? He is not David, or any earthly monarch, but Jesus Christ, the Son of the living God. He is the Lord of Hosts, who rules among the armies of heaven, and does His will among the inhabitants of earth. He is the King of Grace, whose crowning glory it is, to obtain an entrance for Himself into rebellious human hearts long closed and barred against Him, and to set up there His throne.

No doubt David was a glorious king. Victory had attended his arms wherever he went. The old fortress of Jebus itself, which had stood out so long, had yielded before him. And now, amid songs of triumphant thankfulness, he was bringing up to Jerusalem, its lasting abode, the Ark of the Covenant. It was a day of deep religious and patriotic feeling; and no doubt the warrior-king bulked largely in the minds of a devoted people as they bade him welcome to his future capital. But in his psalm,—prepared for the occasion, and sung, as Josephus the Jewish historian tells, by answering choirs that day,—the earthly monarch points his subjects away beyond himself to the Heavenly King, who stood behind him and above him. He cries to the old gates of the hoary, fortressed city to open—not to let *him* in merely, but that Greater One, of whose presence and blessing the Ark would be the symbol.

Christ is the King of Glory. When He came to earth, He was born a humble babe in Bethlehem, and wrought for His day's bread in the carpenter's shop in Nazareth. But He was a Prince, a King, though found in lowly guise. He was the brightness of His Father's glory; and ever and anon His heavenly dignity shone through. Wherever He entered, He brought the true glory with Him, before which, if men had had eyes to see, the glory of the Herods, and even of the Cæsars, would have paled into nothingness. And what a record of glory lies behind Him now, after all these centuries! He seemed a victim on the cross and in the grave. But He rose a glorious conqueror: a Saviour and a Prince. Conquests? Yes; how countless have been His bloodless victories, all down the ages—how many are the hearts He has subdued by love, that He might establish in them His reign of peace for ever!

This is the King you are called to welcome. Will you not obey the summons to let Him in? Bid Him forthwith enter your holiest of all. Throw wide the everlasting doors of your never-dying soul. And the King of Grace and Glory will come in.

Settling Accounts with God.　　October 2

"Because sentence against an evil work is not executed speedily, therefore"
(Eccles. viii. 11).

THEREFORE, what? Is the evil-doer thankful because the execution of the sentence is delayed? Does he become penitent, and sue for mercy from God? Not always so, by any means. Sometimes, because a respite is given, the sinner is emboldened. His heart becomes only the harder. He thinks that sentence, though it has been pronounced, will not be executed at all. And so he goes on in sin.

This is very wrong, and foolish, and dangerous. God has declared that sin shall not go unpunished; and we may be quite sure that He will keep His word. He does not smite down the evil-doer at once with the bolt of judgment. But nobody should conclude from this that the transgressor will escape. What God intends by delaying punishment is, to give the sinner the opportunity of turning from his wickedness, that he may live. Along with delay He sends him the message of the gospel, which offers a free forgiveness to those who seek it in Christ. But if any despise God's mercy and presume upon His long-suffering, so that his heart is fully set in him to do evil, such an one may depend upon it that he will yet have to settle accounts with God.

There is a saying, that—

"Though the mills of God grind slowly, they grind exceeding small;
Though with patience He stands waiting, with exactness grinds He all."

It is a great mistake to suppose that because He is not in a hurry to wreak His vengeance on His adversaries, He is indifferent about their sin. He is long-suffering and slow to anger, *but* He will by no means clear the guilty.

An irreligious farmer in one of the Western States of America, who gloried in his irreligion, wrote a letter to a local weekly newspaper in such terms as these :—" Sir,—I have been trying an experiment with a field of mine. I ploughed it on Sunday. I planted it on Sunday. I dressed it only on Sunday. I reaped it on Sunday. I carted the crop home on Sunday to my barn. And now, Mr. Editor, what is the result? I have more bushels to the acre in that field than any of my neighbours have had this October!" He expected some applause from the editor, who did not perhaps himself profess to be a specially religious man. But underneath the letter, on eagerly opening his paper, he found printed this short but significant sentence —"God does not always settle His accounts in October."

October 3 — Respect unto the Lowly.

"*Though the Lord be high, yet hath He respect unto the lowly*" (Ps. cxxxviii. 6).

THIS verse more literally runs, "The Lord is high—He looks upon the lowly." So that some would prefer to translate it, not "*though*" but "*because* the Lord is high, He hath respect unto the lowly." That is, it is just a part of His greatness, that He has such regard for those who are humble in estate and humble in character.

We find in Nature, that the glory of God is revealed in two different directions. You have the marvels disclosed by the telescope—the countless stars in the heavens—a multitude of worlds, many of them far greater than ours; and, looking upon these you say, "What a great God it must be who has created these, who put and keeps them in their place, and sustains all this vast universe!" Yes, but you also have the marvels disclosed by the microscope, revealing the minute perfection of the Creator's skill and providing care; and, when thus you scrutinise the tip of a butterfly's wing, or even a grain of sand taken from the seashore, you will be far more ready even than before to exclaim in wonder, "How unspeakably great a Being God must be, to hold these immense worlds under His control, and at the same time to give so exquisite a finish to the smallest atoms His universe contains!"

It was this argument of the microscope that Dr. Chalmers turned against those who reasoned, from the magnitude of God's works, that it was absurd to think that He would give much thought to a little world like ours, and actually send His Son to die for sinners here. Chalmers rightly insisted that it is one of the most wonderful things about God, that while His mind grasps without effort the whole of Nature, "He has an attentive eye fastened on the very humblest of its objects, and ponders every thought of my heart, and notices every footstep of my goings, and treasures up in His remembrance every turn and movement of my history."

Whatever others may do, God does not despise little things or little people. He has respect unto the lowly. The proud He knows afar off. They are, as it were, at a distance from Him, and are kept at a distance. But with those of a humble, contrite heart, God will dwell. Remember, then, that to get near to God we must be lowly in this inner sense. Be our outward circumstances high or humble, we must be lowly in heart. You might learn these beautiful lines of the poet Montgomery—

> "The bird that soars on highest wing
> Builds on the ground her lowly nest;
> And she that doth most sweetly sing,
> Sings in the shade when all things rest;
> In lark and nightingale we see
> What honour hath humility.

> "The saint that wears heaven's brightest crown
> In deepest adoration bends;
> The weight of glory bows him down
> The most when most his soul ascends;
> Nearest the Throne itself must be
> The footstool of humility."

On the Way to Greatness.   October 4

"*I am small and despised; yet do not I forget Thy precepts*" (Ps. cxix. 141).

THE great philosopher Isaac Newton compared himself to a boy who had gathered a few shells only, on the shore of the great ocean of truth. There was in him the spirit of genuine humility which always accompanies true greatness. And so the Psalmist here makes a very lowly estimate of himself. "I am small and despised," he says.

But he adds a "yet" which shows that he is on the way to real greatness—"Yet do not I forget Thy precepts." The words breathe humility, but they also breathe ambition. He says in effect, "I know that I am not of much account yet; but, though others may look down upon me, I am looking up to God. And, walking in the way of His commandments, I am very sure that something will be made of me yet by Him."

Now, the greatest men have always been the humblest men. If you think yourself great already, be very certain that you are not so, and are not likely soon to be. But you are not forbidden, but rather encouraged, to aim at being great. Nobody has a right to despise you. You have no right to despise yourself. You should rather seek to improve yourself, in the way that God approves.

Who knows what may become of some of you young people yet? Nobody would have reverenced the baby in the ark of bulrushes on the Nile. Yet he became one of earth's greatest men. Boy, girl, with an immortal soul—what may you not become? President Garfield—who rose from "Log Cabin to White House"—has left this among other memorable sayings—"I feel a profounder reverence for a boy than for a man. I never meet a ragged boy in the street, without feeling that I owe him a salute; for I know not what possibilities may be buttoned up under his coat."

Seek, then, the true greatness. And, if you would attain it, be careful to seek it in the right way, by remembering God's precepts, and shaping your life so as to please Him. The world sometimes seeks greatness in another way; and it may be possible to push a way to wealth, position, and power, while ignoring the laws of God. But the rich man may be a poor soul; the strong usurper, a cowardly caitiff; the man of high degree, low-bred in his tastes, and sordid in his aims. It is only by keeping the divine precepts that you become good—that is, like God—that is, truly great.

The mighty Persian conqueror ordered to be written on his tomb—"I am Cyrus, who brought empire to the Persians; do not envy me, I beseech thee, this little piece of ground." Death reives away all earthly splendour. But eminence in goodness is the imperishable, as well as real, greatness. It is not what a man has, but what a man is, that lasts.

The Christian's Heritage.

"*All things are yours*" (1 Cor. iii. 21).

VERY often in the newspapers there is an advertisement headed, "Heirs Wanted," which goes on to tell that somebody has died, leaving a certain property, and that whoever is connected by kinship with the late owner may, with advantage, apply to such and such a lawyer, who will give due attention to his claim.

Not many years ago, there was a remarkable case of disputed inheritance in England. A gentleman and his wife had both died, leaving a very large estate. Their only son had gone to sea many years before, and was believed to be dead. But, after some time, a man appeared upon the scene, saying, "I am the long-lost heir. I have been away in the Australian bush, and did not hear for a while of my parents' death. But now I am come back to claim my estate."

The case became known all over the world as "the Tichborne Case," and the man himself as "the Claimant." He had a very eager as well as clever advocate. He could apparently recall many things belonging to his boyhood in the ancestral home. There were marks of a peculiar kind upon his body, that seemed to confirm what he declared; and he bore undoubted resemblance in some of his features to the missing man. Numbers of people, too, came forward to swear that this was certainly he. But, after very careful sifting, the judge concluded that the man was an impostor, and that those who spoke for him were either false or mistaken. And, instead of becoming a gentleman at ease, and luxuriating on the Tichborne estate, as he had hoped, he was sent to disgrace and toil in Newgate prison.

But if you are Christ's, and Christ is yours, none can dispute your title to the Christian's heritage, which is a far richer one than any earthly property. "All things are yours." The ministers of Christ,—Paul, Apollos, and Cephas,—with their varied gifts, are yours. The world of outward beauty and fitness—the world of changeful social experience—is yours. Life, not physical or mental merely, but spiritual—a life of the soul, from God and unto God—is yours. Ay, and death is yours,—not the death of others only, as made yours for admonition concerning the unseen, but your death, —made yours, however stern his armour and seeming rough his grasp, as a herald to usher you to the land of reunions, at your Father's time, the land of rest, the land of the full and fadeless inheritance. Things present, sweet or bitter, are yours, working together for your good. And, best of all, things to come are yours —the unbroken presence of Jesus, the regained society of loved ones, the perfection of holiness, the fulfilment of every worthy desire and heavenly ambition. "Eye hath not seen, nor ear heard, nor have entered into the heart of man, the things which God hath prepared for them that love Him."

"*The Sun of Righteousness*" (Mal. iv. 2).

THE Lord Jesus is like the sun, in at least four things that readily suggest themselves.

(1) The sun is *the source of light* to a dark world. And so is Christ. As the rising of the sun in the morning chases away the gloom of night, so the coming of the Saviour brings light to the sin-darkened souls of men. He is called " the bright and *morning* Star," which tells that day is near ; but He is also the Sun of Righteousness, whose shining gives the day. And so He says of Himself, " I am the Light of the world."

(2) The sun is *the source of heat*, and thus the strengthener of healthful growing life. And so is Christ. It would be a cold as well as a dark, dark world without Him. And without His beams to shine on it, the soul cannot thrive or even live. It would be like some poor consumptive people, traces of whose cottages I saw inside the great Kentucky Cave. They were taken there that they might have air of the same heat all the year over, in the hope that they would be cured. But, instead of that, they pined and died, longing for the sun. There is warmth and healing under the Saviour's wings.

(3) The sun is *far, yet near*. That golden ball which you see daily mounting the sky is ninety-one million miles away. Yet, though far away, it is beside you every day ; for its rays lighten your path and warm your heart and bring health to your countenance. And so it is with Christ. He is far away, yet near. He is in Heaven with his Father ; yet He is with you. If you are one of His disciples, you feel His influence every day, according to His promise to be with His people " all the days," even to the end of the world.

And lastly (4) the sun is *always shining*; and so is Christ, whether we see Him or no. Clouds sometimes hide the sun ; men's eyes are sometimes closed that they cannot see him ; the motion of the earth carries them round to a point where, strain their eyes as they may, they cannot see him—and that is what we call night. But the sun is shining on all the same, bright as ever. And depend upon it, if at any time Jesus seems to cease to shine, it is because your own eyes are shut to Him ; or because some earth-born cloud has hidden Him from your view ; or because the whirl of the world has carried you away from Him, to a point from which you cannot expect to see Him. Still, whether you see Him or not, He *always shines*.

Be sure, then, to do two things—*live in the sunshine*, and seek to *reflect the radiance* of Him who says of Himself, " I am the Light of the world," but who also says to His true disciples, " Ye are the world's light."

October 7. The New Testament Passover.

"What mean ye by this service?" (Ex. xii. 26).

THAT is a question which was often put by the boys and girls of Israel, when they were gathered by their parents to celebrate the Passover. "What does it all mean?" God expected them to ask this question, and told His people to be ready to answer it. He loves the hearts and minds of the young to be exercised about sacred things, and eager to get information concerning them.

Now, as you have looked on wonderingly at the solemn celebration by your father and mother, and perhaps by your older brother or sister, of the New Testament Feast, which corresponds to the Passover,—I mean, of course the Lord's Supper,—this same question has, no doubt, often arisen in your heart—"What does it all mean?" It would take a long time fully to answer this inquiry. But we mean by it, at anyrate, these four things—

(1) That there is *a great Event we want to keep in mind.* It is the greatest event in earthly history. If Bannockburn or Waterloo is thought worth remembering, if in America the Declaration of Independence is considered worth commemorating every year, this is an event far more important and deserving to be celebrated. It is the death of God's own Son on the Cross of Calvary, in the room of guilty men. The Passover called to mind a great deliverance wrought in Egypt. But this is an infinitely greater one. We who sit at the Lord's Supper mean to say, "I am guilty, and deserved to die, but Christ Jesus died for me." Our Feast is the "Eucharist," or Feast of Thanksgiving, as we call to mind that saving sacrifice.

(2) That there is *a beloved Friend we want to keep ever near.* The Saviour, who died for us, is not dead, but lives. What He gathers us round is "a Table, not a Tomb." He rose from the dead the third day; and, though in His bodily presence He has gone to heaven, He is spiritually present with His people alway. Although unseen, He is really with us at the Feast; so that it is our "Communion," in which we draw close to the Friend of Sinners as the Best of Friends, and have fellowship with Him and His other guests.

(3) That there is *an honoured Captain to whom we would keep true.* At the Lord's Table we take the "Sacrament," or oath of loyalty, to Christ as our King, while we seek strength from Himself to fulfil it. If the soldiers of great earthly commanders, like Cæsar and Napoleon, were proud to swear allegiance to them, should not we rejoice to serve under the banner of the bravest of all leaders—the Captain of Salvation who never knew defeat? And thus in the Feast we consecrate ourselves to Him, and vow to be true and faithful, even unto death.

(4) That there is *a blessed Hope we wish to keep ever bright.* That hope is the brightest of all hopes to the Christian—"till He come." The Lord we love has gone to Heaven to prepare a place for us. But He has promised to come again to receive us to Himself, that where He is there we may be also. The ordinance of the Lord's Supper is His love-token to us, to remind us that He is not forgetting us, and to fix our thoughts and hearts upon His gracious promise, which is our hope—"So shall we ever be with the Lord."

None like God.

"Who is like unto Thee, O Lord?" (Ex. xv. 11).

This is part of the triumphal song of Miriam by the Red Sea, where Israel's experience had brought out how much Jehovah was to Israel—how He had to be everything to them. Assuredly there is none like God; and He is able and willing to be to us, still, all that He was to His ancient people.

(1) God is His people's Guide. It was He who really led Israel, though He did it by the hand of Moses and Aaron; and He never led them once astray. It seemed as if He had been an unwise Guide, in directing Israel to be brought between the mountains and the sea (verse 2), where Pharaoh might hem them completely in. God's dealings are not always for the time easy to explain. But He never leads any wrong. In Him, His people have the Best of Guides.

(2) God is His people's Commander. He spoke to Israel with a tone of authority, and insisted on their taking His way, not their own. The hearts of the Hebrews were failing them for fear. And little wonder! A hostile band is coming up the valley behind, 600 deadly charioteers, the flower of Egypt's fighting men—pressing on to take their fill of vengeance. In front, the cold sea rages, and licks the shore, as though eager to swallow them up. The stern mountains frown on them at the side, forbidding all approach to their bare, rocky heights. But God gives, through Moses, the word of command—*Go forward*; and it was "theirs but to do, or die." Unquestioning obedience is still our part when He commands, whatever be the seeming hazard it involves. For we are sure to find that—

(3) God is His people's Shield. It is very wrong to run needlessly into danger. But when God sends any of His people on a perilous road, He can protect them. The sea, instead of overflowing the Israelites, stood up like a wall of waters on either side, and made a pathway for their feet. And another strange thing was, that the pillar of cloud now came in behind the Israelites,—that is, between them and their pursuing foes; and that, while for God's people it was bright and helpful, it became dark and hindersome, on the other side, to their enemies. God's look (which brings heaven or hell to the soul) troubled the Egyptians. And then—

(4) God is His people's Song. When Moses and the people, safe across the sea, looked back on the way by which God had led them, and saw what destruction He had wrought on their fierce enemies, their hearts were so thankful that they could not but sing praise. And often since, God's people have been constrained, like them, to join heart and voice in a song of gratitude and hope. So may it be with you! No matter what odds are against you, if God is on your side you are certain to conquer in the end. Cost what it may, be sure to obey Him, and you will not have to regret it. Go forward at Christ's call and in Christ name; and, when you reach the Better Land, you will join in a better song than that of Moses—the Song of the Lamb.

October 9 A Selfish Choice, and what came of it.

"Then Lot chose him all the plain of Jordan" (Gen. xiii. 11).

LOT was the nephew of Abraham. Like his uncle, he was a religious man—to some extent. But he was worldly and selfish in spirit. And he showed that, in this early choice. You remember the circumstances. Abraham had taken Lot with him from Egypt into Canaan. Both of them had flocks, and herds, and tents; and for a time the two companies were able to live comfortably and peaceably alongside of one another. But as the flocks increased, and there was greater difficulty in finding water and pasture for so many together, strife broke out among the herdsmen; and both Abraham and Lot saw that it would be wise to separate. So the former said to his nephew—"The whole land is before you; choose you which part you will take, and I and my herds will go in another direction." And Lot lifted up his eyes, and beheld all the plain of Jordan, that it was well watered everywhere, "as the garden of the Lord." His eyes glistened; and he said, with a wave of the hand, "I'll take that!"

He thought he had made a capital choice; and so to all appearance he had. He had picked out the very best, leaving his uncle to shift for himself. But don't you think it would have been more seemly, if the young man, instead of being so very clever, had asked the older one to choose first? There was in his heart, however, no thought of gratitude, or courtesy even, toward the generous Abraham. He was only bent on grasping all he could; and, instead of politely saying, "After you, uncle!" he rushed at what seemed the prize, crying, "That, then, will be mine!"

But it never pays in the longrun to be selfish. Many a one has learned this, to his cost; as Lot now learned it. His choice led him into very bad company. There were disadvantages about it which he had little dreamt of; and, in the end, he was a case of a man "saved, yet so as by fire."

By going into Sodom, Lot *lost his self-respect*; for he was vexed with the filthy conversation of the wicked, and vexed with himself for having gone among them. He *lost his earthly all*—the property he had loved so dearly. Unlike Noah, who had all his family with him in the Ark, when the fiery trial came he *lost several members of his family*, who stayed behind with their mocking husbands. Having led his wife under the fascination of Sodom, he *lost his wife*, who, looking back as they fled from the doomed city, became a pillar of salt. In short, though we may hope that he was saved for eternity (2 Pet. ii. 7, 8), he *made shipwreck of the present life* through his selfishness. He who had started in life so high in hope and with a prospect so fair, became in his old age a poor, stripped, bare, disgraced, broken-hearted man.

"*Let us go into the house of the Lord*" (Ps. cxxii. 1).

WHAT a power companionship is, among you young people, as well as among those who are older! These words, "Let us" do this or that,—"Let us" go to such and such a place,—have often had an incalculable influence for good or evil, as spoken in another's ear by the lips of some youthful companion. Be sure that you use well the leverage that friendship gives you over the hearts and lives of others. For the way in which you use it, you will have to answer one day to God. This is an additional reason for seeking to do the right thing, and to go to the right place ourselves—that, by our example and influence, we may take others along with us.

The "house of the Lord" in the highest sense is Heaven. How often you have repeated the words, in the close of the 23rd Psalm—"And I shall dwell in the house of the Lord for ever." I hope you are to dwell there for ever. And would it not greatly increase your happiness, not only to see some of your loved companions there, but to know that you had led or encouraged them on the road thither? If this is your desire, I trust you will show them, that you love the house of the Lord on earth; and that you will join hands with some young comrade, who may perhaps have little otherwise in his surroundings to incline him in that direction, in order that you may bring him, with yourself, under the gracious influences of the sanctuary.

"Come with me to our Sabbath school: I am sure you will like my teacher," said a boy one day to another in America. The "let us go" had its effect. The new scholar was not very well dressed, but he was made heartily welcome; and, though at first he was not very well behaved, he became in the end a good student of his Bible. For he was none other than D. L. Moody—afterwards so greatly blessed as an evangelist on both sides of the Atlantic. The boy did a good work, whose "let us go" led to the Sabbath school and the Church one who was honoured afterwards to lead so many souls to the only Saviour.

"Won't you come with me to church to-night?" said an old woman to a youth, whom she saw standing idly on the street one Sabbath evening. He was one of a rough set of boys, who had agreed to meet that night, as was their wont, for frivolous amusement. His companions had not turned up at the appointed time, and in his vexation he said—"Yes, I will go." He went; and the truth as it is in Jesus laid hold of his heart. He became a true Christian, and his fame was afterwards in all the Churches, as John Williams, the great missionary to the South Seas, who accomplished so much both for Christianity and for civilisation among the savage islanders there. A word fitly spoken,—at the right time and in the right spirit,—how good it is. May your "let us go" be such a word!

October 11 — What is your price?

"And I said unto them, Give me my price" (Zech. xi. 12).

THE prophet Zechariah here puts the people to the proof, by getting out of them what they thought he as a prophet was worth. They weighed him out thirty pieces of silver, the common price of a slave. He speaks of it, ironically, as "a goodly price that I was prized at of them"; and he casts the thirty pieces of silver to the potter in the house of the Lord. He takes the liberty of disagreeing with them in their estimate of his worth. And he is right. Yet thirty pieces of silver was all that the wretched Judas got, when he sold his Divine Master—the price of a slave. It, too, went to the potter; for when Judas, in remorse, flung his thirty pieces at the feet of the rulers, they bought with them "a potter's field to bury strangers in." But was it not a paltry price to put upon the Son of God?

Sir Robert Walpole said of his contemporaries in Parliament, "You see with what zeal those gentlemen oppose me; yet I know the price of every man in this House excepting only three." And it is a common remark with the cynical, that "every man has his price,"—by which they mean that, if only you bid high enough, you can buy them, and get them to do what you will. This is not true. There are men who are what Danton claimed to be at the French Revolution—"men beyond price"—men who cannot be bought by unworthy inducements, however great.

It is certain, however, that many people hold themselves far too cheap. They "sell themselves for nought." They give themselves away for next to nothing. At the time, they may imagine they are doing well. But, sooner or later, they awaken to the discovery of how poor a bargain they have made.

As two friends were riding past a beautiful park, one of them asked the other, "How much do you suppose this estate is worth?" The answer was—"I do not know how much it is worth, but I know what it cost its late owner." "How much, then?" "His soul," said the other solemnly: "he died a wretched death, and declared on his deathbed that all his misery was due to his love of money, which had often tempted him into fraud and other sin."

That poor proprietor—poor indeed!—had surely put far too little value on *himself*. He had sold himself for nought. You should learn from Christ, you may learn in the Christian, the value to be set on an immortal soul. "Bought with a price"? Yes, but such a price—"the precious blood of Christ!" If you are Christ's, that is your price; and you dare not, you will not, hold yourself cheap enough to be knocked down for any poor bid the world can offer for you.

Simon Peter. October 12

"Thou art Simon : thou shalt be called Cephas" (John i. 42).

You remember the scene. Andrew had made the great discovery: he had "found the Christ." He had gone with the news to the man he loved best, his brother Simon. And so the Saviour and the warm-hearted fisherman of Galilee are here, for the first time, face to face ; and these are the words Jesus first speaks to him, memorable ever after—"Thou art Simon : thou shalt be called Cephas"—or Peter, the Rock.

(1) "Simon" means *one that hears* or obeys. He who bore it had been well named in this case by his parents. For he was quick to hear, and also swift to act. He was only too ready, sometimes, to obey his passing impulse. But, happily, Jesus claimed his heart ; and "Simon" came to mean, in him, *one that hears Jesus* and follows Him. He still heard other voices, and sometimes obeyed them to his sorrow—as when he yielded to the taunt of the thoughtless maid in the porch of the Judgment Hall. Yet, in the main he was Christ's "Simon"—Christ's hearer, disciple, follower ; and from the moment when he came under the Saviour's influence, he entered on a preparation for a better name.

(2) "Cephas," or "Peter," means *the Rock*. This new name which, in their first meeting, Jesus tells Simon is yet to be his, must often have sounded in his ears like a rebuke. For a long time, there was little of the Rock-Man about him. While none of the disciples was more warm-hearted, none seemed so little steadfast as he. But it was also a name which he felt he must try to live up to ; and the time came when he was the worthy wearer of it. We know, from his after history, what a pillar Simon Peter became in the early Christian Church. The outpouring of the Holy Spirit at Pentecost made a different man of him. How loyally and unflinchingly he who had before denied his Master stood forth in His name, and braved all opposition for His sake. At length he died a martyr's death,—being crucified, it is said, with his head downward,—and received the martyr's crown.

Young reader, "thou art Simon." You are worthy of the first name of the son of Jona ; for you are very ready to hear, and very quick to catch impressions, and to act upon them. May you be a constant hearer and follower *of Jesus*—giving your heart to Him, cleaving to Him as your Saviour, and confessing Him as your Lord. May you, like Simon, have God's Spirit bestowed upon you, to make you strong, and brave, and true, and worthy of your new name of Christian. And at length, when the new nature is perfectly fitted to the new name, you will have the reward which is mentioned in Rev. ii. 17, and which Simon Peter, we are very sure, is enjoying in heavenly places with Christ.

October 13   **Ready for Either.**

" Whether we live, therefore, or die, we are the Lord's " (Rom. xiv. 8).

"READY for Either" is the appropriate motto under the seal of the Baptist Missionary Union. It represents an ox standing between a plough and an altar; and the idea suggested is, that the members of the missionary band are prepared, just as Christ may appoint, either for service or for sacrifice.

This is a good motto for every Christian, whether he is a missionary to the heathen or not. For every Christian should remember that he is, in a true sense, a missionary—a man with a mission, which Christ has committed to him, and expects him to fulfil. What strength and true nobility it gives to any life, to be able to say—" Whether I live, I live unto the Lord; and whether I die, I die unto the Lord." Whoever is prepared, like Paul, to say this, is, in the best sense, "ready for anything."

The great question for each of us here is—and you cannot have it too early decided in the right way—" Am I the Lord's?" Have I taken Him to be mine—my Saviour, my Master? And have I given myself into His hand, that He may keep and govern me? If I have not, then I am not ready either for worthy living, or for peaceful dying. But if I have, then I may be well content to leave all my future in His hand. Whether I am to have a long term of service on earth or not, let it be spent heartily for the Lord I love. And then death to me will mean not separation from Him, but falling asleep in His everlasting arms. In either case, He shall be glorified, and I unspeakably blessed.

You remember the simple lines which Rowland Hill used so often to repeat—

> "And when I'm to die, 'Receive me!' I'll cry,
> For Jesus has loved me, I cannot tell why.
> But this I can find, We two are so joined,
> He'll not be in glory, And leave me behind."

The death of the Christian has been likened to the vacation morning, when children, long absent from their parents, go home. It is a time not for mourning on their account, but for joy and thanksgiving. "School is out; it is time to go home." But they do not go home to idleness. Death sets them free for larger service. "There's another poor fellow got his discharge," said one soldier to another, of a comrade who had died. "Not that," said the other: "only transferred." "Transferred where?" "To the other department." "What for?" "For duty." "What duty?" "I can't tell that: it depends on what he is fit for." This we do know, that those who have lived for Christ here, and died in Him, will live still, and far better, for Him yonder.

"Give attendance to reading" (1 Tim. iv. 13).

In this age of many books and of free libraries, there is a great deal of reading done. But perhaps there never was more need for the apostolic counsel—" *Give attendance* to reading."

There are some people, fond, in a sense, of reading, who seem just to read whatever comes in their way. They are what are called " great readers," or " voracious readers." But they cannot be called wise readers; and what they read does not come to very much after all, for they do not " give attendance " to what and when and how they should read.

The taste for reading is one which it will be well worth your while to cultivate. Those who have it are introduced into a world of which those who have it not remain ignorant, though it is lying all around them. Persons who have books at their command, but do not love reading, are not aware of how much they miss. They are shutting themselves out from one of the most refined and elevating of pleasures ; and they are depriving themselves of what might be a great source of comfort and uplifting in seasons of distress or infirmity, when the active pursuits of life have perforce to be set aside. It is to degrade reading to make it only a means of killing time ; but he who truly loves it will find in it far more than this—a means of filling up time to rich advantage—a means of becoming wiser and stronger and better, through living contact with the wisest and strongest and best who have lived before us.

The choice of *what* we read is of supreme importance in this connection. There are those whose one rule it is to read everything *new*. It is a great pleasure to read some new books. But perhaps the critic was right who said—" I suspect that nine times out of ten it is more profitable to read an old book over again than to read a new one for the first time."

There is one Old Book—old, yet ever new and up to date—which you must not neglect to read, whatever else you may neglect. It is called the Bible. It is the book to make you wise unto salvation ; and even as literature there is nothing anywhere to beat it or to compare with it. Have you ever read the Bible right through ? It is told of Mrs. Booth in her biography that she read it from cover to cover eight times before she was twelve years of age. You read little fragments of it. But it would be well for you to read it right through. This, at a moderate pace, can be done in about fifty hours ; so that, by giving to it one hour per day, you could easily read the Bible in less than a couple of months.

Give attendance to reading the Word of God. So will you lay up a rich store of enlightenment and consolation for coming days.

How God Tempts.

" God did tempt Abraham " (Gen. xxii. 1).

It is said in the first chapter of the Epistle of James, that God does not tempt any man. And yet here we are distinctly told that God tempted Abraham. How do you explain this? It is clear that there must be some explanation; for the Word of God does not contradict itself.

When it is said that God does not tempt any man, it is meant that He does not, like Satan, allure anybody to sin. He abhors sin; and it is the very last thing God would do, to tempt anybody to it. It is impossible, indeed, to think of God as the author of sin; for that would mean His ceasing to be God.

But God did tempt Abraham in the sense of testing him, trying his faith, putting him and it to the proof. This He often does with His people still. Very often He appoints something for them to do or to bear, which sorely tries them. But this is not because He wishes them harm, or because He does not love them. Far from it. It is often those, like Abraham and Job and others, whom He loves best, and in whom He has most confidence, that He puts in this way most severely to the test. And He does it, not in order that they may fall, but that they may come out from the trial more manifestly His, and all the stronger and purer for having been subjected to it.

God tests faith for at least two reasons: to *prove* it, and to *improve* it.

Satan says—" Religion is a sham. There is no such thing as real faith. A man like Job, for instance, is religious just because it pays. He does not serve God for nothing." God answers—" Satan, I will prove that you lie. I will permit Job, in providence, to be submitted to the sorest of trials. You will see that there *is* such a thing as real faith in the world, and that to test it is only to purify and strengthen it." And so, when Abraham and Job and such as they are " tempted," in this sense, God is glorified thereby.

A lady, who had become possessed of a beautifully wrought ring, took it to a jeweller to learn its value. He said the only way to be quite sure that it was genuine, and to ascertain its proper worth, would be to put it into a strong acid, which would no doubt injure it, if it were only an imitation, but which, if it were genuine, would not do it any harm. The lady hesitated. It would be such a pity to destroy the beautiful workmanship! And yet, if, as she believed, the ring was genuine, she would prize it all the more after it had been thoroughly tested. Into the acid the ring was dropped; and, after a few anxious minutes, its owner received it back, looking only the brighter for the ordeal. The tried ring was far more precious to her than before. And, though Christ does not need to get information about any of us in this way, we can readily understand that tried followers who have stood the test are among the most precious of His treasures.

"*The beginning of the sin*" (Mic. i. 13).

It was a wise advice which the old miller gave to the young one, who told him that the water was leaking through his mill-dam, but that the hole was only "a very little one." "I would try to fancy it a very big one," said his experienced friend; "for it will soon be big enough, if it is not attended to." And so it proved; for, the young miller having despised this advice, the water, before long, had broken the mill-dam completely down.

You cannot be too much upon your guard against the beginnings of sin. It may be easy to stop a little hole when it is no bigger than your hand—as the boy in Holland did, when he bravely held his hand, for an entire night, upon a hole which he saw in the "dyke," rather than allow the country to be flooded by the tide. But it will not be easy to hold back the angry rush of waters, when the breach has been fairly made. It may be easy to stamp out a spark with your foot, so long as it is only a spark. But if you allow it to catch hold and burst into a flame, not all the fire-engines in the city may be able to extinguish it until an amount of damage has been done that cannot be retrieved.

That dishonest criminal, whose character is now so completely broken down that nobody can trust him, and who has to be committed to the penitentiary or the jail, did not become a notorious blackguard all at once. He allowed his integrity of character to be sapped away by small, hidden dishonesties, which prepared for the thorough breakdown of which everybody reads in the newspapers. And so with the wretched murderer executed the other day. Had he put out the spark of evil passion long ago, it would never have grown and strengthened to the furious flame, which impelled him to take away another's life, and so brought him to the scaffold.

"Why *will* you not be persuaded to break off those habits of drink?" said a friend to a man who, in bitterest agony, had flung himself despairingly at his feet one day. "*Impossible*," he cried; "I would give everything I have to be able to do it, but the raging fire within demands *another drink*, and another, and another, and another; and so it must go on till *death*. Oh, it is hopeless, hopeless!" Yet his friend remembered him as a noble youth with the brightest of prospects opening out before him. When, a few weeks later, he died miserably in an almshouse, he added only one more to the long roll of the victims of early indulgence.

Remember the old Latin proverb—"*Obsta principiis*," Resist the beginnings; or the modern English one—"He that crushes the egg need not fear the flight of the bird."

October 17 **The Folly of Earthly Greed.**

"For we brought nothing into this world, and it is certain we can carry nothing out" (1 Tim. vi. 7).

NOTHING poorer, so far as earthly possessions are concerned, could be imagined than a new-born baby, unless it be a dead man whose body has been laid aside for burial. The one has his swaddling clothes given to him, and the other is provided with a shroud. But both, in themselves, are utterly destitute of worldly good. Yet the true wealth does not lie in outward things. That is what the apostle is urging here. The life of the soul is the great thing. Every baby that is born is an immortal being, and every person, old or young, who dies, enters upon an endless life beyond, of weal or woe, though no longer seen to mortal view. Therefore do not let us make too much, Paul says, of the mere good things of time. Having food and raiment, let us be therewith content; and let us follow after the higher possessions that will abide with us for ever—righteousness, godliness, faith, love, patience, meekness.

The Bible here, as elsewhere, gives a true account of human life, and offers wise and sound advice as to how to make the most of life. It was in the use of this text that a colporteur in Ireland commended the New Testament to a crowd of Roman Catholics so much, that quite a number of copies were purchased for use both in Ireland and in America.

He said it was a good book and a true; and by way of giving them a specimen, he read this verse—"We brought nothing into this world, and it is certain we can carry nothing out." "Deed and that's true, anyway," said one of the bystanders, with whom most of the others concurred. One of them, however, bent upon his joke, struck in—"Sure, then, and it's not always true; for there was Biddy Malone, who had a half sovereign that she wanted to keep her folks from quarrelling over when she was gone—so she swallowed it just before she died!" The crowd laughed; but the first man earnestly retorted—"Ay, but what about her *soul* ?"

Yes; that is the great question. It is a matter for thankfulness if we have what the Shorter Catechism calls "a competent portion" of the good things of this life. To be rich in earthly possessions is not by any means always a thing to be desired; and there is a way of winning them that is the opposite of real gain. But godliness with contentment *is* great gain. And what we should covet is the unsearchable riches, the imperishable wealth, of those that "win Christ"—who, though He was rich, yet for our sakes became poor, that we through His poverty might be made rich.

Christ the Truth.

"A Teacher sent from God" (John iii. 2). . . . *"I am the Truth"* (John xiv. 6.)

THE Lord Jesus Christ is a Teacher. He is not only, as Nicodemus called Him, a Teacher sent of God, but a Teacher who is God. And since He is so divinely wise, patient, and kind in His training of us, we should ever seek to be humble, eager, and diligent learners in His school. You should make every "Teach me," that you find in the Bible, a prayer. Go with it to Jesus, saying, "Teach me to pray—Teach me to do Thy will—Teach me Thy ways, O Lord"; and He will make you wise unto salvation.

Then, Jesus is the Truth. This he calls Himself: and again and again the term *true* is applied to Him by others. Especially in St. John's Gospel you may find quite a number of instances. And if you look at these you will see that He is called "true" for two reasons—both for what He *says*, and for what He *is*.

Jesus is the "true and faithful Witness," who never speaks false. An untrue word has never once fallen from His lips, and never shall. You may rely on all His statements. You may trust all His promises. He will fulfil to His servants every good word in which He has caused any of them to hope. And then, He is "the true Light," "the true Bread," "the true Vine," because He is so real, so genuine, and never disappoints. The things you see and handle, and taste, dear young people, are not by any means the only real things. Rather are they, by comparison, the shadows. It is Jesus who is the True Light, to lead; the True Bread, to satisfy; the True Vine, union to whom gives real life. Pray that He may be yours.

Since Jesus is so true, how should you regard and treat Him? You are to believe Him, for He never deceives. You are to believe *in* Him, for He never disappoints. And, taking Him as your Teacher and Example, you are not only to *speak* the Truth always, but to *be* ever true like Him—refusing to be unreal, and to act a part.

"What is truth?" was asked of a deaf and dumb boy one day. He drew on his slate a straight line; and for falsehood a crooked line. It was a significant answer. You must beware of crooked ways and crooked character, if you would please, and be worthy of that Master who *is* the Truth.

There is an expression in one of Paul's Epistles, which was the chosen motto of one of my Edinburgh professors,—that remarkable man, John Stuart Blackie,—and which, I think, you might very well take as a motto for your life. You will find it in Ephesians iv. 16—"Speaking the truth, in love." It means, more literally, as the margin has it, "being sincere, in love." Or, as Professor Blackie used to translate it, to show that more than *speaking* the truth was meant—"*Truthing it*, in love."

October 19 ## Lessons from Babel.

"The Lord did there confound the language of all the earth, and scatter them abroad" (Gen. xi. 9).

Perhaps you sometimes think that it would be very nice if everybody spoke the same language still; for then you would not have to learn French or German at school, and you could travel anywhere without having to "get up" a foreign language. There is a man in Europe who is trying this very thing—to have a language adopted by everybody, which he calls "Volapuk." But I do not think he will succeed. Though your grammar and spelling seem hard, I think you would all like English better than Volapuk!

At anyrate, God found it desirable to scatter men and divide their tongues; and this is how it came about. Clubbing together on the plain of Shinar, they began to feel the strength of numbers, and they were filled with pride. Their crowning desire was to make themselves a great name. "Let *us* build *us* a city and a tower," they said, "whose top may reach unto heaven." This was the form their pride took. God was not in all their thoughts, and they did not consult Him about their plans. Some think they meant to scale to heaven; some think they wanted to make a shelter in case there should be another Flood; some think the tower was meant to be an idol's temple. The last supposition is probably right. And the idol was *self*.

But God was looking on (verse 5), and though He was not consulted, He had a word to say to their plans. He had a "Let us"— a resolve—in opposition to theirs, and He broke all their plans in pieces. He scattered the proud in the imagination of their hearts. This He did very simply. He confounded their language, so that they might not understand one another's speech. One man asked for plaster, and his neighbour brought a barrowful of bricks. Another needed a hammer, and was supplied with a hod of plaster, or a trowel. They began to get confused, and then vexed with each other, and angry. The tower became a tower of "Babel," or confusion. The tie between them was broken, and by mutual consent they scattered in families and tribes over the earth.

Let us remember that God looks at all our work, and everything depends on the result of His inspection (1 Cor. iii. 13). See that you have an object in life which He can approve, and take your plan from Him. Then there will be a place for your life-work in His great scheme of service. Otherwise, if self-glory is your object, your life will be a failure: if earthly fortune or fame be your tower, it will come to nought. For, no matter how many you have with you, this will not make a wrong thing right. All the world were united at Babel; but then, God was against them.

Let us not forget that in divine judgment there is often mercy. It was well for the world that men were scattered over the earth; as it was well in the Early Church when persecution sent missionaries everywhere from Judea. As Babel scattered men, so Calvary gathers them. And, as was seen at Pentecost, when the Gospel is preached in every tongue, men of every tribe will learn the one Song, and speak the one language of the Spirit.

"*When the enemy shall come in like a flood*" (Isa. lix. 19).

WHAT shall happen then? Will it be all over with God's people? No. For then "the Spirit of the Lord shall lift up a standard against him." And that, as the margin reminds us, "will put him to flight."

No other standard but the Lord's would do it. When a flood comes in, it makes man feel very powerless. Every now and again we read of deluges of rain swelling the rivers in America and elsewhere, and whole valleys being swept by the torrent—men, and cattle, and houses, and stacks, and everything being carried by the flood to destruction. At such a time, how hopeless a thing it would be for the greatest general to plant his standard down, and say that this would stay the onward rush of waters. Why, the standard, the general, and his soldiers too would have to yield before it.

We read in old British history of a king, Canute by name, saying to the waves, in presence of his courtiers, "Stop!" But the waves rolled in as before. It needs the King of all the earth to say, "Thus far and no farther!" if the tide is to be driven back.

You remember how, in the days of Noah, the rain continued to pour day after day, and night after night, and it seemed as if it never would stop. It rained continuously for forty days and forty nights. But at God's time it ceased. Just so long as He willed it, the waters prevailed; and when He willed it, they began to abate. At His bidding, "a wind passed over the earth, and the waters assuaged, and the rain was restrained" (Gen. viii. 1, 2).

And what God did in Noah's days, and can do still, in nature, He is able to do in the society of men. It is an unspeakable comfort to know that "the Lord sitteth upon the flood, the Lord sitteth King for ever." The supreme control is in the hand of the infinitely wise and holy One. It may sometimes seem as though influences hostile to the cause of truth, and purity, and temperance would altogether prevail. The Church of God has been in circumstances which appeared to threaten utter defeat, if not destruction. But when the floods have lifted up their voice, as in Reformation and Covenanting days, it has been found that the voice of God, though by comparison a still small voice, was mightier than the noise of many waters.

If ever you have to encounter a flood of trial or of temptation that threatens to carry you away, may you find a refuge in God. If He is your hiding-place, "surely the floods of great waters shall not come nigh you." The standard of His Spirit will bid the tempest back. He will compass you about with songs of deliverance,

Self=made Men.

"Fashioning yourselves" (1 Pet. i. 14).

After what "fashion" is your life, I wonder, to be framed? This is a very important question,—the most important of all questions that concern your future, on earth and afterwards.

The word "fashion" means literally *shape* or *make*, from the Latin word (as you boys know) meaning "to make." It is often used of the cut of a person's clothes, which are said to be "in the fashion," or otherwise, according as they conform, or do not conform, to the shape or style that is prevalent and popular at any particular time. And there are people whose great ambition it is to be always "fashionably dressed," and to keep in line, in other respects, with the customs and requirements of "fashionable society."

Here we are reminded that there is something far more important than the clothes we wear, and the outward style we keep up. The question of fashion is a much more serious one than many "fashionable people" imagine. It cuts immensely deeper than the shape of one's garments. It has to do with the cut, not of our clothes only, but of our character—with the shaping of *ourselves*.

Persons who have risen in the world, who have fought their way up from a humble to a prominent position, are often spoken of as "self-made men." Such are sometimes foolishly ashamed of the fact that they have "risen," and do not wish it to be known or remembered that the point from which they started was such a lowly one. Others of them are foolishly boastful about it, like a vulgar rich man, who said in a very impressive style to those he met—"I am a self-made man, sir!" and got as a quiet answer once—"So I should have thought, sir—and rather a poor job you have made of it!" Others of them wear their honour modestly—for it *is* an honour to have come to the front through personal merit and noble effort—and are not anxious either to conceal or to boast about the circumstances of their early life. Such were Lincoln, Livingstone, and Garfield, and scores of others that could be mentioned, to whom there has been accorded universal admiration without their asking for it.

But the great thing my young readers are to learn from the text before us is, that in a very real sense you are all to be self-made men or women. You are to be going on forming habits, good or bad, and shaping your character day by day. See that you "fashion yourselves" in a worthy way. It is a great thing to have a good model to go by in making anything. In constructing a ship or an engine, the artificer would be foolish if he chose an inferior model when he might have the best. Now, remember this—you have the best of all models for character and life in the Lord Jesus Christ, who has "left us an example that we should follow in His steps." He has left us, too, the promise and the gift of His Holy Spirit, to help us so to walk as we have Him for an example.

Confessing Christ.

" Whosoever, therefore, shall confess Me before men, him will I confess" (Matt. x. 32).

If Christ has really the confidence and love of our hearts, we ought not surely to be ashamed or afraid to let this be known. In religion, as in other matters, the brave course is the best course. Many reasons might be given why we should be ready, whatever our circumstances may be, to acknowledge our Saviour. We have time to speak now of only two.

1. It is *due to Christ*. If He is not ashamed to call us brethren, it is the very last thing we should be, to be ashamed to call Him Saviour.

Suppose you fell into the river or the sea one day, and a man you did not know, and upon whom you had no claim, sprang into the water and saved your life at the risk of his own: would you not be very grateful to him—so grateful that you could not but make mention of his name and his noble deed to others? You would think very meanly of yourself if you were to sneak away from the spot, and to bury the remembrance of what you owed to your deliverer as a secret in your own breast. But those whom Christ has saved have far greater reason for gratitude to Him, and open acknowledgment of Him, than in the case supposed. He not only risked His life, but *gave* His life for their salvation. And so far from having any claim upon Him, they were His enemies, and deserved only to be left to their destruction. If Christ has brought you life through His death, and joy through His sorrow, it is the least you can do to acknowledge it.

2. It is *due to yourself*. A brave, open acknowledgment of the Saviour will be good for your own soul. Not only in view of eternity, but in view of time, and of your progress in the divine life, it will be well for you frankly and without delay to avow your Saviour. Secret discipleship cannot expect to thrive. It hides in the shadow, it lives in the darkness, when it ought to be out in the open light of God's reconciled countenance. Shrinking from the duty of confession, it misses the benefit of it.

It was a wise as well as a brave course taken by a United States lawyer, when he was converted from scepticism to the Christian faith. The very evening of the day when he found Christ, he surprised his wife, on arriving home, by announcing, "I must set up my family altar. Let us go into the drawing-room and pray together." There was a company present, including a number of lawyers; and his wife, though a good woman, suggested, in a moment of weakness, that perhaps they had "better have prayers by themselves in the kitchen." "No," he answered; "it is the first time I have invited the Lord to my house, and I do not propose to invite Him to the kitchen." He forthwith explained to the guests the change that had been wrought in him; and added—"While I offer my first family prayer, you can remain if you will. I leave it to your choice." They all remained, and did not think the less of their host, who afterwards became Judge M'Lean, the Chief-Justice of the United States.

October 23   **Be Pitiful!**

"*And be ye tender-hearted*" (Eph. iv. 32).   "*Be pitiful*" (1 Pet. iii. 8).

THE word translated "tender-hearted" in Ephesians is the same word which is rendered "pitiful" in 1st Peter. These two great apostles, Paul and Peter, express to us, in an important particular, the mind of God, when they urge, with one voice—"Be kind."

This is a charge which young people, as well as old, greatly need to have sounded in their ears.

(1) *Be kind to one another.* It is a mistake to suppose that it is manly to be rude and selfish. A boy who delights in bullying those who are smaller or weaker than himself, or in taking advantage of the good-nature of those who are unwilling to retaliate, is a coward at heart. Every real man is a *gentle*-man, however much strength he may have in alliance with his gentleness. A boy who bullies, or a girl who pinches and vexes a companion, and takes pleasure in seeing others in pain or in discomfort, has great need of this apostolic counsel—"Be kind to one another." It is just as easy to be kind as to be unkind; and it is really far more pleasant. What Shakespeare says of mercy is true of what we call "kindness" too. It is twice blessed. Therefore, next time you are tempted to play a saucy trick on a companion or to do him some injury, try to do him some good and give him a pleasant surprise instead. And how happy you yourself will feel!

(2) *Be kind even to your enemies.* This is what Christ tells us to be. This is what He Himself was. It was when we were enemies that Christ died for us. And this is the true way to get the better of a foe. This secures the real victory. "Oh, master, do buy him!" pleaded a favourite slave with respect to a tottering old negro whom they saw in the market. His master rather unwillingly consented. When the old man was brought home he who had got his wish took him to his own cabin and treated him there as tenderly as if he had been his son. "Why is this?" it was asked: "Is he your father?" "No." "Your brother?" "No." "Your friend?" "No; he is my enemy. It was he who long ago stole me from my native village and sold me into slavery; and now, as the good Lord bade me, I am heaping coals of fire upon his head."

(3) *Be kind to the dumb creatures.* Remember that they are God's, and that He is angry with those who in any wise abuse them. There is a Society for preventing cruelty to animals, such as horses and dogs and cats; and it is doing much good. It would do yet more good, if every boy and girl in the country were to join a great league of pity, and to practise all through life the law of kindness toward what we call the lower creatures, both great and small. It is in early youth that dispositions of heart as well as habits of mind are fostered for good or evil. Diocletian, who afterwards became the great persecutor of the early Christians, found in childhood his favourite pastime in torturing flies. Have no kinship with the like of him. But be kind not only to your domestic pets, but to the birds and the bees and the butterflies. Rebuke heartlessness everywhere. "Be pitiful!"

Be Courteous!

"Be courteous: not rendering evil for evil" (1 Pet. iii. 8, 9).

RELIGION has to do with the little things of life as well as with the great. In teaching us to provide for the interests of eternity, the Bible is not forgetful of the happiness of the present life, or of the small details of duty which tend to promote it. The Book which charges us to "flee from the wrath to come," and to "lay hold upon eternal life," also addresses to us this admonition—"Be courteous." We are hereby reminded that the delicacies of the Christian character are of much importance in the sight of God.

"Courtesy," from its derivation, makes us think of Court life, and the manners of the Court. But courtliness and courteousness are not by any means the same. The difference is manifest, and cuts deep. One may be *courtly*, while the heart is all the time unkind and insincere; but one cannot be truly *courteous* unless he is giving expression by look and act to a goodwill that is really within his heart. Courtliness may be merely an affair of outward deportment. Courtesy is an affair at the same time of the spirit within. A person who merely puts on "company manners" now and then, is not a truly courteous person, but only a poor imitator for the time of a virtue he does not possess.

Courtesy has been described as "benevolence in trifles." It is not easy to define it; and this is perhaps as good a description as any. It consists in carrying kindness and the desire to please within the breast, and giving natural and suitable expression to it habitually, *especially in little things.* There are people who would do a big, kind thing for a neighbour when he was hard pushed, because their hearts are really kind. But at ordinary times they are rude and careless in their behaviour to others; and so, through not being courteous, they fail to sweeten society as they might do, and sometimes, in thoughtlessness, cause pain where they could just as easily have given pleasure instead.

The want of courtesy has been sometimes very aptly rebuked. "Do you permit a negro to be more of a gentleman than yourself?" said President Jefferson to his grandson, who did not return a negro's bow. "No, gentlemen," said General Robert Lee, to some soldiers in a tramcar, "if there was no seat for the infirm old woman, there can be none for me." They had left the old woman standing, but had sprung to their feet to give the General a place. His words did not make them very comfortable—especially the officers among them; and soon there was plenty of room in that car.

Courtesy, on the other hand, has often been strikingly rewarded when it was not looking for any recompense. Two boys, a rich and a poor, were going to a merchant's office to apply for a situation. A ragged little girl happened to fall on the icy pavement, and lost her pennies. The first boy only laughed: he was the gentleman's son, too! The other went to the girl's help, found one of her pennies, replaced the other from his own scanty store, and so dried her tears. The merchant had seen it all from his window; and it was the poor boy who secured the situation, though his only testimonial was his courtesy.

October 25

Son Timothy.

"This charge I commit unto thee, son Timothy" (1 Tim. i. 18).

TIMOTHY is one of those Bible characters concerning whom we are not told a great deal, but whom, nevertheless, we seem to know very well. In Paul's two letters, as well as in the Book of Acts, we have glimpses of him, which enable us to form a tolerably clear conception of his history and of his character.

Timothy was a Highlander. I do not mean to say that he belonged to Celtic Scotland; but he was born in the uplands of Lycaonia,—away up among the hilly districts, which the Apostle of the Gentiles visited in his missionary journeys, not less willingly than the seaboard towns in Asia Minor. And it would have been worth Paul's while to penetrate to Lystra, if it had resulted in nothing else than the gaining of this one Highland lad of Asia Minor as a convert to Jesus Christ. For Timothy became a great soldier in the Christian army; and in the second generation of the Church, after Paul himself was gone, he had to fill a notable place.

We cannot give any full account of Timothy's career. But there are several things which we do know for certain about him.

1. He was *a good child*. It was perhaps easier for him to be this, than for some. He came of a good stock. His grandmother Lois was a godly woman; and so was his mother Eunice. The latter was a Jewess, who became a Christian. And though Timothy's father was a Greek, he was perhaps well affected to Christianity, and at anyrate he allowed Christian influences to be very freely exercised on young Timothy's heart. The boy, in our earliest glimpse of him, is seen sitting at the feet of his grandmother, or in his mother's lap, reverently listening to what they have to tell him.

2. He was *a good scholar*. I do not know whether or not he was what is called a very learned man, though it is said he afterwards became a bishop, or overseer of several churches. But very early in life he became very wise: for he was made "wise unto salvation." And what led to this was his early instruction in the Scriptures within his pious home. He was Paul's "son in the faith," so that the apostle was probably the immediate means of his conversion. But Lois and Eunice prepared the way. They set the tinder for the divine spark. And it was then and for ever well for Timothy that there was one book at anyrate which he had learned well—his Bible (2 Tim. i. 5, iii. 14, 15).

3. He was *a good man and a good minister*. Timothy was both. He could not well be the one without the other. None can be a good minister without being first a good man. And none is a good man without being in some true sense a good "minister"—a servant or helper, that is, of the good cause. Timothy was "well reported of by the brethren" (Acts xvi. 2). When he grew up, it was seen that grace reigned in his heart. The child was father to the man. And he not only ministered to Paul, "serving with him as a son in the gospel," but he was what you should seek to be, in whatever sphere of life God may place you, "a good soldier of Jesus Christ."

"It is not hidden from thee, neither is it far off" (Deut. xxx. 11).

THE word of life is not a secret, hidden thing, which few can discover and understand. The way of life is not a path difficult of access and far away, so that few can reach it. Salvation is a secret revealed: it is a blessing near at hand. You have not to get one to climb to heaven to bring it down to you. You have not to cross the ocean in order to make it yours. Salvation is here, just where you stand. It may be yours, as you read this sentence, just for the taking. The river of life which proceeds from the Throne of God and of the Lamb has this peculiarity, that it always will be found flowing just by the side of any poor sinner who is thirsting for it.

You may have heard the story of a vessel, which, through a defect in the compass, or something of that kind, had wandered far out of its course, till the water-supply on board became completely exhausted. The crew and passengers were in the greatest distress. They were under the awful tortures of unalleviated thirst; and as they looked abroad upon the wide ocean, and saw no help for them at all, they were ready to sink into despair. "Water, water everywhere, but not a drop to drink!" It was becoming almost maddening. But at length they descried another vessel on the horizon. As she came nearer, they signalled her. At close quarters, their captain shouted across through the speaking-trumpet —"Give us water: we are dying of thirst." Back came the unlooked-for but welcome answer—"You are in the mouth of the Amazon. Dip and drink!" Oh, how quickly the pails went down; and up came the delightful supply of fresh river-water to slake their burning thirst!

Even so, there are souls in this world dying for thirst, while the water of life is within their offer and within their reach. Has some young reader been thinking of salvation as a thing to be waited for a long time, as something far away, which he cannot hope to secure till he is much older and wiser than at present? Jesus says to such, "It may be yours now, for the taking. The water of life is at your side. Stoop down, and drink, and live!"

God's own children, too, should remember that the provision they have in Christ, is a supply that will not fail, and that the help He promises them is near and available. There is a story told by James Gilmour, suggestive of what sometimes happens under the gospel. A poor old Irishwoman was grieving her heart out because her son was not sending her money to pay her rent. What was his letter to her from abroad without that? She was in the greatest anxiety and sorrow. Yet all the while there was a post-office order in her hand, which the letter enclosed, more than enough for all her need! To her it was a valueless piece of paper, because she did not recognise its worth. Yet it only wanted her signature or her mark to bring the very boon she was most anxious for. Just so, we have in the promise of Christ an order which only needs our filling up to secure for us all needed blessing. It is not hidden or far away. "If ye shall ask anything in My name, I will do it."

October 27   In the Wrong Slot.

" Wherefore do ye spend money for that which is not bread?" (Isa. lv. 2).

THE picture presented in the opening of this familiar and beautiful 55th chapter of Isaiah is a very suggestive one. We see a great crowd of people eagerly seeking after good, but seeking it in vain because they are not looking for it in the right quarter. They are thirsty, but they are turning to wells without water to quench their thirst. They are hungry, but they are spending money for what is not bread—no more real bread than a sawdust biscuit is, whatever appearances may say. They are eager to have their hearts satisfied, but they are expending their labour on that which satisfieth not.

A sorrowful picture, is it not? It is true to life, however. There are multitudes of people all around us who are just doing this very thing—foolishly seeking for true good where they cannot possibly find it. But there is one point of light in the picture, suggestive of hope for these weary toilers. And it is this—that above the crowd there stands One of infinite majesty, but of infinite loving-kindness too, who calls to all who are willing to hear Him, to come to Him and He will freely give them what they elsewhere seek in vain. Are they thirsty and weary? He will give them wine and milk for the asking. Are they hungry? They are welcome to eat from His stores that which is good; and He is quite sure that none who obey His invitation will have reason to be disappointed. It is Jesus, I need hardly say, who thus calls: He who stood on the last, the great day, of the feast, and cried, "If any man thirst, let him come unto Me, and drink." If you come to Him, He will give you the Living Water: He will feed your soul with the True Bread.

Young reader, it is quite natural and right for you to seek for what will satisfy your heart, and to seek it with all the energy and diligence of which you are capable. But take care not to make the fatal blunder of seeking it in the wrong direction. There is many an active life that is quite misspent, just because it is so miserably misdirected.

A little boy of my acquaintance had a great disappointment one day lately. You know "the penny in the slot" machines that are set up at railway stations and elsewhere, which give out in exchange for your coin a biscuit, a stick of chocolate, or something of that sort? Well, this boy was persuaded by a bigger one to put his penny into what looked like a slot one day. But it was really only the slit for a broad latch-key in the lock of a gate. And so, though the child looked eagerly, he got no return for his penny. The elder boy laughed at his disappointment. But it was no laughing matter for the little fellow. It cost him, I rather think, some bitter tears. How many are like him—spending their means and their labour on that which brings no satisfaction in return. They are putting their penny into the wrong slot!

Be Content!

" Be content with such things as ye have" (Heb. xiii. 5).

This apostolic counsel is not meant to encourage indolence or to check worthy ambition. But what it is aimed against is, the covetous spirit which is so bent on getting more of this world's good that it cannot enjoy what it already has.

The story is told of Benjamin Franklin, that, seeing a child looking at a plate of apples as if he wanted them, he handed him the biggest and rosiest of the lot. But he evidently wanted more. Another was offered him; and now both the boy's hands were filled. But still he gazed at the dish. Franklin handed him a third apple, which he eagerly received. But he was not able to hold so many treasures, and all the three apples rolled upon the floor. The child lay down and wept. "There," said the American Solomon, "is a little man, who has more wealth than he can enjoy."

A man who has but a little, with the spirit of contentment, is in reality far richer than the man who is nominally the possessor of a great deal of earthly good, but is filled with a spirit of covetousness and unrest. He is not only himself happier, but he will probably do more for society with his comparative poverty than the other with his abounding wealth. It has been sarcastically said of the covetous man, that he is of service much in the same way as the pig is—after he is dead. "The pig when alive does not carry like the horse, or give milk like the cow, or watch the house like the dog; but when he is dead, he will cut up well. And so is it," says an old writer, "with the covetous rich man." It is after he is dead that people get some good out of him. But what of *him*, then? He knew little or nothing of true comfort or heart's ease on earth. And what of his happiness, when not only that on which his greedy heart was set has been snatched from his sight, but even that which he seemed to have has been taken from his grasp! When the manna was greedily sought in greater quantity, and selfishly kept for longer time, than God desired it to be, it turned to worms. And there are others besides the ancient Israelites who have found this, to their cost.

Godliness with contentment is great gain. The well-known Matthew Henry, whose commentaries are perhaps on your father's bookshelves, had little of this world's good, but that little he used well. His heart was set on higher things, and with his worldly portion he was content. One night, on going to preach, he was met by four men and robbed of all that was in his purse—some ten or eleven shillings. Among his reflections afterwards, in his diary, were these:—"(1) What reason have I to be thankful to God who have travelled so much and yet was never robbed before! (2) What a deal of evil the love of money is the root of, that four men would venture their lives and souls for about half a crown a-piece! (3) See the vanity of worldly wealth: how soon we may be stripped of it! How loose, therefore, we should sit to it!"

October 29 — The Place of Safety.

"*My hand*" . . . "*My Father's hand*" (John x. 28, 29).

It is as if Jesus were anxious here to make the assurance of safety for His people doubly sure. He first says, "They shall never perish, neither shall any man pluck them out of My hand." And then He adds, "And no man is able to pluck them out of My Father's hand. I and My Father are one." If you have accepted Jesus as your Saviour, and are following Him as your Shepherd-King, how safe you are! He and His father are at once about securing you from destruction. It is as though Jesus said—"My hand is about you, as I might clasp in the hollow of it a precious jewel, refusing to let it go. And the Father's hand is about My hand: so that you have a twofold omnipotence for your defence. Who, then, can do you hurt?"

Satan tries hard to snatch or lure the sheep of Christ away to their destruction. He does His best to wrest the jewels of Jesus from His hand. But he cannot succeed. No member of Christ's flock—not even the smallest lamb in it—will be amissing from the fold at last. None of the jewels of Christ—not even the tiniest of all His gems—will be awanting from His diadem in the day when He makes up His jewels. If Satan had only human power to reckon with, he would laugh at such defence, and your soul would not be safe from his malice for a single day. But when it is a case of overcoming the omnipotence of the Almighty Father and the Saviour-Son, the great enemy is completely baffled. He has the will to destroy Christ's people, but he utterly lacks the power to do it.

Is it not a great comfort that our safety depends, not upon ourselves, but upon Jesus? If it were only the hold that your feeble hand or mine could take and keep of Him that kept us safe, alas for our security! Satan would not take long to shake us loose. But, it is Christ's hold of us, and not our hold of Him, that is the secret of our preservation. If He holds us in "the right hand of *His* righteousness,"—that hand so strong as well as tender,—none can pluck us thence.

A story is told of two little girls, whom we shall call Mary and Nellie, which very prettily illustrates this great truth. They had been singing in a corner of the nursery, while their mother was writing; and after giving some snatches of the hymn, "Safe in the arms of Jesus," Nellie was heard to say—"Sister, how do you know you are safe?" "Because I am holding Jesus with both my hands tight!" answered Mary. "Ah! that's not safe," said the younger sister: "suppose Satan came along and cut your two hands off!" Mary looked perplexed for a minute; but the anxiety soon lifted from her face as she joyfully exclaimed—"Oh, I forgot! I forgot! Jesus is holding *me* with *His* two hands. Satan can't cut *them* off; and so I *am* safe!"

"The night is far spent: the day is at hand" (Rom. xiii. 12).

THERE are two sorts of twilight. There is the evening twilight, with its deepening shadows, as the sun goes down beneath the western horizon. And there is the twilight of the dawn, as the first rays of the rising sun are shooting above the eastern horizon—struggling with the darkness of the night, and overcoming it. If you were walking along a road you had never traversed before in the twilight, it would matter a great deal for your comfort, and perhaps even for your safety, which of the two twilights it was that enveloped you. The evening twilight would mean for you quickly darkening night. The morning twilight would mean the speedy dawn of blessed day, when you would rejoice in the sunshine, and see all things clearly as you pursued your onward way.

Now, there are two ways of looking at the swift flight of the earthly life, and the nearer and nearer approach of death, which is to bring so great a change of one kind or another to every one of us.

"The day is far spent: the night is at hand"—so says the worldly heart, if it can be brought to reflect at all upon the matter, and to speak out its thoughts. The man who is living without God and without hope in the world, even when he seems most gay, is haunted by an uncomfortable feeling that every year as it flits by is bringing him nearer to what he dreads. The thought is forced in upon him sometimes—"Life is short; death is coming; what light I have will soon go out in darkness; the gloomy shadow is creeping nearer and nearer to enshroud me; it is verging toward twilight already; ere long I shall be under the total eclipse of everlasting night."

"The night is far spent: the day is at hand"—so says the man of faith, in prospect of death and the endless life on which it is to usher him. Here he is often in darkness. But yonder is the light! Here he is sometimes in sorrow and in gloom—groping if haply he may find the way. But yonder is gladness and good cheer! And though now for a season, if need be, he is in darkness and in heaviness, he is even now a child of the light and of the day. The valley through which he is meantime being led is begloomed with sin and sorrow. But he is to be brought out by and by into everlasting day. Have not some rays at least of the Sun of Righteousness already reached his soul, to lead and cheer him on? The night is far spent. It is twilight now; but the morning, not the evening, twilight. The dawn is near. The dayspring has arisen. The Sun Himself will soon appear. Then all sadness and cheerlessness will be over. Joy cometh in the morning.

October 31. Bread from Heaven.

"I will rain bread from heaven for you" (Ex. xvi. 4).

WHEN the hungry Israelites went out, the morning after Moses told them God would send them bread, they saw the whole ground covered with a small round thing, that looked like hoar-frost upon the ground. And in their astonishment they cried, "Man-na,' *What can this be?* And so the manna got its name.

How very good it was in God to open the windows of heaven and pour out day by day so much blessing on these poor travellers! The supply did not once fail them during all the forty years they had to travel in the wilderness; and for many long generations after Israel were in Canaan a pot full of the manna was kept within the ark of the Congregation, to remind the people of how kind and faithful God had been to their fathers upon their desert march.

Now, I wonder how *you* would have liked to be depending, as these children of Israel were, on the shower of manna, morning by morning, for your food? When you look into your mother's well-stocked pantry, perhaps you are thankful that your case is different; and you think that even if the storeroom were to get empty, your father has only to send an order down the street to some of the shops to have it filled again. Yet your case and that of the Israelites are not so very different after all. Learn from their experience, that—

(1) *Daily bread comes from God.* It is He who has given you your father to work for your support, and your kind mother to plan for your good, and "to get ends to meet" at home. It is He who made the seed spring, and who watered the crop, and sent the sunshine, and gave the harvest. And, moreover, it is He who not only gives you the food, but gives hunger to eat it and enjoy it. The commonness of our "common mercies" should make us *all the more grateful to Him.*

(2) *We should be very thankful if we have enough*, though we may not be what men call rich. The Israelites were taught by God not to be grasping. Everyone was welcome to gather as much as he and his family could eat. But if any man was greedy and tried to hoard up the manna, it bred worms and stank. It is a wise prayer in the Book of Proverbs, "Give me neither poverty nor riches; feed me with food convenient for me."

(3) *Daily bread is needed for the soul.* And God gives that too. Jesus says, "I am the Bread of Life." Do you know what it is to hunger in soul for Jesus, and to have your heart strengthened by feeding daily upon Him who is the true Bread from heaven? Remember that just as the Israelites had to seek and gather the manna day by day, you must seek Jesus daily in prayer, if your soul is to be fed and your heart satisfied.

The True Test.

"*Daily*" (Ps. lxi. 8 ; Luke ix. 23).

This word "daily" is a very important word, in more aspects of it than one. Considering our continual dependence upon God, how important it is that we should receive daily bread from Him. Considering our continual responsibility to God, how important it is that we should remember our daily duty toward Him. Our life ought to be a life of daily faith and daily obedience.

It is this latter point which is emphasised in the two verses chosen for to-day. In the first of them (Ps. lxi. 8), the Psalmist declares his anxiety that he may "daily perform his vows," as one who is to sing praise to God's name for ever. In the second (Luke ix. 23), Christ reminds those who would be His disciples, that in coming after Him they must be prepared to "take up their cross daily," and follow Him.

It is the daily life that is the true test of character. It is not what people say when they are in certain circumstances and surroundings. It is not what people appear in particular places, such as the church or the Sabbath school, on special occasions. But it is what people are in the ordinary run of daily life, when they are off their guard, amid their customary everyday surroundings, that reveals their real character.

"But you should hear his language on the week day!" So said a member of a Sunday-school class to his teacher, who had been praising one of the other boys and pointing to him as a model, for good behaviour in the class, and for always knowing his lesson well. "But you should hear his language on the week day!" With surprise and pain the teacher looked right in the face of his "model scholar." Guilt and confusion were written there. But the teacher's look of grief spoke rebuke more eloquently than words. And, by the blessing of God, such a change was wrought in the boy's heart that none of his companions could point the finger at him any longer and say—"Oh, he is one thing on the Sunday and a very different thing on the week day. You should hear and see what he is from day to day!"

If the Sabbath is made to us what God designed it to be, and if what we learn when in the Sunday school, and otherwise, has its due effect upon us, our whole week will be the better for having the Lord's Day, with its sacred influences, at its beginning. We must not shrink from the application to us of Christ's own test—"By their fruits ye shall know them." And we should seek so to live, that any day that is taken as a fair sample of the rest, may be a day in which we are found "doing justly, loving mercy, and walking humbly with our God." Day by day may we magnify Him, even as we hope to praise Him for ever and ever.

> "The trivial round, the common task,
> Will furnish all we ought to ask,—
> Room to deny ourselves, a road
> To bring us *daily* nearer God."

Shoes or Sermons.

"And they were judged every man according to their works" (Rev. xx. 13).

HIRAM GOLF was a shoemaker, yet a saint, and an eccentric man withal. The young minister, lately set over the congregation, came in to see him one day, and to have a talk with him about the things of God. But he dropped, to begin with, a remark which Hiram did not like, about being "glad that a man can be in a humble occupation and yet be a godly man." "Don't call this occupation 'humble,'" said the shoemaker, looking up. And then he went on—"I believe the making of that shoe is just as holy a thing as the making of a sermon. When I come to stand before the Throne of God, He will say, 'What kind of shoes did you make down on earth?' and He might pick out this very pair, in order to let me look at them in the blazing light of the Great White Throne. And He will say to you, 'What kind of sermons did you make?' and you will have to show Him one of your sermons. Now, if I make better shoes than you make sermons, what then about 'a humble place'?"

The young minister had not meant to hurt old Hiram's feelings; but the lesson taught by the good shoemaker was a useful one. Whatever your earthly place and calling may be, see to it, as the chief thing, that you "therein abide with God." It is not so much the sort of work you are engaged in, as the spirit in which you do it, that should be your great concern. There is, no doubt, a sense in which it is the most honourable of all callings to be a minister of the gospel, an ambassador for Christ. But it is quite as possible to glorify God by the shoemaker's "last," as in the pulpit. All honest work is honourable work, and every sphere in which such work may be done gives room enough for serving and glorifying Christ.

> "A servant with this clause
> Makes drudgery divine:
> Who sweeps a room, as for Thy laws,
> Makes this and the action fine."

It is important for Christians, as for other people, to remember that *every man* is to be judged according to his works, or, as the Bible elsewhere puts it, "according to that he hath done, whether it be good or bad." No doubt all true believers will be saved, for Christ's sake, from death and hell. But some will be "saved so as by fire": the results of their life will be so poor and unworthy, that they will be burned up. Others, though perhaps their place on earth was a very lowly one, will have achieved, out of Christian love, a work that will abide for ever. And, having through grace done well here, they will be ready for a higher place and service yonder. May it be our great desire and endeavour, as it was with St. Paul, that when we come to "receive the things done in the body," we may be "accepted of the Lord."

The Raven and the Dove.

"He sent forth a raven: also he sent forth a dove" (Gen. viii. 7, 8).

You have had a sea voyage perhaps. At first you liked it; but by and by you grew tired of looking at the water day by day, and wished for land. If you had been with Noah in the Ark,—though you might have found great amusement among the animals for a while,—I rather think you would have felt the same. At length you would have grown quite weary, and sighed—"Oh for a sight of dry land again!"

This seems to have been Noah's own feeling by and by: still more strongly, perhaps, his children's. For the voyage lasted—that is, they were in the Ark—more than a year in all. God was not forgetting Noah. He remembered him and his, and even all the cattle with him (verse 1); and when *His* time, the right time, came, He was to lead them forth again, to enjoy the beauty of the fresh, green earth. But we do not wonder that, when Noah saw the waters abating, he thought he would test the state of the earth by sending out two messengers, to see what prospect there was of release again.

The first messenger was *a raven*; the second, *a dove*. Their experience seemed to be different. Away the raven sped from the window of the Ark, and never came back again. It soon forgot all about Noah's kindness, and the comfortable shelter he had given; and, coarse bird that it was, it found plenty of carrion floating on the waters, and so was satisfied. The dove too winged its way from the window, for it was glad to try its wings again after so long a stay. But it soon came back; for it found no rest for the sole of its foot, and was fain to get within the familiar home again.

Seven days later, Noah again sent forth the dove, and back it fluttered to his breast again at eventide, bearing in its mouth an olive leaf—meet emblem of God's peace. It was not till seven days more that the dove could be got to stay away. And then it was that Noah found the earth was dry—the dove heralding his way where he too might go in safety and in peace.

Now this is a beautiful little history. *And what may these two messengers remind us of?* Two souls, I think. The raven, of a soul content to wander, and filling itself with the gross pleasures of the world. The dove, of a soul that cannot have joy away from its home in God—like the Psalmist when he said, "Return unto thy Rest, O my soul, for the Lord hath dealt bountifully with thee" (Ps. cxvi. 7). Is your soul like the raven, or like the dove?

November 4 — Be Reverent!

"*And God smote Uzzah: and there he died by the ark of God*" (2 Sam. vi. 7).

To understand this incident, you must remember what the Ark was, and how God expected it to be regarded and handled. It was a box of Shittim wood, overlaid within and without with pure gold, and ornamented round the rim of the lid with an ornament or crown of gold. The lid itself was of pure gold, and was called the Mercy-Seat. On the centre of the Mercy-Seat the glory of God rested; and at either end of it stood two angels or cherubims in gold, with outstretched wings, looking down upon the Mercy-Seat, as if desiring to look into (1 Pet. i. 12) the wonders which the Ark contained.

And what was inside the Ark? There were *the two Tables of Stone*, on which Jehovah had inscribed with His own finger the terms of His Covenant with Israel: what we are accustomed to call the Ten Commandments. There was *a Roll of the Laws of Israel*, on sheepskin, with an outline of the national history under the leadership of Moses (Deut. xxxi. 24–26). There was *the Rod of Aaron*, whose blossoming had indicated Jehovah's choice of the tribe of Levi, and the house of Aaron, for the sacred functions of the priesthood. And there was *the Pot of Manna*—a golden pot containing some of the food from heaven with which Jehovah had fed His people during their forty years' wandering in the wilderness.

Thus, you see, the box called the Ark was a very sacred object because of what it contained, and especially because it was wont to be the Throne on which the glory of God rested, in token of His presence among His people. Only once a year—on the great Day of Atonement—was anyone allowed to enter the Holy Place, and look upon the Ark. This was the High Priest; and even he could only venture in, as representing the people, with the sprinkling of the blood of the atoning sacrifice. When the Ark had to be removed, the High Priest was ordered carefully to cover it from common view; and the Levites had to carry it, by means of gold-covered staves, upon their shoulders.

Now, in all this, God was teaching His people *reverence* in dealing with Him and the sacred things of religion. But what happened in the case of Uzzah? The Ark was being conveyed, not by Levites, but in a jolting cart. And when the carter put forth his hand to steady it,—evidently doing so in a heedless spirit, as if it had been just some common old box he was handling,—God smote him, and there he died by the Ark of God!

There is an important lesson here for all time, and not least for our own time, and for the young people living in it—*Be reverent!* Reverence *God*. Do not take His name in vain; grieve when you hear others profane it. Approach with reverence *the Mercy-Seat*. Whether it be in God's house or in your own room that you seek it, see that you come devoutly there. Deal reverently with *the Bible*. If the ancient law was so sacred to Israel, what should the Bible be to us. See that you give due reverence to all objects and persons, of whom God expects this of you. He is grieved with irreverence. He is angry with it. In some way or other He will punish it.

The Unspeakable Gift.

"Thanks be unto God for His unspeakable Gift" (2 Cor. ix. 15).

"God so loved the world that He gave His only-begotten Son, that whosoever believeth in Him should not perish, but have everlasting life." That is what the gospel tells us about the Gift of God. And Paul, as he thinks of the exceeding preciousness of this Gift, both in itself and because of all the other blessings it brings with it, exclaims, "Thanks be unto God for His unspeakable Gift." His heart is full to overflowing about it. He wishes to thank God very much. But he feels that he cannot as he would. This is a gift the worth of which never can be told.

It is a gift *unspeakable*, whether you think (1) of what it cost God to give it, or (2) of what good it brings to us who receive it.

(1) It cost God more than tongue can tell, to give up His Son—His only Son—to die. And yet for us He did it. God could have made and given away a star or two quite easily. He could have made a new world for man to live in by a word. But to make new men, with their hearts made new, for living in His world, He had to give up His Son. Yet He did it. It was an unspeakable Gift.

(2) The good this Gift brings to those who receive it tongue can never tell. It brings eternal *life*, with peace that passeth understanding, and joy unutterable. Paul tried to speak his sense of its worth, and could not. Myriads have tried it on earth; hosts are trying it in heaven, and will try it for ever. But they never will succeed. Yet they still will ever try; for that is their chief delight, and it pleases God to hear the Saviour's praise. And it is good for us, both here and hereafter, to try: though the more we try, the more heartily we are led to confess that even when we, and others with us—

>"Join all the glorious names
> Of wisdom, love, and power,
> That ever mortals knew,
> That ever angels bore—
> All are too mean to speak His worth,
> Too mean to set our Saviour forth."

Do you ever try to tell others how much *you* think of Christ? Do you ever try at least to tell it to God? Or is your heart, while thankful for some of your other blessings, cold at the thought of the Gift Unspeakable? Perhaps you have little sympathy with Paul in his fervent ejaculation of thanksgiving? Perhaps you cannot at all account for his enthusiasm, or understand his speechlessness here? Perhaps *you* could soon tell out all the value you really set upon Christ? Surely this is both strange and sad. "He that forgets his friend," says Bunyan, "is ungrateful to him; he that forgets his Saviour is unmerciful to himself." To make light of the Unspeakable Gift is hurtful to the soul. It is grievous also to God. If your brother saved you from death at the risk of his own life, would it not grieve your father to see you thinking more of some toys and trinkets he had given you than of such a brother? Ah, do not thus grieve God; but by lips and life give daily thanks to Him for His "Unspeakable Gift."

November 6 Cursing the Deaf, and Tripping the Blind.

"Thou shalt not curse the deaf, or put a stumblingblock before the blind"
(Lev. xix. 14).

GOD hates meanness; and He will punish it. In giving this charge, through Moses, He adds—"but shalt fear thy God: I am the Lord." That is to say, mean things, which may escape detection by others, are seen by Me; and you will have to reckon with Me about them.

It is a sorry thing to think, how mean people can sometimes be. There were evidently plenty of mean people in the days of Moses; and there are plenty of them still. Just think of God having to make a law, and to issue a warning, against cursing the deaf and tripping the blind! It is very humbling that it should have been necessary, and that something of the same kind should be necessary still.

If you saw a person hurling bad language at another, and wishing him all sorts of evil, and were told, "Oh, he ventures to do that, only because he knows that other person is deaf," you would at once say, What a cowardly and mean thing it is to act like that! Or if you saw a thoughtless or malicious person deliberately laying a stumblingblock in the way of another, knowing that he was blind and was almost sure to fall over it and be injured, your indignation would be aroused. You would, if possible, remove the obstacle before it had done mischief; and you would take the earliest opportunity of talking with him who laid it there, and giving him "a bit of your mind!"

Well, but there are a great many people doing that very sort of thing, only in a different way; and society does not seem to mind it much, or to put on them any serious mark of its displeasure. There are those who are constantly saying cruel, malicious things about others behind their backs, which they would not dare to say in their hearing. That is just as mean a thing as it would be to curse the deaf! There are those who are, in mischief, or sometimes from selfish motives, laying traps for others to fall into—doing it so cunningly that they do not perceive the snare, or know who has set it. That is just as mean as to set a stumblingblock for the blind!

Do not take advantage of anybody meanly! Do not treat even a dumb creature—one of the lower animals—unhandsomely, as you would not venture to do it if it could speak and expostulate with you! "Thou shalt fear thy God: I am the Lord." Many things that escape human observation, and do not come under man's reproach, are seen and noted and will be punished by God. Jacob could successfully deceive his blind old father Isaac; but God had something to say to him, and he sorely suffered afterwards through the deceit of his own children. Haman could cleverly plot in secret against poor Mordecai; but just as he had his gallows ready, he was himself hanged upon it. Ahab could take a heartless advantage of the humble but high-minded and honourable Naboth; but the dogs afterwards licked his blood in the plot of ground he dishonestly acquired. Modern history is full of similar cases of retribution. Ever live as beneath the all-seeing eye. Verily there is a God that judgeth in the earth. And it is with Him, above all others, that we have to do.

An Upsetting Sin. November 7

"*Look not thou upon the wine when it is red*" (Prov. xxiii. 31).

One of the greatest evils of our time, if not the greatest, is the sin of drunkenness. And one of the most promising features of our time is the amount of interest that is being taken in this subject, with a view to reduce, if not to extirpate, the curse. Shrewd heads and loving hearts, both in the Church and in the Parliament, are devising plans with that blessed end in view; and every lover of his race must wish good-speed to every wise and honest effort toward rescuing society from the blight which drunkenness has brought upon so many lives and so many homes. But the great hope for the future lies with you young people. Whether you belong to a Temperance Society or not, the nation looks to you as its mighty Band of Hope,—not only because you *have* hope springing up in your young hearts, and with it high resolve, but because you *are* our country's hope, to whose character and influence, under God, it looks for better days.

There has been a great improvement as respects the drinking usages of our land, even since some of us remember, who are not yet very old. And it will fall to you, beginning with yourselves, to promote yet further, by example and effort, the cause of true sobriety in your own day and generation. May God give you all the wisdom, and firmness, and patience of love which will be needed for the hastening of the day—which seems yet, alas! so far away—when there shall not be any longer such a being as a drunkard known in all our borders!

The heading to this day's talk is taken from a quaint prayer which a Negro once offered in a small meeting of coloured brethren. "Lord, deliver us from evil," he said, "and especially preserve us from upsettin' sin!" "Brudder," remonstrated one of his comrades afterwards, "you ain't got dat ar word. It's *besettin'*, not *upsettin'* sin." "Brudder," was the swift rejoinder, "if dat's so, it's so; but I was speakin' ob de sin ob 'toxication; and if that ain't an upsettin' sin, I dunno what am!"

That Negro was right. Drunkenness is the besetting sin of multitudes. But it is also, by pre-eminence, the upsetting sin. It upsets everything. Not only does it overturn, in a literal sense, and lay low the poor drunkard himself—who ought never to be an object of derisive merriment, but rather of profound compassion, whenever he may stagger across your way. But it upsets family happiness. It upsets character. It upsets the worthy plans of life. It upsets and renders vain noble ambitions, which might have had a glorious issue in eternity. Beware of the deceitfulness of all sin, but especially of this sin, which has destroyed so many, who were of the very flower, as regards qualities of both head and heart, of the families and circles to which they belonged. "Wine is a mocker, strong drink is raging; and whosoever is deceived thereby is not wise."

November 8. Not Worth the Candle.

"Ye looked for much, and, lo, it came to little" (Hag. i. 9).

WE have here a powerful description of a laborious but unsatisfactory life. "Ye have sown much, and bring in little." Yours has not been an idle life. By no means; it has been full of activities of a kind. You have worked, and worried yourself even to weariness. But what is the outcome of all your labour? "You bring in little." The harvest out-turn only mocks the sowing. "Ye eat, and drink, but ye have not enough." Yours has not been a life without enjoyments of their kind. But the world's chosen joys could not satisfy your heart. Over all its fountains you have found it written, "He that drinketh of this water shall thirst again." Always *"to be blessed,"* you have grasped the flower, to find that in the act you have shed its bloom. "Ye clothe you, but there is none warm." Your life has been anything but bare in the ordinary sense. You have been quite surrounded perhaps with what are called "the comforts of life." But somehow they have not been able to dispel the chill upon your heart. "He earneth wages, to put it in a bag with holes." Your labour has not gone without recompense altogether. You have got your wages, such as they were. But anything you have earned has been far more easily spent. You do not feel yourself one whit the better for it. You are as poor to-day, as one who has slipped his money through a hole in the bag in which he sought to treasure it.

The above, dear young reader, is a correct description of many a life. It is not such a life, I am sure, as you would like yours to be. It can hardly be called a life worth living. The game, as the proverb puts it, is not worth the candle.

"Fifty years," wrote one who was high in station, and they found the writing among his papers after he was gone—"Fifty years I have possessed riches, honours, pleasures, friends: in short, everything that man can desire in this world. I have reckoned up the days in which I could say I was happy; and they amount to fourteen!" Something wrong about such a life! What could it be? Just this,—that it is not a life which has sought God as its portion, and His glory as its end. And He has "blown upon it" with a breath that has withered it.

Let yours be a diligent life. Labour as earnestly as one who seeks for hidden treasure. But see to it that you are working in the proper mine—where the true treasure really lies! All is not gold that glitters. "What can you give for that?" said a countryman, laying the contents of his bag upon the table of a gold merchant. "Nothing!" "What!" he exclaimed, "do you not deal in gold?" "Yes," said the merchant; "but that is not gold." It was only some yellow quartz the man had brought. He had spent his labour for nought and in vain. Let it not be found so with your life, when its results are laid out, and their value computed at the last!

"*Fear not, for God hath heard the voice of the lad where he is*" (Gen. xxi. 17).

WHEN the great traveller, Mungo Park, was lying prostrate one day in the desert, overcome with weariness and thirst and on the point of despair, his eye caught sight of a little floweret. Elsewhere it might have gone unnoticed, but the sight of it there brought him hope. "Little flower," he said, "does God take care of thee here, and shall my Heavenly Father forget His child?" Nerved by the thought that God was near, he pushed on till the oasis was reached at last.

The circumstances of Ishmael and his mother were very similar. They were out in the desert—sad, lonely, apparently forsaken, almost in despair. But God was looking on them, and He brought relief. Poor young Ishmael is footsore and hungry—for their little stock of provisions has run out—and he is so parched with thirst that he cannot walk another step. His is indeed an evil case. But there are still two things on his side. The one is, a mother's love; and the other is, the divine compassion.

Mother-love—what a wonderful thing that is! Surely it is a fragrant floweret strayed from Eden. How it grows and flourishes in the most unlikely places, this tender, holy affection. It was not less genuine and beautiful in the breast of Hagar the bondwoman, than in that of Sarah the princess. She had apparently tried to carry Ishmael for a while; but he was too big and heavy for that; and when her strength failed, there was nothing for it but to cast him under one of the shrubs. "And the water was spent in the bottle." It wrung her very soul to hear his moans and see his agony. Alas, for the poor distracted mother, sitting over against her gasping, dying boy! The world might despise him, but he was everything to her. He had been the hero of all her brightest dreams. The only time an angel had spoken to her, it was to tell about his mighty future. But there he lay dying. A mother's love had done its best, its all, in vain!

Divine compassion—that is more than mother-love. Hagar's anguish touched something akin to it in the great heart of God; and though her resources were exhausted, His were not. Unlikely as it might seem, "God heard the voice of the lad." And a tender inquiry reaches the ear of the poor, bewildered, broken-hearted bondwoman, whose heart was so tender, though her skin was so black—"What aileth thee, Hagar?" Her eyes are opened, and she sees a well of water near. Oh, how gladly she runs and fills the bottle, and puts it to the lips of her dear, dying boy! And so Ishmael revived, and Hagar lived to be proud of him, as a true son of the desert—rude and wild, perhaps, but undoubtedly great and strong, able to hold his own with everybody against him, and him against all. "Man's extremity is God's opportunity." You are sure to be taught some time your own helplessness. May you be taught with it the infinite helpfulness of God!

November 10   God Lives.

"The Lord liveth, and blessed be my Rock" (Ps. xviii. 46).

A LITTLE girl, whose mother was sunk in grief, crept up to her side, and startled her by the sudden and anxious inquiry, "Is God dead, mother?" It was the very message the widow needed. Her child's question had an effect the innocent prattler had not intended. The mother felt her faithlessness rebuked. She dried her tears. She lifted up her heart to the Heavenly Father in fervent prayer; and though her grief was still great and her burden heavy, she found new strength to face the world with, from the timely remembrance that "God lives."

So was it once with no less a man than Luther. He was a man of heroic mould, as everybody knows, and was bold as a lion when confronted by the enemies of the truth. But even he had occasional fits of depression and weakness, from which he found it impossible to rouse himself. The gentle Melancthon was sometimes of great service to him on such occasions. And so was his loving wife, Catherine von Bora. Luther himself tells how successfully, by a quaint device, she stirred him once from his fit of melancholy.

"At one time I was sorely vexed by my own sinfulness, by the wickedness of the world, and by the dangers that beset the Church. One morning, seeing my wife dressed in mourning, I asked the reason. 'Do you not know,' she said, 'God in heaven is dead?' 'What nonsense, Katie,' I exclaimed. 'How can God die? He is immortal, and will live through all eternity.' 'Is that really true?' she asked. 'Of course: how can you doubt it? As surely as there is a God in heaven, so sure is it that He can never die.' 'And yet,' she said quietly, 'you are so hopeless and discouraged!' Then I observed what a wise woman my wife was, and mastered my sadness."

We, too, may have our trials and our seasons of darkness and discouragement. At such times let us remind ourselves that *God lives*. Those who have in Him their Heavenly Father never need despair. Whoever may be taken from us, He never can. "When my father and my mother forsake me, then the Lord will take me up." He has said, "I will never leave thee nor forsake thee." And here is firm footing, though all else may seem like shifting sand. Blessed be my Rock! In Him there is a refuge and safety for me. In the secret place of the Most High my soul can find both security and comfort, such as the young brood find under their mother's sheltering wing. "He shall cover thee with His feathers, and under His wings shalt thou trust." So that you may well exclaim with David, "Let the God of my salvation be exalted!"

Heavenly Armour.

' Wherefore, take unto you the whole armour of God" (Eph. vi. 13).

THE Christian life on earth means battle. It involves constant conflict. Hence the figure of war, and the comparison of the Christian to a soldier, is familiar in the writings of the Apostle Paul, who was himself an experienced officer in the ranks.

Here we have a "call to arms," which teaches us that—

(1) *Armour is needed.* It is not for drill merely, or for show on the parade-ground; else the apostle would be the last to urge us to encumber ourselves with it. No; but he recognises that we are in an enemy's country, where every Christian, however peace-loving, has to be a soldier. And since life is real, life is earnest, Paul summons the believer to prepare himself for the fight.

(2) The armour *of God* is needed. Not what another man may invent and recommend, but what God Himself provides, is required for protection and victory in such a conflict. For the enemies we have to contend against are not merely wicked men, but principalities and powers, "wicked spirits in heavenly places," with the devil at their head with all his wiles. And what would human armour be against foes like these?

(3) The *whole* armour of God is needed; what one of our hymns literally translates, "the panoply of God." This includes both defensive armour and weapons of attack. And no part of the panoply which God has provided can with safety be omitted by us. With foes so wary, no single point of advantage must be given; for if but one spot is left unguarded, they are sure to discover the place of weakness, and to operate effectually there.

It is told of Achilles, the great Greek warrior, that to make his body invulnerable his mother dipped him, when a child, in the Lethe stream. The heel by which she held him was the one part of his body not bathed in the preserving flood. Years passed; and the brave Achilles was a hero in the strife, and seemed invincible. But his enemy, Paris, fired an arrow one day which shot him *just there*, in the unprotected heel, to the mighty warrior's undoing.

Let us then give good heed to the apostolic warning, to put on the *whole* armour of God: the girdle, the breastplate, the sandals, the helmet, for the protection of the body, the feet, the head. And in our hands let there be the shield of a living trust in a living and omnipotent Saviour, and the sharp sword whose blade cannot be broken, and with which Satan was put to flight by the Christ Himself—"the Sword of the Spirit, which is the Word of God." If this heavenly armour be not only admired but really *put on* by us, and worn and wielded in a spirit of constant prayerfulness, we shall be more than conquerors, through Him who loved us, and who loves us still.

November 12. Giving to God.

"Of Thine own have we given Thee" (1 Chron. xxix. 14).

THESE are the words of King David, on a notable occasion towards the close of his reign. To the old King's challenge, "Who then is willing *to fill his hand* this day unto the Lord?" so large and willing a response has been given toward the future building of the Temple, that David's heart is made right glad. But, while rejoicing in his people's liberality, he turns to Jehovah and gives Him the praise: blessing Him for both the power and the willingness to give. And he humbly acknowledges, on behalf of himself and the people—" Of Thine own have we given Thee."

There is a sense in which none *can* give anything to God, because all that we have is His already. Nothing which we call ours can be called *our own* in relation to God—excepting only sin. Everything good, everything which has gone to the enrichment of our life, has been bestowed by Him; and we are really stewards rather than owners of all we hold.

Yet there is a true sense in which we may be said to give to Him. Suppose a father grants a son a certain allowance, to carry him through college, or to pay his expenses on a business tour, leaving something over for personal enjoyment. If that son denies himself in certain particulars, that he may have the gratification of bringing his father home a gift—will the father be likely to flout the offering of love, as "not really a gift at all," since the power to offer it was bestowed by himself? Surely not. And if earthly fathers know how to receive and appreciate the gifts of their children, though they may be small things in themselves, how much more graciously and tenderly will our Heavenly Father appreciate whatever we bring to Him out of a loving heart?

David may here teach us at least two things about giving. The first is, that it is *a duty* to be discharged "with *an upright heart*." It is to be honourably done. We must never deal meanly with God, as those do who secretly ask—" How little can I afford to give?" and who fall back on all sorts of petty devices for saving their pockets. The second thing is, that giving to God is *a privilege* to be welcomed with *a joyful heart.* The people, with their king, offered willingly. Giving was for them not a harsh or even a prosaic duty merely, but a joy. All their heart went with it. It was to them not a tax, but a privilege.

"Freely ye have received; freely give." You have sometimes felt very happy in giving something to father or mother. Do you ever claim the happiness of giving to One who deserves of you even more than they? Act upon these two counsels about giving to God, and you will never regret it:—(1) *Begin early.* You have not much to give? But God greatly values even a little gift, if it is the token of a great love. (2) *Continue to give* "*as the Lord shall prosper you.*" As you grow richer, enlarge your gifts. Beware of a growing purse and a contracting heart.

Our Marching Orders.   November 13

"Go ye into all the world, and preach the gospel to every creature"
(Mark xvi. 15).

IF our country were engaged in a great foreign war, every loyal and intelligent citizen would take some personal interest in the progress of the British arms abroad. And if you knew some of the soldiers or officers personally, you would be very likely to take up your newspaper with some eagerness, to inform yourself about their movements and about the course of the campaign.

Now the Church of Christ has a great foreign enterprise on hand—a war not intended to destroy men's lives, but to save them. The soldiers are the missionaries—men and women who have gone forth with the Word of God in their hands and something of Christ's own love within their hearts, to win the world for Him. This is a great campaign, in which you should take a lively interest; and one good way of stirring yourself up to do this, will be to take every opportunity of getting to know the soldiers, the missionaries, for yourself, and of hearing what they have to tell, when they come home "on furlough," about the successes or disappointments of the war.

Nor are you only to take a general kind of interest in the matter, as a bystander and onlooker might. But you must remember that the work of foreign missions is one in which you are called to have a personal share. The Lord of the Church, the Captain of our salvation, looks to you to do whatever you can, by your prayers, by your gifts,—it may be by the gift of yourself,—to carry forward this great cause to victory. Who knows but some of my young readers may yet have their names inscribed on what is, in some respects, the noblest roll on earth—the roll of the great missionaries of the Cross?

There are those who try to laugh at foreign mission work, calling it a failure and a waste of men and means. Some of them have lived abroad, and they pretend to be very sagacious on the subject, though they probably have seen nothing of the work, and have never taken the trouble to cross the street to enter a missionary college or school or church.

But facts are against them. Much has been accomplished through foreign missions; and more has been prepared for. And whatever be the difficulties of the work and the sneers of its opponents, what the Church has to go by is the word of command issued by her great Commander. Here is His claim—"All power is given unto Me in heaven and on earth." Here is His commission —"Go ye into all the world, and preach the gospel to every creature." Here His is consolation—"Lo, *I* am with you always." Hear *Him*, whatever others say. If you hear a professing Christian at any time running down foreign missions, say to him, as the Duke of Wellington, in similar circumstances, said—"What are your marching orders, sir? What are your marching orders?"

Bad Coins.

"Reprobate silver shall men call them" (Jer. vi. 30).

THIS is said of the wicked; and it is true of them, "because the Lord hath rejected them." They are like the dross merely, which the refiner has separated from the precious metal. Or they are like false counterfeit coins, which are refused, because they have not the genuine ring about them.

In the Bank of England, there is a delicately-balanced scale for receiving sovereigns, and testing whether they are of the proper weight or not. Down the sovereigns are dropped upon it by a machine, in a continuous stream, and every one of them is impartially dealt with by the scale. If it is of standard weight, it is passed into one box; if it is of light weight, it is retained in another box upon the other side. That instrument may make us think of the test which God applies to every human soul. Far more unerringly than any machine which man could devise, He who is the Judge of all the earth pronounces upon the life and character of each of us, and deals with us accordingly. The Apostle Paul, in view of this, calls upon us to examine ourselves, to prove our own selves; not to wait till the Judgment Day for testing and for judgment, lest in that great day, when too late to make a better of it, we should be found reprobate (2 Cor. xiii. 5).

It is not only the weight of coins, but the quality of them, that is of importance; and the banks have their own ways of testing this also. Besides the scientific methods of "assaying" or trying the precious metals, there is the popular way of testing coins by striking them on the table or the counter, to see what sort of sound they give out. Anybody who has travelled in Spain knows well about the application of this test. You cannot buy an article in a shop there without the shopkeeper, in the most matter-of-fact way, taking the coins you offer him by way of payment and testing them upon his counter before he will receive them. If you are not very wary in accepting your change from him and others, it is more than likely that you will have quite a collection of "reprobate" coins to carry away with you, when you leave the Peninsula. But God can never be left with false coins upon His hands: He unerringly detects and rejects them.

That was a clever device by which Constantine, when he came to the throne, sifted the characters of those about him. Finding a number of professing Christians in office, he issued a decree requiring all such to renounce their faith or to resign their positions. Many of them valued conscience more than place; but some were base enough to renounce Christianity, in obedience to what they supposed to be the imperial will. Constantine, however, retained the first in office, and dismissed these others. He knew they were not to be trusted. They were not genuine men, but "reprobate silver."

"*So I prayed to the God of heaven*" (Neh. ii. 4).

THE prayer of which Nehemiah here speaks was offered in very peculiar circumstances, and must have been a very brief one. He was standing in the presence of King Artaxerxes as the King's cup-bearer ; and it was between the putting of a question to him by the King and his answering it that he sent his prayer up to the God of heaven and got His answer back. Was not that swifter than the telegraph ?

You remember the circumstances. Nehemiah was in deep distress at the news that had reached him about the condition of Jerusalem and the remnant of his people there. For days he had been weeping and fasting and praying over it ; and his grief had begun to tell on his countenance. The King at length had noticed it, and had asked the reason for it in a tone that had struck terror to Nehemiah's heart. " Then was I very sore afraid." For a cup-bearer to go into the royal presence with a woe-begone face was a serious offence, which might lead to sore punishment, or even death. But Nehemiah manages to stammer out an explanation, which was intended as his apology too. And the King is not only appeased, but, moved to sympathy, asks, " For what dost thou make request?" *So I prayed to the God of heaven.*

Nehemiah *had* a request to make to Artaxerxes. But before stating it, he wisely took counsel with the King of kings, and by an upward desire besought God that his words might be well chosen words, and might have the effect he yearned for on the mighty despot's heart. And so, when Nehemiah immediately stated his wish and plan to Artaxerxes, his prayer was answered—" And the King granted me, according to the good hand of my God upon me." The way by heaven was really the shortest way to reach and move the consent of the King in whose very presence he was standing, and who was looking to him for an immediate answer !

Do you ever pray *short* prayers to God ? Prayer is not to be hurried over in ordinary circumstances. But there are times when a brief word may be all that is either needful or possible ; and it is a great thing to know that God "hears *the desire* of the humble." We are not heard for our much speaking. There may be more prayer compressed into a word or two than in long drawn-out repetitions that have little or no heart in them. Even on the street and among a crowd you may send up a petition to heaven in a moment and get an answer back.

" How do you know your kite is there ? " asked a gentleman at a little boy who, on a foggy day, was sitting on a doorstep with a string in his hand that stretched upward till it seemed lost in the sky. " Because I feel it pull," he replied. There is communica-tion between God and us. We know that He hears us. And we know it, not only because we feel it, but because we get answers back, on the invisible telegraph between our souls and heaven.

November 16. The True Vine.

"I am the true Vine, and My Father is the Husbandman" (John xv. 1).

By the true Vine and its branches, as this chapter explains, is meant Jesus and all the hearts that are united to Him by faith. Have you ever seen a vine? In this country they are generally to be found in hothouses. But in Palestine they grow outside. Perhaps a fair vine trellis overhung the window of the very room where Jesus and His disciples sat. And certainly the Vine of which He spoke is not a hothouse tree, but one which is planted out in the world, and which has sent its boughs unto the sea and its branches unto the river, spreading its growth in every land.

Much care is needed with a vine if there is to be much fruit. A gardener will tell you that every separate branch has to be fed, guided, pruned, watered, and shone upon, if it is to contribute its share to the vintage.

(1) It has to be *fed*. So there must be a free flow of sap from stem to branch. If you were to tie a string very tight round any branch, it would be most injurious, and the gardener would at once remove it.

(2) It has to be *guided*, else it will go in wrong directions, and perhaps get hurtfully intertwined with the other branches. So the gardener is careful to train each branch on its proper trellis, that both it and the others may have a fair chance of growth.

(3) It has to be *pruned*, else its growth may run to wood, and though it may have great appearance of leaf and fruit, there will be but sour and crabbed grapes. So the gardener is careful to "weed" the branches, and with his sharp knife to cut the superfluous wood away.

(4) It has to be *cleansed*, else the dust and the vermin will soon spoil its fair appearance, and leave little hope of fruit. So the gardener takes his syringe and plentifully besprinkles it with water in due season.

(5) It has to be *shone upon*, else it will be at most a poor sickly thing, with a life scarce worth calling life. So the gardener attends to "the exposure," and sees to it that none of the branches are without the opportunity of abundant sunshine.

Dear young reader, may you be a true branch engrafted by faith into the True Vine. Let no bond of unbelief or evil habit interfere with the free flow of His grace into your soul. Pray God to guide the growth of your young life aright. Be content that He should curb your pride and naughtiness, even if need be by the kind though keenly-cutting knife. Ask for daily cleansing from the defilement of the world and the vermin of evil thoughts which prey upon the soul. And, sprinkled by Him with clean water, let it be yours never to hide from the Sun. Then will you not only have life, but have it more abundantly. Instead of being a withered branch, fit only for the burning, you will bear much fruit; and the Divine Husbandman, the Father, will be glorified.

Crossing the River. November 17

"When thou passest through the waters, I am with thee" (Isa. xliii. 2).

God's children have often to go through deep waters of affliction on their journey to the Better Land. Sometimes they come to a stream so deep and dark that they do not know how they are ever to get over it. But if God does not bring them to a bridge, He finds for them a ford; and even if the waters are so great as to threaten to carry them away, He takes them by the hand, or, if need be, carries them through.

There is one river, described as "Death's cold, sullen stream," over which each of us must one day pass, and, so far as earthly friends are concerned, must pass alone. That is a stream over which no bridge has been thrown, or can be thrown, by man. To try to cross it on any frail structure of baseless hope that man might rear would mean most certain doom. Nay, we cannot bridge it; we must needs "pass through." And the friends who love us most can only comfort us, at farthest, down to the river-brink.

A great many people are sadly afraid of that river. Even children of God are sometimes unable to shake off the burden of dread at the prospect of having to cross it. But it is wonderful how, when death actually comes, dying grace is given to such, and all their tremors disappear. God's "fear not" brings blessed comfort to the soul, just when it most is needed.

So was it with Christian, you remember, in the *Pilgrim's Progress*. As he and Hopeful were crossing the river, Christian began to despond, and then to sink; and Hopeful "had much ado to keep his brother's head above water." But Christian suddenly caught a glimpse of Jesus, and heard Him speak. And then he found footing, and the rest of the way was shallow; and thus they got over to the glorious welcome of the Celestial City.

So was it too with that true-hearted but tremulous pilgrim, Mr. Fearing, in the second part of the *Progress*. We read that "when he was come at the river where there was no bridge, there again he was in a heavy case." But what was the result? Something "very remarkable," as Bunyan calls it, yet by no means uncommon. "The water of that river was lower at this time than ever I saw it in all my life; so he went over at last, not much above wet-shod."

> "There are our loved ones in their rest;
> They've crossed Time's river,—now no more
> They heed the bubbles on its breast,
> Nor feel the storms that sweep its shore.
> But there pure love can live, can last,
> They look for us their home to share;
> When we, in turn, away have passed,
> What joyful greetings wait us there,
>   Across the river!"

November 18 — Sin's Bitter Fruit.

"So he drove out the man" (Gen. iii. 24).

THERE is something, dear young people, which follows sin as closely as your shadow follows you, and that is misery. We find this illustrated very plainly in the case of our first parents. Satan had persuaded them of the advantages that would come to them from the little act of disobedience to God which he recommended. But their dream of larger good was quickly broken. The fruit seemed very sweet for the moment; but it soon turned to ashes. They knew *evil* now, indeed; but, alas, it almost seemed as if they never would know good again.

Sin brought with it (1) *shame.* Adam and Eve forthwith felt that they were creatures that needed to be covered from sight. They could not bear to be seen now by one another, for innocence was gone. Much less could they bear to be seen by God. With shame came also (2) *fear.* Before, they had known only the fear of trustful reverence, such as you have toward your father; and when the Lord God used to come to Paradise, their delight had been to run to meet Him. But conscience makes a coward of the sinner. For the fear of the child, they have now the fear of the criminal or the slave. And, see! they flee to hide themselves from Him whose coming used to be their joy. And they justly fear, for sin has brought with it (3) *curse.* Called from their leafy covert, guilty and trembling, into the presence of Jehovah, the wretched pair learn that God's threats are true, and that punishment must follow sin. Faltering excuses are vain. Not only is the serpent cursed, but man's life is blighted. The very ground is cursed for his sake. Adam and his wife, and all who come of them, are to be acquainted now with pain and toil and death. And, last but not least, sin brings with it (4) *banishment.* "So He drove out the man." What a terrible word that is, and what a sad day! Sad, because of the outcast place, and toilsome, guilty life they were driven to. Sad, because it was *He* who drove them out—He, their Father, their Best Friend, the sweetness of whose love they had known, and from whom even a harsh word would once have seemed heart-breaking to them. *Drove* them out—that was what He did now; and they knew in their hearts that He could do nothing less.

What wretchedness sin brings with it! It is the worst of blunders, as well as a crime. The life of banishment from God is a dreary, desolate life. And there is this additional element of misery, that man driven from Paradise cannot find his own way back again. The ways seems hopelessly and for ever barred to his approach. But God amid wrath remembers mercy. He gives a gospel promise, as one ray of light amid the gloom. The sword of justice bars the entrance to the earthly Eden. But it is a sceptre of grace which is stretched from the Mercy Seat, and invites us to enter the better Paradise.

Keeping your Temper. November 19

"*A soft answer turneth away wrath*" (Prov. xv. 1).

A MISSIONARY in Jamaica was expounding in a Sunday school the text, "Blessed are the meek, for they shall inherit the earth." He put the question, "Who are the meek?" and a little black boy answered very well, "Those who give soft answers to rough words."

It is said in the Book of Proverbs, that he who ruleth his spirit is better than he who taketh a city; and one important element in ruling your spirit is to "keep your temper" well. There are very wrong notions abroad about temper. It is sometimes said of a person, "That is a man with a great deal of temper," or, "That is a very strong-tempered woman," when the very opposite is the truth. For what is "temper"? You will find, if you think of its meaning, or consult the dictionary, that it is ability "to mix properly," "to moderate," "to soften." It is the person who has his emotions well in hand, and not the one whose anger is uncontrolled, that should be called a person with a strong temper. And so a boy or a girl who is ready to fly into a passion over every trifle, instead of being a "high-tempered" boy or girl, should be pitied for having a poor temper, a feeble power of self-control.

We should not only seek to curb our own angry feelings, but try to enable others to do the same. There are people who are afflicted with a very excitable and irascible nature. They are like one of the "geysers" I have heard of in Iceland, which is said to send forth boiling water whenever a clod of earth or even a bunch of grass is thrown at it. The very least provocation calls forth a flood of hot, scalding, angry feeling. We should not play upon this weakness, but rather help those afflicted with it to overcome it.

"A soft answer turneth away wrath." This was often illustrated in Bible times. You remember how effectually Gideon by his soft answer turned away the anger of the fierce men of Ephraim, when "they did chide with him sharply" for not giving them a chance of joining him in the victory over Midian? And how Abigail by her soft words calmed down the wrath of David, when he had vowed to destroy not only the churlish Nabal, but all the males of his house? It was a notable instance of "keeping the temper," too, when Paul answered quietly to the rude interruption of Festus, "I am *not* mad, most noble Festus, but speak forth the words of truth and soberness."

The person who "loses his temper" in a dispute is, in nine cases out of ten, the one who is in the wrong and is getting the worst of it. Victory lies with him who rules his spirit. The well-known missionary Francis Xavier, a man of great zeal and warmth of nature, was addressing a Japanese crowd, when one of his hearers came forward professedly to whisper something in his ear. When Xavier bent down his head to listen, the man spat in his face. But the missionary, wiping his face calmly with his handkerchief, went on with his address, and earned not the contempt but the admiration of the crowd thereby. It was only one of many similar victories won by the followers of Him who "when He was reviled, reviled not again." Would you not like to win some such victories too?

November 20   To what purpose?

"To what purpose?" (Jer. vi. 20, and Matt. xxvi. 8).

IN the first case (Jer. vi. 20), it is God who puts the question, concerning some who tried to pass themselves off as very religious people, though in reality their hearts were far away from God. They brought incense from Sheba, and sweet cane from a far country, and they tried to make their sacrifices fragrant. But they were all the time living in sin. They did not hearken to God's law, but rejected it. Therefore He says of their worship—To what purpose is it? "Your burnt-offerings are *not* acceptable, nor your sacrifices sweet unto me."

In the other case (Matt. xxvi. 8), the question is put by human lips, concerning an act of true devotion to Christ, which to some of the onlookers seemed a very foolish piece of useless extravagance. It was Judas, as John's Gospel tells, who gave utterance to the expostulation about Mary's deed of love, when she anointed the feet of Jesus with her costly spikenard, so that the house and the world were filled with the odour of the ointment. But there were others besides him, some of the true-hearted yet mistaken disciples, in whose hearts the question was rising up—"To what purpose is this waste?" And He who read Mary's heart, and who knew His own future too, told them that, whatever they might be disposed to think, Mary's offering was *not* useless extravagance. "She hath wrought *a good work* on Me," He said; "for in that she hath poured this ointment on My body, she did it for My burial."

Thus in the one instance we have men who thought well of themselves, and were regarded by others perhaps as religious people, bringing their rich offerings from afar; yet God says of them, "To what purpose?" In the other case we find a humble, grateful soul, thinking nothing of herself but everything of her Saviour, bringing her alabaster box of very precious ointment to pour it on His head. And though others, in a strain of superior virtue, exclaim, "To what purpose?"—she is accepted of the Lord.

He that searches the heart knows exactly to what purpose we are living, and to what end every single action of our lives is really directed. Let us all see to it that we are living (1) to *a* purpose. An aimless, drifting life is an unworthy, ignoble life. (2) To a *good* purpose. If this be not so, we are debasing ourselves and squandering our opportunities; and the greater our success along that line, the worse will our failure be. (3) To the *best* purpose: to the glory of God and the good of men. A noble aim, patiently and persistently followed, is the secret of true worthiness in any life. No matter what niche of honour we may fill, it will be no place of real honour for us, if we are not laying out our energies and opportunities for Christ. There was a valuable lesson, rather grimly taught, by that most purposeful man Oliver Cromwell, upon seeing twelve silver images perched round the walls of a certain church. Being informed that they represented the twelve apostles, he exclaimed—"Take them down and melt them into the coinage of the realm, that, like their Master, they may go about in society doing good"!

Water from the Rock. November 21

"Smite the rock, and there shall come water out of it" (Ex. xvii. 6).

Do you ever thank God for the water you drink? Perhaps you thank Him for your food, and ask His blessing with it. But water is such a very "common" blessing in our country, that we take it as a thing of course, and hardly ever think of it as a gift from God. Yet if it were withheld from you for two days or so, you would value it more than almost anything else; and if it were kept from you much longer than that, you would lose your senses and go quite mad.

Extreme thirst is even more hard to bear than severe hunger. So many a poor traveller in the desert has found, and many a shipwrecked sailor on a raft. If all the gold in the world were offered to such in one hand and a cup of cold water in the other, they would, without a moment's hesitation, choose the water. Remember this, next time you are thirsty and "get a drink" from the well!

The Israelites were terrible grumblers, and they behaved very badly to Moses at this time under the torture of thirst. They had not learned the lesson of faith yet, but in the hour of need could only grumble, and threaten, and sink into despair. But we must not be too hard on these parched travellers either, remembering the extremity of anguish they were under. You recollect that, when Jesus was on the Cross, the one thing, so far as bodily suffering was concerned, which called from Him an expression of distress was, not the pain of the thorns or of the nail-points, but this—"I thirst." And God had pity on the Israelites. For He is a kind Father; and He told Moses that as He had supplied them with plenty of food, He would enable him to give them plenty of water too.

What a scene followed on the smiting of the rock by Moses, at the bidding of Jehovah! Murillo, the great Spanish painter, has tried to picture it in what is deemed one of the greatest paintings in the world. You see the great rock with the limpid, living stream gushing from it, and Moses standing by, looking up in thankfulness to heaven, while the people, with eager faces, are stooping to drink, and to fill all manner of jars with the precious water. There are old men and women, and fathers and mothers, and fainting boys and girls, and even little children holding out their arms to get a share.

Are not these thirsty Israelites, travelling to Canaan, a picture of you and me as pilgrims upon earth? This world cannot satisfy our soul's thirst. Like the Psalmist David, we thirst "for God, the living God." His presence, His favour, His salvation, His love is what we long for, and must have, if our souls are to be satisfied. And have we not in the Smitten Rock a picture of Christ (1 Cor. x. 4)? From Him, as stricken upon Calvary, there flows the stream of life. In the freeness with which the water was given to the people at Horeb, you may behold the freeness of gospel blessing. All kinds of people have flocked to the gospel fountain—and not in vain. Are you thirsty? Then come and take. The offer is free to all. No price is asked. "Let him that is athirst, come!"

November 22 A Queen who lost and kept her Crown.

"But the Queen Vashti refused" (Esth. i. 12).

You remember the story of the fair young Queen, who was the darling of the great King Ahasuerus, till one day she lost her crown by refusing to do what she believed to be wrong. It was nearing the end of a seven days' feast at Shushan the palace; and the King's heart was merry with wine. He was proud of the beauty of Queen Vashti; and he suddenly bethought him that it would add zest to the entertainment, if he sent for her and displayed her charms to the assembled princes. Now, to stand unveiled in the presence of men was counted a deep dishonour by pure women in the East. And "the Queen Vashti refused to come." Therefore, she lost her earthly crown. But she kept a better—the crown of her virtue and modesty, and self-respect.

There are various lessons for us from this story.

1. *How fickle is the favour of the world!* King Ahasuerus no doubt had professed great love for Vashti. But he was selfish and whimsical in his affection for her. She was little more to him than a mere toy, to be played with at his pleasure. And so when she crossed his wishes his pride was hurt; and he cast her aside like an old shoe. How different it is with another King—one Jesus! If you are His, if your soul is married to Him by faith, if you have committed yourself to His care and keeping, nothing shall be able to separate you from *His* love. Get His favour, and let the world, if need be, go!

> "Earthly friends may fail and leave us,
> This day soothe, the next day grieve us,
> But *this* Friend will ne'er deceive us:
> O how He loves!"

2. *How well it is to keep the conscience clean!* Vashti went down to the grave a poorer woman, after the incident that evening in Shushan, with no crown upon her head. But she had a better right than before to hold her head erect; for she had shown herself prepared to give up everything, rather than have her conscience wounded and defiled. She might have said in her humble retirement afterwards, what a general who had fought a good fight but had been defeated wrote home as his despatch—"All is lost but honour." We may learn from her to suffer anything rather than sacrifice honour and self-respect. Be true to God and conscience, no matter what it may seem to cost. If a prize at school or in after life can be obtained, if a post at school or in the world can be kept, only at the expense of honour—do not pay for it so dear a price! Remember Vashti. Be like Sidney when he was told that by denying his handwriting he could save his life. "When God so places me," he said, "that I must either tell a lie or lose my life, He gives me a plain indication of duty." Vashti was not really a loser by what she did, and her resolute conduct was overruled by God for good. It was indirectly through her courage that Esther became Queen; and she through Esther became the deliverer of the whole Jewish people.

Led at Christ's Chariot Wheel. November 23

"To the one the savour of death unto death; to the other the savour of life unto life" (2 Cor. ii. 14–16).

THE picture suggested in these verses is one which the inhabitants of a Roman Colony like Corinth would readily appreciate. The words would bring vividly before them a scene they might have witnessed in Rome, or which they had often read of at least in the annals of their nation's history.

A victorious general has just returned from a foreign war; and the Senate has awarded him a triumphal entry to the city. In a chariot drawn by four horses, he is passing in State along the Via Sacra to the Capitol, there to offer sacrifices to the gods. The whole population are in holiday attire, and crowd the sides of the pathway or follow the army, chanting songs of victory. Behind the general march his victorious troops, with their military standards at their head. In front of him are led the prisoners of war. And on either side of him, as the procession moves along, the incense-bearers scatter fragrance on his path. Incense likewise smokes on every altar, and every image is adorned with garlands.

When the procession, headed by the Senate, reaches the foot of the Capitoline Hill, those of the captives who have been condemned to death are singled forth to meet their doom. To them, as we can well understand, the mirth of the day is melancholy, and the music of the trumpeters a dirge. The incense of the waving censers has no sweet fragrance for them. They know its significance all too well. In their nostrils its savour is "a savour unto death."

With the captives who are being spared how different! They, too, have perhaps been dreading death. But in clemency their lives are given to them: they are saved from the fate they feared. And there is music for them in the songs of jubilation that rend the air. There is fragrance for them in the incense which is being scattered—and which some of *them* may have been appointed to scatter—round the chariot in its onward path. Its savour is for them "a savour unto life."

Paul here rejoices that God always "*leads him in triumph* (R.V.) in Christ." He is a willing captive in the train of the triumphal progress of the great Captain of Salvation. He is a prisoner of hope. Yes; and he is privileged to be an incense-bearer, scattering abroad on every side the knowledge of the name and the love of the Redeemer. But this is for him a thought of much solemnity, that those who hear the gospel will be either a great deal better or a great deal worse for it. Christ must reign. He reigns over the willing hearts of those who accept the message of salvation. He will crush beneath His feet those who despise and reject it, and thereby deepen their own condemnation. If not a savour of life, the gospel will be to them the savour of death unto death.

November 24   **A Member of the Aristocracy.**

" But let him that glorieth glory in this " (Jer. ix. 23, 24).

IT is counted a great distinction to belong to the aristocracy—whom the dictionary, I see, defines as "the nobility or chief persons in a State." But there is more than one type of aristocracy. Four kinds are mentioned by Jeremiah here ; and of the four he singles out *one*, as that to which it is of by far the greatest consequence to belong. If you belong to *it*, he says, you may well glory ; but not otherwise.

(1) First there is the aristocracy of *learning*. Now it is a great thing to be learned and wise ; yet it is not a thing to be gloried in. The man is foolish who, because he knows a little more than his neighbour, yields to the temptation to intellectual pride. Why, a pin-point driven in upon his brain any day might reduce him to the level of the veriest driveller. He may have in his hand a few shells more than others have gathered upon the shore of the great ocean of truth. But what are they, where the ocean is so wide ! Moreover, when we think how little mere wisdom in the worldly sense can do for a man's character, leaving it possible for him to be " the greatest, wisest, meanest of mankind," we must seek for something better than this to glory in.

(2) Then there is the aristocracy of *power*. Now it *is* something to be in any true sense a mighty man. Power is a great endowment. The heart of man naturally covets it, and in so doing suggests the place of dominion in which God set him at the first. But there is might—*and* might. And even the power of a Napoleon, resting upon force,—through which he had at one time all Europe prostrate at his feet,—was a poor thing to glory in ; as he had often to confess to himself, with bowed head and bitter heart, while he gazed despondently across the sea from the rocky prison he was never more to leave. Let not the mighty man glory in his might !

(3) Then there is the aristocracy of *wealth*. Now, riches justly acquired and generously used may be a great boon. But sought as an end, and valued as the chief good, they will be a curse rather than a blessing, as they have been to many a wealth-blighted, shrivelled soul. Be he never so rich, the rich man had better not glory in his riches. For even if they do not take wings to themselves and flee away, the day will assuredly come when he will be compelled to feel that mere riches are a sorry portion to glory in.

(4) There remains one more—the aristocracy of *faith*. Seek a place among *them*, urges Jeremiah in the name of God. Wisdom—power—wealth—what can they do for us, after all, in the great moments of existence ? With guilt behind us, sin within us, sorrow hanging over us, eternity before us, we need more than these as children of immortality. " Let him that glorieth glory in *this*—that he understande h and knoweth *Me*." The soul can safely make its boast only in od. To be able to say of Him—" I know Him ; He is mine," is something to glory in. He that glorieth, let him glory in the Lord !

Stirring up the Nest.   November 25

"As an eagle stirreth up her nest . . . so the Lord" (Deut. xxxii. 11, 12).

THESE words occur in the remarkable "swan song" or farewell ode of Moses, the man of God. He has been recalling the dealings of Jehovah toward His people, and pointing them to the noble end He has in view for them in all His discipline. And, with a sudden bold flight of poetic fancy, suggested perhaps by the lordly career of an eagle swooping overhead as he spoke, toward the dark neighbouring range of Nebo, the prophet exclaims—"As an eagle stirreth up her nest, fluttereth over her young, spreadeth abroad her wings, taketh them, beareth them on her wings, so the Lord."

Here we have a beautiful picture of the way in which the Lord kindly and patiently educates His people for a higher life. Look at the scene described!

The eagle's fledglings have all along enjoyed her tenderest solicitude. The bird of prey, stern and pitiless as she may seem to others, is only gentleness to them. The fierceness of her swoop as she descends upon her victims is changed into the placidity of affection as she glides down upon her young brood, to feed and cherish them. For is she not their mother, who has brooded them into life, nestled them in comfort, met all their opening and expanding wants, even at the cost of stint and hardship to herself. They have early come to know, to trust, to love her as their dearest friend. Her presence has been the one great joy in their little, uneventful life. Even her absences, they know, have been devoted to their good. Yet the time has seemed long when she was away, and they have been ever ready to welcome her return with "tumult of acclaim." So the days pass by; and the eaglets live on in their high nest in peace, and never dream of danger.

But lo! one day their mother's mien is strangely altered. Sailing swiftly down upon them, she carries nothing to them in her talons as of yore, but in seeming fierceness strikes with them swift and deep into the nest. The well-built structure yields: it is stirred to its very heart. Twigs, leaves, feathers, scattered over the ledge, are all that is left to tell of the once snug and happy home; and the bewildered eaglets find themselves sprawling in the air, trying with poor success to bear themselves up for dear life's sake on their unpractised wings. But now see the mother-bird, how tenderly she flutters over them—taking hold of this one as in its very eagerness it is just going to sink, bearing that other one aloft as it seems ready utterly to fall, gliding once more from beneath it when it is calmed and rested a while, that it may try its skill again. And when at length, by kindly training, by plain example and timely aid, the fluttering brood are taught to rise, far above the eyrie from which with such alarm they had been shaken—will they not be thankful for the apparent cruelty which was real kindness, since it has taught them to rise to the larger life and liberty of the azure sky!

November 26 — Selling the Birthright.

"Esau, who, for one morsel of meat, sold his birthright." (Heb. xii. 16).

Esau and Jacob were twins. But they were very unlike each other, even in bodily appearance—also in tastes, and, as their story shows, in character, and in the end toward which in life they travelled.

In some respects Esau was the more loveable. He was frank, outspoken, rollicking, impulsive, as boy and man. Jacob, again, was quiet and designing, and often very cunning. But Esau's was after all a poor life; and though there was much dross in Jacob's character, God took means to purify it, and he was led onward to a nobler life and heritage. It is not always those who start best who come out best at the end. In Jacob we see what divine grace can do. How good a man he became, and how bright a deathbed he had, though he made in some respects so unpromising a beginning!

Both the brothers were selfish, and both were punished for their selfishness—a vice which seldom prospers in the longrun. But there is this difference, that while Esau, as he went on, became a worse and more worldly man, Jacob, as he went on, became a better man. His face was turned upward toward God, and forward toward heaven, of which he had a vision at Bethel, which never came to the like of Esau. He knew how to value the promises which his brother despised; for there was in Jacob's breast what Esau lacked, a faith in God which strengthened him for work and suffering, in the sure hope of a rich reward.

The truth is, that Esau, with all his dash and free-handedness, was extremely selfish at heart—so selfish that he could never hold himself in check for any length of time, but must needs gratify himself at once, and at whatever cost. He was not a drunkard; but he was just like in spirit to the drunkard who said, "Give me the drink now, although I should go to hell to-night!" He was a spendthrift. "Give me some of *that red* there," he cried, "and let my birthright go." Just because he was hungry and could not wait so much as an hour, he surrendered his precious birthright for a bowl of pottage. He had no high thoughts of God, no liking for religion, no value for the promises of a distant future. Present worldly pleasure was what he was bent upon. So he got what he desired, but lost far more instead of it. He lost both his birthright and his blessing, and had only the portion of the world—not the inheritance of God.

You remember the two children, Passion and Patience, in Bunyan's "Interpreter's House." Do not be like Passion, who was so like to Esau. Little good, depend upon it, will come of the boy or the girl who says—"A bird in the hand is worth two in the bush: give me good fortunes now, and you may have all your fine texts of Scripture, and all your fine glory in the world to come to yourself."

"So Esther drew near, and touched the top of the sceptre" (Esth. v. 2).

THIS is a very beautiful and suggestive scene—Esther drawing near to King Ahasuerus, at what was the supreme moment of her life, and touching the top of the royal sceptre. When we remember that the Persian monarch was regarded by his subjects as a god, and had the absolute power of life and death in his hand, it may make us think of a soul drawing near to the Most High. There is one important difference—that in God we have not to deal with a capricious tyrant, but with One who is just in all His ways, and who delighteth in mercy. But in other respects her experience was very like that of many a supplicating soul.

(1) *Esther's anxiety* was great, and it was far from groundless. She was one of a race under the ban of a royal condemnation. She was one, moreover, for whom there seemed to be no standing-room to plead. For thirty days at least the King had not called her to his presence, and to go there unbidden meant death, if the King should not extend to her the golden sceptre. Yet she felt impelled to adventure herself into the inner court. For it was certain death for her whole kindred, to stay away. It might be life for them and her, to enter. "I will go in," she said; "and if I perish, I perish."

(2) *Esther's hope* in coming to the throne was simply and solely a hope in the possible mercy of the King. She well knew that her action could not be defended upon legal grounds. It was "not according to the law." If Vashti had been degraded for refusing to come when bidden, how could she defend herself for daring to intrude unbidden? From an appeal to the law, there was absolutely nothing to hope. Her acceptance, if accepted she was at all, could only be of the royal grace.

(3). *Esther's mode of approach* was very suitable. She came near in a spirit of deep humility, and she appeared before the King in the robe which he himself had given her. After a three days' fast, we are told, she put on her royal garments, which Ahasuerus had exchanged for the poor attire she had worn as the captive Jewish maid; and clad in these she went within, and standing opposite the throne made thus her mute appeal—saying nought, but thinking in her heart, "If I perish, let me perish thus, and here!"

(4) *Esther's reward* was the reward of simple trust. It touched the monarch's heart; and her silent, modest mien, standing in the robe which was the token of her weddedness to him, was more eloquent than words. No call for the sword of justice to be unsheathed against her! But forth goes the golden sceptre as the token of her welcome. Her person is accepted, her life spared, communion with her lord granted, and a rich promise given that her prayers will be answered, "even to the half of the kingdom."

November 28   God holding our right hand.

"Nevertheless I am continually with Thee: thou hast holden me by my right hand" (Ps. lxxiii. 23).

A CHILD in the darkness finds it sometimes a great comfort to have a loved and trusted one simply clasping him by the hand to tell him he is near. Some people, even grown people, have a great shrinking from the darkness. A silly nurse, perhaps, used to tell them awful stories in their childhood; and they would almost rather anything than stay in the dark alone. This is foolish. None need fear being in the dark, unless those whose bad conscience bids them dread being left "alone with God." The wicked are told to fear, and even in their mirth they are warned to rejoice with trembling. But God's people need not be afraid. They are the children of One to whom the darkness and the light are both alike, and they are continually with Him. Their Heavenly Father is always near.

A little girl once taught her father, in this connection, a valuable lesson. He was in trouble, and thick darkness seemed to lie upon his future. He did not know into what situation his next step in business might land him. As he lay tossing on his bed at night, brooding over his anxieties, his child in the crib close by awoke with a troubled cry: "It's dark, father; it's dark; take Nellie's hand." He stretched out his hand, and clasped the child's in his. Immediately she was comforted, and soon again she sank into a placid sleep. And the parent, as the story ends, remembered that he too had a Father, to whom he could lift his cry, saying—"Father, it is dark: it is dark, Father; take my hand."

Difficulty, too, has sometimes to be encountered in the day-time, which makes it an untold comfort to have a strong, experienced hand to cling to, that it may guide and hold us up, and bring us safely through. A traveller whom I knew was attempting to pass along what is called the *Mauvais Pas*, near Chamounix in Switzerland. The path for a considerable distance is only a narrow ledge about a foot wide, on the face of a rocky height; and below there is an ugly precipice. To a clear head and a strong nerve there is no danger, as there is an iron rail to cling to at the part which is most precarious. But on this occasion the iron railing had got loose in places, and, yielding to the traveller's grasp, it had, as he afterwards confessed, a most unnerving effect upon him. The strong Swiss guide, observing this, however, made his way toward him, and did not let go his hand till he was in the place of safety. Faint symbol of the help afforded by the strong but tender hand of Jehovah; and of the reassurance brought to those who, turning to the Omnipotent One, have thankfully to say—"Thou hast holden me by my right hand."

The Slander Book.

"Laying aside all evil speakings" (1 Pet. ii. 1).

In a certain family there was an account-book kept, which had the above title printed on the outside—"The Slander Book." Inside there was a register kept of the fines inflicted upon the different members of the household every time they were guilty of speaking evil of others. It was instituted on the suggestion of a daughter of the house, who noticed how terribly prevalent the sin of backbiting is, and how readily even "good people" fall into it. I do not know how the filling-up of the book went on. But if it was faithfully kept, and if the fines were rigidly exacted, it would undoubtedly do a great deal of good.

I am afraid that in too many families, and in too many circles of friends, such a book is sadly needed. Slander is a crime which people seem to pardon very readily in themselves. But God does not so lightly overlook it. It is hateful in His sight; for all calumny is of the devil. As his very name suggests, *he* is the prince of slanderers; so that, when we are "running other people down" behind their backs,—saying and suggesting unkind and untrue or only half-true things about them,—we should know whose work we are doing, and what master we are pleasing. Certainly we are not serving and pleasing Christ.

A minister one day gave a well-merited rebuke to some young ladies who were calling at his house, and who, as he entered the room, were discussing—along with his own daughters perhaps—a young lady who was absent. Among the adjectives used, he heard such words as "very odd"—"*so* singular," and the like. Having inquired and been told the name of the person under discussion, he said seriously, "Yes, she is an odd young lady—very odd; I consider her extremely singular." Then, after a pause, he added with emphasis, "She was never heard to speak ill of an absent friend!" The curious thing is, that it is often the best people who are slandered most. This arises partly from envy perhaps, and the desire to drag those who are better than ourselves down to our own level. Bacon explained it quaintly by saying, that "we generally find that to be the best fruit which the birds have been pecking at."

Beware, then, of evil-speaking, this often thoughtless rather than malicious, habit of *de-traction*—of "dragging away" something from the good name of others. It will be hurtful to them, and hurtful also to yourself. Better for you to bite your tongue, than to utter a biting word behind a neighbour's back! Do what you can, at home and among your companions, to make an atmosphere of kindliness. If we can say at a fit time a word of honest commendation, we ought to speak it. If we cannot say what is good about others, the less we say about them the better. Remember what M'Cheyne said to a young convert who was lamenting that he could not speak for Christ. "Then, perhaps," said he, "you can sometimes be silent for Him!"

The Wonderful Name.

"*His name shall be called Wonderful*" (Isa. ix. 6).

AND certainly it may well be called so; and that for many reasons. Of these I will mention only four.

(1) It *means so much*. There is a wealth of meaning in it we can never exhaust. The riches in the name of Jesus are unsearchable. It is more full of significance than all other names together that the world has known. Richard Newton wisely puts "the wonderful name" first among the wonders of the Bible; and after giving at least one hundred and fifty of the titles that belong to Jesus, he says that he has not given them all, and cannot tell which is most beautiful.

(2) It *has lasted so long*. There are very few names that outlast their generation. Of the multitudes of men who lived upon the earth in the days of Jesus, we know now only a very few names; and of those we do know, some are mere names and nothing more. Even famous names fade in lustre as the ages pass. But the name of Jesus shines forth with undying splendour. His memory will never fade. It will grow more and more vivid, if possible, as time goes on. For God has said, "I will make Thy name to be remembered in all generations."

(3) It *has travelled so far*. Some men are counted great in one place who are not so much as heard of in another. The head man in the village is not known in the nearest town; and the town provost's fame has not reached the neighbouring great city; and even the Prime Minister of England's name may not (as Mr. Gladstone found in an outlying part of Norway) be known in some other countries. But where will you find me the land in which the name of Jesus had not been often said and sung? Its glad sound has gone forth unto all the earth. It has travelled to the remotest corners of the world.

(4) It *has so much influence*. While He lived on earth, the name of Jesus brought a spell over the hearts of multitudes who thronged to hear Him. After He departed, many miracles were wrought in the name of God's holy Child, Jesus; and by faith in His name dead souls were made alive. Then, during the dark succeeding ages, amid the overthrow of dynasties and the wreck of thrones, the name of Jesus still lived on, a name of power. And in the world at this moment it has a more commanding influence than ever before. The countless lives of Christ never want for readers. His is a name which men cannot put aside. They feel its influence in spite of themselves. Some rage against Him. Multitudes adore Him. As Napoleon said, "To this day millions would die for Him."

There is no name like that of Jesus! It brings gladness to the heart in life; it gives comfort to the saint in death; it opens for the believer the gate of heaven. It is the name of greatest influence with men; it is the one name of influence with God. Is not Jesus, then, "the Wonderful"?

Surely, and Quickly.

"Surely, I come quickly" (Rev. xxii. 20).

Is this a threat, or is it a promise? It depends on how you stand related to Him who here announces that He is coming, and coming soon. To some the coming of Christ means *that awful terror*; to others it is *that blessed hope.* Quickly, quickly, quickly—thrice repeated in this chapter (verses 7, 12, 20)—so the swift years say, however we receive it, *I come quickly!*

When Saul sent word to the beleaguered men of Jabesh-Gilead—"I am coming; by to-morrow, when the sun is hot, ye shall have help," it was pleasant news to them. But it was disastrous tidings to the Ammonites, whom by the appointed time they scattered, "so that two of them were not left together" (1 Sam. xi. 11), and whom they slew "until the heat of the day." So, too, it was blessed music to our fellow-countrymen awaiting a horrible death in Lucknow during the Indian Mutiny, when the slogan of the Highlanders told them that Havelock and his men were marching to their relief. "Dinna ye hear it? Dinna ye hear it?" cried Jessie Brown; "we're saved! we're saved!" And soon the most unbelieving in Lucknow found that she was right. But the approach of the gallant Havelock was bad news for the Sepoys.

Even so is it with the approach of Christ, foretold in these closing verses of the Bible. It is the worst of news to some; it is the best possible news to others. When He comes, there are those who shall flee from His presence, and shall vainly cry to the mountains and the rocks, "Fall on us, and hide us from the face of Him who sitteth on the throne, and from the wrath of the Lamb; for the great day of His wrath is come, and who shall be able to stand?" But there are others who shall flee not from Him but to Him, saying, "Let me behold the face of Him who sits upon the throne, and enjoy the love of the Lamb; for the great day of His love is come, and who that loves Him would stay away?" A friend said to the late Dr. Andrew Bonar once, "Now, doctor, if you were told that Christ was coming, what would you do?" The simple-hearted saint replied, "I would just run to meet Him!"

A writer tells of a poor Welsh peasant who used to look out every morning from his casement, for years, to see if Jesus Christ was coming. "He was no calculator, or he need not have looked so long; he was no student of prophecy, or he might not have looked at all; he was ready, or he would not have been in so much haste; he was willing, or he would rather have looked another way; he loved, or it would not have been the first thought of the morning. His Master did not come, but a messenger did, to fetch the ready one home. The same preparation sufficed for both; the longing soul was satisfied with either."

May we too be ready for the Saviour's coming. Coming *to* Christ is the best preparation for the coming *of* Christ. We know not when the end of the world shall be. But to us at anyrate Christ is coming, both surely and quickly. May we be of those who can say with John from the heart—"Even so, come Lord Jesus."

December 2. A Dark Path to a Bright Career.

"Ye thought evil against me; but God meant it unto good" (Gen 1. 20).

God meant Joseph's trying experience to turn out for good both to himself and to his brethren.

He needed humbling, and he got it. He had a fond father, who was foolish enough to show favouritism for him—keeping him much beside him, and clothing him in a gorgeous princely coat as a mark of special fondness. Thus Joseph became a vain youth. Though he was a good boy,—pure and upright and steadfast in early and later life,—he could hardly fail to be somewhat "spoiled" by Jacob's treatment of him. As he marched about in his fine robe among his shepherd brethren, the thought of pride would come into his heart, and tell him that he was better than they. Young as he was, he had an ambition to excel which gave colour to his thoughts by day and even to his dreams by night.

Joseph's desire to be greater than his brethren was to be fulfilled in a way he little imagined. God in His providence was to lead him to its accomplishment. But it was to be through much mental suffering; and one influence to be used toward the end desired would be the envy of his brethren.

How terrible a thing is envy! It has often led onward to the blackest crimes. If another excels you in anything, be sure to crush the envious thought, lest the spark set on fire the tinder of corruption within! Perhaps it is hardly to be wondered at, that the feeling of envy rose in the hearts of Joseph's brothers, as he strutted about in his gay coat, and, with a self-satisfied air perhaps, told them of the great things he had dreamed for himself. But they should have put the feeling down, before it had time to pass into hatred. Since they did not do this, however, it changed them into monsters ready for murder or anything.

But for a pang of soft-heartedness on the part of Reuben, Joseph would actually have been put to death. In the end, as you remember, he was sold to a passing caravan of Midianites. Sold into Egypt by his own brothers! Oh how sad young Joseph's heart must have been! As he trudged behind the camels to a foreign land, and thought of his kind father whom he might never see again, his spirit must have sunk within him.

Yet this was a dark path to a bright career. He who leads the blind by a way that they know not was leading Joseph to a place of great usefulness and high renown. His banishment to Egypt punished Jacob's favouritism and Joseph's own vanity, and was made the means of sore humbling to his envious and cruel brethren. But it was also overruled by God for great good to the whole family. For "the Lord was with Joseph," and he rose, step by step, next to the throne of Pharaoh. And when the famine drove Jacob and his family to Egypt, Joseph, the Prime Minister, had a home ready for them there, in the fruitful land of Goshen.

Gathering to Christ.   December 3

"Unto Him shall the gathering of the people be" (Gen. xlix. 10).

It is a touching scene this—of old Jacob, as he lies a-dying, speaking to his sons of what should befall "in the last days." He says in effect—"You are gathering, my sons, about my dying bed for blessing. There are varied experiences awaiting you. Separating influences are sure to assert themselves. There will be a scattering among you yet. My prophetic eye foresees how different the future is to be for some of you from what it is to be for others. But there is One coming, who, though of the tribe of Judah, is to be of common interest to all. He is the One about whom you shall assemble for effectual blessing. Not an old dying man like me, but the Peace-bringer, the Rest-giver. He is coming. And unto Him shall the gathering of the peoples be."

The fulfilment of this prediction has been far more wonderful, I doubt not, than Jacob himself imagined. It was a comparatively light thing to be the Restorer of the tribes of Israel; but He on whom the vision of the Patriarch rested was to be the Light of the Gentiles also, and Salvation to the ends of the earth. Christ was to be the great Gatherer: He was to be the centre of attraction for the souls of men all the world over.

Even in the Cradle, we see the attractive power of Jesus making itself felt upon widely different classes of men—the shepherds, the wise men of the East, and others. So too in the Crowd, during the days of His busy ministry, upon the streets of Jerusalem or by the shores of the Galilean lake, the presence of Jesus acted like a magnet, to draw all sorts of needy seekers after Him. But it is especially through the Cross, as He Himself predicted, that His drawing power is exerted over the hearts of all kinds and conditions of men. "I, if I be lifted up from the earth, will draw all men unto Me." To Him, as the crucified but now glorified Redeemer, shall the gathering of the people be.

Are you among those who have been gathered around the Shiloh? He loves to gather the young about Him. He invites you to gather about Him at the Cross, to lay your sins upon Him there as the Rest-giver who is His people's Peace. He calls you to gather about Him beneath His Banner, that He may lead you on to share with Him the bloodless victories of the gospel. The youth, you remember, are represented in Ps. cx. as flocking to the standard of the Conquering Son of God, thick as the dewdrops that gem the fields at early morn. And He will see to it, if you are His, that you are safely gathered about Him at last in the eternal Fold, where none of His own will be amissing in the great day. When the Christian dies, he is, like old Jacob, "gathered to His people"; and the people to whom he is gathered are the people whom Shiloh has gathered about Himself.

December 4. Seeking One Another.

"He sought to see Jesus . . . And Jesus looked up and saw him"
(Luke xix. 3, 5).

WHEN there is a seeking sinner and also a seeking Saviour, who will prevent them from finding one another? Jesus at the time mentioned here was just leaving Jericho, the City of Palm-trees, for Jerusalem. It was His last journey; for He was going up to the Capital to be crucified. But though He is on the most important business of His life, He has time to think of and to save this poor lost soul Zacchæus, whose heart is yearning after Him more than Zacchæus himself knows.

It is a beautiful story with many lessons, on which we cannot dwell. But let us think of (1) *the Sinner seeking Jesus*. Who was he? A rich man, one of the wealthiest in the neighbourhood, but of the hated tax-gatherer class. What was his desire? To see Jesus; not from mere curiosity, but from a vague sense, too, of his need of this so-called "Friend of publicans and sinners." And how did he satisfy his desire? In a way which showed the sincerity of it very plainly! By pocketing his dignity and overcoming every difficulty in his way: pushing his way through the excited crowd, and (because he was little of stature) actually climbing up into a tree to get a sight of Jesus as he passed. So there he was—peering out from among the leaves of the sycamore (a species of fig-tree with low, hanging branches), with the great swelling crowd beneath—none thinking of him, and he of none, save only One, the One he so greatly longed to see. And who was He?

(2) *The Saviour seeking a sinner.* He was a Man, with a face of wonderful gentleness, yet dignity and power: a face of great serenity, though with a shade of sadness resting on it; very earnest, but very kind and tender, with a look in the eyes that seemed to say that He was hungering to do others good. He was more than man, too; for He was the Son of God. Yet He was not being borne along in State as the great ones of earth sometimes are, but just walking on the dusty highway as a humble wayfarer might. And now what a surprise there is for Zacchæus, up among the leaves! For Jesus looks up (accidentally as it might seem) and recognises him; and, calling him by name, invites Himself as an intimate friend, or else as a monarch, might do, to abide at the tax-gather's house!

And now we see a third thing—(3) the mutual joy between *the sinner rejoicing in the Saviour*, and *the Saviour rejoicing over the sinner*, who had been lost, but now is found. Can we wonder that Zacchæus found joy in Jesus, who put a new hope into his heart and a new meaning into his life? Can we wonder that Jesus rejoiced over Zacchæus, when He saw in him another lost sheep found, another jewel reclaimed from the mire of sin, for a place of beauty in His glorious diadem? It was for this very purpose He came to earth. "For the Son of Man is come, to seek and to save that which was lost."

Epaphroditus. December 5

"*Brother, companion, fellow-soldier, messenger, and minister*" (Phil. ii. 25).

SUCH is Paul's beautiful description of one of the members of the Philippian Church which he loved so well. Philippi was the place where first in Europe he had preached the gospel; and the Christian community there seems to have had a peculiarly warm place in his heart. We cannot wonder at it, if many of the Philippian believers were at all like Epaphroditus, whom he here describes.

An old Roman sage said that "some men, like pictures, are fitter for a corner than for a full light." With Epaphroditus it is different. The fuller the light and the more careful the scrutiny, the more we see in him to admire. The ties that bound him and the apostle together were indeed very close and powerful.

(1) There was the bond of *kinship*, "My brother." What a flood of suggestion this name suggests! Reared under the same roof with ourselves—sharers in our blood—partakers in the nurture and discipline of the same home—having prayed at the same mother's knee and shared in the same father's counsel and blessing—"my brother." The world's poets have often, with good reason, dwelt on the tenderness of this relationship—

"The gnarliest heart hath tender chords
To waken at the name of brother."

But it is in Christ that the true brotherhood of men is realised. And Paul said a great and a true thing of Epaphroditus when he called him "my brother."

(2) The bond of *common service and endeavour*—"My fellow-companion in labour." This name, too, is full of suggestion. Not only had Epaphroditus a warm and brotherly heart, not only was he a man of tender sensibilities, but he was one who could face and go through with genuine hard work. "For the work of Christ he was nigh unto death." In this epistle we are beautifully reminded that the Master Himself, though Lord of all, was found in the form of a servant. And not only for Paul, "the servant of Jesus Christ," but for his "companion in labour," was there, as there is for you and me, a place to fill, and a work to do which the Master could turn to good account.

(3) The bond of *chivalry*—"My fellow-soldier." This may be kept in view along with the other. If there is a lowly side to the Christian life, as a life of labour, there is a heroic side to it as well—"my fellow-soldier." All true Christians are knights—of the Order of the Cross of Calvary. It does not need the sheen of glistening armour to proclaim the hero. Some of the followers of Christ in the humblest spheres are most worthy of that name. The plodding side and the heroic side of Christian life may sometimes be the very same. When it is so, the blessed influence of such a life will shed itself on others. The *fellow*-soldier, going with others, with the one heart and the one step, as messenger, or minister, or anything, will be a beneficent power for which many will have to bless the God and Father of all believers. "Hold such in reputation."

December 6 — **Eyes to the Blind.**

"*I was eyes to the blind*" (Job xxix. 15).

IN defending himself against the harsh accusations of his friends, Job feels himself called upon to rehearse some of his own good deeds; and, in speaking about the kindness he had shown to one class of people and another, this is part of his claim—"I was eyes to the blind." This must mean that when he knew of a blind person, he saw to it that he was guided and cared for, doing by himself and through others what he could to alleviate the distress of those afflicted with loss of sight.

With all due deference to Job, there died not long ago (in the autumn of 1894) a man who, in a far larger sense than the ancient patriarch, might have said of himself—"I was eyes to the blind." This was Dr. William Moon, who lived at Brighton, and died at his residence in Queen's Road there, at the advanced age of seventy-five. It was he who invented the embossed or raised alphabet, which bears his name, and has been of such untold comfort to the blind. Others had preceded him in valuable attempts to provide a type which the blind might read, and some of them, such as Mr. James Gall of Edinburgh, had done noble service in this field. But Dr. Moon's system was found simpler than any other; and the blind, not in our own country only, but all over the world, learn to read his type. It is said to be used now in no less than 476 languages and dialects.

Was not this a noble end to serve in life? And how was he qualified to accomplish it so well? He had other gifts that so far fitted him for it, no doubt; but one chief element in his preparation for his great life-work was, that he himself was overtaken with blindness at the age of twenty-one. This aroused his sympathy and awoke his inventiveness as nothing else could have done, with the result that he has provided the blind with a literature of considerable extent, both in English and other tongues. Thus God brought good out of seeming evil, and made it well both for him and others that he had been so sadly afflicted.

It is interesting to know that it was the longing for the Bible on the part of the blind that principally stimulated invention on their behalf. And when we think how much spiritual light and comfort the embossed Bible has brought to those blind in more senses than one, we perceive in how blessed a sense a man like Dr. Moon has been as "eyes to the blind." It has been his privilege to direct multitudes in this way, who were sitting in darkness, to Him who is the Light of Men. You, young reader, have eyes to read your Bible, and I hope you read it. But what if you are more blind in soul than some of the poor blind people you so sincerely pity?

Pilgrims to Canaan.   December 7

" We are journeying to the place of which the Lord said, I will give it you
(Num. x. 29).

It must have been a strange sight, to see that nation of wanderers crossing the desert ; young and old, rich and poor, man and woman and child, pressing on together with one purpose in their hearts and one goal before their eyes. What could it mean ? What could have prompted them to the journey ? What could be sustaining them in it ?

I have sometimes seen a pilgrim band, hastening from the railway train through the streets of Glasgow, to the emigrant ship that was waiting to carry them to the far-off land they knew but little of. Frequently a motley crew, whose appearance no less than their jargon as they hurry past, tells you they belong to diverse nationalities, and must have been brought together from widely different surroundings. You read something of their past in their very faces. From the honest Norwegian rustic, bone and sinew of the land he has left and a future strength to the land of his adoption, with faith in his heart and strength in his arm to do the right—to the broken-down outcast of the continental town, leaving his country for his country's good, with vice and wretchedness written on his face, and in his heart just hope enough to keep him from despair :—you instinctively feel how widely different the histories of these have been, and of the grades that lie between them and around them.

But amid all the diversity of past experience and of present characteristics, there is that in common which binds them all together to the fulfilment of one purpose, the pursuit of one goal. They have all been brought to feel *some measure of discontentment with their past*; they have all been led to cherish *some degree of hope with reference to their future*—if only they can reach the land they have been told of across the sea, where there is room, they say, for all, and welcome for all, and work for all, and reward for all who rightly seek it. So forth they go, to follow if not to find, to hope and struggle if not to succeed : some to work their way to competence and ease—others to find the El Dorado of their dreams widely different from the sober reality that soon confronts them.

Now look at the Christian band on their way to Canaan. Their past experiences and present characteristics are widely varied. But they are all urged by discontent and lured by expectation to seek one far but friendly shore. Only, their discontentment is mainly a discontentment with themselves ; and their hope rests upon no mere human hearsay. They are going forward on no mere peradventure, but to the sure enjoyment of a glorious inheritance—
" the land of which the Lord hath said, ' I will give it you.' "

Hard to Blot Out.

"Blot out all mine iniquities" (Ps. li. 9).

Sin is a horrible evil; and one of the most awful things about it is, that, once you are defiled with it, it is so difficult to get rid of its stains again. They were discussing once in a Sunday school the conduct of a newsboy, who, in order to sell a newspaper, had told a lie. Dick was asked, "if he thought it worth while for the boy, to tell a lie for a penny?" He promptly answered, "No." "For £1?" He still said, "No." "For £1000?" Dick hesitated. But another of the boys in the class cried out—"No; because when the £1000 was all spent, *the lie would be there all the same.*"

Macbeth is represented by Shakespeare as crying out in anguish, "Will all great Neptune's ocean wash this blood clean from my hand?" The stain of murder was upon his conscience, and upon his wife's too, as it afterwards appeared; and their sense of guilt told them that the great ocean itself would not suffice to cleanse away that stain. What is true of the sin of murder is true of other sins as well. They leave their mark behind them; and nothing we can do, nothing that other people can do, will rid us of the foul stain.

But there is One who can cleanse us, and who offers to do it, if we ask Him. He says, "I, even I, am He that blotteth out thy transgressions, for Mine own sake." God can do for us what no other can do; and He is willing to do it, not because we deserve it, but because of His own great mercy. And so it is to Him that the Psalmist David turns with the prayer—"Blot out all mine iniquities."

David was a great sinner. But there was wrought in him a deep heart-hatred of sin; and he is anxious to make very thorough work of his cleansing from that abominable thing which he as well as God now hates. So we find him praying in this beautiful 51st Psalm, "Hide Thy face from my sins." And not only that, but "Blot out all mine iniquities." And not only that even, but "Create in me a clean heart, O God." He desires to be done with sin; not only to be delivered from the evil of the past, but to have a heart disposed to seek only what is pure and lovely in God's sight, in all the time that is to come.

Are you in sympathy with David here? You have sadly blurred at school, through carelessness or wilfulness, your copybook. Will it content you, if the master does not see, or profess to see, the blot? A better thing will be, if, even while he rebukes you for it, he takes means to remove the blot away. Better still, if he can fill you with an earnest desire, and can give you power and skill, to keep your copy clean. "The blood of Jesus Christ, God's Son, cleanseth us from all sin." And here is the secret of progress and purity for the future. "I will put *My* Spirit within you."

The Three R's.

"These things which are most surely believed among us" (Luke i. 1).

By "the three R's" used to be meant the three subjects taught to those who had any pretension to be educated at all—Reading, (W)riting, (A)rithmetic. A quaint divine, Rowland Hill, who was immensely popular in a bygone generation in London, applied the expression to religion in a way that has been often quoted since. He said, speaking of the foundation truths, or what our fathers used to call "the fundamentals" of Christianity, that they were three—"Ruin by the Fall, Redemption by the Saviour, Regeneration by the Spirit." These, said Rowland Hill, are "the three R's" of Theology.

Rowland Hill was right. Just as nobody could profess to be educated who had not learned to read and write and count, so nobody can be said to have mastered the elements of Christian truth who has not been taught the truth of the ruin sin has wrought, the need of a redemption through the blood of God's own Son, and of a new birth to the soul by the power of the Holy Ghost. These are truths at the foundation of the Christian system. Have you, reader, learned them yet—not only with your head, but in your heart? Have you discovered how terrible is the ruin sin has wrought in your nature? Have you been brought to see in Jesus the very Redeemer whom you need—"in whom we have redemption through His blood, even the forgiveness of our sins, according to the riches of His grace"? Have you been taught anything in your own experience of the renewing power of the Spirit—who gives the new life, and gives it more abundantly? Then happy are you! Your education for a blessed eternity is at least begun. God will not leave your training incomplete. May you abound in knowledge more and more. But never allow yourself for a moment to forget or to despise "the three R's of Christianity," from a firm grasp of which all stable progress in spiritual attainment must ever proceed.

Rowland Hill said many funny things which made people smile. He did not believe that religion consists in wearing a long face always, or that there is anything inconsistent between earnest Christianity and a hearty laugh. He considered rather, that it is the Christian who of all men has the best reason to be happy, and that a smile rests on no face so suitably as on the face of a reconciled God. But with all his humour and mirthfulness, he was a serious man, living for a serious purpose. And you may depend upon it that, as you grow older, you will be made to feel that the happiness to be envied most is the joyous serenity of those who are rooted and grounded in the Love which has conquered sin through the Cross, and which by the Spirit has breathed a new life into what was before a dead soul.

December 10 — Closed Eyes Opened.

"Open Thou mine eyes" (Ps. cxix. 18).

WHEN Isaiah is describing, in language adopted afterwards by Christ, the dreadful condition of impenitent Israel, one of the worst things he has to say of them is this, "Their eyes they have closed" (Matt. xiii. 12). And this is true of a great many people besides the ancient Jews. They have closed their eyes, and more or less deliberately they keep them shut.

One great end for which God's Son came to earth was to open men's eyes (Isa. xlii. 7); and this was one of the duties specially laid upon Paul as Christ's messenger to the Gentiles—"to open their eyes" (Acts xxvi. 18). It is assumed, you see, that the eyes of people are for the most part shut. They are closed sometimes through slothfulness. Sometimes they are intentionally closed, to prevent something from being seen which it is not desired to see.

It is thus a very suitable prayer for the world—"Lord, open their eyes. Awaken them from their sleep of carelessness. Arouse them from their indifference. If they are keeping their eyes deliberately shut, make it impossible for them to continue doing so. Make them see what they ought to see, even if they do not wish to see it." This was the dying prayer of the martyr William Tindal, on behalf of the King with whose concurrence the persecution was carried on against God's suffering saints, "Lord, open the King of England's eyes!"

But the Psalmist felt that it was a prayer to be offered not only for others, but for himself; and so we too should feel, "Open Thou mine eyes." Not merely do men of the world—ay, even those who count themselves most "wide-awake"—need to have their eyes opened; but the most advanced believers still need to pray that their eyes may be kept open, and made more fully open than in time past they have been.

A great theologian said, as he lay dying, "*We are all of us only half awake.*" This witness is true. We are all of us only half awake—

(1) *To the glory of God.* Do we see God in everything? Have we especially seen God in Christ, and are we seeing God in Him every day? "I never see anything like your pictures in nature," said a lady once to Turner. "Don't you wish you did, madam?" was the quiet answer.

(2) *To the depth of our own and of the world's sin and need.* Who can understand his errors? None of us can. And who can measure the need that sin has wrought for us and for the world of men? We can best discover something of what that means by looking at it with divinely opened eyes in the light of the Cross of Calvary.

(3) *To the nobility of the Christian calling.* There is help for men in God. If we have discovered this for ourselves, it is well for us personally to discover more and ever more of the divine helpfulness. And it is also well for us, remembering the shortness as well as greatness of our opportunity, to seek that the eyes of others may be opened (as the young man's eyes were opened at Samaria, 2 Kings vi. 17) to the abundant provision God has made for the safety and blessedness of them that are His.

Partakers of Others' Sins. December 11

"Neither be partaker of other men's sins: keep thyself pure" (1 Tim. v. 22).

WE who live side by side, and are brought into contact with one another day by day, are partakers together in many things. There is a mutual influence constantly at work between us; and we should be anxious that this influence may always be of a good and helpful kind. God has intended us to be sharers of one another's experience in this world; and His word frequently urges the importance of a spirit of earnest practical sympathy between man and man.

But there is a point at which the Bible comes in and says, Stop; there is one thing in which you are not to be a sharer with your brother! You are to share in his sorrow, in his burden, in his anxiety, and also in his happiness and joy. But you are not to share in his guilt. Be not partaker of other men's sins! Here is the one case in which you are to hold quite aloof, and to shake yourself clear of copartnery. The very love which otherwise says, "Share with your brother," says here, "Be not partaker with him!" If you love him, if you love your own soul, be not partaker of his sins.

There are various ways in which young people as well as old may be sharers in the sins of others.

(1) By *a cowardly silence*. This is a very common way of having fellowship with evil, and becoming partaker in unrebuked sin. You would not yourself cheat; but your companion does it and you wink at the fraud. You would not pollute your lips with swearing; but your companion drops an oath sometimes, and you are silent, if you do not smile. You are in company where loose talk is going on; and though you do not join in it you lend a not unwilling ear to the immoral jest and impure tale. How easy and how common it is, in such ways, to be partaker of others' sins! A word of remonstrance in fit season—how good it sometimes would be to a neighbour! How the uttering of it would at anyrate deliver your own soul!

(2) By *a bad example*. Example may make us partakers of the sins of others in two different ways. We may associate ourselves with a neighbour in evil, either by setting him a bad example which he follows, or by following a bad example which he sets. Just in proportion as your companion looks up to you, your influence upon him will be great for good or evil. If he is accustomed to take his lead from you, your responsibility for what he is and does will be greater than you sometimes think. In the way you treat truth, purity, kindness, religion, remember this! If you are indifferent to these, and lead him to be the same, you will be partaker of his sin. On the other hand, you must be specially on your guard against imitating the evil things in those you admire and love. How much more prone we are to do this than to copy what in them is good! Let us not, through imitation, become partaker in the badness of any, however dear they be. But let us only follow others in so far as they follow Christ.

December 12

Be Honest!

"Thou desirest truth" (Ps. li. 6).

THE foundation of all worthy character is truth. It was a poor account the Scotchman gave of himself when he said, "Honesty is the best policy, my friends, for I have tried baith." A slave-boy once said a much better thing, in answer to the question of one whom he was anxious to have for a master. "Will you be honest, if I buy you?" said the intending purchaser. "I shall be honest," he answered, with a look that spoke volumes, "whether you buy me or not."

God desires truth. His Word requires us to be—

(1) *Honest with ourselves.* "Happy is he," says Paul, "who condemneth not himself in that thing which he alloweth"; the man, that is to say, who lives conscientiously, and does not permit himself to do what his conscience condemns. We are to deal righteously with ourselves as well as with others. If we have a high conception of life, we should seek personally to live by it—attempting ourselves what we commend, not holding our ideal slothfully, but goading ourselves when necessary to its attainment, and dealing honestly with our own failure and sin. This was one of the best of the many good things Polonius said—

"To thine own self be true;
And it must follow, as the night the day,
Thou canst not then be false to any man."

(2) *Honest with God.* He desires truth, perfect candour, on our part in dealing with Him. If we give Him that—frank sincerity—He will make us to know wisdom. The Psalmist was not alone in the experience he describes in the 32nd Psalm. So long as he "kept silence," seeking to hide or excuse his grievous fault, he was miserable. But when he was brought to confess his sin, God forgave it, and he was compassed about with songs of deliverance. A prince visiting the arsenal at Toulon had the privilege of setting free one of the galley slaves. Questioning them one by one, he found most of them ready to maintain that their punishment was unjust. But at last he came to one who sorrowfully declared—"I deserve it; I deserve to be broken on the wheel." "This," said the prince, "is the man I wish to set free."

(3) *Honest with our neighbour.* We are to be straight and "above board" in all our dealings. There can be no self-respect or genuine happiness, if we are not mindful of what is due to other people. He who takes a mean advantage of a neighbour may seem to be a gainer. But he will be a loser in the end. Honesty *is* the best policy. A boy accidentally smashed a large and costly pane with his ball, and ran away. But he was ill at ease. "Why not turn back and tell the truth?" He did so, expressing sorrow, and willingness to give work in payment of the glass. His offer was accepted, and he did so well that the merchant would not part with him afterwards, but made him his confidential clerk. Do you think that youth ever regretted being honest? And many have had a like experience.

Using the Means.　December 13

"Except these abide in the ship, ye cannot be saved" (Acts xxvii. 31).

WHAT a stirring description that is of a storm at sea, of a wreck, and of the saving of all the crew and passengers which you have in this 27th chapter of the Book of Acts! You boys will find it difficult to match it in the best of your stories of adventure.

First we see the vessel putting out to sea under a gentle breeze. Then very soon we see her driving before the wind, which rises and rises in severity till it is a perfect tempest—a regular Euroclydon. Then we see every means being taken to save the ship and its cargo by striking the sails, and "frapping" or undergirding the ship by cables passed under the keel and fastened round the hull. Then we see the sailors convinced that the cargo must go, and casting the goods, and even the tackling, overboard for dear life's sake. Then we see general despair settling down upon all faces, excepting only one—even the oldest "salts" on board being fully convinced, as the shattered hulk drifts helplessly on, that it is all over with them. And then we hear a voice of good cheer spoken, by one of the passengers named Paul, who is a prisoner on his way to trial in Rome. He says that the angel of God ("whose I am and whom I serve") has appeared to him during the night and told him that the lives of all on board would be preserved. This announcement brought some comfort to his fellow-voyagers, especially as there were signs soon discovered that they were drawing near to land.

But now occurred the incident which called forth the warning of our text. The sailors very meanly devised a plan for escaping in the ship's boat, under pretence that they wanted to get round to the foreship for the purpose of anchoring it. Paul saw through their trick, however, and instantly told the centurion and soldiers who had him in charge—"You won't be saved without the sailors. If they are permitted to desert their post, you are lost." Quick as thought, the swords of the soldiers flashed out. The boat's ropes were cut, and the sailors were kept on board in spite of themselves. The result was that, after some more adventures, they managed to run the ship into a narrow creek, and all in one way or another escaped safe to land.

Now, did not Paul before declare plainly that all on board were to be saved, and that he "believed God," whose angel had told him so? Why should he then have been so concerned about what the sailors might do, or not do? Simply because he knew that God works through means. As the old proverb says, "God helps those who help themselves." It was not enough, because God had promised safety, to sit down with folded hands and let things take their course, and say that everything would come out right at last. And yet this is what people sometimes do regarding the great salvation—deliverance not from drowning merely, but from death, and hell, and sin. They say, in effect, "If we *are* to be saved, we shall be saved, no matter what happens!" But if they do not avail themselves of the means of safety, committing their souls to Christ and giving Him the guidance of their lives, such a hope is utterly vain.

December 14 — The Filling of the Cup.

"This year also" (Luke xiii. 8).

It is told of an Italian prince who lived in despotic days, that he was celebrated for two things—for his forbearance first, but also for his severity when at length his vengeance was aroused. A servant of his, whom he had repeatedly admonished, seemed to become more reckless and impudent every day. Presuming on the indulgence of his royal master, he entered his presence with his hat on; and when rebuked he saucily said he had a cold. The prince calmly but sternly answered—"I will take care that you never catch cold again." The man was immediately haled away to prison, and the order was given to the executioner to nail his hat to his head. It was a cruel but instructive comment on the Bible declaration—"He that being often reproved hardeneth his heart, shall suddenly be destroyed, and that without remedy."

One of the prince's friends expressed surprise at the severity of the sentence upon one who had survived more serious offences. The prince took a cup, and having half-filled it with water, requested his friend to put an apple in it. The water rose to the brim. "How is it," he asked, "that the small coin has made the water to run over, while the large apple raised it only to the brim?" The friend needed no further explanation. He perceived that the cup of righteous indignation had needed but a very little thing to make it overflow.

Now, there are people who go on for long, provoking the Almighty to anger; for, as the Bible tells us, God is angry with the wicked every day. He mercifully restrains the fierceness of His anger. But if they do not repent and forsake their sin, the flood so long sluiced will at length burst forth upon them and sweep them to destruction.

The owner of the vineyard came year after year to look at his trees, and there was one fig-tree on which he never found any fruit. His patience became at length exhausted, and he proposed to cut it down. But the dresser of the vineyard pleaded that for one year more it might have a chance of doing better. And even he had to admit, that if, with all the care bestowed upon it, there was no fruit upon it then, it ought to be cut down as a mere cumberer of the ground. As our years are lengthened out, let us be more and more in earnest that our lives may be found bearing fruit to the glory of our God. It would be a sad thing—would it not?—if God's sparing mercy, and all His goodness, instead of softening our hearts only hardened them? It would be sad indeed if, instead of accepting at God's hand the cup of salvation, we went on through the years filling up for ourselves a cup of divine anger, which should overflow at length to our destruction!

In His Steps.

"Leaving us an example, that ye should follow His steps" (1 Pet. ii. 21).

CHRISTIANS have not only a book of instructions as to how they ought to live,—what they should do and not do; but they have a bright and glorious pattern to go by, in which they see the will of God perfectly embodied before their very eyes. And so, while the Bible gives us many counsels as to life and character, it sums up all by pointing us to Christ, saying—"Consider Him! There you will find in an actual example everything you ought to seek to be and to do!"

This is a great advantage for us. It is so much easier to understand what is expected, and to strive intelligently to act up to it, when we have a model before us rather than a mere description on paper of the shape our character and life should take. And this is not all. For, with this example before us, Jesus puts His Spirit also within us, to enable us to follow where He leads, to walk through this world as He also walked.

Now, we should be constantly bringing our copy alongside of the original, comparing our handwriting with the headline above it. This may be very humbling to us, as we perceive how far short we come, and what a poor blurred copy ours is at the best. But it will be also very useful; and indeed it is the only way in which to make real progress. Without it, we shall more than likely go back instead of forward, and be found growing worse instead of better. M'Cheyne somewhere speaks about his watch having had a tendency to go slow, and being found more at fault in this respect when he was in the country than when he was in the town. The explanation was simply this, that he was frequently brought face to face with the steeple-clock in the town, which called him to set his watch right; but that there was no such reminder in the country. This he applied to the inner watch—the heart within—which the Christian ought often to compare and set right by Jesus Christ.

Let us then ask often—"What would Jesus do?" and, whether called to act or to endure, let us seek to be like Him. "I will set the Lord alway before me," is a good motto for every Christian. How thankful we should be that Christ goes before us, and that He is willing to inspire us to follow Him. It is said to have been one of the great secrets of Cæsar's influence and conquering might, that he seldom said "*Ite*" (Go) to his soldiers, but "*Venite*" (Come). So is it with a greater than Cæsar, namely, Christ. He cheers His people in face of difficulty by His own example. Like the Hungarian king whose weary men were sinking into a death-sleep among the snow, He says to us—"Arise, arouse ye; follow Me." And as we are awakened and enabled to put our feet into His footprints, it will mean for us life, progress, victory, everlasting reward.

December 16 — The Common Lot.

"And he died" (Gen. v. 5, 8, 11, etc.).

MEN have learned from long experience to speak of death as "the way of all the earth," because everyone, sooner or later, has to pass through its gloomy portal. It is the common lot of man. Only two men in the world's long history have escaped death. Concerning all the rest, it has had to be written, "And he died." This is not a pleasant thing to think of; but it is true, and we need not attempt to conceal from ourselves its truth.

A French preacher at the Court once gave utterance to the commonplace, in presence of the King—"We all must die." The royal brow was observed to be clouded with a frown; and the orator, who spoke mainly to please his audience, stammeringly added—"at least most of us!" Whether this interjection brightened the royal countenance or not, I cannot tell. But that preacher was a base flatterer; and death would not come one moment later to the royal palace for all the flatteries that man might utter, and all the delusive hopes that might be suggested by them.

You have perhaps read the *Vision of Mirza*, by Addison? If not, obtain it, and read it, and think upon it. It is a beautiful and instructive specimen of what is called Allegory—belonging as it does to the same kind of composition as the *Pilgrim's Progress*, though much shorter than it. The Bridge of Human Life, with the innumerable trap-doors through which the passengers fall into the great tide beneath, has its lessons for us, whatever be the stage of the earthly journey at which we have arrived; and, since "the hidden pitfalls were set very thick at the entrance of the bridge," as well as towards its end, there is a lesson even for the youngest.

As you look round among your many class-fellows, with faces ruddy with health and eyes sparkling with the fire of youth, you may think it will be a very long time before your ranks can be thinned by death. Yet as you go on in life, one after another will disappear from the bridge—most of them long before the seventieth arch is reached. I knew a very aged gentleman, who had been in youth a member of a very large class in the High School of Glasgow. In after years, the survivors of that class, he told me, used to meet annually to dine together; and they all signed their names every year in the class album, which was to belong at last to him who outlived all the rest. Fewer and fewer the number grew: 50—40 —30—20—10—5—3; until only two white-haired old men sat down together, and wrote their names in the book. Then my friend alone was left, and became the possessor of the album. And now he too is gone. "And he died" has come true of every one of them. So will it be sooner or later with every member of *your* class. Our times are in God's hand. Happy he of whom it not only has to be written, "And he died," but can be added—"*Nevertheless he lives* the blessed life with God"!

Amid Changeful Weather. December 17

"He abideth faithful" (2 Tim. ii. 13).

WE live in a world that is full of change. You will be more and more impressed with that as you grow older. But there is One who changes not; and I trust that you will learn more and more to value Him as the Friend who in storm or sunshine will abide with you, and undertake for you, and make all things work together for your good.

"He abideth faithful." He is always *true to His own character.* He is a God of unswerving righteousness. He is utterly and at all times to be relied upon. He cannot deny Himself. He is a God also of marvellous loving-kindness. That, you must not, dare not doubt, whatever appearances may say. A good old man had a curious weather-cock made, and set it over his house. It had printed upon the vane the words, "God is Love." So, whether biting Boreas or the gentle Zephyr blew—whether the wind was from the north, south, east, or west—the weather-cock told the same true story still, "God is Love." It was a quaint but useful way of reminding himself and others, that "God may change His dispensation towards His children, but His disposition does not change."

"He abideth faithful." He is always *true to His promise and purpose of grace* to believers. No good word in which He has caused any of them to hope will come to naught. God will be found true, though all men should be found liars, even the best men we have known. He is faithful who hath promised; and what He has promised He will do. As for His purpose, it is sure to be executed. To human view, this may not appear likely; some things may seem to point in quite a different direction. But He sees the end from the beginning, and can control everything to the attainment of His end.

Let us trust Him, and trust Him wholly. He does all things well. He makes "all things work *together* for good" to them that love Him. That word "together" is a very important word. The frosts, the snows, the ploughing, by themselves would not give a harvest; but, together with the seed and the sunshine and the showers, they have their own part to play. That cup in the patient's hand might be poison, were the ingredients taken separately, or were even one of them left out; but mixed together by the skilled physician's hand, it is breath and life.

It is a safe rule to go upon, when we are tempted to pass judgment on God's dealings with us—"Wait till you see the end: do not judge till you know the whole." Stitch by stitch the texture of your life must be inwoven. There may be some dark threads in it which you would fain have had left out. But when the work is done, and you look at the completed pattern *from above*, you will not wish that any single divinely appointed thread or stitch had been omitted then.

December 18. A Helpful Master.

"I will help thee: yea, I will uphold thee" (Isa. xli. 10).

THOSE who serve Christ serve the best and kindest of all masters. He is both just and generous to those who serve Him. He takes a deep personal interest in every one of them. When they are perplexed, He is ready to counsel them. When they are in straits, He is ready to help them. When they are weary and cast down, He not only sympathises with them under their burden, but says to them—oh, how kindly and persuasively!—"Cast thy burden upon Me."

It is told of an old woman, a mill-worker, that as she was toiling up a hill in a hot day, almost ready to faint under the web of cloth she was carrying on her shoulder, she heard a voice behind her, saying—"Roll it off on *my* shoulder; and I will help you." Very thankfully she obeyed. What was her surprise and almost her confusion on seeing that he to whom she had transferred her load was none other than the gentleman she served, the wealthy owner of the mill himself!

Now that deed of kindness, that bringing of kindly succour to one oppressed, was a Christlike deed. Our holy Heavenly Master loves to do things like that. He is doing them so constantly that we need feel no confusion when, at His bidding, we cast our burden upon Him. He is our Master, but He is our Friend and Saviour too. And when His strong hand makes help to us, it both lightens the heart and shortens the way. "I will uphold thee with the right hand of My righteousness." How strong and yet how tender a hand is this—the right hand of our Redeemer's righteousness!

"More than thirty years," said the gallant Havelock, "have I served Christ; and no man ever had so good a Master or so kind a Friend." Havelock's Master is willing to be yours. How well it will be for you, to enter His service early, that you may know from the very outset of your life the joy, which some have grieved that they knew so late, of being "a servant of the Lord Jesus Christ."

They are to be pitied who are toiling and struggling on amid life's burdens, all ignorant of the sympathy and the helpfulness of Jesus. "I used to work single-handed," said one who knew well what difficulty meant; "but now I have a Partner, and He lightens the load for me." The loving Saviour is willing on His part to be the Partner of your life. Are you willing to enter into partnership with Him? "Two are better than one," says the wise man in the Book of Ecclesiastes. And if there are to be two, of whom you are to be one, who shall be the other? Can you for a moment hesitate about the answer? Surely it will be Christ!

I must Work.

"I must work the works of Him that sent me" (John ix. 4).

WHY *must*? When Jesus said, "I must work," did it mean that He was compelled, that He had to work whether He liked it or not? This is the case, we know, with some people—perhaps with a great many; when they work at all, they do it out of sheer necessity.

A gentleman met a tramp upon the road one day, who asked him for some money. The beggar was a sturdy-looking fellow; and the gentleman refused at first to give him anything. But the man looked him solemnly in the face and said—"I am sorry for that, sir; for I shall have to do what my soul abhors." The gentleman, alarmed and thinking that he contemplated suicide, drew a shilling from his pocket, and in handing it to him spoke seriously to him on the sin and folly of even hinting that he meant to take away his life. "Oh," said the vagrant, with more wit than gratitude, as he turned away, "it was not *that* I meant at all, sir; I meant that I should have *to work*!"

That man was one of the sort who count work a great infliction, and exercise far more persistence and ingenuity sometimes in seeking to avoid it, than would have been needful in order to its easy and successful accomplishment. I need hardly say that Jesus was of the very opposite spirit. His life was a patient continuance in well-doing, cheerfully undertaken and carried through. *Must* work, in His case, means, not because He was compelled, but because He loved His Father and His work so much that He could not be idle.

If *you* love your Heavenly Father, you will find some way of pleasing Him, too; and you will have to find it, or you will not be at rest. "What can I do for you, father? What can I do for you, father?" said a little fellow to his parent so often that the latter grew wearied at length, and said rather sharply, "Why do you bother me so?" The boy burst into tears and cried, "Oh father, because I can't help it!" But the Heavenly Father is never "bothered" when His children, under the constraint of love, come to Him for errands.

"I must work *to-day*," said Jesus, "because night is coming." He was still in the vigour of His manhood; but he knew that the working day was short. · So is yours and mine, though life may seem for the present to be stretching out long before us. We must work from love; we must work with a will; we must work for an end; we must work *to-day*. The old are prone to say, *Yesterday*. The young are prone to say, *To-morrow*. Christ says, *To-day*. Remember this—for it is true: To-morrow, if it is yours, will bring to-morrow's duty with it. To-day's duty cannot be done to-morrow.

December 20. There Also.

"There shall also My servant be" (John xii. 26).

JESUS expects His servants to be where He is. He intends that they shall be there. And when He says to us, "Where I am, there shall also My servant be," we should hear in the words both a call to duty and an encouragement to hope.

"There shall also My servant be" has (1) *a meaning for this life.* Where is Jesus to be found on earth? Where there are souls needing to be enlightened, troubles to be relieved, devils to be cast out, there the Saviour loves to be, and is; and there He sends His servants too. Those who are truly His *disciples* (Matt. x. 1) He makes *apostles* also (Matt. x. 2); and each of them has an errand of mercy for the Master. We have not all the same road to run, the same bit of work to do for Him. But there is something for us to do, in enlightening somebody's darkness, alleviating somebody's sorrow, helping somebody in society somewhere to overcome the evil spirit and cast him out. Where the cause of Jesus needs to be represented and His work to be done, at home or abroad, here or anywhere, there also shall His servants be.

You remember what was said to King David by Ittai the Gittite, at a time when David and his cause stood sorely in need of sympathy and help? It was a wonderful expression of devotion for the King of Israel to have drawn from a Philistine. But there was a magnetic charm about David which attracted the loyalty of widely different people to him; and he had charmed the heart of this man of Gath, among the rest. So here is what Ittai said, when it was suggested that he might go back to a place of safety and ease —"As the Lord liveth, and as my Lord the King liveth, surely in what place my Lord the King shall be, whether in death or life, *there also will thy servant be"* (2 Sam. xv. 21). So should we be ready to speak to our yet nobler King, as One we will on no account be parted from. And then we shall find, that—

"There also shall My servant be," as spoken to us by Christ, has (2) *a meaning for the life to come.* Even on earth we shall find the place of duty, ay, or of severest trial for His sake, the place of true inward reward. But that is not all. For Jesus has gone to heaven as the Forerunner of His people; and, one by one, when His own time comes, He gathers His servants home. His presence in heaven is the pledge that all His faithful followers also shall yet be there. "If any man serve Me," He says, "let him follow Me; and where I am there shall also My servant be; if any man serve Me, him will My Father honour."

Is not this a cheering echo from heaven of words such as those of Ittai the Gittite? "There also will thy servant be," says the devoted heart to Christ. And the heavenly echo from the glorified Saviour answers back, "Here also shall My servant be!"

Shutting the Door. December 21

"And the Lord shut him in" (Gen. vii. 16). *"And the door was shut"* (Matt. xxv. 10).

THE shutting of the door in both these cases meant, enclosing some in safety and comfort, and leaving others out to dismay and desolation.

The mockers in Noah's time would fain have had a place at last in the despised Ark. But their day of opportunity was past. The Lord who had shut Noah in had shut them out, and the last of them, even on the highest mountain-tops, had at length to die, amid the plashing rain, with the despairing cry upon his lips—"Too late! Too late!" God gives to you, as to Noah, the invitation, "Come." Take heed lest the same lips have to say to you the heart-breaking word, "Depart." A godly father and pious home will not themselves save you. The invitation runs, "Come thou *and all thy house* into the Ark." Had one of Noah's sons refused to commit *himself* to the Ark, he would have perished like anybody else.

So, too, the foolish Virgins in the Parable would gladly at last have got within to the marriage feast. But their folly and negligence cost them dear. While they were going to buy oil for their lamps, which should have been trimmed and ready, the Bridegroom came. And they that were ready went in with Him to the marriage: *and the door was shut.* Alas! poor foolish ones, they might knock, and knock, now; but they could not enter. The only answer they could obtain from within was the refusal which sounded like a knell—"I know you not."

How much better to be shut in than to be shut out! It was a beautiful answer given by an old man who lived in a cottage upon a lonely moor, when one asked him if he was not afraid at night. "Oh no," he said; "faith closes the door and shutters at night, and mercy opens them in the morning." May such safety and peace be yours in the Ark—that is, in Christ. May perfect joy at last be yours at the marriage feast—that is, in Heaven.

But what if *you*, meantime, are shutting the door? Perhaps the King of Grace has been knocking gently and patiently at the door of your heart to get in, and you have refused Him. He will not force His way in. Unless any man, or boy or girl, *will* open the door, it may remain shut for ever.

What an unkind thing to Jesus, to keep Him standing there outside! And what an unkind thing to yourself, to run the risk of sending Him away! For He is *standing*; and while this reminds us how very very anxious He is to get in, it also reminds us that He may pass on. In sorrow, not in anger, He sometimes has to say— "I will never seek to brighten that door again!" The door, you must remember also, will grow harder and harder to move on its rusty hinges. The company within may be less and less fit for the presence of the King. And you may be less and less disposed even to think of opening it for Him. Alas, you may put off till the case is just reversed—Jesus within and you knocking. What a sad, solemn word to hear, spoken from within and you outside—"Too late—too late—you cannot enter now!"

December 22. NOW.

"Now is the accepted time" (2 Cor. vi. 2).

THAT little word *now* is a very important word for all of us. We can hardly exaggerate its importance; because the future so greatly depends upon the *now*, and the *now* will so speedily be changed into the past which can never be recalled.

The ancients sometimes represented Time as an old man with a bald head that had only one lock of hair upon it—namely, at the front: to remind men that once Time is past it is impossible to lay hold of him again. An opportunity once missed is gone for ever.

It is not to be wondered at that the Bible, since it deals with the most serious of all concerns, is so urgent in its call to us to make the very most of the spiritual opportunities that are given to us. There are people who practically go upon the foolish rule—" Never do to-day what you can put off till to-morrow." But God warns us of the folly of such a course, and what His Word enjoins is—" Never put off till to-morrow what ought to be done to-day." Especially does the Bible warn and entreat us, not to delay, where it is a question of our soul's salvation. "Now," it urges, "is the accepted time: Now is the day of salvation." Do not trust to a to-morrow which may never be yours. It is a very serious thing to pray the prayer, which Augustine confesses that he prayed in his sinful youth—" O Lord, convert me, but *not now.*"

A man was bird-nesting on the face of a high cliff. He was standing on a ledge of rock half-way down the cliff, which rose almost sheer out of the sea beneath. The rope by which he had let himself down slipped somehow from his hand, and though it kept swinging to and fro, he saw to his horror that every time it swung it was a little farther away. To be left on that little ledge meant death by starvation. Quick as thought he perceived that his only chance for life was to spring at the rope and seize it at its next vibration; else it would be for ever beyond his reach. His resolve was taken: he leapt for dear life, and clutched the rope, and was saved. Oh, how thankful he was as he reached the top of the cliff again, and was restored to family and friends, that he had been enabled to seize the *now* before it became a *never*!

"My Lord, these letters contain serious news; and I am requested to ask you to read them at once." The speaker was a messenger who had arrived in hot haste with despatches for Archias, the governor of Thebes, while with a company of boon companions he was seated at a feast. "Serious things to-morrow," cried Archias laughingly, as he put the letters beneath the pillow of his couch. But that same evening the conspirators, against whose plot the letters warned him, rushed into the banquet hall and put him and his guests to death. Delays are dangerous. Let us remember that "every hour added to our life is an hour taken from it"; and that "now is the accepted time."

Heirs of God.

"If children, then heirs" (Rom. viii. 17).

A MAN'S heirs are usually his children. And God's children are His heirs. They will get all their Father has to give them.

Now, the Bible speaks about God's only-begotten Son. And for long ages He had but one Son, who dwelt in His bosom from eternity, and was the Heir of all things. But in wonderful grace it was determined to bring others within the family. And who do you suppose these were? Why, just sinners, outcast and vile, like you and me! God's heart of love went out after us. "I would like to bring these children of men into My family," He said. And the Son made answer, "I would like to go forth, to seek them, and *bring* them to share with Me the blessings of My Father's house. Yea, I will die to take away their sin, and make them meet to dwell with us on high. For I long to make them sharers in My bright inheritance." And so Christ came, and lived, and died upon the earth, that we might become children of God, and joint heirs with Himself. "As many as received Him, to them gave He the right to become the sons of God, even to them that believe on His name" (John i. 12).

The heir to a large estate in Scotland lay dying. He summoned his younger brother to his bedside; and, after talking to him for a little while, he said—"And now, Douglas, in a short time you will be a duke, and—I shall be a king." The dying youth was a believer in Jesus. He was a child of God. He was heir to a richer inheritance than any upon earth; *and he knew it.* Hence he could leave the world without a sigh. He felt that he was not quitting his best possessions, but rather entering upon them.

Peasant or peer—poor or rich on earth—there is none with prospects to compare with those of the heirs of God. It has been said that "all are low-born who are not born from above." The converse is true—that all are high-born who are children of the Heavenly King and have the heavenly heritage in store. If you are Christ's, and Christ is yours, then all things are yours in Him. "Eye hath not seen, nor ear heard, nor hath it entered into the heart of man, what God hath prepared for them that love Him."

Surely this may well be an inspiring thought for us, whatever be the place we are called, meantime, to occupy on earth—"I am one of the children of the King, and I am under preparation here for the prepared inheritance." John Newton says: "If one of the angels was called on to rule an empire and another to sweep a street, they would not wish to exchange places." To be where the Lord puts us should be enough for us meantime here; and we should patiently and thankfully seek to be qualified there for the higher things in store. God forbid that we should ever envy those—

"Who barter life for pottage; sell true bliss
For wealth or power, for pleasure or renown;
Thus Esau-like, the Father's blessing miss,
Then wash with fruitless tears their faded crown."

December 24   The Safe Refuge.

"God is our Refuge" (Ps. xlvi. 1).

THIS is a wonderful thing to be able to say of the high and holy God—that He is our refuge. As you young Latin scholars can tell us, this means that He is *One to run to*: One to whom we may run back, when we are feeling ourselves sorely pressed, that in Him we may find safety, succour, consolation.

Perhaps you have sometimes felt that He was rather One to run *from*, if haply you might hide yourself from His sight, as Adam and Eve tried to do among the trees of the garden. But this is both an unhappy and a foolish course to take. It can never succeed. The sinner has to learn that there is no refuge from God except in God. He only knows true peace who has been brought to say with Augustine—"I fear thee, O God: therefore do I flee into Thine arms."

You remember about the *Cities* of Refuge in the Old Testament? They were six in number, three on either side of the Jordan; and they were placed so that one or other of them might be easily reached from any part of the land. In them there was a shelter for the fugitive from the avenger of blood, and he would at anyrate have the question between them fairly tried before punishment was inflicted upon him.

Now the fugitive fleeing for safety to one of these six cities of Levi, makes us think of the sinner fleeing to the Saviour. Just as there were way-posts along the road,—with the word *Refuge* printed upon them, and pointing toward the City, so distinctly that he who ran might read,—so in the Bible we have many an invitation and promise plainly directing us to God in Christ, that in Him we may find safety. I wonder whether you have fled to the Saviour, and found a refuge for your poor guilty soul in Him? If you have, there is *always* now a Refuge for you in God. He is One to whom you may constantly turn; and, coming to Him in need and in expectation, you will never find Him turning His back upon you and refusing to you His sympathy and help.

We have not *Cities* of Refuge now. But we have still some institutions which teach us what a refuge means. We know what a Home of Refuge is, for the cold and hungry and weary in our great cities. We know what a Harbour of Refuge is, for storm-tossed sailors along our coasts. We know what a Fort of Refuge is, to which hard-pressed soldiers might repair under the stress of battle. Among the cold and want and storm and battle of life, how well it is for us to have, in such a sense, a Refuge in God. But there is something more familiar still than any of these, which may enable the youngest to understand what is meant by having in God our Refuge. A mother's lap! Where, in days of early childhood, did you naturally flee with all your troubles, great or small, that you might be comforted? To your mother's lap! Even so, Jesus says, "Come to Me!" The Eternal God is thy Refuge; and underneath and about thee will be the everlasting arms.

The Young Child.   December 25

"The young child and His mother" (Matt. ii. 14).

On this day, when many are celebrating the birth of Christ, I invite you to think of the name by which He is called at least nine times in this chapter—"The Young Child." The name teaches us—

1. That Jesus *began life at the very beginning*. He did not come into the world endowed at first with the powers of manhood. In that case there might be a great gulf between you and Him. But He came a helpless babe, requiring to have everything done for Him. Mary had to put Him in His baby dress, and feed Him at her breast; and Joseph had to snatch Him away to Egypt in order to save him from the wicked king who sought the young Child's life. He needed food, clothing, protection, training—just like any other child. Thus—

2. Jesus *understands you*. He can enter into all your feelings, and knows your ways. He lived and grew among boys and girls like you, and He knows their temptations, their troubles, their difficulties, as well as their joys; and He can feel for them. He is not a Saviour only for grown-up people; but He is a Saviour —a Friend—a Brother—to the young. And you on your part are to remember that.

3. You may copy Jesus, and *begin to copy Him now*. You are not to wait till you are bigger, and to say, "Ah, when I am a grown man or woman, *then* I'll try to be like Christ; then I'll love God and go about continually doing good." No, no; begin now! The young Child Jesus "hallowed childhood and early youth by passing through them," that yours, too, might be holy. He grew and waxed strong in spirit, filled with wisdom; and the grace of God was upon Him." That is *His* boyhood. And when He grew older, He did not, as lads are sometimes prone to do, try to throw off His parents' authority. Even after exciting the wonder of the doctors in the temple, He went down to Nazareth with His parents and was subject to them. "And He increased in wisdom and stature, and in favour with God and man."

Now that is in the Bible just for you. Some of us are past childhood and youth; and our opportunity for being like Christ in these is over, leaving the record of our failures in the great book of God's remembrance. We may long to bring opportunity back, but cannot. An eminent servant of Christ, whose youth was spent in folly, used to sigh, "O Lord, too late I loved Thee!!" And many an unhappy man has died with the useless lament of the expiring soldier in his heart, if not on his lips, "If I could be a boy again— a boy again!" But youth is still yours, though you are just now reminded that another year of it has almost sped. Do not trifle with it. Do not stain it. Do not waste it. Yield yourselves to God. Grow in grace and in the knowledge of our Lord and Saviour Jesus Christ.

December 26   The Kindest Wish.

"I wish above all things that thou mayest prosper and be in health, even as thy soul prospereth" (3 John 2).

ONE of the Popes made the following remarkable confession on his deathbed—"When I was a common man, I thought I had good hopes of getting to heaven; when I became a Cardinal, I very much doubted it; and when I became a Pope, I had no hope at all." Many a one in humbler circumstances has reason to make a like confession—that his spiritual prosperity has diminished as his outward prosperity has increased. This ought not to be so. Increase in riches or in rank ought not to be allowed to turn the head, or lead the heart away from God. But against so unhappy a result, divine grace is the only proper safeguard. Hence the wisdom of such a prayer as this of the Apostle John for his well-beloved Gaius.

This is a season for good wishes. We should always be wishing one another well, not in words merely, but from the heart; but one of the pleasantest features of this season of the year is, that the air is full of the kind wishes which everybody is uttering so cheerily for everybody else.

Well, now, this Bible wish is like, and yet unlike, what is so common among us. The apostle wishes that his friend may "get on well," and "keep well"—that he may grow richer and stronger, and keep his bodily health. But he is thinking more of his friend's spiritual than of his temporal interests; and so he adds—"even as thy soul prospereth." He loves Gaius too well to desire for him worldly good out of proportion to his spiritual prosperity. He is above all things anxious that Gaius may "get on" and "be in health," in his soul; and then that, along with that, he may have as much outward prosperity as he can safely bear.

Now, dear young reader, the best wish those who love you most can give you is—(1) *that your soul may prosper*—that you may be cleansed from sin's guilt, cured from sin's leprosy, delivered from sin's power—that you may grow richer and stronger every day—richer in faith and love and heavenly wisdom, and stronger to resist the evil and to perform the good. And then, we may safely wish for you (2) *that your outward prosperity may be just as great*—that you may get on in the world, and become richer and more influential day by day, so long as that does not interfere with the well-being and progress of your never-dying soul. Worldly adversity is sometimes the greatest blessing God can send to His children, whose hearts have been growing cold and self-satisfied, and dead through a superabundance of earthly good. It is a searching question for old and young in the closing year—What would my outward prosperity be if it were exactly proportioned to my inward worth?

A Pressing Invitation.   December 27

"Come—Come—Come—Take" (Rev. xxii. 17).

THE closing year is a time for giving and receiving invitations. Here is an invitation for you from the closing Bible. It is the best of all invitations—the call to sinners to accept the blessings of salvation purchased for them by the blood of Christ on Calvary. Come, and take!

You cannot fail to notice two things about this invitation.

(1) How *earnest* it is! The Bible, being just about to close, seems in this last appeal to grow, if possible, more earnest than ever before. The Spirit—the Third Person in the Holy Trinity, whose part it is to strive with men—says, "Come." The Bride—that is, the Church, the Bride of Christ the Saviour, whose will is also hers—says, "Come." And all who have heard it for themselves are urged to join in the glad invitation, "Come." Within the heart—within the bounds of the Church—and wherever there is a living, loving Christian in any corner of the world to give voice to it, the cry is the same—"Come—Come—Come!"

Then (2) How *free* it is! No price is asked. And God means it. I remember hearing the water-sellers on the streets of Cairo shouting—"Ho, thirsty ones, water without money!" But they did not mean it. They only intended to let it be known that they had fine fresh water to sell, for which they would not charge *much*. But when God says "Without money and without price," as in Isa. lv., or "Come and take," He means it. "Let him that is *athirst* come." Are you thirsty? That is all. Here is water for you. Don't hold back! Come and take it, that your soul may be refreshed. Yea, "Whosoever will, let him take the Water of Life freely." Lest you should stop to ask—"Am I so thirsty as to be one of those meant?" this is added—"Whosoever will!"

"Thank God," said the famous Richard Baxter, "for that 'whosoever.' Had it been—'Let Richard Baxter take,' I might have doubted if I were meant; but that 'whosoever will' includes me, though the worst of all Richard Baxters." Why, dear young reader, should it not include you too? Perhaps you are able, humbly but thankfully, to say that it has included you. If not, are you to allow this year also to close, without closing with the offer which God in Christ is making to you, so earnestly and freely now? "*I* am willing with all my heart," He says. But what of *you*?

Hitherto.

"Hitherto hath the Lord helped us" (1 Sam vii. 12) ... *"Hitherto have ye asked nothing in My name"* (John xvi. 24).

WHEN, in answer to Samuel's prayer, the victory was given to Israel over the Philistines at Mizpeh, the prophet set up a memorial stone and called it Ebenezer (the Stone of Help), saying, "Hitherto hath the Lord helped us." Samuel meant it to be a token both of thankfulness and of hope. He declared by it his gratitude to Jehovah for His faithfulness in the past; and likewise his confidence in the divine faithfulness for all the time to come.

Surely we, as we look back on the way by which God has led us during our past life, or even during the bygone year, have abundant reason to praise Him for His mercy and His truth. And when we remember what He has already been to us and done for us, we may well trust Him for coming days. It is ours to set up our Stone of Help, as Samuel did, as a stone both of gratitude and of continued hope in God. "Hitherto hath the Lord helped us." Never once, as yet, has He been found wanting to us. In straits, in times of sorest difficulty, He has always proved Himself a present aid. Therefore will we trust, and not be afraid.

But the word "hitherto," while reminding us of the constant faithfulness of God, is fitted to suggest to us at the same time our past faithlessness. We have not confided in Him as we should have done. We have not always looked to Him for help as He invited us to do. Sometimes we have presumed to fight our Philistines, our spiritual foes, in our own poor strength; which was but to court defeat. Too seldom have we turned to God for the blessings which He was so willing to give us; and so we are much poorer to-day than we might have been. He is faithful; but we have been unbelieving. And Jesus puts into *His* "hitherto" a tone of gentle chiding.

"Hitherto have ye asked nothing in My name." Nothing, that is, in comparison with what you might have asked. If you are a child of God, you have asked something. "Behold, he prayeth," is "the hall-mark" of a real Christian. "None of God's children are born dumb." The new-born soul cries for God as the new-born babe cries for his mother. But hitherto you have asked nothing worth speaking of alongside of what Christ is able and ready to bestow. And so He comes to you now with a fresh challenge to faith—"Ask, and ye shall receive, that your joy may be full."

"When will you cease asking, Raleigh?" said Queen Elizabeth once to her courtly favourite. Sir Walter answered, "When your Majesty ceases giving!" If we are not to stop asking till Jesus stops giving, we shall go on asking much and long. And this is what our Heavenly King desires. He longs to crown the year for you with His goodness, and to enrich you with His best gifts. Do not, like the unbelieving king who was called to smite with the arrows (2 Kings xiii. 18), restrain the blessing. Try to ask in such a way as to satisfy the Great Giver's heart.

"*They who live should not henceforth live unto themselves*" (2 Cor. v. 15).

"GOD has spared my life, and I am going to be God's man now." So cried a poor convict, in fervent thankfulness, in Glasgow prison, on the 16th January 1891, when the news was brought of the respite of the death sentence under which he lay.

The story of the man was interesting, and some of the particulars connected with it were as touching as the incidents in any romance. Loreto Palombo, for that was his name, had been at a marriage in the company of other Italians resident in Glasgow. A quarrel through jealousy arose between him and one of the other guests, whom he stabbed. The wound proved fatal, and Palombo was sentenced to death. But there were certain extenuating circumstances. Petitions were largely signed in favour of a reprieve. And one who loved the condemned man greatly, after seeking help for him without avail in various quarters in Glasgow, made her way to Lord Lothian himself, who represented the Crown in the matter, and sent into him, at his residence at Dalkeith, the earnest message— "If you will spare his life, I will willingly take his place, as I know that but for me the thing would not have happened."

The result was what has been already indicated. After careful consideration of the case, a reprieve was forwarded to the Governor of Glasgow prison. He immediately sought the Lord Provost, and they repaired together to the convict's cell. "They found Palombo," runs the newspaper report, "upon his knees on the floor, engaged fervently in prayer. On seeing the Lord Provost and the Governor, he rose immediately to his feet. His Lordship said he had good news for him, and read the letter intimating the Queen's pardon. Palombo, on hearing the news, dropped on his knees, threw up his arms, and thanked God for his deliverance from death. Addressing his Lordship, he thanked him for his visit, and expressed gratitude to all the good people of Scotland for what they had done to save his life, and added, '*God has spared my life, and I am going to be God's man now!*'"

It was a fit resolve. It was a resolve quite in keeping with the spirit of the Apostle Paul. "Henceforth—unto Him!" It is a fit resolve for you and me. If, as we look back, we are ashamed to see how much we have been living for selfish ends, and degrading our life to mere earthly and sinful uses, let us, as we look forward, say from the heart: "This sort of life must cease. No longer shall I live to the gratification of what is base in me, but to the will of God." If Christ died for us, and thereby, at an infinite cost, secured our reprieve from the sentence of eternal death under which we lay, we should remember that He died, "that we who live should not henceforth live unto ourselves, but unto Him who died for us and rose again." In view of all the future that awaits us, let this, then, be our motto—"Henceforth unto Him!"

December 30.   **The Sin of Ingratitude.**

"Forget not all His benefits" (Ps. ciii. 2).

You cannot remember them all. But you certainly ought not to forget them all; and you should not be unthankful for any of them which memory, as you look back this day, may enable you to recall.

Your blessings are far more than you can count. As a minister was walking along one starry night holding the hand of his little daughter, she began, looking up, to try to count the number of the stars. Bravely she proceeded for a time, but at last he heard her exclaim—"Two hundred and twenty-three, two hundred and twenty-four, two hundred and twenty-five—Oh dear, I did not think there were so many!" And then she stopped. And the minister said to himself—"I am just like my little maiden, when I begin to count the mercies of my God. I can review a great many of them; but when I begin to reckon them up before Him, I am constrained to exclaim in wonder—"I did not think there were so many; they are more than can be numbered!"

There are some people who pride themselves because they never forget an injury. It is a very poor thing to pride themselves upon. There are multitudes who should humble themselves because they never remember a kindness—especially a kindness bestowed on them by a loving and bountiful God. A short memory in such a case is not only an infirmity, but a grievous sin.

"*The river past, and God forgotten,*" is a proverb which reminds us how much readier we are to ask good at God's hand, and to implore help from Him in seasons of extremity and distress, than to pause afterwards to give Him thanks. You remember how, when Jesus had healed the ten lepers who besought His mercy, nine out of the ten straightway forgot all about their obligation to Him. And it was with a reproachful sadness in His tone that Jesus exclaimed—"Were there not ten cleansed, but where are the nine? There are not found that returned to give glory to God, save this stranger."

There are base forms in which ingratitude has sometimes shown itself, from which we would instinctively recoil. Such, for instance, was the conduct of a wounded Russian soldier at the battle of the Alma, whom Captain Eddington heard crying piteously for water. The charitable English officer stooped and gave him a refreshing draught. But as the captain was turning to join his regiment, the wounded man rose upon his arm, and used his reviving energy to shoot and wound his benefactor. Which of us is not ready to say—"Such a wretch was not worthy to live!"

Are any of us base enough to wound by a spirit of hostility the heart of Him who, times without number, has been our Friend in need? Are any of us willing to grieve Him by even a spirit of cold indifference in view of all His benefits? Nay, rather, "Bless the Lord, O my soul; and all that is within me, bless His holy name!"

"*We spend our years as a tale that is told*" (Ps. xc. 9).

THE main idea here is, the swiftness of life. There are other figures in Scripture which lay emphasis on this. In the Book of Job, life is likened to a swift "post." Just as the swift horseman careered along with his message and handed it on to another, and another, who brought it to its destination, so life goes quickly forward to its goal. The "swift ships," too, which pass and hail one another and then vanish beyond the horizon; and the flight of "an eagle in the air," which soon gets quite out of your sight; and the disappearance of "a little vapour," which speedily melts into the air and is no longer seen—these are some of the things which suggest the shortness of man's life on earth.

This 90th Psalm has already compared life to the growth of the grass, which springs up quickly and very soon withers again. Here it speaks of it as *a tale* that is soon told and over, so far as earth is concerned; or more literally, as *a thought* which flashes into the mind and passes—one of the thoughts of God.

Now, if life is a tale, you have this advantage over us who are older, that you are still near the beginning of the story, and have, under God, the writing of your biography upon the tablet of time very much in your own hand. See that yours is a story with a pure moral in it. Have it filled with generous aims and high ideas. Ask Christ to take your hand and guide it to write well all through. Then you will have fewer blots and fewer regrets than some of us have, when we look back upon the pages that are past.

The tale you are telling has years for chapters, months for paragraphs, days for pages, hours for lines, and minutes for words. If the pages, paragraphs, and chapters are to be worthy of you, take good care of the words and lines! And remember this, that when "*finis*" has been written to your story by Death, it is not to be forgotten and cast aside. God is to read off every chapter of it, including the chapter now closing, and the next—or as much of it as you are to be spared to see; and He will pronounce upon its every page.

There are waxen tablets called "palimpsests," because they have been rubbed and written on more than once. When the upper layer of wax has been removed, the writing below has been found legible still. So will it be with your life and mine. Many things crowded-out of our memories by new events and scenes will be laid bare to view again. Our whole career will be revealed as in a panorama before us. All our biography in its connection will be read out in our hearing. The tale we now are telling will ere long be a tale that is told.

God knows how much yet remains untold of our life-story upon earth. But whether it be much or little, let us remember, in the words of Dr. Horatius Bonar, "the sweet singer of Scotland," that—

"He liveth long who liveth well!
　All other life is short and vain;
　He liveth longest who can tell
　　Of living most for heavenly gain.

He liveth long who liveth well!
　All else is being flung away;
　He liveth longest who can tell
　　Of true things truly done each day.

Waste not thy being; back to Him
　Who freely gave it freely give;
　Else is that being but a dream,
　　'Tis but to *be*, and not to *live*.

Be what thou seemest; live thy creed,
　Hold up to earth the torch Divine;
　Be what thou prayest to be made;
　　Let the great Master's steps be thine.

Fill up each hour with what will last;
　Buy up the moments as they go;
　The life above, when this is past,
　　Is the ripe fruit of life below."

www.ingramcontent.com/pod-product-compliance
Lightning Source LLC
Chambersburg PA
CBHW030355230426
43664CB00007BB/607